SIR HARRY JOHNSTON
AND THE SCRAMBLE FOR AFRICA

OKAPIA JOHNSTONI

This painting, made from the sole evidence of two incomplete
skins, errs only in making the eyes brown instead of blue

SIR HARRY
JOHNSTON

& THE SCRAMBLE FOR AFRICA

———◦◉◦———

Roland Oliver

1958
St MARTIN'S PRESS INC
NEW YORK

Library of Congress
Catalog Card number 58-12365

Printed in Great Britain by
T. and A. Constable Ltd.

INTRODUCTION

THIS book has been written, and published, in the full knowledge that the circle of people is small to whom Sir Harry Johnston is even a name. One of the best-known London publishing houses indeed rejected the completed manuscript for this reason alone. Lugard, Milner, Rhodes and Chamberlain, Cromer even, and Kirk, all these enjoyed a fame which has long outlasted their generation. Johnston, despite his forty published works, died in 1927 almost in obscurity. No representative of the government he had served came to stand by his grave in the little Sussex churchyard of Poling when he was buried. Even to near contemporaries who ploughed adjacent furrows he seemed by the middle of the present century but a shadow from the past. 'Sir Harry Johnston', the late Mr L. S. Amery remarked to me in December 1954, 'Oh yes. He was such a failure.'

And yet it would be strictly true to say that in the course of ten years spent mainly in the study of Africa and its history no one personality has more constantly crossed my path. The best attempt at a history of all Africa so far published is Johnston's. It is supplemented by his encyclopaedic works on Central Africa and the Congo, Uganda and Liberia. I have encountered his name almost daily upon the lips of those of my colleagues who are students of African languages. It has always evoked a ready response from ethnographers and botanists, zoologists and museum curators. By the extent and variety of his contributions to learning alone Johnston, it would seem, should qualify as the completest 'Africanist'.

Nevertheless, this book is only in some small part the story of a scholar and a writer. It is as a man of action that Johnston has chiefly aroused my historian's interest. It has been my happy privilege during the last five years to watch and encourage, and above all myself to share in, the work of a group of research students in the University of London, the majority of whom have chosen their special fields of study from the supremely important and richly documented period covering the partition of the continent among the European powers. From the succession of regional situations thus un-covered Johnston emerges, if not as a titan, at least as a ubiquitous and always significant personality. In the course of twenty years spent mainly in Africa he left his mark upon the Congo and Nigeria, Nyasaland and Northern Rhodesia, Tanganyika, Kenya and Uganda. In the intervals between his travels he was the friend and adviser of Lord Salisbury, the intermediary between Salisbury and Rhodes, the friend of Stanley and Kirk, of Goldie and Mackinnon. King Leopold knew and feared his influence. Serpa Pinto met him and turned back from his project of extending the frontiers of Mozambique to those of Angola.

Johnston's active life coincided almost exactly with the international scramble for Africa, and he himself played with intensity and enthusiasm all the most characteristic parts that fell to the 'man on the spot'. He was in turn explorer, concession-hunter, treaty-making consul and pioneer administrator. For this reason alone his unconsummated career is decidedly worth the chronicling. But this is not to say that Johnston was a type. No man was less so. In so far as his public life was cut short by factors other than ill-health, it was mainly that he never learned, as every high official must, to wear a public face. He allowed his rich humour and his extravagant flights of fancy to flow freely on the most formal occasions and on the most serious subjects. He never knew the meaning of discretion. And therefore, as Dame Lillian Penson once remarked to me, his greatest attraction to the historian is that he tells one how things really happened.

Naturally, in writing this book I have made almost daily use of Johnston's own autobiography, as also of the *Life and Letters of Sir Harry Johnston* published by his brother, Mr Alex Johnston in 1929. To Mr and to Mrs Alex Johnston I am further indebted for much kind help and encouragement, both in conversation and by correspondence. The Johnston Papers, as they now survive, descended through Lady Johnston to her residuary legatee, Brigadier J. G. Deedes, who deposited them in the Central African Archives in Salisbury, Southern Rhodesia. I am extremely grateful to the Chief Archivist, Mr V. W. Hiller, and to his Assistant, Mr Burke, for supplying me with microfilm copies of these papers and also of the relevant correspondence from the papers of the Cape Town office of the British South Africa Company. These microfilms have since been acquired by the Library of the Royal Empire Society. Indispensable as they have been, however, the Johnston Papers are but a small and disappointing collection, which have, moreover, in any case been used before both by Sir Harry himself and by his brother. My main new quarrying-ground has been in the archives of the African Department of the Foreign Office, where hundreds of Johnston's original despatches, together with the priceless marginal comments of ministers and officials, lie scattered through almost a thousand volumes of Slave Trade, Africa, and Domestic files. For access to these my thanks are due to the officers and attendants of the Public Record Office, who work with cheerfulness and efficiency in conditions of stuffiness and overcrowding which would certainly have provoked Johnston either to a diatribe against that soulless miser the Treasury, or to a plea that the problem be solved *more Africano* by having the Master of the Rolls exhibited in chains at the junction of Fleet Street and Chancery Lane. I have to thank also the Warden and the Librarian of Rhodes House, Oxford, for access to the papers of Rhodes and Cawston with their valuable collections of letters from Johnston, and the Rhodes Trustees for permitting me to reproduce the portrait of Rhodes by Edward Rowarth; Captain A. L. Kennedy for permission to reproduce his photograph of Salisbury in old age; the Librarian of the Royal Geographical Society for access to letters, drawings and paintings, and that Society for permission to reproduce some of these; Mr J. B. Henderson and Mrs Arnold Dolmetsch for permission to reproduce oil paintings and drawings by Johnston in their possession; the Library of the School of Oriental and African Studies for permission to reproduce the facsimile letter from Johnston to Sir William Mackinnon; and Lord Salisbury for permission to see and quote from the letters written by Johnston to the third Marquess of Salisbury.

Finally, it is my delightful duty to thank those personal friends who have helped me in various ways to make this a better book than it would otherwise have been: Sir Keith Hancock, who first encouraged me to write it at all; Mr John Flint of King's College, who has helped me with his probably unrivalled knowledge of Nigerian history during the 'eighties and 'nineties; Mrs Marie Hemphill, of Williamstown, Virginia, who discovered the Mackinnon Papers, and passed on to me all the relevant by-products of her exploitation of them; M. Jean Stengers of the Université Libre de Bruxelles, who has helped me to understand the enigmatical character of King Leopold II and the far from unsubtle one of Stanley; Dr A. J. Hanna of the University of Southampton, who generously allowed me to see the manuscript of his recent book on *Nyasaland and North-Eastern Rhodesia* in advance of its publication; Mr Anthony Low of Makerere College, East

Africa, who has helped me greatly from his knowledge of the Secretariat Archives at Entebbe, and by lending me a most valuable unpublished paper on the negotiations leading up to the Uganda Agreement of 1900; Professor Malcolm Guthrie of the School of Oriental and African Studies, who has been unfailingly kind and patient in suffering my importunities on linguistic matters; my colleague, Mr R. A. Hamilton, who has read and commented upon the four Nyasaland chapters; Mr Cyprian Blagden, who has read the whole manuscript and advised me on maps and illustrations; Mr H. B. Thomas, who in addition to much other help has been kind enough to assist me in reading the proofs; and my friend and publisher, Mr Peter Calvocoressi. My last and my largest acknowledgment is to my wife, who has tolerated the all but intolerable selfishness of authorship, and who has nevertheless been ready with counsel and encouragement for every fragment as it has appeared.

R. O.

Clugin, Hinterrhein
12th August 1956

CONTENTS

*

PLATES

*

PLATES

With the exception of the photographs of Sir Harry Johnston and Lord Salisbury and the portrait of Cecil Rhodes, all the plates in the text are reproduced from oil paintings and drawings by Sir Harry Johnston.

DRAWINGS IN TEXT

MAPS IN TEXT

Chapter 1

TWENTY-ONE YEARS

HARRY JOHNSTON was born in London on June 12th 1858. He had two older step-brothers from his father's first marriage, and was himself the eldest of twelve children born from the second. His father, John Johnston, was the well-to-do Secretary of a large insurance company, a shrewd, well-informed, widely travelled man of business, whose work took him regularly all over Western Europe and Scandinavia, and occasionally as far afield as Russia, Asia Minor and South Africa. He had some property besides his emoluments, so that despite the size of the family the Johnstons lived comfortably in a series of large suburban houses on the fringes of south-east London. There was leisure for some cultivated interests; there were regular holidays in the country and by the sea.

More than most Victorians of the middle class, the Johnstons were aware of the revolution in communications which was making the world smaller and bringing its remotest corners within the commanding influence of industrial Europe. John Johnston's professional life was intimately linked with the consequences of the opening up by railways and steamships and telegraphs of Australia and South America, Siberia and the United States. In his spare time he was an active member of the Royal Geographical Society. He was deeply read in the literature of African exploration and had followed with understanding as well as enthusiasm the journeys of Dr Livingstone. He knew more accurately than most Englishmen the location of Khartoum or Candahar. Yet all this breadth of outlook, all this competence in material things, was bounded and interwoven with a strange theology which dominated and determined his domestic life. He and Esther Hamilton, his second wife, were both second-generation members of the Catholic Apostolic Church, a body founded in 1831 in London by a Presbyterian minister, Edward Irving, and a Scottish banker, Henry Drummond. Deeply influenced by the Eastern Orthodox as well as by Roman Catholic usages, the liturgy and ritual of the 'Irvingites' had an exotic flavour not wholly inconsistent with the cosmopolitan commercial interests of

A

many of its leading members, but its teaching had developed a prophetic strain more akin to transatlantic Adventism. The man whose week-day employment was to insulate people so far as possible from the changes and chances of this wicked world, on Sundays donned a deacon's stole, believed devoutly that the Tsar was Antichrist and lived in daily expectation of a Second Coming, when a handful of Apostolic Catholics would be caught up into the air and endued with immortality before returning with the Son of God to govern the earth for a thousand years.[1]

In all their changes of residence the Johnstons kept within easy reach of 'the church', situated first in Trinity Square, Southwark, and later in a larger and more ornate building at Camberwell Green; and some of Harry Johnston's liveliest recollections of his childhood were associated with ecclesiastical affairs.

> I liked being an acolyte in a white dalmatic and a scarlet cassock, taught to prepare and reverently to pass into the priest's hands the incense in its splendid censer. I liked the long Sundays, spent so much in church between one enthusiastic service and another, when little picnics of sandwiches, biscuits and sherry took place in the vestries and the corridors, while the clergy moved about in gorgeous eastern vestments which completely transmogrified the meat salesman, the auctioneer or tea-dealer of everyday life. . . . I liked being able, after some unusual, exciting prophecy from the blue-stoled prophet, to slip into the priests' vestry where there was a good reference library, and to read Alison's *History of Europe* and make out in the atlas the changes in political geography which would come about when the ten kingdoms of the Apocalypse were brought into being. I enjoyed the spiritual pride of the consciously elect. As I rode in omnibuses with my feet in their frowsy straw, it thrilled me to think that if only the Last Trump or some other appalling supernatural summons sounded from heaven, I with my mother would soar up without the pain of dying, whereas all the other people in the omnibus, unless they were Adventists in disguise, would remain where they were, only able at best to enter immortality through the very painful death of martyrdom.[2]

This preoccupation of the Johnstons with an extreme and rather merciless eschatology does not seem to have been accompanied by any of the domineering severity of so many

---

[1] H. H. Johnston: *The Story of My Life*, London 1923, p. 12.
[2] H. H. Johnston: *The Gay-Dombeys*, London 1919. Johnston habitually wrote truth in the guise of fiction, and there is no doubt whatever that this passage is intended to be autobiographical.

narrowly religious Victorian households. On the contrary
the Johnstons were, and remained, an uncommonly gentle,
devoted, easy and contented family circle. Yet the very
singularity of their beliefs must have been socially constricting.
Despite their comfortable circumstances, the only family
acquaintance who was in any way well known among his
contemporaries seems to have been the historian, S. R.
Gardiner, whose wife had been born into the same persuasion.
The saints, perhaps, did not mix more than was strictly
necessary, and though the rapidly expanding public schools
were by no means closed to boys whose parents had three or
four thousand pounds a year, young Harry Johnston was put
to school first with the Misses Pace of Camberwell, and then
in 1870 at the Stockwell Grammar School. Not that his education, in the narrow sense, suffered from this choice: on the
contrary Edgar Sanderson, headmaster in turn of Stockwell,
Macclesfield and Huntingdon grammar schools, was one of
the liveliest and most original teachers of his generation.
Under his rule Latin was used less as the means to a classical
literature and more as a philological introduction to the
modern romance languages; geography was taught against a
background of geology; drawing and painting were always
practised from live subjects and never copied from books
according to the method then in fashion. Harry Johnston
excelled in languages. Already, at the age of ten, during a
year's absence from school after scarlet fever, he had discovered
both a definite gift for drawing and a marked preference for
studies of animals and birds. Now, during his vacations and
half-holidays from Stockwell, he began to take his sketch books
first to the natural history galleries of the British Museum and
then to the London Zoological Gardens. Here, when he was
still only fourteen, he sold his first picture, a drawing of a
lion's head. He also attracted the attention of Professor Alfred
Garrod, who, as the Society's Prosector, was just beginning the
brilliant work on the structure and classification of birds which
was to win him at the early age of twenty-eight the Chair of
Comparative Anatomy at King's College, London.[1] Garrod
initiated Johnston into the mysteries of his dissecting-room,
commissioned him to illustrate his zoological papers, and
later introduced him to Sir William Flower at the museum
of the Royal College of Surgeons, where he extended his
anatomical drawings to apes and men.

[1] See the biographical note in W. A. Forbes: *Collected Scientific Papers of Alfred Henry Garrod*, London 1881.

When he was sixteen and a half Johnston left the Grammar School and became an evening student at King's College, where he attended classes in French, Italian, Spanish and Portuguese. By day he worked at the South Lambeth Art School and continued his visits to the Zoo and the College of Surgeons. The next year he passed into the Royal Academy Schools as a student of painting. It was a much desired achievement, but though he accepted the vacant place with alacrity, he was now, as throughout his life, most uncertain as to his real capacities in this field.

> My desire to choose painting as a profession was already unconsciously modified by doubts whether I should ever develop into a great painter; to be a second-rate artist did not attract me. I achieved facile triumphs in 1876-9 as a Royal Academy student, because I was a good draughtsman and had some skill as a painter from actuality, as a colourist, as an appreciator of the exact values of chiaroscuro in a scene. But as a composer of pictures, as anything more than a predecessor of photography, I began to doubt whether I should ever make a name.[1]

It is a curious and interesting reflection that Johnston, who by no means underrated his abilities in other directions, should have been so hesitant about the one in which he came nearest to being a master, and that he strove from the outset of his career as an art student to keep open other much less clearly marked avenues to success. It was evidently with the deliberate intention to put his linguistic studies to the test that he persuaded his father in the summer of 1876 to finance a three months' expedition to Spain and the Balearics. Dieppe, Paris, Marseilles, Barcelona, Palma, Soller: it was his first real escape from the amenities of suburban London, and it was not at once an agreeable experience. He was travelling cheap, and the dirt, the diet and the solitude of the Majorcan inn utterly oppressed him. Then he found a donkey for hire, and riding up El Puig Mayor by night, painted the dawn from its summit. Soon he had taken discomfort squarely in hand and found he enjoyed it, riding and walking over the island with no luggage but his paintbox and with the youthful owner of the donkey as his companion and guide. From Soller he went on to Valencia, Madrid, Cordova, Seville, finding hospitality and making friends. He returned to London by sea from Malaga, content to pursue his painting, but determined to travel again, and if possible more ambitiously.

For more than three years it was not to be. The session of

[1] *Story*, p. 32.

1876-7 was a strenuous one at the Academy, and throughout it his mother's health gave increasing cause for anxiety. In November 1877 she died, in her twelfth childbirth. For months he was too stupefied with grief even to go on with his work. Then there was a large family of younger brothers and sisters to be cared for and comforted. At last, in the early summer of 1878, he decided to try the art-schools of Paris; but he disliked the hurly-burly of French student life and soon moved south to Provence. Avignon caught his imagination and he stayed there painting hard for two or three months and making expeditions to Nîmes, Tarascon, Barbentane and Vaucluse. He returned to England by way of Savoy and Switzerland, only to find himself plunged within a month in a second domestic tragedy, the death from typhoid of his step-brother George at the age of twenty-four.

In after years Johnston was to see this event as the terminal point of his childhood's faith. 'There are millions of similar deaths every year, showing—as at any rate it showed me then —that in this incredibly vast universe the overruling, intelligent power, if there be one, has no conception of what agonies of grief we poor human ants on this tiny planet can suffer from the cessation of life in those we love. The researches of Astronomy can discover no pity anywhere in the ruthless processes of Nature'.[1] It was not of course either a profound conclusion or an original one. To identify God with 'Nature red in tooth and claw', and then to judge Him non-existent by the superior standards of humanity, not to say of Christianity, as if these were in some way independent of creation and the Creator, was a fault of reasoning peculiarly characteristic of the late nineteenth and early twentieth century. It resulted from the first crude impact of evolutionary theories upon an almost equally crude biblical aetiology which dated the act of creation to the year 4004 B.C. In Johnston the impact of Garrod's dissecting-room and the bottled embryos at the College of Surgeons upon the doctrines of Trinity Square, Southwark, must have been exceptionally severe. Yet in Johnston the abandonment of Christianity, which he paraded more publicly than most of his contemporaries, and in which he persisted to the end of his life, did not result in a merely negative cynicism. Illogical though it might be, he believed in Evolution as in a God, and in himself as its devoted, and perhaps its only intelligent, servant. Moreover, though he rejected for himself its metaphysical doctrines and its systems

[1] *Ibid.*, p. 46.

of worship and prayer, he regarded Christianity and the
Christian virtues as among the highest manifestations of the
evolutionary process, a manifestation which it was his duty to
support and defend against all the lower religions which were
competing for man's allegiance in different parts of the world.
He retained also many of the abstemious habits of his strictly
religious upbringing. He always preferred tea to alcohol,
sweets to cigarettes, conversation to cards. He married late
and was beforehand a blameless bachelor, fond of solitude,
parsimonious of time. The most self-advertised of unbelievers
became the most unqualified advocate of Christian missions,
and by temperament was always more at home on a mission
station than in an officers' mess or a Government House.

To lose his faith was in these circumstances not to lose but
to strengthen his ambitions and calculate even more carefully
how they were to be fulfilled. He was beginning to achieve
some outward success with his painting. He had rented a small
studio in Chelsea, to which he repaired daily from the family
home, now at Champion Hill. He worked up several pictures
which he had begun the previous year in Provence: one of
them was accepted for the Academy in 1879 and others were
hung in the Dudley Galleries. He continued to illustrate for
Garrod at the Zoo, and he sold some of his studies of birds
and animals to *The Field* and other illustrated papers. But he
was still doubtful of his real abilities as an artist; and under
Garrod's inspiration he was considering seriously whether he
should not leave the Academy Schools and go instead to
Cambridge. Had Garrod lived to help him, he would probably
have done so. He would have read the new Natural Sciences
Tripos and would very likely have made a more satisfying
if less singular career as an academic zoologist or botanist.
But Garrod's life was already threatened by phthisis, and he
died the following autumn in his thirty-third year.

Johnston was already given to hypochondria, and Garrod's
death intensified it. The diary which he kept day by day from
November 1879 to January 1881,[1] is packed with references,
not as a rule to any specific ailments but with imaginative
and at times querulous comments on his general state of
health. About one day in three was 'completely spoilt by
ill-health'. He was forever 'feeling wretched' or 'returning
home quite knocked up'. It was, according to his own much

---

[1] This diary is preserved, together with the rest of Johnston's private papers,
in the Central African Archives at Salisbury, Southern Rhodesia. There is a
microfilm copy in the Library of the Royal Empire Society, London.

later account, to shake off this tendency that he decided in the autumn of 1879 upon a long voyage to the Mediterranean, the particular choice of Tunis being due to the accident that the British Consul-General there, Mr Thomas Reade, had been an old acquaintance of his father's. Both these considerations were doubtless real. The diary, however, adds something else. Tunis was certainly intended to be much more than a convalescence. It was a much cogitated, carefully planned breakaway from the dearly loved but too encircling influences of his home. It was a venture into the unknown in search of fame and fortune, by his brush if possible, but failing that by his wits. It was a deeply significant act of faith in himself as an individual adult being, which he debated with himself in his diary with all the anxious self-scrutiny one might expect of a novice on the eve of taking perpetual vows. The full nature of his project he evidently did not communicate to his father until just before he left:

This is a day [reads the diary for November 30th] that may be a turning point in my life. Woke rather late, but after a scramble got to church in good time. Douglas and Aunt Betty came to dinner. Church again in the afternoon. Went to Butterfields to tea. Back to church, where I heard Mr Askey preach. Evening at home—fairly pleasant. Caught Papa before going to bed and spoke to him with some premonitory apprehensions about the monetary arrangements in re Tunis. Found him most delightfully sympathetic. Acceded so fully and quickly to everything I proposed, that I was quite startled and relieved at not having to argue my cause. So I am to start this day fortnight, the 14th. Shall I ever regret having taken the leap and started once more on my travels? Shall I ever look back with longing regret to the quiet happy home I have left and sigh for the thousand miles of land and sea that separate me from it?

These were scarcely the words of an invalid, and during the next few weeks the note became more insistent. 'Church twice. Parted cheerfully with everybody. Don't much care if I never see them again.' 'Oh, if only I could be famous some way or other.' 'Ah, how I do hope my trip may be a success: otherwise how wasted all this expense and worry will seem.' And on arrival in Tunis: 'I do hope I shall do something successful here.'[1] No doubt he was genuinely upset about Garrod; no doubt it brought him as he later claimed to a turning-point

[1] Diary: December 7th, 10th, 14th and 21st, 1879. In Alex Johnston: *The Life and Letters of Sir Harry Johnston*, London 1929, p. 27, 'way' is cited as 'day'. The difference in the sense of the two readings is considerable.

in his career; most certainly, however, that turning-point represented a very clear, definite decision on his own part to make his way not by the orthodox path of a University education but by the devious, dangerous, uncharted, but possibly more rapid route of an adventurer.

It was a momentous choice. It brought him to meteoric success and almost as meteoric decline. Brilliant gifts but little training, wide knowledge but no recognized qualifications, middle-class origins unredeemed at any stage by an expensive education, these were the liabilities arising from his decision. And to them must be added one over which he had no control, a fully grown stature of five foot three inches with a rather high-pitched voice, adding to the impression of precocity in youth, but faintly ridiculous in maturity and middle age. These handicaps produced a certain lack of composure which made his success always precarious. It was not enough for Johnston to succeed: he had to dazzle. His speech must be shocking, his despatches arresting, his actions dramatic. It was never enough to do one job and do it well: he had also to do it faster than anyone else and with less apparent effort. Naturally versatile, he cultivated his versatility to the point of exhibitionism: political business must be despatched before breakfast, so that the morning could be divided between linguistics and anthropology, the afternoon between taxidermy and painting. In conversation he had to shine, frequently at the expense of discretion, sometimes of good taste. If you were twenty years older, he was so unusually intelligent, vivacious and amusing that you laughed and forgave him; if you were ten years older and in danger of being left behind, you were pompous and outraged; if a contemporary, you heaved a sigh of impotent regret—'poor Harry'; if a junior, you first worshipped and then learnt your lesson.

Johnston's primary purpose in Tunis was to test himself as a painter. His way of doing so was to attempt a project far more ambitious than any he had tried before. After only three or four rambles round the town with an Arab guide, he fixed upon the subject which was to occupy him day in day out for nearly seven months. It was to be an enormous canvas depicting as a background the gateway of the Olive Tree Mosque, with its early and splendid example of the Saracenic horseshoe arch. The foreground of steps and street was to be filled with a cosmopolitan crowd of worshippers, built up from a long series of individual studies. It was to be a picture which, if successfully completed, would establish him forever, which would carry him forward at a single bound from the mass of struggling students each seeking by small successes to build a livelihood and then a name. And certainly, despite continuing hypochondria, mounting financial embarrassment and the steady growth of other interests, he made a serious and disciplined attempt to carry his conception into effect. His occupation defied the susceptibilities of the thronging Muhammadan populace, but morning after morning he continued his work in the same crowded thoroughfare, completing numerous detailed studies, and finally setting up the full canvas in a perfumer's shop facing the mosque. He learnt the colloquial Arabic of the Tunisian street. He jostled with beggars, not with the thrusting impatience of one who in half an hour will be safely back in his ship's cabin or his military cantonment, but with the restraint of one who knows that day after day he must share their wonted beat. He chaffered with shopkeepers and leather-workers with the comradeship of a fellow artificer and not with the insolence of a passing patron. He learnt the comings and goings of an oriental metropolis, the grave grandiloquent greetings due to prince and preacher, the complicated ethnology of Berber and Bedouin, Moor and Jew. After lunch he retreated to his simple suite of ground-floor rooms rented from a certain Madame Eliza in the Moorish quarter of the town. For the late afternoons there was an island in the lagoon connecting Tunis with the sea, where he could gaze across a vast green landscape to the purple forms of distant mountains, and, concealed among the crannies of a ruined Spanish fort, watch the waterfowl—herons, cranes, storks and flamingoes—'slowly returning to the island, to plume themselves, to forage, to quarrel or make love'. In the evenings, but not as a rule before, he would call upon his European friends, or, when he could afford it, attend 'the pretty little theatre whose performances often rise above the mediocre'.[1]

It was an excellent régime for one who was beginning to study the political as well as the visual scene. For Tunis at the time of Johnston's visit was enjoying its last year as a practically independent principality under the nominal suzerainty of Turkey. Already a French army was mustering in eastern Algeria, and even within the Tunisian borders France was quietly but surely possessing herself of the land. The railway from Tunis to Bône was being built by a French

[1] Cf. 'A Winter in Tunis', *The Globe*, 26.i.80.

A*

concessionaire company, whose engineers, nominally in the service of the Bey, were diligently surveying the country in all directions. Other French companies managed the telegraphs and gas-works. Frenchmen were becoming large landowners in the countryside round the capital. The Vizier, a fading Adonis of twenty-seven, was in French pay along with other important officials. Not that these preparations went unnoticed or un-challenged by Italy, whose Consul made unceasing but unavailing attempts to outshine the French Minister and Plenipotentiary on public occasions and to outbid him in his private transactions with the venal underworld of Tunisian Jews and outcast Maltese and Italians who circled on nefarious errands around the Vizier's palace. An Italian company made an offer for the little British-built railway which ran the nine miles from Tunis to Goletta and protested vociferously when the prize was knocked down to their French rivals. Italian diplomats were active in Constantinople, and not unhopeful of support from London—at least in keeping the French out.[1]

In this, however, they were mistaken. Consistently and successfully as successive British governments had based their Mediterranean and Near Eastern policies through the middle years of the century upon the doctrine of maintaining the in-tegrity of the Ottoman Empire, that empire was seen by the 'seventies to be tottering to a state in which it could no longer be shored up even by such ill-disguised props as the Italian, French and British control of Tunisian finances instituted in 1869 or the nominally international, but in fact Franco-British, control established over the finances of Egypt in 1876 through the *Caisse de la Dette*. It was of course the expansion of Russia that English statesmen chiefly feared—Russia in the Mediterranean, Russia in the Persian Gulf, Russia in India, Russia in the Far East. Consequently, with the massacre by the Turks of 12,000 of their Bulgarian Christian subjects and therefore with the imminence of another Russo-Turkish war, Lord Salisbury, then serving his apprenticeship in foreign affairs at the India Office, decided that 'the old policy, wise enough in its time, of defending English interests by sustaining the Ottoman dynasty' had become impracticable and must be replaced by a more direct one involving 'some territorial re-arrangement'.[2] Disraeli, bred in an older school of diplomacy, told him he was immoral; but nonetheless appointed him Foreign Secretary

[1] *The Globe*, 5.vi.80.
[2] Salisbury to Lytton 9.iii.77, cited G. Cecil: *Life of Robert Marquis of Salisbury*, Vol. II, p. 130.

in March 1878 when the Russians were at Adrianople, and in June took him to the Congress of Berlin, where the territorial re-arrangements were to be adumbrated. When the Russian delegates announced their intention to retain the Turkish provinces of Kars, Ardahan and Batum, Disraeli countered by revealing a secret convention with the Porte, whereby England was to occupy Cyprus as a base from which to defend the remainder of the Sultan's Asiatic dominions from Russian aggression. At the same time Salisbury, in conversation with Waddington, then French ambassador at Berlin, intimated that while Great Britain claimed a dominant influence in Western Asia and especially in Mesopotamia, she had no intention of establishing an exclusive footing in Egypt, while further west in Tunis she had no wish 'to contest the influence which the geographical position of Algeria gave to France'.[1]

By the autumn of 1879 rumours of these conversations had leaked out. Johnston had known of them at the time he planned his journey,[2] and if they had not determined his destination, they had certainly entered into his calculations. A fellow art-student, Carmichael Thomas, had introduced him to his father, William Thomas, the proprietor of *The Graphic*, who had invited him to submit sketches of Tunis for publication; and doubtless through the same friends he had obtained a small (and uncertain) commission to write a monthly article for *The Globe* newspaper. He was not therefore uninterested in copy. On the boat from Marseilles to Goletta he had been lucky enough to fall in with two French officials, the Comte de Sancy, a member of the three-power commission controlling the Tunisian national debt,[3] and the Vicomte Maurice de Roumefort, a young diplomat working on the staff of M. Roustan, the French Minister. Neither had made any secret of French intentions, and on discovering an agreeable and highly intelligent young Englishman with journalistic interests they had determined to make a supporter and not an enemy. Arrived in Tunis, Johnston was invited to mess regularly with them at de Sancy's house. It was beyond his means, but he accepted, and in de Roumefort at least he made a fast friend, from whom he accepted small loans and even advice on the niceties of evening-dress. This arrangement made him *persona grata* with the whole circle of French officials. Roustan himself was kindly, helping him with small commissions for portraits

[1] Salisbury to Sir Henry Layard 29.x.78, cited Cecil, *op. cit.*, II, p. 332.
[2] *Story*, p. 60.
[3] *Supra*, p. 10.

and criticizing his articles for *The Globe*. So also were MM.
Géry and Lemaire, two directors of the Bône-Guelma and
Extension Railway, who were in Tunis seeking a concession
from the Bey to dredge and widen the harbour at Goletta.
In March 1880 he was invited to travel seventy miles up the
new railway line which was being built at the Bey's expense
to carry the French troops with convenient speed from the
Algerian border right into the capital.[1] In April he made an
extended visit to the borderland between the two countries,
where the Kroumirs, a tribe of nomadic Berber pastoralists,
were already the subject of French complaints on account
of their depredations inside the Algerian boundary. From
the railhead, then at Ghardimau, Johnston rode first to the
headquarters of the Tunisian army sent to subdue the bandits.
There were five thousand soldiers assembled against perhaps
five hundred Kroumirs, but the place had more the appearance
of a country fair than of a military encampment. A general was
in command, but acting under the direction of one Yusuf
Allégro, the son of an Italian colonel and a Tunisian princess,
now officially Tunisian Consul-General at Bône, but also in
league with the French. At twenty-one, Johnston was not
above the pleasure of being implicated in a plot. Securing a
guide and an armed escort, he rode up out of the Tunisian
plain into the delicious, densely wooded scenery of the Majerda
mountains, to where on a three-thousand-foot eminence domin-
ating the Kroumir country the French *Corps d'Observation* was
at work with its lorgnettes and field-glasses. The hospitality
of the officers, French officers in the informal conditions of
active service, was even more congenial and flattering than
that of de Sancy and de Roumefort. Johnston lived with them for
a week in the clean, airy booths built by the Algerian soldiers.
By day he rode through 'magnificent virgin forests of oak,
covering the mighty hills with waves of dark, velvety green'.[2]
In the April evenings talk under the stars was gay, and the
spice of excitement was added by the lions and leopards,
not then extinct, which growled about the kraals of captured
Kroumir cattle. He returned to Tunis for May and June,
sure of what would happen, but also a willing believer in the
mission civilisatrice de la France.

It does not appear from his writings at this time that
Johnston seriously considered the coming occupation of Tunis
as a moral question. Many years later, after a second and

---

[1] *The Globe*, 3.iv.80.
[2] 'Into the Country of the Lion', *The Globe*, 5.v.80.

longer residence there as British Consul-General, he was to condone it in a formidable indictment of Islam and all its works.

All human knowledge, especially the most marvellous developments of the human mind in the nineteenth and twentieth centuries have to be subjected to the intolerable sieve of the narrow mentality of Muhammad, an illiterate, uneducated bandit mystic of the seventh century A.C. . . . who derived his knowledge of the Hebrew Bible from oral information imparted by Arabian Jews and his conception of the Christian tenets from Ethiopian slaves. . . . Most of the great names of the golden age of Islam between the eighth and the thirteenth centuries were not those of people of Arab or Turkish descent but of Jews, Persians, Berbers, Copts, Greeks and Italians, whose conformity with the Muhammadan religion was that of more or less unwilling converts, if indeed they did not by special favour retain the profession of Judaism or Christianity. The Arabs and Turks by degrees killed all that was noteworthy in Islamic culture. . . . In short, judged by the test of output in science and art, literature, material well-being, control of disease, sexual morality, public works, subdual of recalcitrant nature, can any comparison be sustained between the countries professing the Christian religion or governed by Christian nations and the lands which remain more or less independent under the sway of Muhammadan rulers.[1]

No doubt this view, which he held consistently and which was confirmed by his experience of Islam in other parts of Africa, was originally formed in the decadent Turkish Tunis of 1880. But in the spring of that year he was too preoccupied with the inevitability of the coming occupation to consider its moral grounds. Within a matter of months Tunis must become either French or Italian: any other alternative was precluded by the fact that every Tunisian of importance had been bought by one side or the other. For an Englishman, therefore, the problem resolved itself into one of imperial strategy. Ignorant as yet of the great natural harbour at Bizerta, Johnston argued that Goletta, dredged and fortified, would one day become the Constantinople of North Africa, commanding the Sicilian Channel. Under Italy, already in control of the Straits of Messina, it would neutralize Malta and endanger the route to the East. Under France, the narrows of the Mediterranean would be guarded by rival powers, and England from Malta would continue to balance the scales.[2]

[1] H. H. Johnston: *Views and Reviews*, London 1912, p. 185.
[2] *The Globe*, 26.i.80.

Over and beyond the problem of Tunis itself, Johnston gained from his stay in North Africa two very fundamental insights into the strategy of European expansion in the Mediterranean and beyond. He saw, in the first place, the strength of Italian reactions to the French plans. He saw, in fact, that the cycle of annexations begun by Russia in the Caucasus, and continued by Great Britain in Cyprus, would not by any means be completed by the French occupation of Tunis. The three powers which had been actively expanding through the middle years of the century would each have had a bite at the Ottoman cherry, but there were new powers in Europe whose appetites were developing, and old powers whose failing appetites might be sufficiently rejuvenated to stake a claim in any general share-out of uncolonized territory. Italy in particular, newly united, and with nationals in every North African town, would not sit down under the French occupation of Tunis, but would shift her ambitions east to Tripoli. Spain might take alarm at the eastward extension of Algeria and try to forestall a corresponding extension into Morocco. There was above all the question of Egypt and the Suez Canal, where an already most delicately balanced equilibrium of European interests might at any time be upset by internal disturbances.[1] There had been a serious crisis in 1879 when the Khedive Ismail, voicing the rising nationalism of the Egyptian army, had dismissed the English and French ministers appointed to his government to control its finances. The two powers had procured Ismail's deposition by the Porte, but it was far from certain that the new Khedive Tewfik, though personally more amenable to the controlling powers, would be any more capable than his father of restraining his countrymen from revolt against the irksome conditions of foreign interference. Military intervention and direct political control might therefore be necessary at any time, and when it came would almost certainly provoke a crisis involving not only France and Britain but also the members of the *Caisse de la Dette* not ministerially represented in the Egyptian government—Germany, Austria and Italy.

So much, it might be argued, would have been plain to any realistic student of Mediterranean affairs. A second insight, however, Johnston gained, and this time from his contacts

---

[1] To support the claims in *The Story of my Life*, p. 77, that he was already thinking of these things, there survives among the Johnston Papers a manuscript treatise on Tunis, written during the autumn of 1880, the sixth chapter of which touches on these matters.

with the French officials. He learned, as few Englishmen ever did, to look on the Mediterranean, not as a theatre in itself, nor even as a sea-lane to the East, but as the beginning of Africa. He saw earlier and more clearly than most of his contemporaries that a breakdown of the old system of international restraints such as was occurring in the Mediterranean would spread far beyond the nominal confines of the Ottoman Empire. Frenchmen were less inclined than Englishmen to think of the Sahara as a natural barrier bounding the Mediterranean world. A policy of expansion in North Africa had to them as its logical complement a policy of expansion in West Africa by which the two would be joined.[1] Such a policy, conducted simultaneously from Algeria and Tunis, the Senegal and Lower Guinea, from Porto Novo and Gaboon, was in fact to be put into practice by the ministry of Jules Ferry in 1883 as a direct consequence of developments in Egypt, and it was to loosen what British statesmen regarded as a separate system of restraints operating from the Senegal to the Congo. Britain and Portugal would then be forced into a corresponding drive for expansion from their existing bases, Germany would intervene, King Leopold of the Belgians would get the opportunity by skilful diplomacy to turn a commercial and philanthropic enterprise into an internationally recognized state. The scramble would be on, and it could not abate until all but the most impenetrable or unwanted corners of the continent had been shared out among the European powers.

Naturally in 1880 Johnston could not foresee the detailed moves; but it is certain that he had more than an inkling of the immensity of the forces which would be unleashed, of the size of the vacuum to be filled. 'Europe', as he later put it, 'seemed poising for a great attack on Africa, a great plunge into Asia.'[2] In that plunge, in that attack, his own country to maintain its position must take a leading and not a following part. That realization, he subsequently claimed, had altered the bent of his life. Taken alone, such a claim might perhaps be written off as a preening trick of the human memory. On two occasions, however, separated by each other by at least twenty-five years, he connected it with an outstanding mental experience caused by a specific historical event. On April 21st, 1880, the Beaconsfield ministry fell. Gladstone resumed from Lord Hartington the leadership of the Liberal Party.

[1] Cf. 'The French in Africa', *The Globe*, 9.v.81.
[2] *Story*, p. 77.

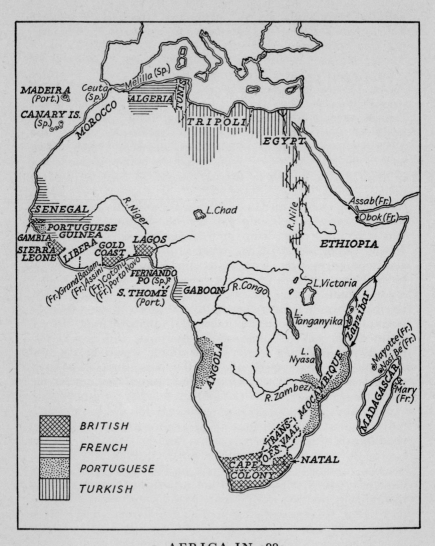

1. AFRICA IN 1880

Showing the extent of Alien Rule.

Salisbury was succeeded at the Foreign Office by Granville.[1] The news reached Johnston just after he returned from his Algerian excursion.

I was in Tunis at the time and in my twenty-first year. For some time I had taken an increasing interest in foreign politics, and the idea of Gladstone's advent to power, pledged by his speeches to withdraw from Candahar and to give up Cyprus, filled me with such dismay and regret that I said to myself 'Why, if you take such an interest in the Empire, do you not yourself become an active agent for its extension?' I resolved that I would, and the whole tenor of my life has been changed by the resolution taken that morning under the Moorish arcades of my dirty but picturesque abode in Tunis.[2]

Basically, it would seem, Johnston's imperialism was, like Lord Salisbury's, intellectual and opportunist, not congenital or romantic. The expansionist tide was flowing, and if Gladstone or any other Liberal Canute tried to stop it, England would simply be swept along by it instead of using and directing it. Much later, when the tide had reached its flood, Johnston was to clothe this opportunism with a philosophy based on his own anthropological conceptions which would make him more of a Whig than a Tory. For the moment, however, he confined himself to remarking in his final article for *The Globe* newspaper that echoes of the English general election had penetrated even to the orange-groves and cypress-avenues of the Vizier's palace, the proprietor of which was said to be much concerned at the retirement of Lord Beaconsfield and even more at the lamentable weakness of character which he had displayed in not having had Mr Gladstone strangled while he was still in office.[3]

---

[1] E. Fitzmaurice: *Life of Lord Granville*, 1905, Vol. II, p. 193.
[2] Johnston to Sir Percy Anderson, no date, cited Alex Johnston, p. 30 *sq.*
[3] *The Globe*, 5.vi.80.

Chapter 2

ANGOLA AND THE CONGO

THERE survives among Johnston's private papers a curious document, belonging evidently to the period immediately after his return from Tunis, entitled 'The Future of the Human Race'.[1] It is a fragment merely, and obviously intended solely for his own use; but it contributes much to the understanding of a character, apparently subtle and even at times deceitful, which was nevertheless really more straightforward and co-ordinated than many of his contemporaries supposed.

The parable of the mustard seed is among the most beautiful of those apt and touching similes attributed to Jesus Christ, and with the substitution of the Kingdom of Man for the vague and less satisfactory Kingdom of Heaven, it may serve for all time to illustrate the History of the Human Race. Sprung from so little. And man a mere accident. The chance combination of certain elements, as accidentally combined perhaps, as endued with that mysterious property we call life. This original cell, this protoplasm, has in the course of time, and almost inevitably, given rise to man, who individually illustrates in his embryonic development the stages he has passed through in his progress from the uncomplicated structure of the single cell to the complicated combination of many cells. . . .

Such being the origin of man [the paper goes on], what is to be done with him? How can he, just entered into his heritage, employ his inherited powers with the utmost advantage? How can he sufficiently apply the great lesson he has been learning all his life in such a way as to most profit by his precepts?

It is clear to begin with that both for the individual and the community there is no surer help towards improvement than a great ambition. The greater the ambition, the greater the advance. Though the goal may seldom or never be touched— perhaps never, for the more we advance, the higher mounts our ambition—yet ere our efforts cease we are sure to find ourselves considerably further on the road than when we started, and can at least leave the task to be continued by our descendants. The very fact of *willing* an advance is an immense progress in itself, for the desire brings about the accomplishment of the thing desired. One can recognize the immense power of will in the

[1] It occurs in the Tunis MS , referred to on p. 26, between chapters 4 and 5.

development of specific differentiation. . . . [Here follow several pages on the development of species in animals, all pointing to the dangers of over-specialization. Versatility is the mark of the highest types.]

Education [the youthful author concludes] will save many more men from the wicked misuse of their own faculties (which is the real sin) than all the imaginary pains and penalties of an offended God. Show a man through his education that all excess is hurtful, that all waste is hard to repair and you will greatly aid him from a selfish point of view to employ his life to the best advantage. In spite of all the precepts and all the beautiful theories in the world man is strictly selfish. He knows that his first duty is to himself. Prove therefore to him that in wasting his time or his health or his powers he is inflicting on himself an irreparable loss, and you will touch him more surely than if you paint the wrath his excesses cause to a second person, albeit dignified with the name and attributes of God. Let man learn that it is Nature he offends, and that Nature means himself and his children, and he will hesitate before erring. Education will also teach him that great Law: Do unto others as you would they should do unto you. He will then be deterred from stealing *par example*—not because it is wrong—stealing is the most natural thing and goes on in Nature all day long—but because he would not like to be stolen from himself. . . . That the ultimate effect of education is selfishness I do not deny. Selfishness arightly read is one of the greatest contributors to mutual improvement. If each individual strives to perfect and to advance himself, the more general and united will be the advance of the community. It seems evident to me that man's first duty is to himself. . . . After you have secured your own position to help others is often beneficial to yourself—but obtain your own position first, otherwise none will help you.

Man an accident, and yet capable by the exercise of will of controlling his own future evolution. Man for whom sin was to misuse the faculties given him by Nature and whose rational self-interest should yet teach him to rise superior to the natural morality of the jungle. It was a muddled piece of thinking. And yet the qualities of moderation, versatility and personal ambition which Johnston deduced to be chiefly necessary, and which he cultivated sedulously through his life, in failure as well as in success, produced a personality surprisingly simple and well-rounded, objective and truthful at least in intention, self-sufficient, cheerful and brave, showing at its best when alone in some remote corner of Africa, at its worst in the convivial company of its social superiors.

Though the resolution so stirringly taken in Tunis no doubt

marked the end of his ambitions to become great by painting, there could be no question at this stage of throwing it up dramatically and starting life afresh. The huge picture of the Olive Tree Mosque had proved a failure in composition; but he had stayed on two more months in Africa working furiously at models in order to save it from total disaster, and when he had at last returned home it had been to resume work in his Chelsea studio. During the year that followed he exhibited and sold many of his smaller Tunis studies, and one rather charmingly formal picture of a group of ten flamingoes poised around a Moorish patio was accepted by the Academy.[1] He next turned his hand to English landscapes, painting in Devon and the Wye valley, in Kent, Hampshire and Dorset. Lord Ilchester's swannery at Abbotsbury became a favourite haunt. Increasingly, however, he was looking around for other openings. In the autumn of 1880 he spent much time on an artlessly written and excessively tedious treatise on Tunis, topographical, historical, ethnological and linguistic, which was fortunately turned down by the publishing house of Macmillan long before it was completed. In a lighter vein, he attempted a number of short dramatic scripts, which, despite the fact that Apostolic Catholics did not patronize the theatre, all had their first and only performances in the large family circle at Champion Hill; and there also on Sunday afternoons while his father slumbered over the *Church Times*, he would regale his young brothers and sisters with the latest Gilbert and Sullivan tunes, played slowly and with solemnity to sound like hymns. Above all, he continued to frequent the Zoo, where he struck up a warm friendship with Garrod's successor in the Prosectorium, William Alexander Forbes, who shared his passion for birds and his ambitions to travel in the remoter places of the earth. In the summer of 1881 they separated, Forbes to study the ornithology of Brazil, Johnston to pay a prolonged visit to the de Roumeforts at their château in the Charente, where, clad in a Tunisian fez and gandura, he painted river scenes and temporarily lost his heart to a beautiful and congenially *libre-penseuse* cousin of the family. Tearing himself away in October, he rejoined Forbes in London, and together they half seriously planned a journey

---

[1] 'The Pets of an Eastern Palace: a Tunisian Study', reproduced in *The Graphic* of 28.i.82. 'The idea was taken from the charming household of Sidi Bakkoush (formerly Minister for Foreign Affairs), who kindly allowed me to make sketches in his palace of Aricana. . . . The main features of the marble entablatures and the general arrangement of the scene were taken from the deserted palace of Khairredin Pasha at Manomba.'

to Central Asia, even engaging a tutor to teach them Russian
in the evenings.

Then suddenly in November came the opportunity which
was to give Johnston his second African adventure. The
seventh Earl of Mayo, then in his early thirties, a keen sportsman and an amateur geographer and zoologist with an exciting
journey in Abyssinia already behind him, wrote asking Forbes
to accompany him on a sporting expedition to the interior of
Portuguese Angola. Lord Mayo was in touch with a hunter
called Jordan, who in 1879 had encountered in Ovamboland
a remarkable community of Trek Boers, the founders of which
had left the Transvaal in two parties in 1874 and 1875, and,
travelling by Lake Ngami and up the Okovango River, had
finally settled in a little known highland country some fourteen
stages inland from Mossamedes, the southernmost port in
Angola.[1] The lower country to the south-east of the Boer
settlements, between the Kunene and Okovango rivers, was
said by Jordan to be abounding in game; and it was Lord
Mayo's plan first to visit the Boers in order to buy horses,
oxen and wagons, and then to spend three or four months
encamped in the Kunene hunting-grounds before returning
to his customary winter pursuits with the Kildare hounds.
To Forbes, or any other Portuguese-speaking naturalist, he
offered a free trip saving only the cost of a steamer passage
from Liverpool to Mossamedes. Forbes could not be spared
from the Zoo. Johnston had both the desired qualifications,
and quickly persuaded his indulgent father to advance the
required two hundred pounds. Without even waiting for
Lord Mayo's reply, he fell to work, studying the works of
Monteiro and Serpa Pinto, the maps of Ivens and Capello,
preparing a *Report on the Natural History of Mossamedes and
District*, and discovering, in the reading-room of the British
Museum, the greatest and most lasting interest of a very
varied life: the comparative study of the Bantu languages.[2]

Although some examples of these hitherto only spoken
tongues had been captured and written down by Roman
Catholic missionaries as early as the seventeenth century,[3]
it was not until about 1800, with the penetration of the

[1] D. R. W. Bourke, Earl of Mayo: *Proposed Expedition to Ovampoland*. Printed
for private circulation by William Clowes, London 1882. Includes, at pp. 37-64,
a 'Journal of the Trek-Boers', by W. W. Jordan.
[2] J. J. Monteiro: *Angola and the River Congo*, 2 vols., London 1875; A de Serpa
Pinto: *How I crossed Africa*, 2 vols., London 1881. Johnston's report is included in
Bourke, *op. cit.*
[3] C. M. Doke: 'The Early Bantu Literature. I. The Age of Brusciotto', in
Bantu Studies, Vol. IX, p. 87.

continent from the south, that it had started to dawn almost simultaneously upon a number of students that all the languages so far discovered from the Cameroons right round to Mombasa, with the exception only of the Bushman and Hottentot enclaves of the extreme south-west, were members of a single vast family, with grammatical characteristics as consistent as those of the Indo-European family and with lexical affinities almost as close as those of the Romance languages of Western Europe. The realization of this great fact gave an altogether new point and zest to the philological penetration of the interior. Every explorer who wrote down a short vocabulary as he passed through the territory of some hitherto unvisited tribe, every missionary who pushed inland to some new district and attempted his first translation of the Lord's Prayer or of the Sermon on the Mount, added a new detail to the growing design. By the early eighteen-eighties, when Johnston entered the field, examples of a hundred and sixty-seven languages all belonging to the same group had been collected and mapped by the great amateur philologist Robert Needham Cust[1]: Johnston in his own summary, published nearly forty years later, was to pass in review two hundred and seventy-six.

Johnston's immediate object in 1881 was to qualify himself as a collector of representative vocabularies in the field. As he worked at Bleek's great *Comparative Grammar of the South African Languages*, however, he could not fail to be fascinated by the grand intellectual problems of comparison and classification which lay behind the work of recording and compilation. So little was known of the indigenous peoples of Africa south of the equator, of their origins and history, that the classification of their languages might well supply the best available evidence for their migrations and dispersions, while a reconstruction from the most common word-roots of the parent Bantu tongue from which all the modern languages had descended might point the way to the cradle-land and to the primeval culture of the race.

It was in all probability his early realization of this great Bantu problem which made Johnston so decisively an Africanist. His other interests, his painting, zoology, botany, anthropology, even his empire-building, could all have been carried on in other continents, and he might easily have considered it a duty to his versatility to spread his travels thus widely. It was the Bantu problem which made him content with tropical Africa, which lured him back there long after it was good for

---

[1] R. N. Cust: *The Modern Languages of Africa*, 2 vols., London 1883.

his health to go, and which finally occupied and gave some sense of purpose to his long retirement. At least as important an influence in Johnston's life as any intellectual interest, however, was the respect for African people almost invariably inspired by an understanding of the range, subtlety and logical precision of the Bantu languages of Africa—'vehicles of speech', so Cust described them, 'unparallelled in melody and comprehensiveness, able by their grammatical method to express every shade of thought, and out of the wealth of their word stores, when properly developed, sufficient to convey every idea, however abstruse, without demanding loan words from more cultivated languages'.[1] Even the practical business of collecting vocabularies, which Johnston pursued as assiduously in the days of his greatness as in his early travels as a freelance naturalist, provided a contact with African life and thought seldom achieved by the administrator or the employer of labour. The evening hour after the days' march or the brief relaxation from official business spent in interrogating linguistic informants—signing, acting, imitating, using every histrionic substitute for speech to overcome the linguistic barrier—all served to establish the bond of common humanity which left its mark upon his attitude to Africans and did much to explain the Johnston who, though he never hesitated to extend the range of British rule, yet remained at heart a liberal idealist in his views of how that rule should be exercised.

In January 1882 Johnston and Mayo met in London and made their decision to travel together. In April they sailed from Liverpool in an old and uncomfortable steamer, the *Benguella*, which pursued a long lingering course around the coasts of Guinea and West Central Africa. It was an instructive voyage and made at a memorable moment. For although in 1882 West Africa was on the eve of great political changes, and although at many points along the coastline and behind it the forces of European expansion were already at work, they were still operating more or less in separate and secret compartments, and the outward aspect of the land was much as it had been since the beginning of the century. After a fearful tossing in the Bay of Biscay, followed by repairs at Madeira, the *Benguella* sailed on down the still unclaimed Mauritanian coast, past St Louis and the other historic French trading-posts between the mouth of the Senegal and Cape

[1] R. N. Cust: *An Essay on the Progress of African Philology*, London 1893.

Verde. Now that Faidherbe had conquered and developed
the valley of the Senegal, their days of stagnation were over,
and the new town of Dakar was shortly to become the largest
of the West African ports. Though the fact was still unknown
in England, France was already taking active steps to extend
this possession still further. For two years past, Galliéni had
been in the interior surveying the course for a railway which
would join the Senegal to the Upper Niger: in 1883 he was to
establish a permanent post at Bamako, the future capital of
French West Africa.

After the Senegal, the Gambia: a series of small trading-
settlements up the course of the navigable river, with a rudi-
mentary government at Bathurst. Portuguese and French
Guinea were represented by isolated commercial posts.
Sierra Leone was a congeries of settlements of freed slaves
from all parts of West Africa, directly administered from
Freetown, and surrounded by a scarcely delimited protectorate
area within which a kind of *de facto* jurisdiction was exercised
by the colonial government. Liberia was a stretch of coastline
better known for its indigenous 'Kru-boys' than for its self-
governing settlements of American Negroes. The Ivory Coast
was a no-man's-land. On the Gold Coast the process of developing a British colony out of a string of long-held coastal forts
had barely commenced. East of the Gold Coast and south as
far as the Angola frontier at the Loge River there were in
1882, with the exception of the Spanish island of Fernando Po
and the Portuguese islands of São Thome and Principe,
only two small European possessions—Lagos, which had been
ceded to the British Crown in 1861, and Libreville at the mouth
of the Gaboon River, which had been maintained by France as a
freed slave settlement and naval station since the reign of
Louis Philippe. Finally, southward from Angola there extended
another unclaimed stretch of coastline from the Kunene to
the Orange River, punctuated only by the naval station at
Walvis Bay, where British sovereignty had been formally
proclaimed in 1878.

It was the central section of this West African coast, from the
Niger to the Congo, that was to be, with one brief interlude,
the main focus of Johnston's interests for six years to come.
As he first saw it from the decks of the *Benguella*, it was the
West Central Africa which had grown up out of Great Britain's
long war on the slave trade. It was a coast patrolled regularly
by British and occasionally by French warships, visited as
occasion offered by the two British Consuls stationed at Old

Calabar and St Paul de Loanda, but where the principal
European activities were commercial and missionary, and were
carried on almost independently of any government control.
Ranged along it at intervals of fifty miles or less were small
unofficial settlements, consisting each of a group of 'factories'
or trading-posts of European commercial houses, mostly
British and Dutch, occasionally American, Spanish or
Portuguese. In eastern Nigeria: Akassa, Brass, Bonny, Opobo
and Old Calabar; in the Cameroons: Victoria, Dualla and
Batonga Bay; in the Rio Muni: Batta, Elobe and Mundah;
in Gaboon: Libreville, Ogowe, Sette Cama, Mayumba,
Loango and Blackpoint; in the Congo estuary and on each
side of it: Landana, Cabinda, Banana, Ponta da Lenha,
Boma, Ambrizette, Mussera, Kinsembo; at all these places
there were settlements, visited regularly by merchant shipping
from Europe, where the resident factors of firms like John
Holt, Hatton and Cookson, or the Dutch Handels Genootschap,
lived up the creeks on moored hulks or in riverside warehouses
and carried on a wholesale trade with the coastal peoples,
who acted as middlemen and retailers to the tribes of the
interior.[1]

Many of these trading-stations were also missionary centres:
in some cases, as at Victoria, it had been the mission which
had brought the factory and not vice versa. By 1882 there
were Anglicans and Methodists in the Niger Delta, Presbyterians on the Cross River, Baptists in the Cameroons, French
Fathers of the *Congrégation du Saint Esprit* at Libreville and right
down the coast to Angola, and up the Congo estuary, more
Baptists. By using native agents, who were often freed slaves
evangelized and educated at Freetown or Libreville and later
returned to their homes in Nigeria or the Gaboon, missions
had in some places, and especially in Yorubaland and the
Niger delta, penetrated further inland than the traders; but
in general the missions, too, had built up their first Christian
communities at the coast, while waiting for trade and politics
to open the way to the interior.

The very existence of all these jostling interests on the coast
of West Central Africa was apt to create a misleading impression
that the *status quo* of unrestricted commercial competition
would prove a difficult one for a would-be political annexa-
tionist to upset. Yet both West and East Africa were to provide
examples of how the older balances of power and interest in

[1] D. R. W. Bourke, Earl of Mayo: *De Rebus Africanis. The Claims of Portugal to
the Congo and adjacent Littoral*, London, W. H. Allen 1883.

the coastal regions were time and again to be upset by
determined initiatives taken in the unfrequented interior;
and in West Central Africa in 1882 there were already three
such initiatives afoot. The first of these, and that which was of
the least immediate concern to Johnston, was on the Niger,
where Taubman Goldie's National African Company, having
created a successful cartel out of the British firms trading up
the river, and having had the resulting monopoly challenged
by a politically inspired French concern, was now openly
seeking powers to consolidate its commercial hold by a network
of political treaties with the riverain tribes. The second was
on the Ogowe, where de Brazza, who had been exploring the
region almost continuously since 1875, was just completing a
special and still secret mission entrusted to him by Jules Ferry
—that of obtaining treaties and founding small military posts
all over the area between Libreville and Stanley Pool, which
was shortly to become the colony of the Gaboon and the
gateway to French Equatorial Africa. The third was on the
Congo, where Stanley had been employed since 1878 as the
executive head of an organization directed by King Leopold
of the Belgians and called first the International African
Association and later the *Comité d'Etudes du Haut Congo*, which
was known to be driving a road from the head of the estuary
round the cataracts to Stanley Pool and the upper river. It
was with the last of these three enterprises that Johnston's
first tropical African journey was to be chiefly concerned.

After stopping four days at Bonny, the *Benguella* next dropped
anchor in the Cameroons River, and here Johnston, who had
been suffering from acute indigestion, thankfully accepted the
hospitality of the naval survey ship *Rambler*, which happened
to be proceeding in the same direction. It was a fateful transfer,
for half-way down the coast, at Cabinda, the *Rambler* picked up
Mr Augustus Cohen, the British consul at Loanda, who had
been travelling on business in the northern section of his
district. Perhaps the consul was intrigued by the frail and
childlike appearance of the Commander's guest; perhaps he
was secretly grateful for some dilution of the exclusively
nautical company: at all events he found time to make friends
with Johnston, to enter into the spirit of his adventure and to
suggest a more promising opening than big game hunting on
the Kunene. No doubt, as the *Rambler* churned southwards
through the clear sunlight of the southern autumn, Cohen
speculated freely about the future of the Congo basin, about
the significance of de Brazza's mission, about the objectives

of the International Association, about Portuguese aspirations and British interests; no doubt at all, he found in Johnston a responsive and flattering listener. Certainly, before they parted at Loanda, he had proposed that Johnston, so soon as he had fulfilled his obligations to Lord Mayo, should return to the Congo with a letter of introduction to Stanley. Perhaps the youthful naturalist would find it easier than others to discover what was really happening on the river. Perhaps Stanley would offer him a job. Perhaps, however, Johnston would prefer to seek a nomination to a consular post in Africa under the British Foreign Office.

At Loanda, the *Benguella* having arrived late and the monthly mail steamer for the southern ports having already left, Lord Mayo joined Johnston in the *Rambler*, which landed them at Mossamedes on June 22nd. Here, while they waited for Jordan to bring down oxen and wagons from the Boer settlements, they stayed in great comfort with a Portuguese doctor, quite a worthy of the town, who, having had marital relations with each of his four mulatto daughters, was now on honeymoon with his eldest grandchild.

> The boys as they grew up became officials, officers in the police force; but most of the girls remained in their father-grandfather's household. The house was comparatively large. There was no disorder. Lord Mayo, his servant and I all had separate, nicely tended bedrooms, quite clean. There was only a crowd over the two big meals of the day; breakfast at eleven and dinner at sunset. The voices of the girls and women were pleasant-sounding, and their manners were irreproachable.[1]

At last on July 9th their transport was ready and they set out across the seventy miles of arid waste which separated them from the steep scarp of the Serra de Chella and the fertile tableland, draining gently south-eastward to the upper Kunene, which lay beyond. Johnston seems to have been from the start a somewhat wayward member of the expedition, lingering far behind the caravan to sketch and botanize, frequently failing to reach the camp by nightfall. On at least one occasion he lay down to sleep alone in lion-infested country; on another he sought the hospitality of a Portuguese farmhouse, the occupant of which was in exile for murdering his uncle. The northernmost of the Boer settlements at Humpata was reached on July 25th, and from here the expedition turned southwards, following an affluent of the

[1] *Story*, p. 93.

Kunene, the Kakulovari. The country was uninhabited and sport good, and for nearly two months they drifted slowly from camp to camp amid herds of elephant and buffalo, zebra and giraffe, with the occasional rhinoceros to spice the excitement. An idyllic life, Johnston called it; but as August turned to September, and as Lord Mayo strayed ever further afield, he grew impatient and rode on down to the Kunene alone. He visited the most south-easterly of the Portuguese garrisons, at Humba, and spent some days at the celebrated Ovambo Mission of Father Duparquet. On his return to the camp he found that Lord Mayo had decided to prolong his trip still further, so taking advantage of the company of a Swedish white hunter who was returning to Mossamedes, he said his farewells and departed.[1]

He was now independent. He was also all but penniless. He had what was left from two hundred pounds after paying for his journey out, and eighty pounds of this had to be set aside for his return passage. If he was to succeed in reaching the Congo he would have to use all his good manners and all his wits. His first objective was Mossamedes, his second Loanda and Consul Cohen. He painted his way to the first, earning his hospitality from Boer farmers and Portuguese garrison officials; to the second, thanks possibly to his association with Lord Mayo, he was conveyed in a Portuguese gunboat as an official guest. At Loanda he met with kindness not only from Cohen but from his vice-consul and deputy, Mr Newton, who owned a general store in the capital and managed a fleet of small steamers plying up and down the Kwanza River. For a happy and instructive fortnight Johnston was the guest of Newton's company. He made the journey of two hundred and fifty miles to Dondo, the principal market for the trade of the interior, and was fascinated by the variety of native races there represented—colobus-capped Bangalas from the Upper Kwango, Balunda from the Kasai, Baluba from the kingdom of the Mwata Yanvo half-way across Africa, Quissamas and Libollos from the south and south-east. From the Scottish engineers of the steamer he was able to supplement his own hurried observations on the state of Portuguese rule. The owner of a lime kiln near Dondo openly boasted that he paid the local Quissamas five shillings a head for returning his

[1] Cf. Lord Mayo: 'A Journey from Mossamedes to the River Cunene', *Proceedings of the Royal Geographical Society*, 1883, p. 458, and Johnston in *The Graphic*, 17.xi.83.

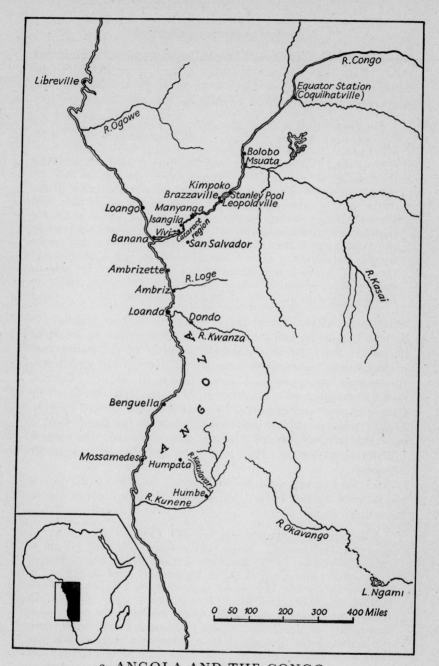

2. ANGOLA AND THE CONGO

To illustrate Johnston's journeys of 1882-3.

runaway slaves. The whole stretch of country for a hundred miles to the south of the Kwanza was quite unoccupied and ungarrisoned; travellers from Loanda to Benguella and the southern settlements could go only by sea.

But [wrote Johnston in an article for *The Graphic*[1]] even as it is we must not forget to give the Portuguese their due. Of all the European powers that rule in tropical Africa none have pushed their influence so far into the interior as Portugal. And the Portuguese rule more by influence over the natives than by actual force. The garrisons at Dondo, Malange and other places in the interior range perhaps from fifty to two hundred men, and these are nearly entirely native soldiers. The country is so thickly populated that the inhabitants could in a moment sweep away the Portuguese if they disliked their rule. What Portugal wants for the development of her magnificent colonies is money and men. She is too poor and too thinly populated to be able to supply these essentials herself and she is too much afraid of foreign aggression to invite them from other nations.

Johnston liked the Portuguese whom he met in Angola. He had no colour prejudice himself, and, though not unaware of its darker sides, he was a sincere admirer of the easy-going, unpretentious ascendancy over the native people which was the basis of Portuguese rule. In particular, the idea of a Central African empire, still Portuguese in name but fertilized by British capital and remotely controlled by the British Foreign Office, was one which seeded and grew in his mind until it was stunted by his diplomatic contacts with Portuguese officials in Lisbon in 1889; and even then it was not finally uprooted.

Back in Loanda, and before starting on the second lap of his journey to the Congo, he wrote in triumphant terms to his father.

I do hope my pictures may be sold. One success, one act of notoriety—let me only cross Africa—and they will go off at twice their value. In the meantime I could not be living cheaper or to greater advantage. I am so happy, and have never been so unailing in my life. Do you know how much I have spent since landing in Africa last May? Remember I have reached the borders of Ovamboland, have visited the great Cunene River, thoroughly explored the Chella Mountains and have been 250 miles up the Quanza. I have a hundred sketches and two thick books with notes on Natural History. I have an exceptionally fine collection of plants and birds, and how much do you think

---

[1] *The Graphic*, 17.xi.83.

it has cost me? Four pounds only—and spent in buying curiosities, giving tips and the little etceteras of daily life. In Africa, when a traveller with a civil tongue is also an artist, ordinary kindness gives way to enthusiastic hospitality and everything is done to aid him and to save his purse. I have been the guest of Englishmen, French, Portuguese, Dutch, Swedes, Belgians, Germans and even Negroes. For three weeks I was an indulged guest on a man-of-war, living like a petted child for nothing, whilst Lord Mayo was charged the regulation pound a day. The Boers lent me horses for nothing. The Portuguese Governor of Mossamedes sent me to Loanda in a Portuguese man-of-war, charged me nothing for my passage, and described me as a distinguished person in his official letter. I have just returned from a journey of five hundred miles as the guest of the Quanza Navigation Company. This expedition cost me exactly seven shillings. I am very hard worked, and think it is that which keeps me so well. I study Portuguese and the native languages, ride, boat, fish, shoot.[1]

In the same exuberant mood, at the end of October, he set off northwards, not knowing, not much caring, where his travels would eventually lead him. He took a Dutch steamer from Loanda to Ambriz, then landed and pursued his way across the Portuguese frontier in a hammock. The arid coastal belt of south-west Africa was now narrowing to a mere mile or so in width and he exulted in the beautiful park-like scenery, studded with splendid baobabs, spangled with yellow convolvulus and tall yellow orchids, and scented with the blossoms of aloe and jasmin. At night he camped out with his carriers on the dry sands by the sea, or found hospitality at one of the many trading-factories along the coast—Kinsembo and Mussera, where trade was mainly in native-grown coffee, Ambrizette, which was the terminus of the great ivory route from San Salvador and the Upper Congo. At all these places the landward trade was in the hands of Africans, and the European merchants did not wish it otherwise. Their sole political concern was to maintain their independence from all civilized governments, and so to be free from customs duties and from officials who might pry too closely into the nature of the labour supply which they used about their settlements.[2]

[1] Cited Alex Johnston, *op. cit.*, pp. 40-1.
[2] For the journey from Loanda northwards and up the Congo, Johnston's manuscript notebooks and sketch-books survive and can be used to check his published accounts: *The River Congo from its mouth to Bolobo*, London 1884; 'An Artist on the River Congo', *The Graphic*, 13.x.83; 'A Visit to Mr Stanley's Stations on the River Congo' and 'The River Congo from its mouth to Bolobo', in *Proceedings of the Royal Geographical Society*, 1883, pp. 569-81 and 692.

Things were very different on the Congo itself, whither Johnston now took ship from Ambrizette. There every European, whether merchant or missionary, understood quite clearly that the days of private enterprise free from any political control were coming to an end. A road was being driven round the rapids, above which, on the Congo and its tributaries, there were known to be some four thousand miles of navigable waterway. Once steamers were operating on this vast, fan-shaped river system, the whole trade of the interior, instead of passing by carriers over a large number of lateral routes to a long stretch of coast, would be channelled through a single bottle-neck at Stanley Pool—and then everything would turn upon the political control of the limited number of practicable routes from Stanley Pool to the estuary and the sea. For, despite King Leopold's professions, it was inconceivable that an organization which was prepared to sustain the vast expense of opening the Upper Congo to navigation would not seek to recoup itself by establishing a commercial monopoly, which in the long run would be enforceable only by political control. Meantime, while the International Association was consolidating its position locally by buying sites and founding stations, and while its various component interests were still jockeying amongst themselves for the internal direction, an elaborate curtain of secrecy was being maintained over the whole Congo estuary to prevent any but interested parties from seeing what was going on. At the Dutch factory at Banana Point Johnston encountered Dr Pechuel Loesche, the head of the German section of the Association, who informed him that Stanley was in Europe and would not be returning, and that in present circumstances it would not be possible for him to travel any further up the river.

It was one of those occasions when Johnston's varied talents served him well. He stayed at Banana a fortnight, painting the scenery assiduously from breakfast till tea, giving most ostentatious attention to his botanical specimens and also to a tame cuckoo which he had brought with him from Ambrizette. He even painted Dr Pechuel Loesche's portrait. Meantime there arrived at the factory a Mr Butcher, a member of the Baptist Mission, who in whispered conversations suggested to him that since the Association's activities were confined to the north bank of the estuary he should attempt to reach the Pool from the Society's station at Underhill on the opposite shore. Butcher then departed in the mission boat, and after a few more days spent in lulling suspicion and in talking of

OLD CALABAR IN 1882

THE CAMEROONS MOUNTAIN FROM MONDOLE

his forthcoming departure for Europe, Johnston was permitted to cross to the Portuguese factory at Kisangwe on the south bank, whence he was able after some further delay to attract the attention of a British steamer carrying building materials upstream to Underhill. There the situation changed suddenly for the better. One morning the missionary company was seated at breakfast when a native rumour flew round the station that *Bula Matari*—the breaker of rocks—was returning. At noon a small steamer passed, making only two knots against the swirling stream, and Johnston had his first sight of Stanley, in a large helmet, seated on a chair, gazing intently towards his Congo capital at Vivi, which was just coming into view.[1] Cohen's letter of introduction was quickly despatched, preparations for the south bank expedition deferred, and on December 18th Johnston with beating heart was climbing Vivi Hill, which, 'rising high above the rushing stream, the white houses gleaming out in their brightness on the great gaunt cliff', looked less like a peaceful settlement than 'the stronghold of some river pirate and the storehouse of his booty'.[2]

It was evening and Stanley was seated on a camp-chair at the door of his house. Round him in a semicircle squatted the chiefs and other delegates of the villages round Vivi, come to pay their respects to *Bula Matari* after his return from Europe. It was a courtly little scene, enacted with all the ease and slow composure that go with nakedness and illiteracy. Questions were being asked about the white man's country, and as Stanley's answers on the marvels of Western science came back to them quaintly clad in the similes and paraphrases of the interpreter, the pipe stems were gently removed and they clapped their open mouths in polite expressions of wonder. It was a sight which made an instant appeal to Johnston's artistic sense.

> I paused involuntarily to look at this group, for Stanley had not yet seen me approaching and was unconscious of observation. Perhaps he never posed better for his picture than at that moment, as he sat benignly chatting and smoking with the native chiefs, while the bearing of his head still retained that somewhat proud carriage that inspired these African chieftains with a real respect for his wishes, and a desire to retain his friendship.[3]

Johnston greeted, the conference went on; but an hour later twenty-seven Europeans sat down to dine at a long table laid out of doors near the edge of the cliff, with the moonlight playing on the mountains and the river rushing beneath. There, while

[1] *Story*, p. 107.   [2] *The Graphic*, 13.x.83.   [3] *The River Congo*, pp. 46-7.

B

the wine circulated and the cigar smoke curled towards the stars, Stanley talked long of past African experiences, and Johnston felt himself at last in the company of the great.

Stanley was welcoming, even fatherly. Doubting perhaps the young explorer's physical powers, he counselled him strongly against attempting the south bank route, which had defeated two experienced Baptist missionaries, Grenfell and Comber, in 1878. But he did not at this stage offer any alternative, so Johnston returned nettled to Underhill and started immediately for the interior. His health had never been better, but it proved to be no expedition for a poor man. The carriers were expensive as well as mutinous, and with the exorbitant blackmail levied at every village, he found that his progress was costing him a pound a mile. There was nothing for it but to swallow his pride and return to Vivi.[1] This time he met with a more helpful reception. Vandervelde, the *chef de station*, was all kindness. Stanley talked to him much and got his measure. Soon the rugged chief of the expedition was to be writing him intimate chatty letters, confessing that he had enjoyed his company more than any he remembered, and chaffing him boisterously about his personal appearance.

And did you really step up to the big Dankelman, and conquer him at last by your suavity? A delicious story it would have been could you have added that with the confitures he kissed you! Fancy Comber on one side who is certainly not remarkable for bigness, jamming and biscuiting you and Dankelman too, both seeming to think that this was the staccato thrust or probe for your love. I wish I had Tenniell or Leech's pencil to put you in an Eton boy's dress with the broad white linen collar and short jacket, smilingly receiving jam and sweet biscuits from Comber in Newmarket breeches and Dankelman in tall boots, shirt sleeves and broad-brimmed Jim Crow hat. But perhaps you are clever at this sort of thing and can see precisely what I mean. The very thought of it makes one laugh.[2]

There was no difficulty now about a journey to the upper river, and on January 7th Johnston set out by the official route to Stanley Pool, taking with him eleven of the Association's carriers, loaded with provisions and camping-equipment, arms and ammunition, and even a flag, all supplied from the stores at Vivi. To these as a parting thought Stanley added three of his own Zanzibari bodyguards, armed with Snider rifles, and enjoined to protect the child of *Bula Matari*.

[1] *P.R.G.S.*, 1883, pp. 569-81.
[2] Stanley to Johnston from Leopoldville 9.vii.83, *Johnston Papers*, cited Alex Johnston: *op. cit.*, p. 49.

The line of communications which Johnston was now to follow from Vivi at the head of the estuary to its highest point at Bolobo nearly five hundred miles up the river was that established by Stanley during the first phase of his Congo mission between September 1879 and July 1882. The first half of its course, as far as Stanley Pool, was a temporary one, dictated solely by the problem of moving the steamer sections and the building materials for the higher stations with no other means of land transport than light, porter-drawn wagons, for the passage of which a road had first to be constructed through some of the most unpleasant country in the world, steep stony hillsides and narrow, baking valleys, each with a belt of tropical forest to be cleared and a rushing river to be bridged. In these circumstances it was necessary to use every mile of navigable water, and to cleave straight through the cataract region instead of skirting it as the railway was soon to do. It had taken Stanley nearly a year to drive his road the fifty-two miles round the lower stretch of cataract to his second station at Isangila, a distance which Johnston now walked comfortably in four days. From Isangila there was a navigable reach of eighty-eight miles to Manyanga, the third station, where, since the north bank beyond it was within de Brazza's treaty area, the Association's route now crossed the river and by-passed the upper cataract from the south, through ninety-five miles of somewhat easier country to Leopoldville at the south-western extremity of the Pool.[1] Johnston loitered a week at Manyanga, staying with Nilis at the station, and paying two visits to Malamine, the capable, French-speaking Gabonese sergeant whom de Brazza had left behind him to look after French interests; then, with a developing ulcer in the leg, he performed an uncomfortable march to Leopoldville, limping into the station early in February and resting there nearly three weeks, with the Baptist pioneer Comber for physician.

Leopoldville perhaps marked the end of Johnston's apprenticeship as a traveller. So far he had made an interesting and unusual journey on remarkably little money. He had been in remote places with Lord Mayo and he had returned through them with the Swedish hunter Eriksson. But in so far as he had travelled on his own, it had been in the main from one European station to another by fairly well-known routes. His one attempt to blaze a private trail had petered out in less than a week. In a geographical sense all that he was now

[1] H. M. Stanley: *The Congo and the Founding of its Free State*, 2 vols., London 1885, Vol. I, pp. 160-356.

to do had been done several times before; he was always to
have a European habitation somewhere ahead of him; but
it was nonetheless travelling that required a high order of
self-reliance. From Leopoldville onwards the stations were
widely spaced and fitfully occupied. There were no doctors.
There was little European food. On a river frequently lashed
by sudden squalls to the violence of a stormy sea, his vehicle
in one direction was to be an open whaleboat, in the other a
native canoe. He would have to lead in a completely new way
his crew of Zanzibaris, and in their company to trust himself
to the good nature and hospitable instincts of African villagers,
some of whom had not yet seen a European at closer quarters
than on a boat in midstream. He would have to talk his way
out of difficult situations and to judge when it was prudent to
retreat.

Judging by the scattered notes which he kept in default of
a diary, he came through most tests in high spirits. Certainly
he seems to have been at all times singularly free of that
ranting exasperation at all delays and other petty annoyances
which so frequently afflict the European in the tropics. Faced
by the unexpected and uncomfortable, he kept his powers of
observation and his sense of humour.

The rain increases and the sky is covered with a dense pall of
cloud. The boat is put into a little creek and we dispose ourselves as best we can under shelter. The Zanzibaris knowing
better the indications of the weather than I, invite me to
descend and take refuge in a house, but foolishly wiser than they,
I persist in remaining where I am. At length such is the deluge
that descends that I am compelled to take their advice—and we
scramble on shore through the wet grass to a neighbouring house
which is put at our disposal. Here the comfort is for the first
few moments delicious—perfect dryness and a comfortable bed
of matting to sit on. The other occupants of the house, excepting
the many and constant visitors, are a middle-aged man with his
wife suckling a baby whose forehead is ornamented with a
band of scarlet pigment, and an old man who might be a poor
broken-down uncle of the family. There is a wood fire in the
middle, the smoke of which is very disagreeable. The house is
clean and tidy and round the walls are ranged many neatly
made articles—long pipes with little bowls, a clarionet, a white
mug, a collection of skilfully made little pouches of goat skin
containing I know not what, hippopotamus harpoons, fishing
nets, horns and a multitude of odds and ends. . . . We open our
case of provisions, lay the cloth on the bed and sit down with
considerable appetite to our frugal repast. All this time visitors
are flocking in. Many children, some of them pretty little things,

have made friends with me and are wonder-stricken at my watch. Then comes a wicked old gentleman with a wife and two marriageable daughters. He is most anxious I should become his son-in-law, *moyenant* several lengths of cloth. He mistakes my prudish reserve for scorn, and hastens to point out the manifold charms of his girls, notably patting and squeezing their plump breasts. But I remain unmoved. A happy thought seizes him—perhaps I like maturer charms and his wife is dragged forward. . . .[1]

Despite this experience, which occurred on his first night out of Leopoldville, Johnston acquired and kept a strong preference for sleeping in native huts to camping out of doors. They were drier and freer of insects; he enjoyed his social contacts with the lenders, and the furniture nearly always provided some curious object for his pencil to record. Apart from such night stops, however, he did not dally on his journey upstream, but pushed straight on to Bolobo, completing the two hundred and forty miles in fourteen days. It was an interesting place, the centre of a dense population of Bayanzi people of distinctly superior culture to their neighbours, their leaders wealthy and sophisticated ivory traders, who travelled great distances both eastwards up the river and westwards to Stanley Pool and beyond. An extended stay there might well have been profitable; but unfortunately Lieutenant Orban, the *chef de station*, was only waiting for the whaleboat to descend the river, and not relishing the company of the two commercial agents who were to remain, Johnston elected to accompany him to Msuata, the station a hundred miles downstream, where he had already met and taken an instant liking to the sole occupant, Lieutenant Eugene Janssen. Here, at the confluence of the Kwa with the Congo, he would be for linguistic purposes within reach of three important tribes, the Bayanzi, the Wabuma and the Bateke; here, too, he could live in congenial company so long as his resources lasted and then, choosing his weather, make a quick dash by canoe for the Pool.

At Msuata Johnston passed the most blissful, certainly also the most significant, six weeks of his whole journey. The incumbent, Janssen, was a resourceful pioneer, a young man whose steady, single-handed work rejoiced the critical eye of Stanley himself, a true colonist who could not only endure hardship but create comfort. His station was the neatest on the river, his table the best served. His kitchen garden abounded

---

[1] Congo Notebooks, 20.iii.83, *Johnston Papers*. A rather more elaborate account of this incident appears in *The River Congo*, pp. 175-7.

in European as well as African vegetables; his poultry yard and his milch-goats, though a constant temptation to the forest leopards, insulated the station from local scarcities and famine. He had invented his own method of extracting oil from groundnuts, so that his cuisine was various and appetizing.[1] Johnston learnt much here of the art of living alone, much that he was to practise with success during his own six months on Kilimanjaro and during his eighteen months on Mondole Island in the Cameroons.

The material side of life apart, it was above all at Msuata that Johnston founded his reputation as a naturalist and ethnographer. It was from here that he brought back his thousand-word comparative vocabularies of Iteke, Ebuma and Kiyanzi, and his notes and drawings on the customs and material culture of these tribes. It was in his daily rambles through the surrounding forest on both sides of the river that he had his first real opportunity of applying the knowledge he had gained as the pupil of Garrod and Forbes. His botanical and zoological notes, his collections of butterflies and fish, above all his classified list of a hundred and forty-six distinct species of birds, which turned his book *The River Congo* from a mere traveller's log into the credentials for his next African journey—all these owed much to his stay at Msuata. Though active, they were also eventless weeks. They were marked in his personal notebook only by the notice of a sudden storm, which caught him in a canoe in mid-Congo and nearly led him to disaster. It was an entry which he was to work up in *The River Congo* into one of the finest passages of descriptive prose he ever produced, fluid and conversational in style, cumulative in effect, deeply influenced by Stanley, yet lighter and more artistic than Stanley's majestic literary hammer-strokes.[2] By the time he did this, his recollection was inspired by a double emotion, for Janssen had been drowned in just such a storm as he had experienced, and in his imagination he was associating Msuata always with the memory of a very real friendship. 'What a happy life we led. We were all by ourselves, each one with his attentive retinue of Zanzibaris. What merry picnics we had in the primeval forests. What hunts of hippopotami, crocodiles, leopards and antelopes. How eagerly we searched for rare butterflies. What aviaries we formed of the birds we entrapped and tried to tame.'[3]

At last, however, the time came for his return, and on a

[1] Congo Notebooks, 27.ii.83, *Johnston Papers*.   [2] *The River Congo*, pp. 265-9.
[3] *The Graphic*, 13.x.83.

bright Sunday morning, April 15th, 1883, he bade farewell to
Janssen, and slipped swiftly downstream in a couple of hired
canoes.

> Everything seemed propitious to my journey . . . the sun shone
> out of a pale blue sky unspotted with the slightest cloud. His
> heat was tempered with the tenderest breeze blowing from the
> west and according to me a message from the sea I was longing
> to greet. There was a general sense of bright activity in all
> things. The kingfishers and the bitterns had never fished with
> such avidity nor squeaked so lustily at every capture. The grey
> parrots were setting out for their day's excursion and whistled
> melodiously as they whirred over our heads. Even the very fish
> leapt in silvery shoals round the prow of the advancing canoe.
> The men sang and the paddles clove the water so energetically
> under their vigorous strokes that my contentment was at times
> disturbed by the occasional showers of spray they flung at me
> and my goods. But I could not check their exuberance, it was
> consistent with my own joy at being homeward bound.[1]

On the 17th he reached the Pool, where, at Kimpoko, he
found to greet him 'the pleasant face of Coquilhat', who in a
few months was to be transferred to the new Equator Station,
three hundred miles beyond Bolobo, which now bears his
name. On the 18th, while paddling gently round the southern
shore of the Pool towards Leopoldville, he saw a multitude
collected at the village of Kinshasha, and landing to investigate, found Stanley in full ceremonial parley with the
chiefs and elders of the people.[2]

Now, if not before, Johnston must have realized what were
the real aims of the International Association. His arrival at
Vivi three months before had coincided with Stanley's return
from Belgium. He had travelled up-river ahead of him; and
he had visited stations which were still, as they had been since
their foundation, fortified warehouses built on plots of land
specifically purchased from the chiefs, where from one to three
Europeans lived with perhaps thirty Zanzibari or West Coast
soldier labourers, cultivating trade relations with the locals,
but making not the slightest attempt to govern. The garrisons
were in fact regarded by the people simply as the domestic
slaves of the white men; and there was an interesting example
of this in the early days of Equator Station, when a chief
having died and some slaves being required to be sacrificed

[1] *Ibid.*, 15.iv.83, *Johnston Papers.*
[2] *Ibid.*, 18.iv.83.

at his obsequies, Coquilhat was confidentially approached
about the purchase of some members of his bodyguard.[1] On
the overland sections of the route the villages situated between
one station and the next had entered into agreements, sealed
usually by the ceremony of blood brotherhood, to respect
the road and its users; but along the river reaches there were
whole communities still unvisited, and nowhere was there
any consolidated area where agreements existed in territorial
depth.

So far the Association's claim to be a philanthropic, non-
political body opening the Congo basin for the benefit of its
inhabitants and the world at large could be at least negatively
substantiated. But it was Stanley's mission between January
1883 and May 1884 to change all this. 'The second phase',
in his own words, was 'the consolidation of the work by
obtaining the concession of their authority from all the chiefs
along the route, and such other rights as they may possess,
which could be obtained by others to oppress us who pioneered
the way'.[2] Accordingly, while Johnston had been working
his way inland, Stanley had been despatching expeditions
from Vivi, westwards along the north bank of the estuary to
Banana Point and eastwards along the south bank of the
cataract region, and now he himself had moved up to Stanley
Pool and was engaged, when Johnston refound him, in the
same task of obtaining the title deeds for European government.[3]

When Stanley talked of 'others who might oppress us', he
meant of course not only the French but the Portuguese: in
fact, the most immediate spur to his activities in 1883 came
not from de Brazza but from the rumours of an impending
treaty between England and Portugal, whereby England, in
exchange for a promise of limited tariffs and freedom for
missionary work, would recognize an extension of Portuguese
sovereignty in Angola so as to include both banks of the
Lower Congo. In truth, so far as the British Foreign Office
was concerned, the proposed Anglo-Portuguese treaty was not
directed against the Association. It had originated several
years before, after a series of scandals connected with slave-
owning by commercial houses on the Congo estuary, as a
scheme whereby Portugal should declare a protectorate on
the south bank and England on the north. It had been revived
as an issue in November 1882 solely as a defensive measure

---

[1] H. M. Stanley: op. cit., II, pp. 180-2.   [2] Ibid., I, pp. 464-5.
[3] Ibid. I, pp. 470-97.

against French expansion. Since French rivalry on the Niger, so ran Granville's argument, was likely to necessitate the declaration of a British protectorate between the Niger delta and the Cameroons, and since Gladstonian finance would not permit two extensions of territory in the same part of the world in a single year, better the Portuguese in the Congo on terms that would not exclude British trade than the French on their own terms which certainly would do so.[1]

The Association did not even enter into these calculations as a possible alternative to either Portugal or France. The Foreign Office officials were still quite in the dark as to Leopold's ultimate intentions. They could not guess that he was out to found an independent political power. They were beginning to suspect that his motives were commercial rather than philanthropic, but that only made it the more likely, in their view, that he would end by selling out his interests to the French. All this was an entirely different view to that of Stanley, and indeed of every English or American trader or missionary working on the Congo. To these, the danger from France seemed remote, a few treaties in the interior, un-supported as yet by any commercial or political activities; and consequently the Anglo-Portuguese treaty appeared to show an incomprehensible preference on the part of the British Government for a nation which had always excluded Protestant missions and impeded foreign trade, as opposed to the Association which was already encouraging the British Baptists and boosting the sales of Manchester cotton goods by British commercial houses.

During the fortnight they spent together at Leopoldville station at the end of April 1883, the relations of Stanley and Johnston ripened into real friendship. Stanley, to judge by his subsequent letters, seems to have thrown aside discretion and to have talked freely to the young man of twenty-four, not only about his own hopes and disappointments on the Congo but also about the affairs and personalities of the Association. Johnston, to judge by his books and other publica-tions, seems to have scrupulously respected these confidences, to the extent of keeping silent about many, many matters which he could honestly have attributed to his own observations and not to Stanley's talk. There is indeed no more convincing proof of his loyalty to Stanley than the fact that he left no record, even for posterity, of what must have been for him at the time a portentous body of information, which the outside

[1] E. Fitzmaurice: *Granville*, II, pp. 341-6.

B*

world was eager to learn, which he could repeatedly have used for his own advantage, and of which he only communicated under pressure a few brief and general comments to two senior officials of his own Foreign Office.

He did not, however, feel bound to carry his obligations to Stanley to the length of decrying his good friends the Portuguese; and in view of the fact that Stanley later felt that Johnston had betrayed him by giving his support to the Anglo-Portuguese treaty, it is interesting to find, in the earliest and most completely friendly letters which they exchanged after Johnston's departure, that there existed a clear difference on this score which Stanley was trying most persuasively to resolve.[1]

LEOPOLDVILLE
July 23rd, 1883

MY DEAR MR JOHNSTON,
You have aroused me by your remarks on the Portuguese. . . . I hope you will not be tempted by the self-interested hospitality of the Portuguese to give your vote that the Congo shall

[1] *Johnston Papers.* As Professor J. Stengers of the Université Libre de Bruxelles has pointed out, this letter is very carefully written. The only area to which Stanley explicitly suggests that British protection should be extended is the Lower Congo, where the International Association had as yet no treaties, and where the Portuguese danger was greatest. For the rest, for all the high-flown language about the British Empire, all the letter need be read as saying is that opportunities which would be open to British subjects under a régime conducted by the International Association would be closed by a Portuguese régime, whatever the professions made in the treaty. Finally, says Stengers, there was the fact that King Leopold's sovereignty on the Congo had not yet been recognized by any of the powers, and it was still doubtful whether it ever would be. 'Imaginons Stanley à Léopoldville en juillet 1883. Il est là, isolé, manquant de nouvelles. . . . Il sent que des menaces étrangères pèsent sur le Congo—menaces françaises d'un côté, menaces portugaises de l'autre. L'œuvre qui est en si grande partie la sienne est en péril. Pour la protéger, il faudrait un drapeau devant lequel l'étranger soit obligé de s'arrêter. Celui que l'expédition arbore—le drapeau bleu étoilé d'or—a peut-être quelque prestige moral, mais il n'a encore aucune valeur politique: aucune puissance étrangère ne l'a reconnu. Peut-on en vouloir à Stanley, angoissé, de songer au drapeau britannique qui sauverait tout, qui sauverait, croit-il, Léopold II lui-même, dont l'entreprise pourrait désormais se développer sur un plan non-politique, à l'abri des convoitises?' Stanley, Léopold II et l'Angleterre. *Le Flambeau*, No. 4, 1954, p. 384.

Professor Stengers' reasoning is amply confirmed by the following extract from a letter of Stanley to Sir William Mackinnon dated 10.v.84, *Mackinnon Papers*, School of Oriental and African Studies, for which I am indebted to Miss M. de Kiewiet: 'I frankly tell you that despite the comparatively strong position of the Association on the Congo, any energetic officer of Portugal or France, with 50 men, is stronger on the Congo than we with a thousand. Why? Because we do not understand whether we have a right to resist by force of arms an aggressive act of Portugal or France. And should we do so, what power will uphold us or sympathize with us? . . . It was the fear of something like this arising on the Congo that stimulated me to make adherents in England on behalf of the Association. Hence my speech in Paris against de Brazza, my talk with the *Telegraph* correspondent, my reception and treatment of Johnston, my letter to him, etc., etc.'

1. LEOPOLDVILLE IN 1883

From the original drawing by Sir Harry Johnston in the possession
of the Royal Geographical Society, London.

be given to them. If England but waits a little she will see sufficient cause to judge that she has as much right as any other nation which only seeks to exclude British trade from this outlet to Central African trade. Despite every prognostication to the contrary, this river will yet redeem the lost Continent. By itself it forms a sufficient prospect, but when you consider its magnificent tributaries which flow on each side of it giving access to civilization to what appeared hopelessly impenetrable a few years ago, the reality of the general utility and benefit to these dark tribes and nations fills the sense with admiration. Every step I take increases my enthusiasm for my work and confirms my first impression. Give a thousand miles to the main channel, three hundred to the Kwango, a hundred and twenty to Lake Mantumba, three hundred to the Mobindu, probably eight hundred to the Kasai, three hundred to the Sankuru, five hundred to the Aruwimi and a thousand more to the undiscovered rivers . . . and you have 4,520 miles of navigable water, Such an ample basin . . . with its unmeasured resources would you bestow on the Portuguese, who would but seal it to the silence of the coming centuries? Would you rob the natural birthright of the millions of Englishmen yet to issue, seeking homes similar to those which their forefathers built in the Americas and the Indies? For what? Is the robust Empire called the British in its wane that you will put a limit to its growth? Such an idea is simply self-murder, and a present confession of impotence. Follow the dictates of Nature. Statistics tells us that Englishmen are increasing fast, that ships are building more and more every year, that trade is extending, that the revenue is augmenting, that colonies are forming, that wealth incessantly flows from all lands to England, that education creates thousands daily of men fit to cope with life's best work viz. to thrive and multiply. . . . Then why lock the gates of a promising field against yourselves? Let it be. Keep the gates open. Let him who seeks to enter do so without let or hindrance and leave it to Time. Time will teach the British Government where its interest, lies. Meantime observe your treaties with the native chiefs of the Lower Congo. Protect them as you promised to the chiefs as far back as 1845 through your naval chiefs. If you deliver these people into the hands of the Portuguese, the past as well as the present teaches us what to expect. You deliver them—soul and body—to Hell and slavery. To avoid the imputation of being false and faithless, proclaim a Protectorate over the Congo, and rescue these poor people from their present impending fate.

You can write and that well. Set to work—the very fact that you are fresh from our work will give what you say an importance. Lend one hand to the present movement so that neither French nor Portuguese nor any other particular nation shall defraud England of her rights and privileges in Africa in broad daylight.

It was Livingstone, an Englishman, who discovered this river, it was Anglo-American money which explored it and made it known. It was international money, part of which is English, which began the task of making it useful to the world. They are English goods, products, manufactures, which enable us to move on and win the love of the Congo nations. Will you still vote that we shall sacrifice all this in honour of Diego Cam whose countrymen allowed the pearl of African rivers to lie idle for nearly four centuries?

Yours ever,
HENRY M. STANLEY

Despite his profound and continuing admiration for Stanley himself, however, Johnston wrote no such book as this letter suggested. He went on his way homeward, marching down to Vivi, rowing down the estuary in a whaleboat, taking ship from Banana to Loanda, and thence again to Lisbon. The ship was a Portuguese one, which gave him generous stops at the island colonies of São Thome and Principe, where the labour supply for the quinine and cocoa plantations was obtained from Angola, as everyone admitted, by a most dubiously administered system of contract hire. Yet he wrote freely in praise of the Portuguese administration, as he never did of the organization directed by Stanley. When he reached Lisbon, he found awaiting him a telegram from the private secretary of King Leopold, and he travelled direct to Brussels. There were long interviews at the palace at Laeken, in which he answered the King's questions and undertook to assist in recruiting some young Englishmen for service in the Congo. There was a second visit to Brussels in September, to discuss a possible journey from the Congo to the Benue at the King's expense. But of these exciting episodes in a young man's life he kept no record and made no public mention until forty years later when he wrote in his memoirs that 'these and other things which I heard encouraged me to believe Stanley's projects of a British Congo interior would be carried out, though I was puzzled to understand why the King of the Belgians should spend hundreds of thousands on such a quixotic idea'.[1]

Only once during the autumn of 1883 did Johnston break silence on a political question. At a meeting of the British Association at Southport at the end of September he concluded a paper on the geography of the Congo by reading, apparently without comment, extracts of Stanley's letter to him of

[1] *Story*, pp. 115-17.

July 23rd. In doing so, he was breaking no confidences. The letter was obviously written for publication, and Johnston took this occasion to publish it. 'Unexpected interest', says *The Times* report, 'was aroused by the reading of a characteristic letter from Mr Stanley himself, making appeals to public sentiment, which were met with enthusiasm by many members.'[1] But there is no indication, either in *The Times* or in the official report of the proceedings, that Johnston associated himself in any way with Stanley's appeal.[2] Equally in his book, *The River Congo*, published at the end of the year, it is significant that, apart from acknowledging the hospitality which he had received, Johnston made no comment at all upon the work of the International Association. In fact, were it not for the survival in the archives of the Foreign Office of two short manuscript memoranda which tell a different story, one would be forced to conclude that Johnston at this time had no eye for political affairs. One might even be tempted to suppose that many of the tantalizing allusions of his autobiography were the exaggerations of a self-important memory.

Certainly it was as an artist and naturalist that his name now began to be known in England. *The Graphic* did him proud, publishing a series of four articles with perhaps thirty of his own drawings, no longer anonymously like his Tunis studies, but as 'An Artist's View of the River Congo—by Mr H. H. Johnston, F.R.G.S., F.Z.S., author of *The River Congo*'. The Royal Geographical Society invited him to give a full-dress evening lecture, with Lord Aberdare in the chair and Ferdinand de Lesseps beside him on the platform. 'Quel pays', remarked de Lesseps, 'où même les petits enfants sont des explorateurs.'[3] He lectured to the Society of Arts on the West African colonies of Portugal, and was introduced by Sir Frederick Goldsmid, who had just returned in ill-health after two months in King Leopold's service on the Lower Congo, as possessing all the qualities of an eminent explorer.[4] He was interviewed by W. T. Stead, the influential editor of the *Fortnightly* and the *Pall Mall Gazette*. Best of all, P. L. Sclater, the Secretary of the Zoological Society of London, was impressed enough by his work on the Congo to recommend him for the leadership of a collecting expedition to Mount

[1] *The Times*, 25.ix.83.
[2] *Report of the Fifty-third Meeting of the British Association for the Advancement of Science*, pp. 593-4.
[3] Alex Johnston: *op. cit.*, p. 23.
[4] *The Times*, 15.ii.84.

Kilimanjaro which was being jointly organized by the Royal Society and the British Association in response to a hint by Sir John Kirk, the Consul-General at Zanzibar, that British scientists were not as numerous or as active as those of some other nationalities on the mainland of East Africa.

It was in connexion with the preparations for this journey that Lord Aberdare gave him in the late autumn of 1883 a letter of introduction to a member of the Foreign Office, Henry Austin Lee, who was then acting as private secretary to Lord Edmond Fitzmaurice, the Parliamentary Under-Secretary of State for Foreign Affairs. It was a trifling matter in which he wanted help—a further introduction, which would enable him to stay in Aden at Government House while waiting for the steamer connexion to Zanzibar, there being as yet no hotel in that place—but he arrived in Downing Street at an opportune moment. The Portuguese treaty, after a full year of delicate negotiation, was approaching signature. Portugal had agreed that, in exchange for the recognition of her sovereignty over both banks of the Congo estuary for a hundred miles inland, there should be free transit to the interior both by land and water, that the Congo basin above the cataracts should be a free-trade area with the navigation on the river controlled by an Anglo-Portuguese commission. Yet, just as the end seemed to be in sight, there were signs that King Leopold, whose aims on the Congo were still largely unknown, was using his influence, not only internationally to stop the acceptance of the treaty by other powers, but even in England, through his contacts with the cotton and shipping interests in Manchester and Liverpool, to prevent its ratification by the British Parliament.

Johnston's first recorded visit to the Foreign Office was on February 22nd, 1884, when he was introduced by Austin Lee to T. V. Lister, an Assistant Under-Secretary, and to H. P. Anderson, the head of the African Department, who consulted him about the best site for a new consulate on the Congo estuary. In an able memorandum submitted the following day he suggested a place within the proposed Portuguese sphere on the south bank, at the same time arguing strongly against the selection of Vivi, where 'the Consul would be unable in any way to supervise the questionable slave trans-actions on the extreme Lower Congo, and would also be more or less dependent on the good will of the International Association. Now in parenthesis I might remark that while holding the highest opinion of Mr Stanley and desiring to express the greatest appreciation of his personal dealings with the natives, I cannot say the same of his subordinates especially at Vivi.'[1] It was a guarded comment, but its significance was not lost on Lister.

I have seen Mr Johnston again [he wrote a few days later] and have obtained some more information about the doings of the so-called International Association as regards slavery. He begged that he might not be quoted as he had received much kindness and hospitality from its agents. He declares, however, that the agents directly encourage S[lave] T[rade] by buying Krumanos [slaves] from the chiefs, and that, although the K. of the Belgians asserts and possibly believes that these men are bought in order to give them freedom—a system wh. necessarily encourages slave raids as much as avowed S.T. wd. do—the men so bought are worked and treated as slaves—that they are brutally flogged for slight offences—and that on one occasion when some of them ran away from the station at Isangila and were retaken, they were given each 100 blows with the manatee or hippopotamus-hide whip wh. draws blood at every stroke, and that the ringleader died under the infliction of 600 lashes. . . . Mr Johnston was implored at Brussels not to mention this circumstance to the King on the ground that it would affect H.M. so much that he wd. be unable to sleep. The King volunteered the remark that it was delightful to think of the number of Krumanos who were restored to liberty by his agents. . . .[2]

Meanwhile, on February 28th, the Anglo-Portuguese treaty had been signed; and three days later Anderson in a confidential minute informed his colleagues in the Office that King Leopold was obviously getting up an opposition to the treaty in the House of Commons, and suggested that the best way of countering it would be to show up the character of the Association's work.

I think [he went on] the proof that it is really a commercial enterprise is sufficient. My story is this. Some time ago d'Antas [the Portuguese Minister in London] sent us three treaties which had come into the hands of the Portuguese. They had been concluded with chiefs near the Lower Congo by an agent of the Company. The Portuguese denounced them, and reasonably enough, for they not only conceded sovereign rights to the Company, but gave it an absolute monopoly of trade. Our consul at Loanda afterwards obtained copies of the same treaties —he spoke in equally strong terms against them, but said he

[1] Memorandum 'for the use of Ld Edmond Fitzmaurice', enclosed in Johnston to Austin Lee 23.ii.84, *F.O.84.1809*.
[2] Memorandum by T. V. Lister dated 3.iii.84, *F.O.84.1809*.

believed that so far no attempt had been made to act on them —that in fact they were only irons in the fire for future use. When Sir F. Goldsmid returned I spoke to him about these treaties and asked him if they were made on authority as they were utterly inconsistent with the professions of the Co. He did not like the subject, but rather pooh-poohed them saying that they were only made to keep others out (by others meaning the Portuguese.)

When I saw Johnston on Thursday last I pressed him to tell me what he knew about the Co.'s proceedings. He was unwilling to speak as he said he had been hospitably treated by the agents and did not like to turn tale-bearer, but on my promising to treat what he said as confidential he spoke openly. He said that no one who had seen the agents at work could doubt that the aim of the Company was a gigantic commercial monopoly, that so far from the roads, stations etc. being open to all, they are jealously closed against all; that the sham aim of scientific objects was frankly discarded; that in fact a German man of science coming up the river had been promptly turned back; that he himself wd. never have got up if Stanley had not taken him under his special protection; that his appearance was unwelcome and created much astonishment, and that he was frequently told that he was a spy. In answer to my enquiry as to what was done at the stations he said that the principal work was making treaties with the surrounding tribes. I asked him what sort of treaties they made. He said 'I know them so well by heart that it used to be said of me sometimes that if a treaty was wanted I might be tapped for one'. I asked him to repeat the form. He did so. It was the form of one of the Lower Congo treaties I had by me. I put one in his hands which was rather a mild one as it had not the exclusive clause. He said that was not the right one. This confirmed my conviction that he was speaking the truth, and I showed him one with the exclusive clause which he at once recognised.

I then said to him: Do you think it is possible that the King does not know that the work of his agents is the conclusion of these treaties? His answer was: When he was talking I wondered whether he was marvellously simple or marvellously deep. . . .[1]

The records of these two confidential conversations, besides marking a definite step forward in the Foreign Office's appreciation of the Congo problem, are essential to an understanding of the tensions created in Johnston himself by his first West African journey. On the one hand there was his belief in Stanley, his friend and helper, with his apparent optimism that the Congo basin would become at best a

[1] Memorandum by H. P. Anderson entitled 'The Nature of the King of the Belgians Co.', dated 2.iii.84, in *F.O.84.1809*.

British Protectorate, at worst an open and profitable market for British trade. On the other hand there was his distrust both of Stanley's masters in Brussels and of his subordinates in the field, which seemed to confirm the official fears that the Congo was destined to be French and to be closed against British trade by hostile tariffs. There is no doubt that Johnston shifted his position slightly as a result of his contacts with the Foreign Office, but it was a tortured shift, from one kind of negative to another. Whereas in February he had been prepared to argue that Portugal's West African colonies were already more extensive than she could manage.[1] in March, when the terms of the Anglo-Portuguese treaty had been published, he was prepared to defend them on the grounds that an extension of Portuguese sovereignty over a hundred miles of the Congo estuary would not injure the interests of the International Association or those of a possible successor state, providing that these did not develop along anti-British lines.

Such at least was the burden of a letter which he addressed to *The Times* on the very eve of his departure for East Africa.[2] No doubt the writing of it had been suggested to him in the Foreign Office, in all probability by Fitzmaurice, who had the difficult, as it turned out the impossible, task of mobilizing parliamentary support for the treaty. But though far from a literary masterpiece, it was not the letter of a stooge or a turncoat, and even Stanley, who had most reason to be offended by it, cleared him from any charge of personal infidelity. 'I completely exonerated you at all times—there never was a question of it—from having been unfaithful to me. But "if you love me then you love my work"—and you will see how odd your conversion to the Portuguese doctrine must have been to me who was unaware what frenzy had possessed you.'[3] One would like to see the letter of Johnston's to which this was a reply. Unfortunately it has perished. Was Stanley really justified in referring to a 'conversion' or a 'frenzy'? Without doubt he had liked Johnston. He had regarded him as a friend and *protégé*. Equally without doubt, he had tried to fashion him into the instrument of a political intrigue. But Johnston had refused to be thus fashioned. He had never pretended to see eye to eye with Stanley about the Portuguese. The utmost obligation he could possibly have undertaken

[1] In an address to the Society of Arts entitled 'The West African Colonies of Portugal', *The Times*, 15.ii.84.   [2] *The Times*, 8.iii.84.
[3] Stanley to Johnston from Berlin 1885, no date, *Johnston Papers*.

towards Stanley in exchange for letting him into the Congo was that he should confine his *rapportage* to scientific matters. That obligation he appears to have strictly observed in all his public utterances. His public defence of the Portuguese Treaty was not based upon any overt disparagement of the work of the Association. As to what had passed in the Foreign Office behind closed doors, could Stanley, had he ever known, have been justly offended?

Chapter 3

THE MOUNTAIN WITH THE UNREMEMBERABLE NAME

IF it was by accident that Johnston had been involved in the politics of West Africa, his entry into those of East Africa was clearly by his own design. It is interesting that by the time he came to write his autobiography he had forgotten this fact, that he had come to picture for himself a situation in which he had acted throughout as the confidential agent of the Foreign Office officials on one hand and of Sir John Kirk on the other. Yet there is no evidence either in the official archives or in his own contemporary papers that the real object of his mission was other than the purely scientific one of making collections of the flora and fauna of Mount Kilimanjaro with a view to ascertaining their relationships with those of other African regions. It is true that the expedition owed its origin to Kirk, the Consul-General at Zanzibar. But Kirk was himself an ardent botanist; and probably it was quite genuinely in this capacity that he proposed the idea of an expedition to his friends at Kew, which had led to Johnston's employment for the purpose by the Royal Society and the British Association.

This is not to say that Kirk was oblivious of the fact that the expedition might have political consequences. No doubt he had it in mind that Kilimanjaro, besides being a botanist's paradise, was very strategically situated for the political future of East Africa, a great geographical landmark, barely two hundred miles from the coast, yet beyond what could be seriously claimed as the dominions of the Sultan of Zanzibar and therefore of what could be in some measure protected from political interference by the position of Zanzibar as an internationally recognized state. Moreover Kilimanjaro, with its temperate upper slopes and its fertile, well-watered and densely populated foothills, was as yet unoccupied by any of the four British missionary societies then working in East Africa whose inland stations lay strung out along the main Arab trade-routes to Buganda and to the slave and ivory hunting grounds around the Nyasa and Tanganyika Lakes. No doubt Kirk, who was beginning to be aware of the danger that European annexations might start in the rear of the

Sultan's dominions, reflected that in this case the recent presence of a British scientific expedition might be a better diplomatic counter than nothing at all. But he had certainly not asked for a political agent in disguise, and there is on the contrary definite evidence that Johnston's initiative in this direction took him completely by surprise and temporarily aroused his resentment and even hostility.

As for the Foreign Office officials, Johnston in his autobiography seems to have antedated the commencement of his close and confidential relations with them by at least a year. He was right of course in thinking that when he had called upon them for an introduction to the Resident in Aden, and when they had pumped him for information about his Congo journey, he had found himself in the presence of like-minded men who shared to the full his vision of the coming partition of Africa and his ideals of what should be the British part in it. In particular Sir Percy Anderson, who was to become one of his closest friends and posthumously his father-in-law, and Sir Villiers Lister, who was to be another of his warmest and most consistent supporters in his consular career, were both of them men who in the course of long service in the old Slave Trade Department had gained as intimate a knowledge of African problems as anyone then living, who had indeed come to regard most of the continent as an unclaimed appendage of the British Empire, awaiting only the recognition of its value by the mercantile classes and the abandonment of national policies of parsimony for its formal incorporation. Finally Lord Edmond Fitzmaurice, the Parliamentary Under-Secretary, had already taken an interest in the young traveller who had proved so well informed on Congo matters and had expressed, with what result will appear, a wish to be kept in touch with his future exploits. Yet so far were the men at the Foreign Office from regarding the Kilimanjaro expedition as crucial to their purposes that they entrusted Johnston, on his outward journey, with a bag for the Cairo Consulate and with a letter to Sir Evelyn Baring suggesting that he might care to take the bearer into his own, or into Egyptian, employ.

Fortunately for the Kilimanjaro expedition, Baring's reaction was characteristically and mortifyingly abrupt. He wanted no more young men sent out by the Foreign Office with no qualifications but a smattering of Arabic, and Johnston, having delivered his bag, retreated quickly to Shepheard's Hotel to nurse his wounded pride.[1] There was a month till

[1] *Story*, pp. 126-7.

the Aden boat left Suez, and he spent most of it in the congenial company of Ernest Floyer, the postmaster-general, to whom he carried a more fruitful introduction from H. W. Bates of the Royal Geographical Society. Floyer was busy organizing the postal communications for General Wolseley's army, just then mustering in Upper Egypt in preparation for the relief of General Gordon; and with him Johnston travelled up the railway to Asiut, six miles beyond the southernmost military post, where their carriage was attacked by an angry mob and extricated only with the help of a company of Hussars. After this escape they toured the delta on horseback for a blissful fortnight, and, while Floyer attended to his postal business, Johnston sketched the illustrations for two *Graphic* supplements which recorded his impressions of the Egyptian scene.

> Behind us lie the white minarets, the melon-shaped cupolas, the mud-built houses of an Egyptian city. Before us a level plain stretching uninterruptedly to the sharp horizon, variegated by brilliant streaks of emerald green, patches of yellow, bands of white and strips of purple red, according to the diversified cultivation and the stretches of ploughed land, and further dotted by clumps of tamarisk trees and date palms, which, though sparsely scattered in the foreground, yet with increasing distance and perspective close up to the sky in a dark green dotted fringe: such are the prospects before and behind us as we ride along an Egyptian country road. . . . And if it be, as I forever imagine it, a sweet spring morning in Lower Egypt, with the air full of fragrant scent from the bean crops and clover, and the many wild birds uttering joyous cries, we shall take in the simple features of a landscape in the Nile delta with placid enjoyment and approbation.[1]

Johnston's next contribution to *The Graphic* was from Zanzibar, where he had spent three weeks as the guest of Sir John Kirk, and it illustrates better even than his correspondence with Stanley the relations of easy familiarity and genial banter which he was usually able to establish with very much older, and to his contemporaries remote and frightening, men. Salisbury, Anderson, Lister, Rhodes, Kitchener, Harcourt, are all examples of people who reacted to him in the same way as Stanley and Kirk. Expecting no doubt yet another in the long list of aspiring explorers, healthy and upstanding, alert and keen, with intellectual qualities masked by a respect for seniority, they encountered something that fell outside all the categories they were accustomed to

[1] *The Graphic*, 8.x.84.

2. ZANZIBAR: THE HARBOUR

From the original drawing by Sir Harry Johnston in the possession
of the Royal Geographical Society, London.

employing, a disarming presence, fragile and singularly innocent, the face at once youthful and grave, quaintly puckered like a child wise beyond its years, yet quick, talented, resourceful, with no upper-class reserve, no exaggerated sense of the differences created by age or rank. Johnston aroused interest. He was also a perfect guest for the busy and the great, requiring no entertainment, yet turning up to every meal with a new drawing, an amusing caricature, a lampoon, a rare flower or insect illustrating some then outrageous evolutionary theory, an artistically executed map of how Africa should be partitioned. He had much to give, much that was near the surface and came away easily. Above all he could be teased, and thereby he escaped impertinence.

Kirk to his contemporaries was an almost legendary figure, once the companion of Livingstone on the Zambesi, now the majestic oriental diplomat who for nearly twenty years had represented British interests on the eastern coast of Africa, building up an ascendancy over the Omani sultanate at Zanzibar which had enabled him gradually to abolish the overseas trade in slaves without forfeiting the trust of its rulers. By the 'eighties even his masters at the Foreign Office held him in a certain awe. Yet in three weeks he gave Johnston the confidence to write of him in more human terms than any of the distinguished travellers who had enjoyed his hospitality.

Like most great men who have helped to extend the British Empire, Sir John has one dark blot on his escutcheon. Warren Hastings exterminated the Rohillas, Governor Eyre was accused of too summarily suppressing the Maroons; Sir John Kirk, more perhaps in the interests of British science than of British rule, has entirely destroyed an innocent species of monkey. The *Colobus Kirkii* had disappeared from nearly every part of the island of Zanzibar, but a rumour prevailed that it still lingered in a clump of forest as yet unvisited by hunters. Thither Sir John sent his chasseurs to report on the monkey's existence. After a week's absence they returned, triumph illuminating their swarthy lineaments. 'Well, did you find them?' asked the British Consul-General. 'Yes,' replied the men with glee, 'and we killed them every one'. Wherewith twelve monkey corpses were flung upon the floor and *Colobus Kirkii* joined the list of species extinguished by the act of man.

When Sir John Kirk gets conscience-troubled and the manes of the avenging colobi . . . tamper with his health; when Zanzibar gets stuffy and feverish and the official routine tryingly monotonous; he steals away, often on foot, to a little paradise he has created among the groves of Mbweni, a tiny settlement on the coast of the island. Here he lives a life that is to him ideally happy. He chats with his tenants, who lead arcadian lives with nothing to do and plenty to eat; he wanders in a shooting coat amid the groves of cocoa palms and the clumps of pandanus that border the sea; he photographs; and above all he gardens. Here, among his cycads and his orchids, his ensetes and his dracaenas, spade in hand, wide-awake hat on his head, a rare flower in his buttonhole, and rustic contentment irradiating his face—here, amid scenery which typifies the botanist's paradise, Sir John Kirk is emphatically at home.[1]

Of what passed between the older and the younger man on the subject of the forthcoming expedition we have unfortunately only Johnston's very much later memories. Certainly Kirk gave him letters of introduction to Mandara, the chief of the Moshi sub-tribe, who had developed closer and more regular relations with Swahili traders from the coast than any of the other Chagga chieftains, ruling each a valley in the mountain's complex outworks. It would seem that they had some further conversation about the course which Johnston should pursue in the event of his encountering the representatives of any foreign power who might be bent on making annexations in the interior. There was at Zanzibar in April 1884 a French traveller named Révoil, whose presence had, in view of recent French operations in Madagascar, excited Kirk's suspicions. It is just possible, as Johnston claimed, that Kirk supplied him with a form of treaty to be signed by the appropriate chiefs, by which 'if the Sultan of Zanzibar waived his suzerainty over Kilimanjaro', they would agree 'to accept the Queen of England instead'.[2] Though no such treaties can now be traced, Johnston was very definite in asserting that he had concluded them with Mandara of Moshi and with Miriali of Marangu, and it must be admitted that such a formula would not have conflicted with the cardinal point of Kirk's policy, that British interests throughout East Africa were to be furthered so far as possible by extending the dominions of Zanzibar and that direct action was to be resorted to only if such an extension were limited by the intervention of a foreign power. Whatever may be the truth about the treaties, it is certain that Johnston had other plans in mind which he did not communicate to Kirk, which constituted a direct assault on Kirk's whole policy and which could easily have cost him Kirk's friendship. It is therefore an

[1] *The Graphic*, 9.v.85.   [2] *Story*, p. 145.

astonishing tribute to their three weeks' association that when
two years later Kirk left Zanzibar for good, he wrote to
Johnston: 'I do wish you could have taken my place. Between
us we might quietly have kept British interests safe even after
all that has happened.'[1]

From Zanzibar Johnston sailed in mid-May to Mombasa,
whence in a farewell letter to the Secretary of the Geographical
Society he set out some of the difficulties and expenses of East
African travel.

DEAR MR BATES,

I write to tell you of my welfare. Within three weeks of arriving
at Zanzibar I have organized my caravan and now within two
or three days when the beads are strung and the loads weighed,
I shall be ready to start for Chaga. My caravan consists of
approximately 120 men. . . . My ordinary equipment (tent, guns,
powder, cartridges, provisions, instruments) require 64 men.
Then 30 more for cloth, beads, wire etc. And lastly 20 or 30
men for carrying men's food, as there is a complete dearth on
the line of march. . . . The wages of my men are $5 (about 18s.)
each a month. . . . This is much less than Thomson paid. Food
for the men cost £30. Their wages £130 to £160 for the journey
from Mombasa to Chaga. I keep about 35 men with me for six
months, which comes to £30 a month and £180 to £200 for
six months. I have spent about £130 in goods for exchange. The
cost of the equipment in London came to about £300, the
journey out here to approximately £100 (Mackinnon's bland
promises have not saved me a penny). £100 for the return
journey and all things added up £10 remain for transporting
me back to England. If I had £500 more I could visit and collect
on Mount Kenia, but while £1,000,000 has been freely granted
to these Missions at Mombasa from first to last, few are the doles
meted out to atheistical Science.

Sir John Kirk has been the kindest friend and the most
agreeable host. The three weeks I spent in his palace at Zanzibar
did much to create the splendid health I am now enjoying. I
start my journey in great hopefulness and with every seeming
prospect of success. Dear Bates, farewell. Think of me at luncheon
time.[2]

In East Africa there were no ox-wagons, no navigable
rivers. Every item of luggage had to be carried on a human
head. And for a hundred miles behind Mombasa there
stretched almost as horrid a wilderness as it was possible to
pass on foot, a spiky desert of blanched thorn scrub with here

---

[1] Kirk to Johnston 1887, cited Alex Johnston, *op. cit.*, p. 69.
[2] Johnston to Bates from Mombasa 14.v.84, *Royal Geographical Society's Archives*.

and there a dying baobab lifting shapeless limbs to the torrid
sky, glaring, shadeless, foodless, almost waterless, necessitating
forced and thirsty marches, offering every inducement to the
stragglers of a long caravan to elope coastwards with their
precious loads and their as yet unearned advance of pay.
Few were the travellers who passed this way without encountering threats of mutiny, and Johnston, like many another
peaceful-minded man, had at least once to thrash and threaten
his way forward as the only alternative to defeat. 'Congratulate
Joseph Thomson,' he wrote. 'Travel on the Congo, in Angola
or most parts of West Africa is easy and civilized compared
with what it is in these countries.'

With the Taita hills came a change for the better both in
scenery and in comfort. The marches settled down to the
routine ten miles a day, accomplished early, and leaving
plenty of time for sketching, language study and nature
rambles. His men now knew their master and could be left
to forage in the afternoons with an ell of cloth apiece for
currency; and as he worked his way round the southern base
of the great mountain he developed that fastidious routine of
hard exercise and good living which marks off a good traveller
from a bad.

Apart from a brief rest among the friendly but primitive
Taita people of Taveta, Johnston's route round the mountain
lay through the sparsely inhabited belt of no-man's-land
which separated the Chagga on their mountain from the
semi-nomadic Masai pastoralists of the plains to the south.
But as he approached Moshi, the path climbed to 3,500 feet,
the forests were left behind, and the caravan wound its way
past evenly scattered homesteads, each with its plantation of
bananas and its tiny strip of mountain pasture. Cow-bells
tinkled as in an Alpine valley, and everywhere water plashed
gaily in the artificial channels skilfully diverted at different
levels from the natural streams and rivulets of the mountain.
'All around are signs of agriculture, and though the people
are naked, one can see that they are anything but savages.'[1]
Mandara's messengers met him at the borders of the inhabited
area and conducted him with much ceremonial musket-fire
to the settlement of their chief.

The fortunes of Moshi among the other Chagga states were,
as Johnston soon discovered, intimately bound up with the
Arab slave-trade. Mandara had been the first chief to receive
the traders from the coast, and following a pattern familiar

[1] *The Graphic*, 13.vi.85; *Daily Telegraph*, 10.i.85, 16.i.85, 19.i.85.

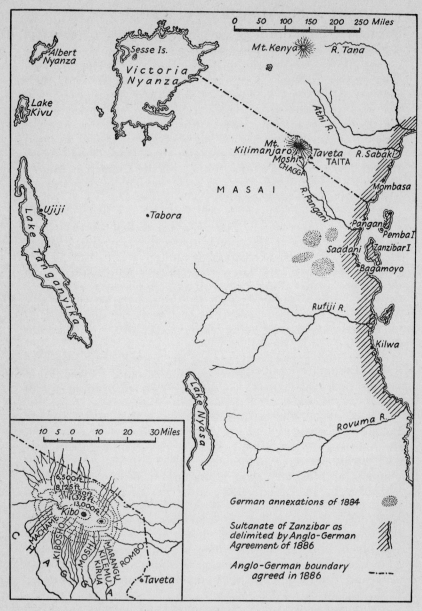

3. KILIMANJARO AND EAST AFRICA

Showing the earliest German annexations, and the partition line of
October 1886.

throughout East Africa in the nineteenth century, he had succeeded, by monopolizing the import trade in firearms and ammunition, in establishing a practical hegemony over all the Chagga of the mountain. This empire had, however, been short-lived. Some ten years before Johnston's visit the vassal sub-tribes had formed a league against him, defeated his armies and driven him temporarily out of Moshi. He had since reclaimed the throne of his fathers, and now occupied as Johnston put it, 'somewhat the position in Kilimanjaro politics of a Napoleon who has returned from Elba but prudently avoids a Waterloo'.[1]

To such a chief allies in the world outside the group of mountain states were of some importance, and the advent of a European visitor bearing letters from so great a personage as Kirk, though in some ways unwelcome, was an event to be treated with much circumspection. Doubtless the small white man was, as his Swahili advisors were quick to point out, a spy. On the other hand his death in Moshi might be avenged by the troops of Zanzibar, and if he had to survive and eventually return to the coast, it was on all accounts to be preferred that he should learn to see the affairs of Kilimanjaro through the eyes of Moshi rather than through those of a rival state. Besides, the small white man was rich, and with a little patience and ingenuity, and by the timely use of threats, he might be well fleeced and released only as a pauper, compelled to follow the shortest route home.

Johnston's request for land on which to build was therefore granted. It was not quite where he wanted, only two miles from Moshi and only five thousand feet above sea-level. But, as Mandara explained, the higher slopes were liable to be ravaged by the Kibosho enemies of Moshi, and Johnston, though half aware that he was entering a trap, accepted the offer, paid off all but thirty of his carriers and despatched them with some misgivings back to Mombasa. With them he sent a letter to Bates setting out most clearly both his sense of exultation and his premonitions of future trouble.

> For nearly a week now I have been settled on Kilimanjaro, camped on one of the loveliest sites in the wide world. Above me towers into the unfathomable blue the snowy head of Kibo, around me are green hills and forested ravines in whose profound depths great cascades of water leap from rock to rock and splash the fronds of lusty ferns. Before me lies spread out a vast blue plain, 'all the world', as Mandara proudly says, and my vision

[1] H. H. Johnston: *The Kilimanjaro Expedition*, pp. 94-8.

southwards is only bounded by the rotundity of the earth.
Perched as I am up here on the shoulder of a great buttress of
the mountain I seem to be on a level with the vultures who
hardly soar higher than I and who poise themselves and wheel
in circles over the awful depths at my feet. When the first cares
of my installation are over, I am going to set to work on a picture
such as I see before me and call the view 'À vol de vautour'.

This is the bright side of my affairs. . . . The darker prospects
are the being in the power of and subjected to the capricious
interference of an African tyrant whose favour at present shines
on me but who may in a moment change his mind and shatter
all my castles in the air. Many people will be disposed to ask me
'Why did you put yourself in his power? Why not go to some part
of the mountain where the country is uninhabited and where
you will be in complete freedom to pursue your investigations?'
To this I reply that *there is no habitable part of Kilimanjaro without
ownership.*[2] In theory it may seem very nice to go and live in a
primaeval forest 10,000 feet above the sea and feed on wood-
pigeons and guinea-fowl, but it hardly answers in practice.
When you have thirty lusty men to feed they object to such
slender fare as the forest provides. Consequently a settlement
must be formed sufficiently near a native village for food to be
easily procurable. Then also it is not possible for these inhabitants
of the warm coast-lands to endure the severe cold at night which
is met with at an altitude of 10,000 feet. . . . Finally in going to
Mandara I have but one tyrant to deal with—in the Taveita or
Masai countries their name is legion, every petty chief must
have his present. . . . Mandara too holds Sir John Kirk in great
awe, and has treated me much better than my predecessors
purely because I come with two formidable letters of recommendation from the Consul, one in Swahili and one in Arabic.
Let us hope therefore that he will leave me in peace to roam over
the hills, to shoot and skin my birds and animals, collect my beetles
and butterflies and press my plants and paint my pictures. . . .

I think of you very often—much more often probably than
your thoughts dwell upon me, for you have a hundred visitors
in a day perhaps, and I see nobody much above the mental
status of a brute, and must perforce feed on the memories of the
past where intellectual conversation is concerned. Still, when I
sit in my shady nook and watch the monkeys coming down to
drink in the rocky pools, when I climb to some frowning height
and see the vultures flocking in the air below me, when I see the
snowy cap of Kibo in the sunrise, or note the roving herds of
game that cross the prairies of the Rufu—then when my social
instincts draw me back to Europe, my stronger love of natural
beauty ties me here.[1]

[1] Johnston to Bates from Mandara's 18.vi.84, *R.G.S. Archives.*
[2] Underlined in the original.

Love of beauty, however, was not the only thread which bound him to Moshi, and even his friend Bates might have been a little surprised to know the scale of the operations that were being carried out at the naturalist's base camp. For while Johnston and his two principal assistants ranged the hillsides and the forests in search of specimens, and while his Chagga neighbours streamed into the camp with live monkeys and hyraxes tied to poles to sell to the egregious stranger, twenty-eight Swahili labourers were constantly at work, levelling, raising *pisé* walls, thatching roofs, hoeing gardens, making roads, cutting irrigation channels, sowing, weeding, gathering, grinding, and generally settling down to all the varied tasks of a self-supporting community. Johnston himself was soon housed in a long three-roomed cottage comprising a laboratory, dining-room and bed-sitting-room to which was later added a wing of storesheds and a wing for his men, the whole forming three sides of a square. A poultry yard was quickly started and the kitchen garden sown with seeds brought from Europe, mustard and cress, radishes, potatoes, turnips, onions, tomatoes, borage, sage, cucumbers and melons. Within a week he was eating a home-grown salad; a month later his root crops were nearly ready and he was staking his young peas and beans. There was a daily market in the compound, to which the Wachagga brought sheep and goats, milk, honey and bananas, to be exchanged for exiguous strips of cotton cloth and strings of glass beads.

Meantime Mandara watched the proceedings from his settlement in the valley beneath, and daily sent his messengers to claim more and yet more presents. To one of these Johnston imparted with some care the tale of the goose with the golden eggs. He returned the following day with his master's appropriate retort: 'When I plant a seed in my land and it begins to come up above the soil, I wait until it is fully grown before I pluck its leaves and fruit.'[1]

After this exchange relationships temporarily improved,

---

[1] I give the story as it is told in Johnston's manuscript diary for June 21st, 1884, in preference to the very much more artistic version which appears on pp. 134-5 of *The Kilimanjaro Expedition*. In this the exchange is described in the form of a personal interview: '. . . Now wasn't that a foolish man, Mandara?' 'Ye-es,' replied the chief thoughtfully, 'perhaps he was.' Then he sipped more tembo, and reflected. After a pause he turned to me and continued, 'And now I will tell *you* a tale. When I plant a seed or sapling here in my plantation, I let it grow quietly at first—I do not pull it up to look at its roots, and I do not pluck its early blossoms or its tender leaves. I wait until it is mature, and then,' he added thoughtfully, looking straight before him, 'if it fails to bear abundant fruit, I cut it down.'

and Johnston felt safe enough to despatch twenty of his men as far away as Taveta in order to pick up some loads which he had left there on his outward march. A fortnight later they returned, having narrowly escaped molestation by marauding bands from the neighbouring Chagga states of Marangu and Kirua, who had pursued them across the border into Moshi territory. Since his own men appeared to have been the cause of the hostilities, Johnston went at once to Mandara's and 'offered to help him in the war'. The chief and his advisors were in a state of panic, for news had come that, in addition to the raiders from Kirua and Marangu on the east, a simultaneous attack had been launched by the Wakibosho from the west. The warriors of Moshi were said to be in retreat, and the civilians were busily driving their sheep and cattle to refuge in Mandara's stockaded settlement. Gradually, however, messengers arriving from the several frontiers brought better tidings. Soon it was the enemy which was retreating, and individual warriors started to come, as was the custom in most East African tribes, to boast their deeds of valour in person before their prince.

At first [reads Johnston's diary] Mandara wanted me to remain and protect him and then when he heard the enemy was retreating, proposed I should follow him up and turn defeat into a rout. I started with my men and some askaris [soldiers] and walked in a blazing sun through terribly hilly country for about three hours until we were almost out of Chagga. We encountered eight bodies of the slain, all the Kibosho people, and they were mostly killed by spear wounds. After our fatiguing walk we began to ask where the enemy was and were informed he had returned to his own country, upon which we thought it better to return as all the men were tired and fasting.[1]

It is not clear from the diary just why Johnston's assistance was reckoned by Mandara to be of decisive importance. It is possible that in such warfare a dozen new rifles in the fairly practised hands of his Swahili servants might have turned the scales of battle. It is just possible that Johnston intended, had the fighting been prolonged until nightfall, to stage a firework display which would strike terror into the hearts of the invaders. It would, however, seem almost certain from the wording of the diary that the stirring scene described by Johnston in his book *The Kilimanjaro Expedition* and also in a series of articles on the expedition published in the *Daily*

[1] Kilimanjaro Diary, MS. *Johnston Papers*, 3.vii.84.

THE FATE OF A FREE TRADER, OPOBO 1887

JOHNSTON AT THE AGE OF THIRTY

Telegraph[1] did not, as a matter of historical fact, ever take place.

As we were seen marching to the field of action [reads the first of these later accounts], guns firing and flags flying, Mandara's men pressed on their enemies with renewed valour, encouraged by our approach, and the disheartened Wakibosho yielded and fled up the hillside till they reached the summit, where they turned and halted, met by reinforcements. The men of Moshi were too exhausted to follow, and when I arrived on the scene I found them crouching down at the foot of the hill, watching their foes. Had the Wakibosho now charged down the slope on us, whom they greatly outnumbered, the consequences for our side might have been disastrous. . . . I resolved to fall back on a rather fantastical method I had preconceived of scattering my enemies, and striking effectual terror into their foolish hearts. . . . No sooner had darkness set in than I blazed forth upon the astonished natives with Bengal lights, red fire, Roman candles, serpent squibs, and lastly a magnificent flight of rockets. The terrified Wakibosho scarcely waited to see the last of these. When the first rocket rose with a flaming shower and a shrieking rush into the air, and then broke well over their heads into a mass of blue and crimson falling meteors, our astounded foes fled in dismay, and we found ourselves alone on the field, whence we journeyed peacefully home by the light of a late-rising moon.[2]

Making every allowance for the fact that Johnston only kept a diary when he was travelling and then only as an aid to memory, written up in odd moments of spare time and used merely as the basis for his published works, there yet remains a fundamental difference between these two accounts which it is impossible to explain away. The diary explicitly says that he made no contact with the enemy; the book and the article, both written less than a year later, describe in elaborate detail how he put them to flight. The diary fortunately provides one further clue: on June 22nd, a fortnight before the episode in question, Johnston had, at Mandara's special request, laid on a display of fireworks from his own settlement on the hillside above the royal town, in order to help in entertaining some distinguished visitors from the coast. No doubt on that occasion the people of Moshi who were not in the secret had behaved much as the warriors of Kibosho in Johnston's imaginary picture of the battle. Johnston, it would seem, deliberately wove the two incidents into one. According

---

[1] Story of the Expedition to Kilimanjaro by its Leader. *Daily Telegraph*, 10.i.85, and succeeding issues.
[2] *The Kilimanjaro Expedition*, pp. 117-19.

C

to the standards of a large number of English people both then and now, he lied. According to the subtler and possibly less philistine standards of, say, Southern Europe, he merely exercised poetic licence. Whichever may be the truer judgment, it is impossible to understand the character of Harry Johnston without realizing that he was capable of this kind of deception. There were probably very few of his contemporaries who, whether or not they caught him out, did not sense in his company that he was capable of something of the kind. In some it bred incurable distrust; there were others who judged that it was not inconsistent with a singular honesty of basic purpose.

Whatever his precise part in it, the one day's war with Kibosho still further cemented the relationship between Johnston and Mandara. The country, Johnston noted two days later, was still in a disturbed condition, and Mandara lived in dread of a concerted attack by all the other mountain states. 'I have found out a lever by which to work him now, and since he knows that I am aware of his limited power, his pretensions have been less.'[1] On the third day after the battle Mandara sent up loads of wood and men to help Johnston to build a more permanent house. On the seventh day he agreed to send a present of two tusks of ivory to Sir John Kirk. On the eighth day Johnston committed to his diary the first real hint of his secret purposes: 'Wrote to Ld. Edmond Fitzmaurice to-day and sent to Zanzibar for forty more men and many trade goods. I have now taken two decided steps towards the colonization of Kilimanjaro. *Nous en verrons le résultat.*' The letter, of which Johnston kept no copy, and the original of which now reposes innocently in the Public Record Office in a file marked Foreign Office, Slave Trade, Domestic Various, July 1884, is a good deal more explicit. It is dated Chagga, July 10th, 1884.

My Dear Lord Edmond Fitzmaurice,
    You asked me when taking leave of you last March to let you know occasionally my impressions of the countries I visited in the course of my travels. I therefore send you a hasty sketch of this interesting district of Kilimanjaro, where I have fixed my residence for six months or so. . . . [The letter goes on to describe Mandara's lively desire for British protection, a fact of which the author has informed Sir John Kirk.] What I feel impelled to say to you myself is this:
    Here is a country as large as Switzerland, enjoying a singularly fertile soil and healthy climate, capable of producing every

[1] Kilimanjaro Diary, 5.vii.84.

vegetable production of the tropical and temperate zones, free from the tzetze fly, and inhabited sparsely by peaceful agriculturalists, skilled in native manufactures and capable and desirous of instruction: here is a land eminently suited for European colonization, situated near midway between the Equatorial Lakes and the Coast. Within a few years it must be either English, French or German. The German traveller Dr Fischer and the French explorer M. Révoil have both directed the attention of their respective governments to the project of colonizing Kilimanjaro, while that idea is not even beyond the scope of action of the International African Association. However all these are still hesitating, while I am on the spot, the first in the field, and able to make Kilimanjaro as completely English as Ceylon, should I receive the necessary authorization. Moreover this might be done without exciting any notice or involving any responsibility for a cost not exceeding £5,000. I have only to invite a certain number of chosen colonists, already desirous of joining my expedition, to come and occupy the beautiful sites which will be given them gratis, and there to cultivate the vine, the coffee plant, the sugar-cane, rice, wheat, oranges and limes —and the principal points of this healthy district will soon be in the hands of Englishmen. A road to the Coast will be made, 170 or 180 miles distant; trade will flow entirely into English hands; the ivory, wax, iron, hides of the interior will come to our markets. And this without any overt act beyond the making of an agreement with Mandara and permitting him to fly the English flag. He desires all sorts of European things—forges, sewing-machines, guns, ammunition, tables, pictures, etcetera. In return he will trade in the fine ivory, wax and gums of his country. Think of the cultivation of quinine in a region singularly adapted for its favourable growth. Think even of the preserves of African elephants which might be formed in the forests of this mountain. Think what a commanding position this hilly district, with its European climate, occupies in Eastern Equatorial Africa. All the trade from the Coast and the far interior would gravitate hither as at present it flows to Zanzibar. Situated only 180 miles from the Coast, with an intervening district offering no difficulties whatever in the construction of roads and railways, Kilimanjaro offers an admirable centre for that occupation and colonization of Eastern Africa that must inevitably come from one of the European powers. . . . What is wanted is £5,000 only with which to engage a hundred workmen (Zanzibaris) to make a good road to the Coast, clear the forests here and build timber houses. Then in a year's time, when all is ready, missionaries and colonists might be invited to take up their abodes on Mandara's territory. A careful selection should be made, so that no debauchees, or drunkards, or fanatics should disturb the peace of the rising colony, nor break the pleasant intercourse which at present exists between the natives and the little known white man. Nor should Kilimanjaro be made the subject of speculative companies—it is for this reason that I address myself privately to you before proclaiming to the world at large the advantages of this region. What should first be done is to introduce European cattle, livestock, vegetables, etcetera, build houses and then invite the colonists and let every man henceforth cultivate and trade on his own account. Here amid my natural history and anthropological studies I shall wait inactive until I receive the reply with which I hope you will favour me, and any suggestion you may make, whether it be in accordance with my own wishes or not, I shall strictly carry out.[1]

So that was the plan. Mandara, the lord of twenty-four square miles, surrounded on all sides by hostile states whose subjects he made a practice of capturing and selling as slaves, was to hoist the Union Jack, while the visiting naturalist, in the intervals of working at his collections, was to become by insensible gradations, first Mandara's guide, philosopher and friend, and then the founder of a select colony of British settlement. Kilimanjaro was to become an African Ceylon placed like a bastion to guard the hinterland of Zanzibar from annexation by Germany or France. It was of course, in the terms in which Johnston presented it, a dream. Six months later he admitted to Kirk that his colony would have needed an army of five hundred trained men to protect it. Road or no road, communications with the coast would have been confined, until the advent of mechanized transport, to head porterage in heavily armed caravans. Ivory would have remained the only product which would have stood the cost of such transport, and even that would have had to compete with the slave-carried ivory of the Congo and the great lakes. Not the least naïve feature of the plan was the supposition that his fellow-settlers would prove fit to be turned loose to farm and trade without the restraints of law and government. Groups of missionaries, living under the strict discipline of their orders or societies, were known to survive conditions of such temptation, but even they had their moral casualties leading to violence and scandal.

Still, Johnston's dream was on the whole pleasantly conceived, in love of adventure and not in greed of gain. It was a dream which recurred to him for many years to come: finally in 1921 he used it for a novel, his best novel, called *The Man Who did the Right Thing*. Roger Brentham, a consul

---

[1] Johnston to Fitzmaurice from Chagga 10.vii.84, *F.O.84.1687.*

at 'Unguja' on the eastern coast of Africa, offended the social
susceptibilities of his Foreign Office employers by marrying
the widow of a missionary killed in the interior of German
East Africa during the Arab rebellion in 1888. Refusing
transfer to a minor consulate in Norway, he resigned his
commission and became the manager of an Anglo-German
development company which was exploiting the natural
resources of 'the Happy Valley' located somewhere in the
mountainous country between Kilimanjaro and the Victoria
Nyanza. At the time of the Jameson Raid and the Kruger
telegram, the great imperialists of England—the Directors
of the Chartered Companies, the editors of the financial press,
the starry-eyed idealists like Albert, Earl Grey, who 'believed
that once a backward country had been painted red on the
map there was nothing more to be done'—all these tried
to bring Brentham back to British administration. 'Roger,
however, was not going to risk the substance for the shadow
. . . and of one thing he was jolly well sure—thinking back on
his faithful Somalis, his cheery Wanyamwezi, on the well-
mannered manly Masai, the graceful Iraku and the obedient
Wambugwe; he would see that the Black Man and Brown Man
reaped full advantage for the White Man's intrusion into their
domain. They should receive compensation for disturbances
and be brought into partnership not only of labour and effort,
but of profit.'[1]

As a practical venture in the year 1884, however, the Happy
Valley of Moshi was a reality for a shorter period than it took
for Johnston's letter to travel to England. Indeed, the first
blow fell only three days after its despatch, when Johnston's
two senior Swahili assistants, with whom in his solitude he had
probably spoken too freely of his intentions, deserted him for
Mandara's, where they earned an easy living by traducing
their former master. Thenceforward, though there were
negotiations for land and plans for joint ivory-trading, there
was no more real trust, and at times Johnston and his men
were literally besieged in their settlement. Even when they were
free to come and go within the state of Moshi, they were strictly
forbidden to transgress its boundaries, and this of course meant
that they were cut off from the higher slopes of the mountain
to which their scientific mission was chiefly directed. 'I am beginning to long for my deliverance,' he wrote; 'no game to
shoot, no fish to catch, no alpine plants or insects to collect.'[2]

[1] H. H. Johnston: *The Man Who did the Right Thing*, pp. 352-4.
[2] Kilimanjaro Diary, 8.viii.84.

At last after six anxious and wasted weeks he obtained permission from Mandara to go in search of his return caravan long overdue from the coast. He marched accordingly back to friendly Taveta, and there left two men to intercept the caravan on its way through, to have the loads deposited in safety and to bring on to Moshi only forty well-armed men. Mandara's manners had mended in his absence, and early in September he even detailed a small force to conduct him safely to the snows. At barely 10,000 feet, however, they were threatened by hostile Wakibosho and forced to turn back. It was this event which finally determined Johnston to leave Moshi. Mandara's was a chiefdom entirely of the foothills: all the upper slopes were controlled by his enemies, the Wakibosho on one side the Wamarangu on the other. To work above 6,000 feet, Johnston must abandon his promising settlement, his buildings and his gardens, and form a new set of political alliances. And so, his men arriving on September 22nd, he forged a letter from Kirk ordering his return to the coast, which Mandara, impressed by force if not by fraud, did not attempt to dispute. He left for Taveta on the 25th.

Meanwhile, in the same week that Johnston was leaving Moshi, his letter to Lord Edmond Fitzmaurice was, perhaps rather undeservedly, making history in London. It had arrived at an extraordinarily opportune moment: otherwise it could never have been, as in fact it certainly was, the turning-point between a static and a dynamic policy in East Africa. For it reached Fitzmaurice just when the whole of British African policy, indeed the whole scheme of British diplomacy, had been thrown into the melting-pot by the sudden and entirely unexpected entry of Germany into the colonial field. In June 1884 Granville had, under strong German pressure, formally abandoned the very foundation of his earlier West African policy, the Anglo-Portuguese treaty concerning the Congo. In the same month he had been forced, after two years of bungled negotiation between the Cape and the metropolitan governments, to recognize German sovereignty at Angra Pequena in South West Africa. In August he suddenly realized that the Germans interpreted this as covering the whole south-west African coastline from latitude 26° south to the Angolan frontier, with the exception of the fifteen-mile stretch of British protectorate at Walvis Bay.[1] Next there arrived the news that the famous German explorer Nachtigal, travelling in the gunboat *Möwe*, who had been officially

[1] E. Fitzmaurice: *Life of Lord Granville*, Vol. II. pp. 347-8.

recommended to British colonial and consular assistance for a trade reconnaissance tour in West African waters, had signed treaties and raised the German flag at Bageida in Togoland, and at King Bell's town in the Cameroons River. The latter exploit had been doubly irritating in that Nachtigal had forestalled by a matter of hours the British Consul Edward Hewett, who was under instructions to do the same thing. Granville's plans for West Africa were therefore all askew. He had been too slow in South West Africa; he had been cheated in the Cameroons; his Congo proposals had been denounced by all the powers, and he had agreed to an international reconsideration of the future of the region at Berlin at the end of the year, at which the initiative would lie not with him but with Bismarck. No wonder, therefore, that the Foreign Office should be more attentive than usual to a definite suggestion for anticipatory action in East Africa.

Johnston's letter went first to Lister, who could always be trusted to back a proposal for extension.

> Kilimanjaro [he wrote] seems admirably suited for a British colony and I have no doubt that an agricultural colony so near the E[ast] C[oast of] A[frica] wd have a most powerful effect in putting an end to S[lave] T[rade] beyond the seas. If Johnston's account is to be trusted, there wd be no difficulty in establishing a Brit. protectorate at once—a Co. might be organized to start the place and make a cheap railroad to the coast without Govt. assistance, and annexation and a Govt. wd follow when the settlers cd afford to pay for such a luxury.[1]

Wily Sir Villiers Lister. How easy, how inexpensive he made it all sound: not even the modest £5,000 which Johnston asked for need be found by the Government. Lister must have known very well that the project would cost the Government hundreds of thousands, perhaps millions, before it was through. He also knew, however, that once committed, no British Government would turn back; that once British subjects were clearly involved in a situation Parliament would pay a hundredfold what it would sanction for an abstract scheme. Lister was used to working for ministers who counted the financial costs and feared above all things the debates on Supply: but if the ministers were so rattled by their failures on the West Coast of Africa that they were suddenly prepared to do something rash on the East, it was no business of his to remind them how far they had forgotten themselves.

[1] Lister to Fitzmaurice 17.ix.84, encl. in Johnston to Fitzmaurice of 10.vii.84, *F.O.84.1687.*

From Lister the letter went on to Granville. 'It seems to me a very important letter,' wrote Fitzmaurice in an accompanying note, 'as coming from a man who is not a fanatic or an enthusiast, but from one who, as his book shows, is above all things a scientific man. . . . The proposal, as I understand it, is that either he or Sir John Kirk or somebody should be allowed to hoist the British flag and forestall the French, the Germans and the International Association. Could we not send out to Sir John Kirk empowering him to communicate with Johnston at once and have the British flag hoisted if he thinks the opportunity a good one? I would like to pay off the Germans for the Cameroons.'[1] Granville was evidently as upset about the Cameroons as Fitzmaurice, for three days later there went out to Zanzibar a telegram which must have caused Kirk more surprise than any other single event in his long tenure of the Consulate. 'Johnston reports King Mandara wishes for British flag and protection. He gives highly favourable report of people, country, climate and suggests establishment of a British colony. What is your opinion? Reply by telegraph.' When Kirk suggested in reply that a decision might be postponed till Johnston's return to the coast, another and even stronger telegram followed within twenty-four hours of the first: 'Johnston's scheme. It would probably be too late if you await his arrival to report, as French and Germans are believed to have designs of annexation. He is waiting at Chagga for answer of H.M.G.'[2]

Had Kirk at this moment had the opportunity of one hour's private conversation with Lister and Anderson, it is possible that the history of East Africa might have followed a very different course. There is no doubt at all that for a few weeks in September and October 1884 the responsible ministers were in a mood to authorize action which would have irretrievably committed the Government. The project would not have worked out so easily in practice as in Johnston's optimistic opinion; but it might easily have been carried so far that even a Gladstonian Cabinet would have preferred the expense of going on to the disgrace of turning back.

But Kirk at his outpost could not, even at this juncture, free himself from the habits of thought of nearly twenty years. British paramountcy in East Africa had rested ever since 1842

---

[1] Fitzmaurice to Granville 20.ix.84, encl. in Johnston to Fitzmaurice 10.vii.84, *F.O.84.1687.*

[2] F.O. to Kirk 23.ix.84 and 24.ix.84, *F.O.84.1676*; Kirk to F.O. 23.ix.84, *F.O.84.1674.*

upon paramountcy of influence at the court of Zanzibar. Kirk knew, and in several despatches admitted, that this system could not continue to be effective for much longer. He had realized the danger that another power might make annexations in the interior, behind the Sultan's possessions. He had realized that this in turn would lead to the demand by the annexing power for a port on the coast, and therefore almost certainly to a partition of the Sultan's mainland dominions. He would not however face, or bring the Sultan to face, the plain implication of all these arguments, that the only possibility of maintaining the integrity of Zanzibar was for Great Britain, with the Sultan's full agreement and co-operation, to protect by annexation the key points beyond the Sultan's landward frontiers. Kirk's attitude continued to be that though an international scramble for East Africa was clearly coming, there was nothing to be done about it until it came. To Granville's second telegram he therefore replied that no rival annexations appeared to be immediately threatened; and to this the Foreign Office at last gave way, only ordering him to use his own discretion if the situation were to change and warning him that 'at the present moment the attention of European powers is directed to an unprecedented extent to the question of the formation of settlements on the African coast, that action had been in recent cases prompt and secret, and that it is essential that a district situated like that of Kilimanjaro . . . should not be placed under the protection of another flag to the possible detriment of British interests'.[1]

Johnston, therefore, when he reached his new base at Taveta, had received as a result of his intrusion into imperial politics, no word either of approbation or reproof. His time was limited by his financial resources, and with forty extra men to pay he would have to be back at Zanzibar in seven weeks. If he was to fulfil the scientific objects of his mission, he would have to work quickly and with skill. His first action, however, was to provide at least some small scrap of land over which, in place of Moshi, the British flag might be raised, should instructions arrive to authorize it. Accordingly, on September 27th, 1884, there was signed an 'agreement entered into between Henry Hamilton Johnston and the chiefs of Taveita, whose names are given below' whereby Johnston acquired absolute rights over a tract of uninhabited

[1] F.O. to Kirk 9.x.84, *F.O.84.1676*. The draft is in Anderson's handwriting and is marked 'approved by the Col. Ctee' [of the Cabinet].

C*

forest, measuring perhaps three miles by two. The 'concession' had three clauses[1]:

I. The said Henry Hamilton Johnston, being anxious to cultivate a district lying within the township and tribal territory of the Ua Taveita (situated between Lat. 3° 20'-3° 23' S and Long. 37° 41'-37° 43' E) and also to found a settlement and town within which his servants or *employés* may reside, and where he may also invite friends to settle, agrees once and for all to pay the chiefs of Taveita four gora of Merikani, five gora of Sahari, and one gora of Handkerchiefs together with one frasilah of beads as a commutation of any land tax or road fees they may have a right to demand.

II. The immunities, rights, and advantages of this agreement will extend and be extended to anyone or to any persons whom the said Henry Hamilton Johnston may designate.

III. Within the limits now purchased the Government and entire rule and possession will belong exclusively to the said Henry Hamilton Johnston or anyone whom he may designate as his representative.

Signed   HENRY HAMILTON JOHNSTON,
SIGARA, SUMWALO, NYOSHEWU,
MELEI, NDALENGWE, MGOSE

This little piece of business transacted, he next called a conference at Taveta of representatives of the neighbouring Chagga states: from them he discovered, what he had previously only half understood, that Moshi was the outcast of the Chagga community, allied traditionally with the Arabs and also with the Masai of the southern plains, its hand turned against its own kindred and its kindred's against it. From them too he learned that the easiest way to the snow lay through the valley kingdom of Marangu. To Miriali of Marangu, therefore, he despatched an embassy laden with the richest gifts he could afford and upon receiving a favourable reply he followed with his company with five weeks of the seven still in hand.[2]

Miriali's motives towards Johnston were not basically different from those of Mandara; if anything, they were even more crudely covetous. But there was on this occasion no question of land or settlement; Johnston's sole purpose in Marangu was a speedy passage to the upper slopes, and by dint of lavish promises in response to exorbitant demands, he was able to gain his object. October 10th found him

[1] Copy enclosed in Kitchener to F.O. 6.xi.85, *F.O.84.1746.*
[2] *The Kilimanjaro Expedition,* p. 204 *sq.*

encamped at 10,000 feet, his men shivering and irritable, but plentifully supplied with food by their former enemies the Wakibosho, who as friends of the Wamarangu made daily journeys up the mountain bringing for sale goats, bananas, sweet potatoes, honey and tobacco. For a week every hour of daylight was spent in collecting. On the 16th, with bronchitis already rampant in his camp, he made his one and only attempt on the summit. The weather was quite unsuitable. At 14,000 feet he encountered mist and hail, and even his picked team of personal servants refused to accompany him further. At 16,300 feet, with patches of snow appearing round him, he turned back. On the 18th he evacuated his high-level camp, striking due eastwards round the central mass of the mountain, so as to come down the Rombo valley to Taveta and avoid Marangu, where he felt it possible the greedy Miriali might hold him to ransom.[1]

At Taveta there was, to his bitter disappointment, still no message from Kirk. He had left there twenty of his men to clear a token acre of his concession, and these had worked well during his absence. Experimental plots had been sown with wheat and coffee, a number of young ostriches had been captured and enclosed, and rough buildings and store-sheds had been erected. Now all these would have to be abandoned to the white ants, the wild beasts and the resurgent bush.[2] For ten days he hung on, cataloguing plants, stuffing birds, packing up his collections, and hoping against hope that even now help might come. At last on October 31st his caravan wound eastwards out of Taveta, leaving the settlement in charge of four men, who had instructions to follow in three months unless relieved.

On his return march Johnston took the southerly route through the Usambara highlands to Pangani, reached on November 12th. Two days earlier, unknown to Kirk or any of the British consular staff, Carl Peters and three companions, representing the Society for German Colonization, had landed fifty miles further down the coast, at Saadani.

Kirk was away on a visit to the southern ports and returned to Zanzibar only two days before Johnston's departure on the monthly mail-steamer. From the available evidence it is difficult to tell whether their brief meeting was friendly or strained: certainly it did not alter Kirk's opinions by one jot or tittle. Back to England by the same boat as Johnston went a

---

[1] *The Graphic*, 27.vi.85.
[2] *The Kilimanjaro Expedition*, pp. 256-80; *Daily Telegraph*, 14.iii.85, 2.iv.85.

despatch to Granville and a private letter to Anderson, rehearsing all the possible objections to the scheme, though
still proposing no alternative which was in any way adequate
to the situation. Referring to 'the sudden change from extreme
caution and deference to the susceptibilities of others to an
action quite the contrary . . . on the strength of one letter from
a traveller who had then only a limited knowledge and
experience', he asserted that Kilimanjaro would be useless
without a port, that a European colony there would probably
have to establish itself by force, and even then would very
likely succumb to the climate. 'Our taking Chagga,' he
concluded, 'would be the signal for the general scramble and
there would be little left of Zanzibar.' And then, rather lamely,
he added that one could not expect things to go on indefinitely
as they had done, that if division came, Chagga would be the
most attractive point to go for; nevertheless, if England took
the first step her relations with the Sultan would be ruined;
therefore let missionaries go in, and sportsmen; but the time
for planters and a Protectorate was not yet.[1]

Kirk, one must conclude, had been too long at one job. He
had been given by Granville a clear mandate to initiate a
new policy, and his response had been to plead for a con-
tinuation of the old one. Three valuable months had been
lost, and what was worse, the forward party in the Liberal
Cabinet lacked, at the vital moment, the support of the man
on the spot. As a result of the deliberation and controversy
brought on by the delay, Gladstone and the Little England
group were able to impose a check so definite that, when Kirk
himself was ready to move on, it was impossible to do so.

The sequel at the Foreign Office to Kirk's earlier hesitations
had been to work out a compromise scheme by which the
Sultan would be invited to send an armed embassy inland
from Mombasa to Kilimanjaro to negotiate treaties with the
Chagga chiefs formally incorporating the district into the
Zanzibar dominions. The expedition would be accompanied
by a member of the consulate staff empowered to supervise
matters of protocol and to take independent action on behalf
of Great Britain in the event of difficulties. The British Navy
would fill the void in Zanzibar defences caused by the
temporary absence of so large a proportion of the Sultan's
military forces in the interior. This plan was embodied in a

---

[1] Kirk to Granville 23.xi.84, and Kirk to Anderson 24.xi.84, both in *F.O.84.1679*.
The argument of both letters is similar, and no attempt is here made to distinguish
between them.

directive and sent by Granville to Kirk on December 5th.[1]
An office minute recorded the fact that it had the support
of Lord Derby, the Colonial Secretary; of Lord Kimberley,
the Secretary of State for India; of Sir Charles Dilke and
Mr Chamberlain. Probably all these genetlmen hoped that,
slipped unobtrusively into the bottom of one of the routine
despatch-boxes, this document would escape the Prime
Minister's eagle eye; but if so they were mistaken, for a day or
two later Clement Hill, as the Foreign Office apologist, was at
work on a *pièce justificative*. 'The despatch . . . on which Mr
Gladstone asks information, contains some formidable phrases,
but it is not so serious. . . .'[2] Nevertheless in Cabinet on
December 14th Gladstone 'broke out against the proposed
annexations in . . . the Kilimanjaro district' and wrote to
Dilke: 'Terribly have I been puzzled and perplexed on finding
a group of the soberest men among us to have concocted a
scheme such as that touching the mountain country behind
Zanzibar with an unrememberable name. There *must* somewhere or other be reasons for it which have not come before
me. I have asked Granville whether it may not stand over for
a while.'[3] On the 20th, as Johnston's ship was nearing England,
a telegram went out to Kirk, which in the event lost Kilimanjaro to British rule for another thirty-two years. 'Suspend
action on my No. 86 and on receipt of it report by telegraph
whether the mountain district referred to can be considered
as actually under Sultan's sovereignty and whether he would
take steps to declare it without support from us.'[4] Johnston
had narrowly missed historical eminence as 'the founder of
British East Africa', which would certainly have come to him
deservedly or otherwise had the British Government acted
more decisively on his letter to Fitzmaurice. But although
Kilimanjaro itself was lost, his travels there, and in particular
his absurd concession at Taveta, had still an important part
to play in shaping British destinies further north, in Kenya
and Uganda.

Back in London during the last few days of December 1884,
Johnston installed himself in a top-floor flat in Victoria Street
and at once fell to work with pen and ink. Stanley had introduced him after his Congo journey to Edwin Arnold of the

[1] Granville to Kirk 5.xii.84, *F.O.84.1676*.
[2] Memo by Clement Hill 9.xii.84, *F.O.84.1693*.
[3] S. Gwynn and G. M. Tuckwell: *Life of Sir Charles Dilke*, London 1917, Vol.
I, pp. 83-4.
[4] Granville to Kirk 20.xii.84, *F.O.84.1676*.

Daily Telegraph. Johnston had been precluded by his after-thoughts on the International Association from making any immediate use of the contact; but now there was no such cause for reticence, and on January 10th there started a series of centre-page articles on his Kilimanjaro journey which continued weekly, sometimes fortnightly, until the end of April. His drawings made during the expedition were published, along with some much shorter narrative articles in four *Graphic* supplements in June and July. By the autumn he was able to send to his new friend and publisher, Kegan Paul, the completed manuscript of *The Kilimanjaro Expedition*, in which the narrative section was followed by chapters on botany, zoology, anthropology and linguistics.

By the rather unfair means which a consciously dishonest person would not have left open to his biographer, of comparing his private diary with his printed work, it has already emerged that Johnston, as a narrator, was on occasion capable of some measure of, presumably artistic, falsification. A more chronic feature of his writing, which appeared not only in his books but also in his reports and despatches as a government official, was a marked tendency to enthusiastic exaggeration. A small clump of blue flowers was liable, if it caught his interest, to become 'a magnificent lake of blue'. His descriptions of his two Kilimanjaro settlements convey the impression that they were the outcome rather of a thousand men's labours for a year or so than of two dozen for a few weeks. Where, in relation to the Moshi-Kibosho battle, his diary remarks that he had observed eight bodies of the slain, *The Kilimanjaro Expedition* has 'quite a typical field of carnage' where the earth was 'pappy with oozing blood', and 'lovely butterflies, blue and black, gold and black, metallic green and saffron yellow, paused intoxicated on the blood-soaked ground'.[1] It was to be the same with official correspondence as with his letter to Fitzmaurice: if Johnston was enthusiastic for any plan he was advocating, he would outspokenly play up the advantages and let the disadvantages disappear. It was not dishonesty. It was an excessive desire to please, to enchant, to persuade; a fault certainly, but a fault not necessarily less excusable than the more typically English fault of understatement leading to inaction.

Certainly, if Johnston, pen in hand, sometimes failed to control his teeming imagination, there is no suggestion that he ever skimped or cheated in his wonderful and various

[1] *The Kilimanjaro Expedition*, p. 176.

contributions to natural history and linguistic science, which were an invariable feature of his travels, and in which it was necessary in a much more strict and material sense to bring back not merely the interpretation but the detailed evidence on which the interpretation was based. From his botanical collections on Kilimanjaro the experts at Kew Gardens listed nearly six hundred species, many of them new and three belonging to new genera.[1] The conclusions to be drawn from the analysis of this flora were not perhaps as exciting as had been hoped. The species found there proved to be almost equally divided between the Cape and Abyssinian forms; and in place of the almost unique species that might have been expected to inhabit the temperate upper slopes of a mountain with its base in the tropics, the main lesson proved rather to be the astonishing powers of adaptation shown by tropical species in modifying themselves for life at high altitudes, and of temperate species in pressing down into the surrounding foothills and plains.[2] To ornithology the expedition brought the knowledge of six new species—three sun-birds, two chats and a flycatcher, of which the first group, all found at great altitudes, shared with the insects the function of pollinating flowers. Among mammals Mr Oldfield Thomas identified a new variety of the Abyssinian colobus monkey. Small collections of butterflies and beetles showed a high proportion of new species; while zoological reports also waxed eloquent on a new variety of river crab and an example of a nematoid worm which during its early life is parasitic on a species of Mantis.[3]

As on the Congo so during his East African travels, Johnston had given much of his time to linguistic inquiry, and it was in the Kilimanjaro narrative that he gave his most graphic and amusing account of what this involved.

I want particularly to ascertain the form of the eighth prefix (a plural one). Unfortunately I cannot ask one of my friends, 'What is your eighth prefix?' . . . I have to get at it in some other way. 'What is this?' I ask, holding up a knife. '*Ki-oso*,' they reply. 'Just so,' I reflect, '*Ki* is the seventh prefix, and the plural must give the form of the eighth.' 'How do you say many knives?' I continue; '*Ki-oso* is for *one*, what is for many?' '*Singi*' (many), they reply. 'No, but many *knives?*' '*Singi*' is again repeated. Then I ask, 'See, this is one knife—*ki-oso ki-mo* (holding up one finger). What is for *two* knives?' (holding up two fingers).

[1] *Ibid.*, pp. 337-49.   [2] *Ibid.*, pp. 334-5.
[3] *Ibid.*, pp. 364-94.

'Two fingers,' they reply, looking up very much puzzled. Then in despair I send for another knife, and placing it beside the original one, again ply them with a question. This only elicits the word for 'another'; but at length after many disappointments, they are induced to say '*Si-oso si-vi*' (two knives), which gives me . . . *Si-* as the form of the eighth prefix.[1]

In *The Kilimanjaro Expedition* Johnston published extensive vocabularies and grammatical outlines of two Bantu languages, Kichaga and Kitaveta, and also of the quite unrelated Nilo-Hamitic language of the Masai of the southern and western plains. He also introduced them with a chapter of much more general interest on the historical implications of linguistic classification, in which he set out the principal hypotheses about the origins and dispersion of the Bantu peoples, which were to be the main inspiration of his linguistic researches during the next forty years, and which, even though they may now be regarded by scholars with considerable reserve and caution, have nevertheless deeply influenced the thinking of at least two generations of Africanists, to whom even unproven dogma is more compelling than a void. He put forward two main reasons for supposing that the original Bantu race, which gave its form of speech to so much of central and southern Africa, must have sprung from a cradleland towards and perhaps beyond the north-west corner of their present habitat, between the Shari basin and the northern tributaries of the Congo. The first reason was grammatical, in that the only other prefix-governed languages in Africa were to be found in little isolated pockets running westwards from Nigeria to Sierra Leone. These languages, which Johnston later labelled the Semi-Bantu and to which he gave much attention in the second half of his *Comparative Study*, were in his view not offshoots of the Bantu, but descendants, collaterally with the Bantu, of a very much older stock. They were each of them what the Bantu once was, and might have remained, had it not been for the historical accidents that caused its users to expand and become the ruling race of southern tropical Africa.[2] The second reason was lexical.

By studying the comparative vocabularies of the Bantu languages, many interesting conjectures may be made as to the original home and primitive condition of this people. Thus the fact that similar words are used in the remotest and most widely separated members of the group to express leopard,

---

[1] *The Kilimanjaro Expedition*, pp. 161-2.   [2] *Ibid.*, p. 480.

elephant, hippopotamus, buffalo, pig, ape, monkey, grey parrot, bee etc. leads us to believe that these creatures were familiar to the primitive Bantu race; while we may infer that because the rhinoceros, giraffe, lion, ostrich and zebra are known by many different and varying terms in the dialects of those tribes acquainted with them, they were unknown to the forefathers of the people in their ancestral home. Now the first mentioned list of creatures (with many others which might be cited but for want of space) suggest a well-forested and well-watered country in West Central Africa as the original abode of the Bantu race. The grey parrot, for instance, is found as far east as the Victoria Nyanza, and as far south as Angola, but otherwise is confined to Western Africa. The leopard, elephant, apes and monkeys mostly affect densely wooded regions. The hippopotamus only inhabits big rivers or lakes. The buffalo is rarely found westward of the Niger. On the other hand the lion, giraffe, rhinoceros, zebra, or ostrich decidedly prefer the sparsely wooded steppes and savannahs of Eastern and Southern Africa; so that on the whole we may conclude that the primitive Bantu being unacquainted with them, and knowing other creatures (such as the grey parrot) confined to the forested districts of West and Central Africa there had his primeval home, and thence started on his career of conquest and colonization over Western, Southern and Eastern Africa.[1]

Thus far Johnston's argument, though not conclusive, was not ill-founded. In developing it further, however, he trespassed on to very unsafe ground. Having located the cradleland of the ancient Bantu, he proceeded by the same means to describe their state of culture before their great dispersion. 'From the fact that there is a common name for ox throughout nearly all the Bantu languages, we may safely infer that cattle-keeping was a feature of the primitive life of the race; and also that they were agriculturalists because the terms applied to various implements for tilling the soil, to ploughing, sowing, digging, reaping, are retained very little altered by some of their remotest descendants.' On the same principle he asserted that the primitive Bantu were acquainted with the use of iron and copper; that they fought with bows and arrows, spears and knives; that they made pottery, plaited baskets, and hollowed the trunks of trees into dug-out canoes; that, besides the ox, they possessed among domestic animals the goat, the sheep, the dog, the pig and the fowl. And from the proposition that the Bantu had the domestic fowl before the original Bantu language had given way to its numerous and varied progeny,

[1] *Ibid.*, pp. 484-6.

Johnston went on to argue that the great dispersion could not have started until well on in the first millennium B.C.

> The era of the domestication of *Gallus Bankiva* is not a very remote one . . . even in Malacca and Indo-China, its original habitat. Hindostan seems to have known it as a domestic bird about 2000 years B.C., China about 1200 B.C., and the Polynesians possibly carried it with them when they started about two thousand years ago to colonize the Pacific Archipelagoes. From India it spread to Persia, and the Persians made it known to the Greeks about 1000 B.C. . . . It was not known to the Romans till much later and the Ancient Jews ignored it till long after the Babylonian captivity. It was introduced into Egypt, as far as we can tell, during the early part of the Ptolemaic rule . . . and thus probably reached the ancestors of the Bantu race not more than some two thousand years ago.[1]

To modern linguistic scholars, equippd with a knowledge of phonetics which was not available in Johnston's lifetime, his arguments about the ancient Bantu appear flimsy indeed. For instance, the words for chicken in the modern Bantu languages, which Johnston assumed were traceable to a single root, are now considered to be attributable to no fewer than five different roots, which, when plotted on a map, run in five vertical, north-south lines, and so suggest a word of non-Bantu origin which was introduced into the Bantu world from the north in five different forms and followed the diffusion of the fowl and not that of the Bantu. For this and other reasons the Bantu dispersion is seen to-day as a very much older and a very much more gradual process than as Johnston described it. Nevertheless, as the confessedly speculative conclusions of a twenty-seven-year-old artist and naturalist, who had never been to a university and whose linguistic knowledge was entirely self-taught, Johnston's remarks on the Bantu problem in *The Kilimanjaro Expedition*, written in 1885, are not unimpressive.[2]

While he was thus engaged in earning a still precarious living with his pen and pencil, 'Kilimanjaro Johnston', as he was now called, was beginning to make friends and to dine out in that late Victorian Society, dominated by wealth and caste but recognizing also achievement, performance in which was apt to be as important for success as ability and attention

---

[1] *The Kilimanjaro Expedition*, pp. 483-4.

[2] In this and other passages touching upon Johnston's linguistic work, I am deeply indebted to Professor Malcolm Guthrie, who has during several years been generous and patient in discussing Johnston's work with a layman in linguistic matters. Needless to say, however, I am solely responsible for what is here printed.

to business. Some of the senior men at the Foreign Office
took him up socially: first Lister, a nephew of Lord Clarendon,
a cousin of Lord Ribbesdale, a brother-in-law of Sir William
Harcourt; Lister, who as Lansdell in Johnston's novel *The
Gay-Dombeys*, 'painted flowers and interiors quite as well as
Alfred Parsons and Mr Orpen; he spoke eight languages,
including Persian, and played the French horn extremely
well. His wife (a sister of Lord Belhaven, "so good, so kind,
she deserved to live for ever") was a magnificent accompanist
and together they made delicious music at their house in
Brinsley Gardens.' Next, Anderson, who as Sir Mulberry
Hawk 'was the dearest old dear and the best whist player that
ever refused to play for money'; he had married, first a
daughter of Lord Teignmouth, and second the dowager
Lady Boston, whose daughter, Winifred Irby, was one day
to be Lady Johnston.[1] Also from the Foreign Office, and a
near neighbour in Victoria Street, there was Oswald Crawfurd,
the British Consul in Oporto, who introduced him to a very
highly valued friendship with Sir Richard Burton. There was
the brilliant Edward Fairfield, the Arthur Broadmead of
The Gay-Dombeys, 'the only Colonial Office man who knew
anything of Africa'. There was Kegan Paul, the Eton master
turned publisher on account of his heterodox religious beliefs,
and his partner, Alfred Chenevix Trench, son of the primate
of Ireland. There was Knowles of the *Nineteenth Century* and
Stead of the *Fortnightly* and the *Pall Mall Gazette*.

Such were his immediate friends and his social patrons, the
people through whom he penetrated to wider circles. He was
still of course active in advocating the claims of Kilimanjaro
to colonization; and since Government policy had been
immobilized by Gladstone's démarche, hope centred upon
that curious borderland between commerce and philanthropy
inhabited by people who, while they expected a return for
their money, were nevertheless prepared to venture it further
abroad and at greater risk than most of their kind if the object
to be achieved was one which corresponded with their ideals.
Such people were to be found among the promoters and later
among the Directors of all the Chartered Companies which
in the eighteen-eighties and 'nineties rushed into parts of
Africa and Borneo where the British Government still feared
to tread. The proportions of self-interest and philanthropy
varied infinitely between individuals. At one end of the scale
were great figures like the Baroness Burdett-Coutts, Albert

[1] *The Gay-Dombeys*, pp. 142-4; *Story*, p. 120.

Grey and T. F. Buxton; at the other men who though vision-
aries of a kind retained strong commercial instincts, like
J. F. Hutton, the Manchester cotton magnate, Mackinnon
the 'British India' shipowner, and Taubman Goldie, the
founder of the Royal Niger Company; Cecil Rhodes, not yet
well known in London, was to show a mixture unique in the
intensity of both ingredients. It was this world which in the
early months of 1885 Johnston strove to enter and persuade.

His task was the harder in that eight years previously a
group of these people headed by Buxton and Mackinnon had
negotiated and carried almost to the point of signature a
concession under which the Sultan of Zanzibar would have
made over to them for ninety-nine years all but the bare
nominal sovereignty over his entire mainland dominions.
The project had fallen through. The Sultan, at whose request
the negotiations had been started, had at the last minute,
and to all seeming deliberately, introduced wrecking amendments. The syndicate had dissolved, loudly protesting that the
Foreign Office had failed to afford them the requisite support:
only one or two very senior officials knew how more than
justified was their allegation, knew how Lord Salisbury,
during his first few weeks as Foreign Secretary and for reasons
which can now only be surmised, had secretly approached the
Arabic interpreter and used him to make mischief with the
Sultan.[1] It was natural that the victims of such a fiasco, even
if they did not know the whole story, should be unwilling to
expose themselves to a second. Still, it was not long before
Johnston, as a recent eye-witness of the slave trade in East
Africa, had the entrée to the Baroness's drawing-room at
No. 1 Stratton Street, and once there politics were not always
separable from philanthropy. Especially was this so after the
publication on March 3rd of the Emperor Wilhelm's *Schutz-
brief*, taking under German protection the territories in East
Africa acquired by Dr Carl Peters on behalf of the Society for
German Colonization.

It was soon after this event that Johnston, meeting Albert
Grey at Stratton Street, poured out his schemes for a colony

---

[1] For this fact I am indebted to Miss M. de Kiewiet, who in a thesis entitled
'The Imperial British East Africa Company 1876-95' (London, Ph.D., 1955) has
notably supplemented the account of the Mackinnon Concession in Coupland:
The Exploitation of East Africa, pp. 300-18. The document which establishes
Salisbury's complicity in the breaking off of negotiations is Badger to Salisbury
of 3.vii.78, *F.O.84.1528*. 'The Sultan was most grateful for the hints which your
Lordship conveyed to him through me, and it is not impossible that they co-
operated to induce him to use greater caution in the matter of the proposed
concession.'

on Kilimanjaro. Grey bore him off at once to Mackinnon's suite at the Burlington Hotel. 'We were admitted *sans phrase* and Grey urged Mackinnon impetuously to take up my concession and send men out to settle on it and make East Africa British. Mackinnon declined. He refused to have any faith in East Africa.'[1] However, on March 19th, the same day on which the location of the German annexations was communicated by the German Consul to Kirk in Zanzibar, the Foreign Office received a letter from Hutton, a close friend of Mackinnon's, announcing that the directors of the Manchester Chamber of Commerce had recently had under consideration a scheme for the construction of a railway from the Zanzibar coast to the Kilimanjaro district. His colleagues, Hutton added, felt that in order to carry out such an undertaking it might be best 'to combine it with other enterprises for the commercial development of East Africa'.[2] However feebly, the idea of the Mackinnon Concession was alive once more; and there can be no question that Johnston's journey, if not his personal propaganda, had been the largest factor leading to its resurrection.

During the remainder of March and April Hutton and his colleagues concerted their plans. At this time they relied much for their technical information and advice upon Frederick Holmwood, Kirk's senior assistant in the Consulate at Zanzibar, who happened to be at home on leave during the spring of 1885, and who on April 10th submitted in the form of a private letter to Hutton an account of the commercial prospects of the northern part of East Africa and a scheme for their exploitation in terms so attractive that they should, as Anderson remarked, have been sufficient 'to empty any pocket'.[3] Of direct contact between Holmwood and Johnston there is no evidence, but it would certainly seem that the correspondence between their ideas was too close to be accidental.[4] On April 22nd a copy of this scheme was forwarded to Lord Granville by a powerful group, including, besides Mackinnon and Hutton, Lord Aberdare, the Chairman of Goldie's National African Company, John Slagg and Jacob Bright, two financier politicians with strong West African interests,

---

[1] *Story*, p. 149.
[2] Hutton to Anderson 19.iii.85, *F.O.84.1735*.
[3] Holmwood to Hutton 10.iv.85, *F.O.84.1737*. Filed under April 20th.
[4] Compare, for example the Humble Petition of David Baird Lindsay, who was 'desirous to explore the mountain ranges of Usambara with a view to form a Company for cultivating them under European management', and who quoted at length from an address given by Johnston to the Foreign and Colonial section of the Society of Arts on April 14th, 1885, *F.O.84.1738*. Filed under 23.v.85.

Henry Lee, Baron de Rothschild, Henry Broadhurst and
W. H. Houldsworth.[1]

> This [maintained Anderson] is the climax of a long story
> which . . . I have made out through interviews with Holmwood,
> Mackinnon and Hutton. The origin of the scheme was fear of
> the Germans cutting us out in Zanzibar—a fear not unfounded.
> The first idea is to occupy Kilimanjaro with British settlements
> —when occupied, British Protectorate is claimed. The next is
> to make a railway to it from the coast. It is to be constructed
> by a British Co. and the latest estimates give the cost at £700,000.
> Holmwood was sanguine that the money wd be found for
> speculation on his prospectus . . . but . . . I can say with perfect
> confidence that Manchester will not advance a sixpence unless
> the money is safe. The necessity of finding security led to the
> revival of the idea of the Mackinnon Concession of 1878 . . .
> restricted so as not to touch the southern part where the Germans
> have placed themselves.[2]

Thus there began to take shape the project which three
years later was to emerge in public as the Imperial British East
Africa Company, the fortunes of which are writ so large upon
the early history of Kenya and Uganda. It was always a sickly
child, only fitfully nurtured by those who brought it to birth,
suspected and despised by the British Government, which
only a year before had been on the point of itself taking
responsibility for something still more embryonic and lightly
conceived. In 1885, especially, Great Britain occupied
temporarily an embarrassed position in international affairs.
With the fall of Khartoum to the Mahdi aggravating her
difficulties in Egypt and her relationships with Egypt's
creditors, and with the possibility of war with Russia over
Afghanistan, Granville could not risk the slightest brush with
Bismarck in East Africa. As between Kirk and the Foreign
Office the rôles were now reversed from what they had been
a year before. Now it was Kirk who was pressing on: he had
at last persuaded the Sultan to send his European commander-
in-chief General Mathews with an armed expedition to annex
Kilimanjaro to Zanzibar; instead of encouragement he received
the warning that, while his zeal was appreciated, any marked
opposition to German action would 'convert a mere commercial speculation into a political question'.[3] In the same
way Mackinnon and Hutton were unreasonably suspect of

[1] Above signatories to Granville 22.iv.85, *F.O.84.1737.*
[2] Memo by H. P. Anderson dated 24.iv.85, *F.O.84.1737.*
[3] F.O. to Kirk 20.v.85, *F.O.84.1722.*

wishing to embroil the Government in their project; they were offered no help with their proposed concession, except the discouraging information from Kirk that the circumstances were not propitious for its negotiation. One thing only Granville consented to do, and that was to inform the German Government that some prominent capitalists had originated a plan for British settlement in the country between the East Coast of Africa and the great lakes and to suggest very cautiously that there existed a case for arbitration of British and German claims in relation to the still undelimited possessions of the Sultan of Zanzibar.'[1]

Bismarck in his drive for German colonies had not hesitated to trample upon British pretensions whenever it suited him to do so. Even as this message was being discussed in Berlin, agents of the German Colonization Society were setting out to annex the Kilimanjaro massif, to which the British proposals primarily related. Bismarck, however, knew that before German East Africa could be of the slightest value there would have to be a reckoning with Zanzibar about the coastline, in which British co-operation would be essential, and must be bought with partition. He therefore accepted in principle the British proposals, on condition that they were not to apply to any territory already annexed by Germany.

With the fifteen months of complex negotiation leading up to the agreement of October 1886 delimiting British and German spheres of influence in East Africa, Johnston was concerned only in one particular. In November 1885, at Anderson's prompting, he transferred his Taveta concession to Hutton.[2] Thenceforward this faintly ludicrous piece of paper acquired an importance out of all proportion to the area of land involved. It was the only 'treaty' which could be put up against those which the Germans brandished in support of their annexations. It was the only document on which the British claim to a sphere of influence behind the Zanzibar dominions could be based. Hastily a copy of it was despatched to Kitchener, the British representative on the Anglo-Franco-German Commission set up in September to delimit the possessions of the Sultan. Meanwhile Hutton and

---

[1] Lord Granville to Sir Edward Malet 25.v.85, Hansard (H.C.) 1886, XLVII, 4609.
[2] Memo by H. P. Anderson of 3.xi.85, *F.O.84.1744*, with Hutton to Johnston 1.xi.85 and 4.xi.85, Hutton to Mackinnon 2.xi.85 and Hutton to Salisbury 5.xi.85. Also Johnston to Hutton 31.x.85, *Mackinnon Papers*, explaining that he has been advised by Anderson (i) to transfer his rights to Hutton, (ii) to ask Hutton to inform Kitchener of his interest in the claim.

Mackinnon formed a company to exploit it, and in May of 1886 actually sent up two agents to occupy it. Consequently, when in October 1886 Bismarck decided to settle the English claim in exchange for diplomatic aid with the Sultan, it was between the Kilimanjaro massif and Taveta that the line dividing the two spheres of influence was drawn, from the River Umba to the first degree of south latitude on the eastern shore of Lake Victoria. Of course, by the time of the Anglo-German agreement British interests were not confined to a strip of forest three miles by two. As a result of Kitchener's recommendations the British Government had discovered a strategic interest in the port of Mombasa as a counterpoise to the Germans at Dar-es-Salaam and the French at Diego Suarez in Madagascar. Mackinnon's interest, too, was shifting further inland than Taveta to the person of Emin Pasha, the German governor of the former Equatorial Province of the Sudan, who in letters passed through the British missionaries in Buganda was suggesting that a considerable reward in ivory as well as a central African province awaited whoever was the first to reach him with aid from the west or the east. But Johnston's expedition and its aftermath, if it had failed to secure Kilimanjaro, had nevertheless served to arouse and maintain some British interest in the parts of East Africa beyond the Zanzibar dominions through the vital two years during which the Germans, with their surprise tactics, might quite conceivably have gained the whole.

Chapter 4

A RESOLUTE BUT SINGULARLY
LAWLESS PERSONAGE

BY October 1886, when the Anglo-German agreement
about spheres of influence in East Africa was initialled,
Johnston had been for nearly a year on the West Coast. His
friendship with Anderson and Lister had borne fruit, and he
had applied in July 1885 for nomination to an expected
vacancy in the consular service, at Mozambique. This vacancy
did not in the event occur; but in late October or early
November he accepted the offer of a double Vice-Consulship
in the Oil Rivers District and the Cameroons at a combined
salary of £500 a year, which, with fairly generous office and
travelling allowances, placed him, status and prospects apart,
in considerably easier circumstances than he had before
enjoyed.[1] In the first capacity he was to act as assistant to the
Consul for the Bights of Benin and Biafra in the coastal district
stretching from the eastern limits of Lagos to the German
frontier at the Rio del Rey. This, the coastal region of what is
now Eastern Nigeria, had been recognized at the Berlin
Conference as a British sphere of influence, and had been
gazetted as a Protectorate in June 1885. In the second capacity
he was to be the British representative accredited to the
government of the new German protectorate of the Cameroons,
with the special task of watching over the affairs of a small
British-protected enclave at Victoria in Ambas Bay, the
sovereignty over which was intended to be, but had not yet
been, ceded to Germany.

His appointment should therefore have been no sinecure.
The Bights Consulate had never, since its establishment in
1849, been one of the more purely decorative of diplomatic
posts. Its early incumbents, John Beecroft and T. J. Hutchin-
son, Richard Burton, the explorer and orientalist, and Charles
Livingstone, the brother of David, had all led strenuous, often
dangerous, lives in the service of the campaign against the
slave-trade and the promotion of legitimate commerce. With
the steady growth in the 'sixties and 'seventies of the demand
for palm-oil, the volume of trade passing in and out through

[1] F.O. to Johnston 2.xii.85, *F.O.84.1702.*

the creeks and lagoons of the Niger Delta and the Cross River
had assumed proportions far greater than for any comparable
stretch of the African coastline. The arbitration of disputes
between the European traders and the African merchant
princes of the coast had become a task far beyond the powers
of a single man, stationed either at Fernando Po or at Old
Calabar, with no regular means of transport other than dug-out
canoes, with no defined judicial powers except over British
subjects, and with no force at his disposal other than the
occasional presence of a gunboat of the West African Squadron.

So long as the problem had been primarily one of European
and African relations, it had been solved with surprising
success by the establishment at all the main trading settlements
of 'Courts of Equity', in which the resident factors of the
European firms sat with the principal African chiefs and
traders and enforced their decisions by refusing to trade with
convicted offenders until the fine or restitution imposed by
the court had been paid. Although they usually functioned
in his absence, the Consul belonged to all the courts, and
on exceptionally important occasions, as when the court at
Bonny unanimously requested the deportation of King Pepple,
he could call upon a man-of-war to add an element of armed
force to what were otherwise only economic sanctions. But
such a makeshift system, however satisfactory in the days when
the European side of the trade was predominantly British and
when traders of other nationalities were content to join the
British Courts of Equity, was totally inadequate to conditions
of acute political as well as commercial rivalry between the
European powers. Moreover, the fact that the Foreign Office,
even after the Oil Rivers had been recognized as a British
sphere of influence, was still able to muster only two officials
to prove 'effective occupation', was a startling measure of how
far expansion was limited by the principles of Gladstonian
finance.[1]

The observance of these principles had already lost Great
Britain the Cameroons. As early as November 1883 the
Cabinet, moved by French attempts to penetrate the Niger
Delta, had decided to declare a Protectorate over the Oil
Rivers and the Cameroons coast as soon as the necessary
treaties could be obtained from the chiefs.[2] In a letter to a
colleague in the Foreign Office, dated January 15th 1884,

---

[1] For the earlier history of this region the reader is referred to K. O. Dike:
Trade and Politics in the Niger Delta 1830-1885, Oxford 1956.
[2] F.O. to Pauncefote of 29.xii.83, *F.O.84.1655.*

Anderson had unfolded the full plan: 'The Cabinet has decided that, to assist in carrying out a certain policy, Vice-Consuls shall be appointed under the superintending Consul, who will be practically Residents. The expenditure is estimated at a maximum of £6,000 a year. This is to be met by funds raised from the traders. . . . It is proposed that Consul Hewett [then on sick leave] should quickly return to his post and should unostentatiously conclude the necessary treaties. . . . When he has done this, the Vice-Consuls should be appointed and the whole machinery set in motion. . . .'[1]

Four months, however, had been lost in fruitless haggling with Liverpool merchants about the raising of the £6,000 a year before the Foreign Office reluctantly decided that the sum must be reduced to £3,625, to be saved out of its own Vote by abolishing the consulates in Sumatra and Ragusa and reducing the emoluments of those in Helsingfors, Brindisi, Bremen, Cayenne and Portland (U.S.A.).[2] Meanwhile Consul Hewett had returned to his post late and single-handed, had concluded most of the required treaties, but had been forestalled on the Cameroons estuary by the totally unexpected action of the German Imperial Commissioner, Nachtigal. 'It was very treacherous of the Germans', wrote Lister, 'to ask for introductions and assistance . . . when going on this anti-English raid.'[3] So it was, but if British imperialism in the 'eighties had been anything but the hobby of a handful of statesmen and officials, traders and philanthropists, if it had been something which the people as represented in the Parliament at Westminster had been prepared, however modestly, to pay for, the treachery would have been foiled. Indeed, considering the manpower which the British Government, in comparison with others, was prepared to deploy, the astonishing thing was not the success of the German irruption but the fact that Great Britain was able at the Berlin Conference to secure the inclusion of so much of the Nigerian coastline within an internationally recognized sphere.

The only part of this region in which British traders had penetrated beyond the coastline was up the Niger itself, and this too was the only part where commercial interests had been successfully amalgamated into a single concern ready and anxious to assume the responsibilities of government. The National African Company, under the direction of

[1] Anderson to Sanderson 15.i.84, *F.O.84.1681.*
[2] F.O. to Treasury 6.v.84, *F.O.84.1685.*
[3] Minute on Admiralty to F.O. 26.viii.84, in *F.O.84.1688.*

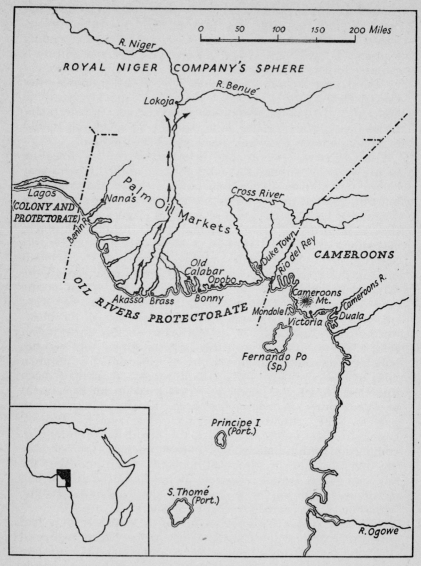

4. THE BIGHTS OF BENIN AND BIAFRA

George Taubman Goldie, had for some years been engaged in establishing its own system of treaty relations with the riparian states and communities of the Niger and the Benue. Although it did not actually receive its Royal Charter until July 1886, the grant of it was already a foregone conclusion, and Consul Hewett had been informed by the Foreign Office that it was no longer necessary for him to travel up the river.[1] The Government was undoubtedly hoping that the National African Company would also succeed in abolishing the many small firms which traded with native middlemen along the Oil Rivers coast from the Benin to the Cross River, and so enable it, by extending the geographical limits of the Charter, to shed its administrative responsibilities in the whole region.[2] Meantime it was not prepared to be prodigal in the provision of expensive officials. In November 1885 the Foreign Office coolly instructed Hewett, who was once again on sick leave, that when he returned to his post he was to concentrate on restoring order, good administration and judicial work in the Oil Rivers territory, although no land forces would be available to support him and he must rely on the moral effect of the occasional presence of one of Her Majesty's ships of war. He was to notice especially the state of affairs on the Brass River, where traders were being impeded by native chiefs and conditions had become so unruly that outbreaks of cannibalism had been reported.[3]

It must in these circumstances have been extremely provoking for Hewett to learn that he was not even going to have his one assistant at his beck and call in Old Calabar. For Johnston had persuaded the Foreign Office to let him have his own residence well out of reach, on a little island called Mondole three miles off the Cameroons coast, which had taken his fancy during his return journey from the Congo two and a half years before. It was a romantic retreat. 'The views from it in all directions were superb—the ghost-like island of Fernando Po westward of Mondole, rising ten thousand feet from a blue, white-breakered sea; the superb range of the Cameroons to the east towering thirteen thousand feet skyward from the shimmering tranquillity of Ambas Bay.'[4] From a

---

[1] F.O. to Hewett 30.xi.85, *F.O.84.1701*.

[2] 'We have been waiting in the hope that the Niger Company would be able to come to terms with the Oil Rivers traders and bring the district within their system. . . .' Minute by Anderson on a Memorandum by Consul Hewett, dated October 1887, in *F.O.84.1828*.

[3] F.O. to Hewett 30.xii.85, *F.O.84.1701*.

[4] *Story*, p. 171. See Plate 3, facing p. 33.

tiny, natural harbour on the eastern side, where his man-of-war's boat could be safely beached, Johnston cut a winding path up the steep, densely forested slopes of the island to a grassy shelf some six hundred feet above the bay; and here his first business was to superintend the erection of the consulate house, which had been sent out in sections by a firm of Liverpool contractors. Always fastidious in solitude as in civilization, he had been at some expense with the furnishings; and with 'a blue room, a red room and a green room', he soon settled down with his books and papers, with his paints and canvas, his bird-guns and his scalpels, his preserving bottles and collecting cabinets, to a life which to most people would have seemed full enough without the intrusion of consular duties. He still had a Tamil servant, Virapan, whom he had engaged in 1884 at Aden, and who had accompanied him to Kilimanjaro and then to England. He had in addition a cook from Accra and a Liberian boat's crew of six; and some months later he was joined by a locally engaged English clerk from Old Calabar, who kept his accounts, copied his letters and manned the station during his frequent absences. Half a mile from his settlement was a village containing the hundred or so indigenous inhabitants of Mondole, a peaceful community of the Bakwiri tribe of the Cameroons Mountain, whose language interested him greatly on account of its borderline relationship to the Bantu family. Otherwise his domestic peace was invaded only by occasional visitors from the mainland or from passing ships.

Johnston's first official task was to present his credentials at Duala to Baron von Soden, the Governor of the Cameroons Protectorate. His next was to visit the little colony at Victoria, which had grown up round the Baptist mission on the shores of Ambas Bay, to which in 1852 Alfred Saker had transferred his followers, many of them by origin British subjects from the West Indies, when the Spanish authorities had expelled him from Fernando Po. The question of Victoria, situated as it was in the middle of the coastline allocated to Germany, had been discussed at Berlin, and it had been agreed that if the Baptist Missionary Society were to be offered suitable compensation for their buildings, the mission would be withdrawn and the settlement transferred to the German protectorate.[1] Despite prolonged negotiations conducted through the British and German Foreign Offices with the Basel Missionary Society,

[1] Memorandum by H. P. Anderson on Pending Questions in Africa dated 23.vi.85, *F.O.84.1739.*

the suitable compensation had not yet been forthcoming, and the question now arose as to whether the British were still bound to their side of the bargain.

Naturally Johnston was an ardent advocate of retention. With a degree of wishful thinking and with an astonishing blindness to the even greater limitations of the administration he himself represented, he argued that the new German protectorate was a castle built on the sand. Disgusted with the behaviour of his countrymen, Baron von Soden had decreed that no white colonist would in future be permitted to settle on German territory unless he could show that he possessed a capital of £2,000, of which £500 must be deposited with the administration as a guarantee of good conduct. With restrictions of this kind to contend with, there was unlikely to be a rush of colonists to the Cameroons. Take away the commercial houses of Janssen & Thormählen and Woermann & Co. with their twenty white employees, and the four or five German officials, and not a vestige of German interests would remain. Compare this, he said, with six firms of good standing and two hundred British subjects. 'My own impression is that Germany has undertaken more than she can manage with the relatively poor support received from the mother country, and that when she has had a little longer experience, she will be glad to agree to some arrangement by which the Cameroons Mountain may be taken over by Great Britain.'[1]

It was a dangerous argument, the more so in that it coincided so exactly with Kirk's estimate of German prospects on the east coast of Africa.[2] On the one hand it encouraged the forward-looking officials at the Foreign Office to go on employing their limited resources in nebulous schemes for expansion instead of concentrating them on the administration of recognized spheres of influence. 'I agree', wrote Lister on the back of a letter received from the Baptist Missionary Society, 'with Mr Vice-Consul Johnston in wishing to retain Ambas Bay. I believe that the German Colony in the Cameroons will fail, and that the whole district will become British if we keep a footing at Victoria.'[3] On the other hand it agreed too well with the preconceptions of Liberal ministers of the Manchester school as an excuse for total inaction by the Government. 'What Mr Johnston says of the Cameroons', minuted Jacob

---

[1] Johnston to Rosebery 28.iii.86, *F.O.84.1762.*

[2] E.g. Kirk to Granville of 8.iv.85 in *F.O.84.1725:* 'Whatever plans were at first in view have entirely failed.'

[3] Minute on A. H. Baynes to Lord Rosebery 26.v.86, *F.O.84.1785.*

Bright, 'is likely to prove true of other German and French colonies. They will turn out to have been made more in the interests of Britain and British trade than in those of the ruling country. *Sic vos non vobis*.'[1]

It was not long before all these prognostications were proved false. The Germans, far from retreating, continued to assert themselves all along the Cameroons coast. Johnston himself was warned off the mainland, and von Soden, without even troubling to deal through him as the accredited British representative, imposed a collective fine of £10 upon the inhabitants of Victoria for an alleged attack on the neighbouring town of Batake.[2] A formal apology for this incident was extracted after prolonged negotiations at Berlin; but when the Baptist Mission at last closed with an offer from the Basel Society of £4,000 for its land and buildings, the British Government confirmed its intention to cede Ambas Bay as a part of the general settlement of problems between the two countries achieved in October 1886.[3] By the end of the year Johnston found himself at Mondole on territory that only awaited the formalities of transfer to make it German soil.

Still he had not been appointed in order to obstruct the cession of Ambas Bay; and if he had been able to fulfil the programme which Anderson had evidently mapped out with him before he left England, the whole matter would have been of comparatively minor importance in his affairs. Anderson, it seems, had encouraged him to hope that the Cameroons would absorb but a small portion of his time and energies, and that Mondole would serve him mainly as a base from which he would be able to undertake frequent exploring expeditions of a semi-political character into the hinterland of the British sphere of influence. The dealings of both consuls and traders had hitherto been confined to middlemen communities situated in the river mouths of the Delta and up the main stream of the Niger and Benue; consequently very little was known either of the primary producers of the palm-oil which passed out through these trading-centres, or of the other natural resources which their countries might contain and of the value of which they might still be ignorant. It was certain that European rivalry, now temporarily stilled by the partition of the coast, would break out again in the interior as soon as

---

[1] Minute on Johnston to Rosebery 28.iii.86, *F.O.84.1762.*
[2] The history of this wearisome dispute is to be found in *F.O.84.1788.*
[3] Memorandum by Sir Philip Currie dated 15.ix.86, *F.O.84.1790.*

forces sufficient for penetration had been mustered; and it was important to be ready with convincing claims for interior lines of partition, which would ensure that up-country markets were not cut off from their seaports and that valuable resources were not unwittingly bartered away by the bargainers at conference tables in Europe. Reminding Anderson of their parting interview in London, Johnston in a private letter written in April 1886 had proposed that he might employ three of the summer months, when the rivers would be in flood, in a reconnaissance of the Oil Rivers hinterland, 'to ascertain whether these countries do or do not possess in themselves the materials for their future prosperity'. His daring plan was to ascend the Lower Niger and the Benue and then to return overland to the Cross River, 'making studies in economic botany and other branches of natural history, besides taking up as far as possible the study of the native races'. It is interesting that the letter passed round the Foreign Office without prompting any comments on the personal risks which would be involved in such a journey. 'I think', wrote Lister, 'it would be an excellent plan, for we could believe all he told us and his knowledge is so varied that his reports are sure to be useful. Tell him to write officially through Consul Hewett.' Lord Rosebery indicated his assent with an initial and a large red tick.[1]

While these comments were being written in London, Johnston was making his first real contact in Old Calabar with Consul Hewett, upon whom the issue of this and of so many other schemes was to depend. At the end of April tragedy had overtaken the little community at Mondole. The faithful Virapan had contracted blackwater fever, and in a sudden, gusty fit of madness had seized a knife and stabbed first one and then another of the Liberian Kru-boys as they had sought to restrain him from rushing in upon his master. On reaching Johnston's room he had thrown the knife away and become as suddenly calm; but of the Kru-boys one had died and the other was seriously wounded, and Virapan had to be removed to Old Calabar for trial and ultimate repatriation.[2] While staying with Hewett, Johnston developed blackwater fever: it was the first of six attacks of that dreaded disease which he was to suffer and survive. Hewett nursed him tenderly, and Johnston's later memories of him were so coloured by gratitude that in *The Story of My Life* there appears an account of their

[1] Johnston to Anderson from Mondole 13.iv.86, *F.O.84.1762.*
[2] *Story*, pp. 164-5.

D

relationship which is misleading in many particulars.[1] For in the year which followed before Hewett went again on sick leave and Johnston took over the whole district as Acting Consul, the younger man remained virtually a prisoner on parole, confined without work on his tropical island in Ambas Bay.

It was not apparently that Hewett bore him any grudge on account of his powerful friends in London, or even that he regarded him as a dangerous young man to be kept in his place. Rather it seems that, as with Stanley and perhaps also with Kirk, Johnston's frail build and childlike appearance, combined in this case with the memory of a dangerous illness, aroused his protective instincts. He could not prevent him from returning to Mondole, but as Consul in charge of the British sphere he could, and did, make it almost impossible for him to go anywhere else. He was constantly solicitous about Johnston's personal comfort, occupying himself with the minutest details of his household, such as the equipment of the kitchen and the layout of the domestic offices; but to his travelling plans, when they came before him officially, he replied flatly that his assistant could not be spared for so long, a decision which the Foreign Office had perforce to accept.

It was the same with every other proposal which Johnston put forward. He might be wanted. He could not be spared just now. In June 1886 he made two brief excursions, one to the summit of the Cameroons Mountain, the other a boat journey up the Duala River, confessed to only in despatches written after the event; and from then on Hewett sent him regular instructions 'not to go away in case I want you' or 'not to leave Mondole till you hear from me'. In November Johnston addressed himself in exasperated terms to Anderson. He had been out almost a year, and thanks to Hewett nothing, even in the way of procuring information, had been done. Their personal relations were of the pleasantest, 'almost of a filial and fatherly character'; but in official matters 'Hewett's wish seems to be to show that he can manage all the work of his wide district himself and he would prefer to decide every detail by his own judgment. . . . If I were idly disposed Hewett's superintendence would suit me to perfection. I should then merely pass my time agreeably on that beautiful Mondole, employed in reading, writing, painting and botanizing with . . . an occasional water-picnic with the officers of one of H.M. ships.'[2]

To Johnston 1886 seemed a wasted year. In retrospect,

[1] *Story*, pp. 185-6.   [2] Johnston to Anderson 13.xi.86, *F.O.84.1750.*

however, and from the scanty correspondence which survives
from this period of enforced idleness, it appears as perhaps the
most decisive in his upward path—as the year in which he made
himself no longer merely the Vice-Consul with the interesting
artistic and scientific accomplishments but one of the very
small company of people who were thinking about the coming
partition of Africa on a continental scale and who were
thinking in advance of events. He was now thirty-four years
old. He had already a record of travel in widely separated
parts of Africa—Tunis, Angola, the Congo, Egypt, East
Africa and now West Africa—which in variety was unrivalled
among his contemporaries. He had met many both of the
men of action and of the men of affairs who had been most
influential in moving the African scene—Stanley and Leopold,
de Lesseps and Baring, Kirk and Burton, Mackinnon and
Manning, Stead and Arnold, Granville and Aberdare. He
had witnessed the colonial aspirations of Frenchmen and
Italians, Portuguese and Belgians, Germans and Spaniards.
He had scientific interests which covered the continent, the
pursuit of which had given a range and accuracy to his
geographical knowledge rare even among the most well-
informed students and promoters of discovery. It remained
that all this insight, all this varied expertise, should be formed
into a synthesis projecting forward from the events of the past
decade into that which was to come. It was just this synthesis
which Johnston achieved in his solitude on Mondole; and it
was this effort, an effort above all of the imagination, which
was shortly to win him the recognition not merely of Anderson
and Lister but also of Salisbury and Rhodes.

It was the novelty and the daring of Johnston's speculations
about the political future of Africa that he carried the logic
of international frontiers right into and across the heart of
the continent. It was a type of logic which had already been
applied by geographers to the watersheds and the drainage
systems, by natural scientists to the distribution of species, by
linguists and ethnographers to the classification of peoples
and tongues. Philanthropists were applying it to their studies
of slavery, and missionaries in their plans for the extension of
the Kingdom of God. But in the fields of economics and
international politics its application had been much slower.
Business men were still paralysed in thinking of the interior
of Africa by the apparently insuperable problems of communications. The imaginations of statesmen and diplomats
were still bounded by concepts of 'coast' and 'sphere' and

'hinterland', which tapered towards the centre into the vagueness of ignorance and precluded anything but a series of regional approaches.

Johnston's imagination was by contrast one that rushed impetuously to the centre, regarding the coastlands merely as an obstacle that had to be overcome on the way. The experience of all his travels, the conclusion of all his reading, had been that the riches of Africa lay in the interior. The healthy uplands were there, as also the mountains and lakes which gave rise to the great river-systems. There, too, must be fertility and an evenly distributed rainfall; and there, near the mountains, the main mineral resources would probably be found. Among the peoples of Africa the levels of the indigenous cultures seemed to rise in proportion to their distance from the sea. The coastal peoples were by indigenous standards barbarians, who had acquired some crude wealth as traders and middlemen by exporting the produce of the interior, but had done so by erecting a barrier between the producers and the outside world, a barrier which in the interests both of commerce and of civilization must be speedily broken down.

The superiority of the inland producer to the coastal middleman had been a constant theme in Johnston's *River Congo*, and now in his official capacity he lost no opportunity of pressing it on the authorities. His very first despatch, written from Bonny in January 1886, had referred to 'that curse of Western Africa, the middleman, who is resolved to prevent any intercommunication between the white traders on the coast and the industrious, thrifty tribes of the interior'.[1] In confessing to the brief journey he had made on his own initiative up the Cameroons River in June, he had pointed the same moral. 'I was certainly impressed with the fact that in many particulars the people of the interior were in a more satisfactory state of civilization than the population dwelling near the coast. . . . With the products of their forests they are tolerably well acquainted, and know how to procure rubber, ebony and camwood. . . . But the Duala traders never buy anything but palm-oil, palm-kernels and ivory. . . . When the tyranny of the middleman is over and the German Government permits the white traders to trade direct with the producers . . . a great impetus will be given to the civilization of this region.'[2] With the detailed application of this thesis in the Niger Delta Johnston's year as Acting Consul in 1887-8 was to

---

[1] Johnston to Salisbury 15.i.86, *F.O.84.1762*.
[2] Johnston to Rosebery 17.vi.86, *Ibid.*

be almost wholly preoccupied; meanwhile he employed his opportunities of recollection at Mondole to developing its wider relevance to British imperial aims.

I am more and more convinced [he wrote to Anderson in November] that we are assisting at the birth of a new India. West Central Africa lies within the same limits of latitude as India, possesses similar conditions of soil, climate, inhabitants and productions, and will doubtless offer the same obstacles and rewards. . . . If we could only set before us some such map as the enclosed, and stick as resolutely as possible to securing that position which is marked in red. . . . We need not rush at the consummation of such a plan. . . . Our policy may for the present chiefly assume a negative character. So long as we keep other European nations out, we need not be in a hurry to go in. But my last two visits to Africa have impressed on me the necessity of backing up the chief courses of English trade, existent and about to exist, by English political control. The French in the Gaboon and the Germans in the Cameroons furnish excellent examples of the way in which British commerce may be subtly harrassed, choked, cribbed, cabined and confined without actually or definitely transgressing international agreements.[1]

The map which Johnston sent home was nothing less than an imaginary partition of the continent, in which the British share, South Africa apart, was represented as a single block fanning outwards from Egypt, westwards through the Libyan and Sahara deserts to the Niger bend, and southwards up the Nile Valley to the Central African lakes. The Atlantic sea-board of this imaginary empire stretched uninterruptedly from Sierra Leone to the Niger Delta: the Gambia had been bartered to France in exchange for the renunciation of French claims on the Ivory Coast and Dahomey. In its southward extension it took in the fertile crescent between Lakes Victoria, Tanganyika and Nyasa, but tapered, neatly including Kili-manjaro, to a single outlet on the Indian Ocean at Mombasa. German claims in East Africa were settled, reasonably enough for one who had studied the activities of the Society for German Colonization but who had no knowledge of the agreement of October 1886, by two large spheres, one north and one south of Mombasa. The angle between the western and southern arms of this empire was filled by a German Cameroons, a French Gaboon and a Congo Free State, to the south of which stretched a Portuguese band, joining up the two provinces of Angola and Mozambique. Southwards

---

[1] Johnston to Anderson (private) from Old Calabar 13.xi.86, *F.O.84.1750.*

5. HOW AFRICA SHOULD BE DIVIDED—1886

From the original drawing by Sir Harry Johnston in the Public
Records Office—Johnston to Anderson 13.xi.86., *F.O.84.1750.*

again, a generously conceived German South West Africa marched with a British South Africa, which had swallowed the Boer republics and pushed up to the central Zambezi.

A detailed plan for the division of a continent submitted privately to an Assistant Under-Secretary in Whitehall by a Vice-Consul in his first year of service is not, of course, a document which need be taken completely seriously. It is unlikely that Johnston ever intended it as more than a sort of slogan, designed as much for the amusement as for the edification of his kindly patron. He was no doubt aware that his excellent relations with the head of the Foreign Office Africa Department would not suffer by being spiced with an occasional sprinkling of vivacious impertinence, and he may even have imagined the old man's chuckle as he slipped the map, with feigned absence of mind, into a pile of papers destined for the Secretary of State. Nevertheless, the prank, if such it was, provided clear evidence that its author was an expert as well as an artist. Given the illogical, fragmentary way in which claims to the coastline had been staked and recognized, a surprising number of Johnston's internal frontiers bore some relation to geographical realities. Nor was his assessment of the realities of European power politics so wildly in error. It is true that the share allotted to Great Britain was optimistic —to the point of utter unrealism in regard to French claims on the Upper Niger. But in other respects his recognition of the aspirations of Germany, Portugal and Italy was not that of an unmitigated jingo who could see no further than his own country's ambitions. Indeed, considering how short a way the process of partition had been carried in 1886, it is impressive to see how few radical adjustments would have been needed in Johnston's blueprint to make it correspond with the *fait accompli* of, say, 1914. Certainly it is easy to understand how the man who could throw off so accomplished a supplement to a private letter to his chief could become during the decisive years between 1888 and 1891, when the major international agreements on African partition were being planned and negotiated, a valued consultant even to a Prime Minister of England, who was himself no mean performer in the intricacies of African geography.

Meanwhile, in the eighteen months that remained of his West African tour, there were at last some less academic duties for Johnston to perform. Towards the end of November 1886 came a welcome letter from Hewett telling him to prepare an expedition to explore and map the so-called Rio del Rey which formed the boundary between the German and the British protectorates. Immediately he sent off to the French Gaboon coast for a party of oarsmen and carriers, and having assembled them at Mondole for Christmas, he embarked them on December 27th in his consular gig, with a dugout canoe in tow, and sailed for Old Calabar. The order for the survey had come from the Foreign Office, and Hewett had had no option but to pass it on; but now, true to form, he could only with difficulty bring himself to give Johnston his independence on the mainland. The visit to Old Calabar was hardly necessary at all, but Hewett managed to spin it out over three or four weeks, and the expensive carriers sat idle while Johnston was employed on this and that piece of consular routine which Hewett suddenly found to be of urgent and overriding importance. In London Anderson sensed what was happening: 'This is too bad of Hewett. Plessen [of the German Embassy] was asking a few days ago why we had not explored the Rio del Rey as promised.' A curt telegram was despatched: 'Delay Rio del Rey expedition most inconvenient. Send Johnston at once.'[1]

Johnston had gone, but only just. He had borrowed from 'Yellow Duke', one of the big Efik traders of old Calabar, a huge travelling-canoe, 'more like Noah's ark than any other vessel', carrying forty paddlers fore and aft, and in the middle a little house with a shaded verandah and a table screwed to the deck, on which the leader of the expedition could draw, write or map, surrounded by his personal servants, his two milch-goats, his Muscovy ducks, his laying-fowls, his tame monkey and his pet birds. With this strange but not altogether unpractical equipage he had set off eastwards, following the routes of the Calabarese palm-oil traders through the intricate maze of inland lagoons connecting the two main estuaries of the Cross River and the Rio del Rey; and he had barely started his work on the easternmost affluent of the latter estuary when, to his vast amusement, he was 'rescued' by Hewett, who had heard an entirely false rumour that he was in trouble with the little-known inhabitants of the region, and had come post haste in a gunboat. It must have been an entertaining encounter for the gunboat's crew to witness: Hewett motherly beneath his outward formality, feeling as ridiculous as possible in the *dénouement* of his wild-goose chase; Johnston bland and puckish, well conscious that

[1] F.O. to Hewett 14.ii.87, *F.O.84.1828.*

fortune had played into his hands. At least from now on there would be no more interference.

During the whole of February and March 1887 Johnston was in his element. The first and basic part of his task was to explore, survey and map every affluent of the Rio del Rey estuary, the course of which was at that time only known for a few miles from the sea. From his survey one of these affluents would be selected as the Anglo-German frontier, and from its source the line would run to the cataracts of the Cross River and thence to the great bend of the Benue.[1] The geographical course of the affluents would clearly be the paramount consideration, but there would also be others. A river which happened to be in addition an ethnic frontier would be a likely one for the final selection; it was important also that the trading frontier of the Calabarese middlemen should as far as possible be repeated in the international settlement. The strict object of the mission apart, the region was unknown, and no piece of information about the inhabitants, the soil, the flora and fauna could be regarded as irrelevant to a government which was preparing for the task of penetration and administration. To Johnston in his little houseboat the days were full of interest. On one of them, chosen at random from his diary, he worked in the morning at a drawing of a small arum-lily, while his men were cutting a rough track round a cataract which had brought navigation to a halt. In the afternoon he walked a few miles up his new road and made a drawing of river scenery. 'Saw a large, white-crested hornbill and a great blue plantain-eater. This bird makes curious, braying, baaing noise, cross between a sheep and a donkey. Caught one small snake and a lovely crimson and green bug. Curious chameleon, exactly marked and coloured like a dead leaf . . . a well-spent day.'[2] Other days were less carefree. There was fever, sickness and insomnia. And there was rain.

Awoke very seedy and depressed after horrible night. Followed up the River Beke to-day and, thank goodness, got out of mangroves and mud. In the late afternoon, just as we were entering most romantic scenery in a rocky gorge where the forest trees towered hundreds of feet into the air, a terrific thunderstorm broke on our defenceless heads. I continued nevertheless obstinately to follow up the river against the stream, but when at length the shallows obstructed further progress, we turned

[1] Minute by Anderson on Johnston to Salisbury 14.vii.87, *F.O.84.1839.*
[2] Diary, 26.ii.87, *Johnston Papers.*

D*

back and sought shelter in a place whither we had seen some Calabar traders direct their course. By the time we had arrived at the beach the Kru-boys were blue with cold and wet, I despatched them *instanter* to the village, invisible in the forest, and shortly after followed myself to see to their comfort. I mounted and mounted a precipitous, hilly path, which had become for the time a voluminous torrent which sometimes reached to my knees. At last I desisted as, no village appearing, and fearing the night would surprise me in the forest, I returned to the canoe, shut myself up in my little house, ate a not badly cooked dinner, and forgot the horrid, rainy night in reading the *Revue des Deux Mondes*.[1]

Five days later he attempted the shallows again. The Beke, or Mbomanjinga as it was called by the Bantu inhabitants of the district, was the last and most easterly of the affluents he had to survey, and he resolved to try dragging the canoe from the banks. He himself remained on the deck to direct the tug-of-war; and the obstacle was nearly past when suddenly the rope slipped from the Kru-boys' hands, the boat spun round and went tearing downstream. A fallen tree spanned the downward course, and to its branches Johnston was left clinging, while the Noah's ark sank under his feet and his little wooden cabin containing his maps, his notebooks, his collections and all his personal belongings splintered into fragments and was swept down with the rest. For a moment the work of two months seemed irretrievably lost. Twenty paces downstream the Muscovy ducks rose to the surface and swam away; then miraculously they were followed by the bows of Yellow Duke's canoe, carried by the torrent well up upon a friendly sand-bank, from which it could be easily rescued and its precious contents quickly dried in the tropical sun.

His mission completed, Johnston returned to Old Calabar on April 2nd to find that Hewett was once again a sick man, waiting only to hand over the Consulate to his subordinate before proceeding on extended leave of absence. He left Johnston in the middle of the month, so overwhelmed with the accumulation of consular routine that it was more than three months before he could reduce his survey notes into a map and present the report on his expedition. However, a large case of natural history specimens was despatched in May for transmission to the Cameroons sub-committee of the British Association and the Royal Gardens at Kew. And his map, when it finally arrived in July, was a model of thoroughness, though

[1] Diary, 20.iii.87, *Johnston Papers*.

it caused some consternation as to whether there was a room
in the Foreign Office large enough to accommodate it unfolded.
The accompanying report was short and admirably clear in
its recommendations. The Rio del Rey was non-existent
except as the recipient estuary of a number of small streams,
all originating some forty miles inland on a single range of
hills which formed an extension of the Cameroons Mountain.
Of these rivulets one, the Ndiang, marked an ethnic
boundary between Bantu-speaking tribes on the east and
Efik and Ibibio peoples on the west. The latter groups were
producers of palm-oil, which they exported through the
lagoons to Old Calabar, and the Ndiang was therefore an
economic as well as a racial frontier. 'Throughout my journey',
was Johnston's brief and dignified summary, 'I have been
received with the utmost kindness by the few natives that
form the sparse population of the country. The only difficulties
and dangers I encountered were those normally attending the
navigation of unknown rivers and the crossing of trackless
forests and treacherous swamps.'[1] On Lord Salisbury's instructions he received the compliments of the Foreign Office
for the careful and exemplary manner in which he had carried
out his task. It was an auspicious beginning to a year of full
and sole responsibility in a post which was certainly at the
time the most arduous in the whole of the African service of
the Foreign Office, a year in which he was to pass through the
fires of controversy and emerge, even if with reservations,
respected and marked out for further promotion.

For no sooner was the Rio del Rey inquiry completed than
Johnston was plunged into an acute political crisis, which on
the one hand raised the whole question of British control in
the Oil Rivers Protectorate, and on the other touched the
deepest animosities existing between the British commercial
interests operating in the region. At the end of June 1887 the
Foreign Office received urgent representations from five
Glasgow and Liverpool firms, banded together for political
and economic purposes as the African Association, that their
agents in the Oil Rivers were being obstructed from trading
up one of the more important Delta rivers by Ja Ja, 'king' of
Opobo. In the facile way of the Office Johnston was instructed
to proceed to Opobo and have the obstacles removed.[2]

[1] Johnston to Salisbury 4.iv.87, 14.v.87, 14.vii.87, *F.O.84.1839.*
[2] Couper, Johnstone & Co. to Salisbury 23.vi.87, *F.O.84.1865;* F.O. to Johnston
24.vi.87, *F.O.84.1828.*

The drafter of the telegram must have realized that this was no ordinary piece of consular routine. Ja Ja, the most enterprising and accomplished of all the African merchant princes of the Niger coast, had been a thorn in the flesh of every Consul for the Bights of Benin and Biafra since he established his settlement near the mouth of the Opobo River in 1872. Handsome, efficient, rich, fluent in English, with manners that were almost polished, and a taste for good, dry champagne which was unanimously approved by his European guests, Ja Ja was the very antithesis of the typical Calabar chief who, when rebuked by Johnston for calling at the Consulate in a state of nudity, disturbed the consular gravity by appearing from then onwards dressed in pink tights, a cabman's many-caped coat, blue spectacles and a bright red chimney-pot hat. Along with his other western ways Ja Ja had developed a nice sense of European logic and legal forms which he had employed with remarkable prescience to defend his commercial interests against future encroachments. In 1873 he had signed a treaty with Consul Livingstone which, in exchange for the limitation of the export duties known as 'comey', explicitly recognized his right to act as the sole middleman between the producers of the interior and the European trading firms; and though this treaty had been denounced by the Foreign Office on a technicality, he had reasserted his claim by refusing to sign the Protectorate Treaty form in use for the Oil Rivers District in 1884 until the clause providing for freedom of trade within his dominions had been deleted from it.[1] At the same time he had further extracted a letter from Consul Hewett stating that 'with reference to the word Protectorate as used in the proposed treaty . . . the Queen does not want to take your Country or your Markets but at the same time is anxious that no other nation should take them. She undertakes to extend her gracious favour and protection which will leave your country still under your government.'[2] Ja Ja, as he thought, had made permanent a very comfortable source of income. Palm-oil and kernels to the annual value of £160,000 were exported through Opobo, upon which the European traders paid him 'comey' at the rate of four puncheons in every twenty, or £30,000 a year, in exchange for the questionable service of keeping the routes open and supplies flowing.

Had the British Government understood the Protectorate

---

[1] Memorandum on the history of Ja Ja by Clement Hill, filed at 31.iii.88, *F.O.84.1918.*

[2] Hewett to Ja Ja 1.vii.84, enclosed in Ja Ja to Salisbury 5.v.87, *F.O.84.1862.*

Treaty, together with Hewett's commentary upon it, in the same sense as Ja Ja, it would have been in an extraordinarily difficult position. For in the middle of its Protectorate, devoted according to the terms of the Berlin Treaty to free trade, it would have had not merely one small enclave but one whole line of river communication monopolized for private profit by the chief of a settlement near its mouth; and while the practical effect might not have been very different from the commercial system of the Royal Niger Company upon the main stream of the river, the monopoly of the Niger Company was an evasion of the law and could be stopped by the revocation of its Charter, whereas Ja Ja would have had the law on his side. Somewhat casuistically, therefore, the Foreign Office had consistently chosen to interpret Ja Ja's monopoly as applying only to his own territory and had warned him several times that he must not interfere with traders who wished to pass up the river and buy direct from the Ibo producers beyond the limit of his dominions.

On the strength of Consul Hewett's reference to his 'markets', Ja Ja could probably have denounced the treaty of 1884, but he did not. Instead, he made practical difficulties for the traders, by placing a boom across the river and by terrorizing his up-country producers into refusing to trade direct with the white men, whilst reserving his legal defence against the time when he was arraigned. For a time the traders acquiesced in the situation. Then, in 1885, as a result of a fall in world prices, the five member firms of the African Association clubbed together to reduce Ja Ja's 'comey' from four puncheons in twenty to three. The one remaining firm, Miller Brothers of Glasgow, having agreed to join with the others, suddenly backed out, paid Ja Ja's price and secured the bulk of his trade. The oil which Millers could not carry Ja Ja shipped on his own account to Liverpool in the mail steamers and made a handsome profit. To these moves the African Association could make only one reply, which was to send out small shallow-draught steamers and make active preparations to trade upstream. It was the arrival of these steamers coupled with Ja Ja's successful obstruction of their activities which had occasioned Johnston's instructions to intervene.[1]

The issue between Miller Brothers and the African Association was in fact as sordid as the language in which it was conducted was hypocritical and high-flown. The African

[1] Memorandum by Hill cited above; Johnston to Salisbury 15.i.86, *F.O.84.1750*; cf. Ja Ja to Salisbury with enclosures 24.i.87, *F.O.84.1857*.

Association, which was fighting Ja Ja under the banner of free trade, was in fact a group which had formed a cartel to depress the prices paid for oil, which was anxious to obtain a Royal Charter, similar to but distinct from that of the Niger Company, to govern the Oil Rivers District, and which if it had succeeded would certainly have imposed a commercial monopoly similar to that in force on the Niger. Miller Brothers, on the other hand, who were parading as the philanthropic defenders of native interests against the encroachments of the African Association, were of course making an excellent profit out of their partnership in Ja Ja's monopoly, and were in addition large shareholders in the Royal Niger Company, whose object was to force the African Association into amalgamation with itself and to bring the Oil Rivers District within the sphere of its own Charter.[1] Johnston's attitude in the case was not the result of any prejudice in favour of one or other of these commercial factions. On the broad issue between monopoly and free trade British Government policy was already quite clearly defined. Apart from Hewett's one incautious reference to 'markets', it had consistently refused to admit that Ja Ja had any monopoly rights outside his own dominions. Within Opobo territory he was entitled to prevent European traders from settling or doing business, but if they were merely using the river as a highway to pass through Opobo to the interior, he must not obstruct their passage.

Within this broad field of agreement there were differences as to what line of action was immediately expedient. The Navy, which in the absence of any land force would have to protect the traders if they penetrated to the interior, and which detested the responsibility of navigating gunboats on uncharted creeks and rivers, was inclined to argue that the time for free trade was not ripe. 'I am distinctly of opinion', Admiral Richards had written to Lister, 'that the time has not come for our government to take the initiative in disturbing the present system of trading in the Oil Rivers. . . . The "middlemen", as you term the chiefs with whom for the most part we have treaties, have a clear and decided use, insomuch as they are now responsible for the protection of the European traders in their districts and for the security of their factories

[1] See especially Anderson to Pauncefote of 10.ix.87, *F.O.84.1869*. 'The African traders of Liverpool who support the middlemen of the Brass River against the Niger Co., wish to break Ja Ja in order that they may trade freely in the Opobo and Eboe creeks, which are outside the Niger Co.'s operations. In each case they follow their own interests. . . .'

and goods. . . . The so-called "monopolies" I look upon as being dues fairly leviable for the security of the traders.'[1] The Consuls on the other hand, Hewett even more so than Johnston, felt that Ja Ja's was the test case by which the whole nature of their authority along the Oil Rivers coast would be determined. Their personal views on free trade apart, Ja Ja had been in a number of smaller issues quietly ignoring their instructions, questioning their judgments and writing behind their backs to the Secretary of State. Meanwhile he was laying out a considerable proportion of his profits on arms and ammunition, which might at any time be used for the conquest of his neighbours or the defiance of the British Government. Their greatest fear was that, unless he was dealt with quickly, Ja Ja would organize a regular base in the interior, from which his advance forces could continue to blockade the river, but to which they could retreat as soon as a disciplinary gunboat made its appearance. Their formula for Ja Ja was therefore deportation as soon as any pretext for such an action could be found.

In reporting Ja Ja's agreement with Miller Brothers in January 1886, Johnston had written: 'I venture with all due deference to suggest to your Lordship that the most effectual aid to peace and commerce in the British Protectorate of the Oil Rivers would be administered by the humiliation or banishment of Ja Ja. It would be a fatal blow dealt at the assumptions of the middlemen, and it would necessitate no other display of force than the action of a gunboat.' The Foreign Office did not dissent from this opinion; indeed they sent a copy of the despatch to the Admiralty in order to prove that Hewett's estimate of Ja Ja was not unique, with the result that Admiral Hunt-Grubbe, who had succeeded Admiral Richards at the Cape, authorized the Senior Naval Officer on the West Coast, in the event of Hewett's further application, to capture Ja Ja and send him to Ascension, only warning him that 'Ja Ja is heavily armed, and unless you can see your way to capturing him with the minimum risk to life, you are not to attempt it'. In other words, in his conduct of the interesting events which followed between July and September 1887, Johnston, though he undoubtedly forced the Government's hand as to method and timing, did nothing which prejudiced the basis of its policy.[2]

---

[1] Admiral Richards to T. V. Lister 5.xii.84, *F.O.84.1693*.
[2] Johnston to Salisbury 15.i.86, cited above; Hunt-Grubbe to Admiralty 13.iii.86, copy in *F.O.84.1784*.

Johnston arrived at Opobo in the gunboat *Goshawk* on July 27th, and for a time it seemed as though Ja Ja would once again outwit his opponent. He pleaded illness, but was at last persuaded to come to a meeting. His tactics were now to delay. Johnston made two conditions: that he should immediately remove the boom he had placed across the river, and that he should send his emissaries upstream to release the people of Ohombela, a market beyond the limits of his own territory, from the 'ju-ju' which he had placed upon them to prevent them from trading with the Europeans. Ja Ja replied that he was sending a deputation to see Lord Salisbury. 'I simply referred Consul Johnston to my chiefs at home and gave him to understand that I would give him a decided answer on their return.'[1] On the 29th, therefore, Johnston despatched *Goshawk* to Fernando Po to fetch Captain Hand, the Senior Naval Officer, and meanwhile himself took a trip up the river in one of the merchants' launches. He landed at Ohombela and tried to see the chiefs, but was prevented by Ja Ja's men. On the 31st he returned down-river to Esene creek, where he saw, and made a drawing of, the skeleton of a woman, 'who for attempting to interfere with the trade by buying palm-oil at a higher price than the market value, was tied to a tree and left till she expired of hunger and thirst'.[2] Then till Captain Hand arrived on August 3rd he spent his time 'principally in drawing plants'. Ja Ja was now faced with two gunboats, and after two long interviews on the 5th he gave way. On the 6th Johnston steamed to Bonny in *Goshawk* to telegraph the news. On the 7th an impressive little flotilla, consisting of the gunboats *Goshawk* and *Alecto* and the five steam-launches of the associated firms, set off upriver from Opobo to open the interior trade. At Ohombela on the 9th four of the independent Ibo chiefs were with some difficulty collected on board one of the launches, and there an Opobo dignitary solemnly dissolved the ju-ju in Ja Ja's name. On the 11th Captain Hand sailed away in *Alecto*, leaving *Goshawk* temporarily at Johnston's disposal.[3]

The news of these events was favourably received at the Foreign Office. Only Lord Salisbury, with an application to detail truly amazing in one who combined the offices of Prime Minister and Foreign Secretary, scored the despatches with a string of searching questions. 'Are we sure Ohombela

---

[1] Ja Ja to Salisbury 1.viii.87, *F.O.84.1867.*
[2] See Plate 4, facing p. 64.
[3] Diary fragment running from 25.vii.87 to 11.viii.87, *Johnston Papers.*

is not his country? . . . If Ohombela is really under the dominion of Ja Ja, he is only doing what a few years ago was done by France, China and Japan, and what is still done by Nepal, Thibet and Formosa.' And against a recital by Johnston of Ja Ja's history since the time when he was a slave of the king of Bonny, he wrote good-humouredly, 'Why should we object to such an honourable termination of his career?'[1]

Then suddenly the situation became serious. On August 19th a telegram from Johnston announced that Ja Ja had broken the agreement and that he had accordingly placed a ban on all trade in the Opobo River.[2] Lister, sensing the scepticism of his chief, sought out Hewett to write an urgent memorandum recommending Ja Ja's punishment and deportation. 'Ja Ja', he himself summed up at the foot of the document, 'is a false and cruel chief under our protectorate, who interferes with British traders and missionaries, breaks treaties and laughs at H.M.G. His cup of iniquity is now full.' On the same day a letter was received from Miller Brothers coolly informing the Foreign Office that four of Ja Ja's sons were on their way to England and that meanwhile they had instructed their agent at Opobo to ignore the Vice-Consul's fiat. The African Association on the other hand wrote saying that they cordially approved Johnston's action and offering to bring a deputation from the member firms to urge some decisive step with regard to Ja Ja. 'Lord Salisbury would probably prefer to deport Ja Ja,' minuted Lister. 'On the whole,' came back the reply in red ink, 'I should prefer to deport the deputation. S.' The debate continued at the end of Hewett's memorandum. 'We can do nothing', wrote Salisbury, 'till Ja Ja's embassy has been heard.' 'I am afraid', replied Lister, either wilfully or unconsciously mistaking the deputation to which the Prime Minister had previously referred, 'you will have to receive the deputation *and* to deport Ja Ja. . . . We must support our Consul and if a severe lesson is not given to Ja Ja all the other chiefs will become uncontrollable and civil wars and destruction of trade will ensue.' The conclusion was grudging and still indecisive: 'I will speak to Ld. George [Hamilton] in Cabinet. These West African expeditions are most unremunerative. S.'[3]

Shortly after he had thus delivered himself, Salisbury

[1] Minutes on Johnston to Salisbury 1.viii.87 and 12.viii.87, *F.O.84.1828*.

[2] Johnston to Salisbury 20.viii.87, *F.O.84.1828*.

[3] Hewett to Salisbury 20.viii.87, *F.O.84.1828*; Miller Bros. to Salisbury 19.viii.87 and African Association to Salisbury 23.viii.87, *F.O.84.1868*, with accompanying minutes; cf. Memorandum by Hill of 31.iii.88, cited above, *F.O.84.1918*.

removed to Puys, his French home on the cliffs above Dieppe. It was there that he read Johnston's explanatory despatches and on September 9th penned an interesting minute expressing his final judgment.

> Nothing in the memorandum of the Department or in the papers sent with it throws much light upon the most important issue, namely whether Ja Ja is in any sense ruler of the territory of Ohombela, from which he has excluded our trade. If he is ruler, then, assuming we are dealing with him according to strict law, he is in his right. If he is not ruler, and is merely making use of his power as a waterside king to stop the highway, then he is in the wrong. . . . The only thing that can be done under the circumstances is to ask the Admiralty to send a gunboat, and that the Captain should be instructed to inquire into the case: if there is any evidence of an attempt to block the highway, that he should inflict whatever punishment he thinks right: but that if Ja Ja's action has been confined to excluding us from countries which are under his control, that then he should negotiate and make the best terms he can: and that in all matters he should act on his own judgment or if in doubt should refer to his superior officer.
>
> I am not satisfied with the entire impartiality of Consul Johnston's judgment, though he has gone less astray than Consul Hewett; but I think his action may be approved by telegram and he should be informed at the same time of the application we are making to the Admiralty.[1]

Lord Salisbury's decision had to travel by courier from Puys to London. Consequently it was not until 3.45 p.m. on September 12th that a telegram left the Foreign Office for Johnston, and even then the message was much abbreviated: 'Your action re Ja Ja approved. Further instruction will be sent after communication with the Admiralty.' Almost simultaneously,[2] an incoming telegram was received from Johnston: 'Ask immediate permission remove Ja Ja temporarily Gold Coast. Organizes armed attacks. Obstructs waterways, markets. Intrigues render this course imperative. Am awaiting your reply at Bonny.' It was the holiday season in Whitehall. Lister and Anderson were both away. Had the official in charge of the African Department been a little more in tune with Salisbury's intentions, he might have taken upon himself

---

[1] Minute by Salisbury dated 9.ix.87, *F.O.84.1869*.

[2] In fact its arrival was registered 22 minutes *before* the despatch of the outgoing telegram. But, allowing for time taken in registration, coding and decoding, and circulation within the Foreign Office, it would seem almost certain that the outgoing telegram would have left before any responsible official set eyes on the incoming one.

the responsibility of an immediate and cautionary reply. Instead, he repeated the telegram to Puys: 'Does this modify your Lordship's Memo received last night?' The response was prompt. 'Adhere to my instructions already given. Consul's language and proposals do not inspire me with confidence. Naval officer will be less under influence of the merchants.'[1] But it was too late. Johnston, faced with an urgent situation at Opobo, and having received what he imagined to be an assent to his request, had not waited at Bonny for the 'further instructions', but had decided to concert his own measures for naval assistance and to put his plan into action forthwith.

The Senior Naval Officer, Captain Hand, though he had in August co-operated with Johnston in opening Ohombela to European trade, had made no secret of his sympathy with Ja Ja and of his disapproval of the Consul's decision to force an issue. When he had left with the *Alecto* on August 11th, he had warned him that to threaten Opobo effectively would require at least two gunboats, and that it would be impossible again to reinforce *Goshawk* before the middle of September. Ignoring the disapproval, Johnston had worked strictly to this time-table. He had made further visits to Ohombela, where he had, as expected, found Ja Ja's agents again at work among the people. He had then concluded a treaty with the chiefs of Obako, another important market well up-river from Ja Ja's settlement, formally placing the area under British protection, declaring freedom of trade and conceding permission for the European traders to build store-houses. This action had been the signal for further interference by Ja Ja, and on a second visit to Obako in one of the merchants' launches, he had been stopped and turned back by an armed force. It being by now nearly the middle of the month, he had gone to Bonny and telegraphed for permission to act. On receiving the supposed approval, he therefore wired to Hand at Sierra Leone: 'Government order Ja Ja's removal Gold Coast. Await arrival second gunboat Opobo before acting. Prompt assistance necessary.' The reply was disconcerting: 'Remember our last conversation. Impossible.' 'I made up my mind', wrote Johnston in a lengthy despatch describing his proceedings, 'that I must do my best with the little force at my disposal, as I knew delay was dangerous and that Ja Ja was preparing to escape to a district where fifty gunboats could not catch him.' He accordingly arranged with the chiefs

[1] F.O. to Johnston 12.ix.87; Johnston to Salisbury 11.ix.87, with minute by Salisbury dated 13.ix.87, *F.O.84.1828.*

of Bonny, who were the trade rivals of Opobo, to block the creeks at the rear of Ja Ja's settlement, and then himself returned to the Opobo river, where he had in Lieutenant Pelly of *Goshawk* a readier ally than Hand, and one who was prepared to take the risk of acting alone.

Johnston now opened proceedings by summoning Ja Ja to a meeting to be held on Harrison & Company's 'beach' on September 19th. The messenger brought back an affirmative answer, but reported that all the big Opobo canoes were being made ready for a journey, that the women and children had already left the town, and that all the remaining inhabitants appeared to be packing up and removing their goods. The next day Ja Ja wrote that he feared to come unless a white man should be handed over to his people as a hostage. This Johnston refused, but he sent a letter pledging that, if Ja Ja refused his terms, no force should be put upon him to prevent him from leaving the meeting and returning to his town. And so, on the morning of the 19th, with the entire European community assembled at Harrison's factory and *Goshawk* with her seventy blue-jackets standing offshore, her guns trained and ready for action, Ja Ja, escorted by twenty-seven war canoes with seven hundred men aboard, crossed the river to meet the Consul. Only the chief himself and his immediate advisers were allowed to land at the merchants' beach: the remainder of his following either landed further upstream or sat waiting in the canoes. At eleven o'clock Johnston entered the improvised court-room and read out a long ultimatum, presenting Ja Ja with two alternatives: he could either surrender himself and accompany Johnston to Accra, there to undergo an open and impartial trial for his misdeeds, or he could depart freely to Opobo as an enemy of the British Government, to be mercilessly pursued and hunted down, his town bombarded, his goods confiscated and himself treated as a declared outlaw. The statement concluded, Ja Ja was bidden to withdraw with his advisers and to return his answer within one hour.

The choice was admittedly a hard one, and indeed the timing of the whole policy which had led to its imposition was perhaps of questionable wisdom. It might have been better to wait until the forces of law and order were stronger before forcing the issue of free trade in any of the Delta rivers. But this granted, there does not seem to be any evidence to support the subsequent claims of Ja Ja's followers that their leader was entrapped and the safe-conduct dishonoured. There is no reason to believe that, had Ja Ja refused Johnston's terms, he would not have been allowed time to return to his settlement and evacuate it before the guns of *Goshawk* opened fire. Indeed, had he been prepared for the dangerous life of an outlaw it would in all probability have been many years before the final retribution came. But in point of fact Ja Ja was far-sighted enough not to pit his strength against British power. Within ten minutes of the ultimatum he announced his surrender, and in full sight of his armed escort went quietly on board the *Goshawk*. There he occupied Lieutenant Pelly's cabin and was allowed four visitors at a time throughout the next two days. On the 20th Johnston held a full meeting of all the Opobo notables, at which he explained all that had happened, reiterated the demand of the British Government for freedom of trade, and set up a 'Governing Council' of European traders and Opobo chiefs to regulate the affairs of the river in the Consul's absence. On the 21st he left for Bonny in the *Goshawk* with Ja Ja and eight members of his household, and there transferred into the mail-steamer for Accra. Throughout the voyage Ja Ja appeared to be on the friendliest terms with his 'captor', sitting beside him while he wrote his despatch to the Secretary of State, turning over the pages of Johnston's books, examining his botanical drawings and asking intelligent questions about natural history.[1]

It was on September 22nd that the Foreign Office first learned how Johnston had interpreted the telegram sent to him on the 13th. Sir James Fergusson, the Parliamentary Under-Secretary, had meanwhile received Ja Ja's deputation, consisting of his two sons, Albert Ja Ja and Sunday Ja Ja, and two of his chiefs, Cookey Gam and Shoe Peterside. The party had been introduced by a director of the firm of Miller Brothers, and had withdrawn with a promise that a full investigation of the situation at Opobo should be undertaken by one of the naval officers on the West African station.[2] The news of Ja Ja's arrest, therefore, however welcome it might be to the permanent staff of the Office, meant the certain prospect of parliamentary questions and agitation which could hardly be so pleasing to the responsible Ministers. Without waiting for the explanatory despatches, Salisbury ordered the naval Commander-in-Chief, Admiral Hunt-Grubbe, to come up

---

[1] Johnston to Salisbury (teleg.) *21.ix.87* and *23.ix.87* and despatch of *24-28.ix.87*, *F.O.84.1828*; cf. F.O. to Johnston falsely dated *25.xi.87*, *F.O.84.1828*, for which *infra*, p. 123.

[2] Memorandum by G. M. Wylde of *15.ix.87*, *F.O.84.1869*.

from the Cape and conduct the trial at Accra. It was more than a month before Johnston received the most guarded approval of his action. Anderson and Lister both did their best for their protégé. 'Mr Johnston acted under a misconception . . . but I have little doubt that his firm and prompt action saved us from a native war within our Protectorate, which would have been costly and troublesome to prosecute, involving temporary stoppage of the Liverpool trade and exposing us to unpleasant criticisms from the Germans who are now working the Cameroons peacefully. . . . I think that with a little pressure we may induce the Colonial Office to add the Oil Rivers district to the Lagos Protectorate. H. P. A.' 'Mr Johnston no doubt mistook his instructions, but the removal of Ja Ja had become absolutely necessary to prevent great evils and it is impossible not to admire the pluck, coolness and straightforwardness of all his proceedings. T. V. L.' Lord Salisbury, however, was bleakly unimpressed. On the despatch describing the circumstances of the arrest he wrote: 'Simply approve his conduct. We need not discuss the principles developed in this despatch. They amount to this, that when a merchant differs from a native chief as to their respective rights, the native chief is to be deported.'[1] And to another rather desperate plea from Johnston for some expression of his confidence, the Prime Minister was, if possible, still more coldly hostile: 'I suppose he must receive the assurance for which he asks, as he has put us in the position where we shall do more harm by dropping than by supporting him. He is a resolute but singularly lawless personage.'[2] Among the privileged few who read these comments, not even Johnston's most ardent well-wishers could have predicted that he would have a brilliant career in the Consular Service and still less that he would be within a year a week-end guest at Hatfield House.

With Admiral Hunt-Grubbe's arrival in December the tide began to turn. The trial, it seems, was fairly held, Ja Ja being supported by the members of his embassy recently returned from London and defended by a coloured lawyer practising at Accra. Johnston was able to prove non-observance of the Protectorate Treaty, direct instigation of the armed attack which had turned him back from Azumara Creek and complicity in the opposition at Ohombela. Ja Ja was sentenced to

[1] Minutes on Johnston to Salisbury of 24-28.ix.87, cited above.
[2] Johnston to Salisbury 4.x.87, *F.O.84.1828*.

deposition and to five years' banishment in the West Indies, with full enjoyment of the income from his private property and a pension of £800 a year. Better still, the Admiral entered with sympathy into the wider issues which were at stake in the Ja Ja controversy. Johnston was determined that the principle of free trade for which he had been fighting should include not merely the freedom of European firms to buy direct from the interior markets but also freedom for the African traders to operate widely all over the Delta waterways and not, as formerly, only in their own rivers. Also if they wished to export directly to England they should be at perfect liberty to do so. Thus the producers would get a fair price for their oil, the trade of the middlemen would be competitive and the danger of price-rings among the European firms would be averted.

Again, with the disappearance of their commercial monopoly there would inevitably be a loosening of the political responsibility of the middleman communities of Brass, Bonny, Opobo, Calabar and the rest, to maintain some semblance of law and order not only within their own settlements but upon the waterways leading inland to the markets. It would be necessary to extend from the coastal communities to those at the inland markets the network of treaties securing the recognition of the British Protectorate and the authority of the British Consul; and it would also be necessary to establish some system of local authorities which could settle the ordinary run of trade disputes in the Consul's absence. Johnston's formula for this was the 'Governing Council', a development from the old 'Courts of Equity', to be composed equally of European and African traders, and with powers to impose fines up to £5 and imprisonment up to one week, and to levy a periodical tax of a shilling a head for essential public works upon the inhabitants of the riverside settlements.[1]

To all these proposals Admiral Hunt-Grubbe was prepared to lend his support and influence, and at the conclusion of the trial he spent ten days cruising with three gunboats along the whole stretch of coast from Brass to Opobo, addressing public meetings at all the principal ports and finally delivering from the poop of H.M.S. *Raleigh* off Bonny a discourse on free trade to a vast gathering of chiefs and notables of the Oil Rivers Protectorate assembled in canoes around his ship. In a despatch written from the *Raleigh* at Fernando Po on the

---

[1] Regulations for Opobo Governing Councils, enclosed in Johnston to Salisbury 24-28.ix.87, *F.O.84.1828*.

conclusion of the tour Johnston reported that he had already instituted Governing Councils at Old Calabar, Bonny, New Calabar and Brass, that he would be proceeding to Mondole for Christmas and that in the opening months of 1888 he would devote himself to a systematic extension of the treaty network on the upper Cross River and in the markets at the rear of Opobo and Bonny. It was becoming evident even to Lord Salisbury that if Consul Johnston was apt to be a law unto himself, he was at least pursuing a coherent policy with an energy and a sense of purpose which Hewett in his long tenure of the post had never displayed.[1]

Johnston's next big despatch, written from Old Calabar early in February 1888, must be one of the most bizarre documents ever received at the Foreign Office. After having the honour to inform his Lordship that on January 5th last he had started on an expedition up the Cross River for the purpose of making treaties with the peoples living beyond the already familiar Efik communities round Old Calabar, the author reported that he had signed treaties with three new districts—those of Umon, Akukuna and Iko Morut— but that he had thereafter desisted from further treaty-making pending a decision by Her Majesty's Government on the best means of governing this country. Above Iko Morut, he explained, the people were in many places rather wild and excitable.

> They are inveterate cannibals, and are continually fighting among themselves. They accorded me a boisterous reception at first. In some cases they began by firing at my canoe . . . then they would wade out through the shallows armed with all kinds of weapons and compel me to stop. They would nearly sink the canoe in their excitement, but to do them justice they never plundered me of the veriest trifle. In one instance I was dragged out of the canoe by a score of cannibals, mounted on the shoulders of the biggest, and carried off at a run to the town, where I was put in a hut with the door open and had to submit to being stared at for an hour by hundreds of entranced savages. Almost over my head, hanging from the smoke-blackened rafters of the house, was a smoked human ham, and about a hundred skulls were ranged round the upper part of the clay walls in a ghastly frieze. Despite these sinister surroundings, however, as soon as my interpreters rejoined me, I entered into friendly conversation with my captors and we soon got on excellent terms. . . . Finally the same big savage that had carried me out of the canoe carried me back, to the surprise and relief of my

[1] Johnston to Salisbury 2.xii.87, 5.xii.87, 13.xii.87, *F.O.84.1828.*

frightened Kru-boys. The town gave me a hundred yams and two sheep, and the old chief presented me with a necklace of human knucklebones from off his own neck. After leaving the place where this incident occurred (it was called Edadama), the banks of the river were thickly populated and the people became increasingly turbulent. Although all our enforced interviews (for we were captured and released every few hundred yards) ended in boisterous friendship, yet to begin with they were almost undecided as to whether they should not kill and eat us—or at any rate eat my Kru-boys. Under these circumstances I thought it better not to pursue my explorations any further, but to make a judicious retreat while the natives still doubted how to deal with us.

I have made a careful survey of the Cross River as far as I ascended it. . . . I have also made collections in Natural History which will be forwarded to Kew and the British Museum. I have the honour to enclose three treaties and a sketch map explanatory of the results of my expedition.

I have the honour to be,
Your Lordship's most obedient humble servant,
H. H. JOHNSTON

It was an astonishing escapade, and it served to establish Johnston as a 'personality' in the Consular Service, to whom, even if he took much upon himself, much could also be forgiven. 'He exercised a wise discretion about the treaties,' wrote Lister. 'I know of no explorer who has such a wonderful influence with savages as Johnston. To those who are acquainted with his refined, gentle and child-like manner and appearance the scenes described in this despatch are almost grotesque, but they show his wonderful courage, coolness and forbearance.'[1] Such a tribute was important at a time when the Foreign Office was being bombarded with complaints from the Miller interest of the Consul's high-handed behaviour, and when the legal experts of the Department were shaking grave heads and writing terse minutes about the validity of his system of Governing Councils. Indeed, when he moved west from the Cross River to Bonny in the middle of February Johnston found quite a sheaf of stern inquiries awaiting his explanations. On what authority, it was asked, had he claimed the right to impose a censorship on Ja Ja's telegrams? Again, by what right had he written to Mr Farquhar, the Opobo agent of Miller Brothers, accusing him of aiding and abetting Ja Ja, and threatening to deport him and to close Miller's factory if there were any further signs of such

[1] Johnston to Salisbury 9.ii.88, with minute, *F.O.84.1881.*

behaviour? 'You must be aware that you have no power arbitrarily to deport a British trader, nor to close his factory . . . and Lord Salisbury would be glad to learn on what grounds you felt justified in addressing such a letter to Mr Farquhar.' Finally, he was told, the regulations which he had submitted for his Governing Councils presupposed 'a totally different régime politically and legally to that which is now in force. In these circumstances Lord Salisbury would be glad to receive further explanations of your scheme and also to be informed whether the provisions of the Order in Council of 1885 have been fully kept in view.'[1]

It seemed a formidable list of charges against a very junior Acting Consul, yet Johnston stood his ground and emerged victorious. The censorship had been imposed for six days only and that after careful inquiries as to his rights under the International Telegraph Convention of 1885, and the result had been the important discovery that on his way from Opobo to Accra Ja Ja had telegraphed a large order for arms and ammunition to be delivered at Opobo by Miller Brothers. The letter to Mr Farquhar had been sent with the knowledge and approval of Admiral Hunt-Grubbe, who like himself was convinced that 'but for Messers Alex. Miller Brothers' greed of gain and their desire to maintain the monopoly of the Opobo trade, King Ja Ja would never have maintained his policy of obstruction. . . . Ja Ja believed to the last that Miller Brothers were stronger than consular authority and his belief is not shattered yet.' Johnston moreover maintained that he had a right of deportation under the Order in Council of 1885, and the Foreign Office, though remarking that such a right had never been exercised against a British subject, did not contest the point. On the question of Governing Councils, Johnston, while enclosing the regulations of a new one which he had just instituted at the town of Nana of Benin, claimed no more than that they were working well on the basis of consent if not of law; and his masters in London, by now either mollified or openly admiring, reacted with indulgence. 'This despatch', minuted Anderson, 'gives an insight into the difficulties in attempting to govern, alone, a district which he describes as being as large as Burma. . . . It seems to me that in view of our hopes of a permanent administration our object should be to temporize, not upsetting what is working well unless pressed by complaints, but on the other hand not adopting or approving plans of doubtful validity.' Lord Salisbury

[1] F.O. to Johnston 16.ii.88, 1.ii.88, 10.ii.88, *F.O.84.1881.*

endorsed his view. 'No interference or directive is necessary at present. S.'[1]

Meanwhile, in response to numerous parliamentary questions inspired by the Miller faction, the Government was preparing a White Paper on the deposition of Ja Ja. It was pointed out to Lord Salisbury that Johnston's emergency action had never been ratified. The reply in the Prime Minister's hand, showed a preparedness in the political field to suit the means to the end in a way that was scarcely more exactly scrupulous than the conduct of Johnston in the administrative field about which he had recently been so scathing. 'Of course then we must ratify. Draft an historical despatch in which ratification is expressed.'[2] A long draft was accordingly prepared, rehearsing the sequence of events leading up to Ja Ja's arrest. It informed Johnston that 'in view of the exigencies of the case, and subject to any further course which may be resolved upon after the reports of Sir W. Hunt-Grubbe have been received, H.M.G. consider that the circumstances fully justify them in ratifying your proceedings.'[3] In the White Paper it bore the date November 25th, 1887, just a week before the opening of Ja Ja's trial at Accra. The manuscript instruction which led to its composition was dated April 6th, 1888.

[1] Johnston to Salisbury 16.ii.88 and 19.iii.88, with minute, *F.O.84.1881*.
[2] Memorandum by Sir Julian Pauncefote with minute by Salisbury of 6.iv.88, *F.O.84.1881*.
[3] F.O. to Johnston dated 25.xi.87, *F.O.84.1828*.

Chapter 5

WORSE ON LAND THAN AT SEA

JOHNSTON did not have the opportunity of directing for long the new phase of British policy which he had initiated in the Oil Rivers Protectorate. Two and a half years on the West Coast of Africa was a considerable spell for any European in the insalubrious conditions of the eighteen-eighties, and when Hewett was at last ready to return to his post in May 1888, his deputy was at once given leave of absence.

It was a different homecoming, this, from the last two. Then he had been an adventurer, charged with experience it is true, but with no certain future, his only assets the wasting ones of his memory and his notebooks. Now he had the security of an official position, the right to a fixed period of rest on full pay, the certainty of employment at the end of it. Then he had had to seek his audiences, to accept with gratitude the invitations of a few learned societies, to fashion and refashion his wares to suit the varying tastes of editors and public. Now he could think more of reputation and less of guineas. He could turn his many talents to the cultivation of a more limited but also a more influential circle. Curiously enough, he was still painfully lacking in self-assurance. 'I do believe in myself,' he had written to his father only a year before, 'more because of my strong will and intense ambition than for any particular qualities I imagine myself to possess. Indeed I am saddled with many disadvantages—my insignificant appearance, my poverty, my lack of family interest in Government circles. I have to fight the world alone. I must creep when I would fly. But if I live, I will be great some day, and may you live to see me so.'[1]

He had, however, an unusually friendly base in the African Department of the Foreign Office, which did not under Anderson's kindly rule regard Vice-Consuls on leave as unwanted strangers who had best keep away until their next assignments were near. He spent much time at the Office and he also made his home near it. He had struck up an enduring friendship with Oswald Crawfurd, who when not in London occupied the delectable post of British Consul at Oporto, and

[1] Alex Johnston, *op. cit.*, p. 115.

at his suggestion Johnston became his neighbour on the sixth floor of Queen Anne's Mansions, at that time still the tallest residential building in Westminster. Here he installed himself with a man-servant called Challenger, and soon covered every wall with the contents of his sketch-books. The Moorish architecture of Tunis and Cairo vied for space with the snowy peaks of Kilimanjaro, river scenes from the Congo and the Niger Delta, seascapes from Mondole and Zanzibar, flowers rare or dainty, animals shy or savage, birds gorgeous or grotesque. The ante-room was his Chamber of Horrors, devoted to the barbarities of untamed Africa. There he hung the all too realistic drawings he had made near Taveta of slaves abandoned in the East African bush by the Arab caravans on their coastward march, children starved to death, dying women half-eaten by hyaenas, vultures hovering in anticipation of their feast. Here too he hung the illustrations he was preparing for a picaresque novel entitled *The History of a Slave*, first published as a serial in *The Graphic* and afterwards in book form, telling in the first person the fast-moving, exciting, somewhat indelicate story of an imaginary Mbudikum slave from the Upper Cross River who worked his way, in and out of slavery, across the Western Sudan from Adamawa to Timbuktu and then across the Sahara to Murzuk and Tunis.[1]

To his surprise and delight Johnston found that he was socially much in demand. London had heard of him in connection with the Ja Ja case and it was curious to see the 'prancing proconsul',[2] who was the centre of so much controversy. Soon, however, it was to know him as the expert on cannibalism, as the dinner-table raconteur who could always be relied upon to shock the ladies. The rumour went round that in the course of his Consular duties he had actually partaken of human flesh, and after this it became socially essential to have had the experience of sitting next to him. In the biography published by his brother, Mr Alex Johnston, in 1929, the story is told of a banquet near Edadama on the Cross River at which 'a great shell filled with a pinkish paste was passed from hand to hand. First the elders of the tribe partook and then presented it to their white brother. He put a big pinch on his tongue and swallowed it as they had done, and noted that it was saltish and pleasant to the taste. . . .

[1] H. H. Johnston: *The History of a Slave*, London, Kegan Paul, 1889.
[2] Cf. Alex Johnston, *op. cit.*, p. 113. It seems that this *sobriquet* was first invented by a propagandist of the Miller faction in the Ja Ja controversy. It was taken up later by Rhodes and his friends in connexion with Johnston's administration in Central Africa.

'Is this goat that I have eaten?' 'It is not.' 'Is it pig?' 'It is not.' 'Is it fowl, or perhaps tender monkey?' 'It is neither.' 'With what then have you regaled me?' 'It is man. It is our great Chief and Father, with whom you are now one—bone of our bone and flesh of our flesh, a blood brother to us indeed.'[1] It is perhaps a slight relief to discover that, as with the battle of Moshi described in *The Kilimanjaro Expedition*, Johnston's private diary supplies no confirmation of this tale. Indeed, it would seem that a memorandum written for the Foreign Office soon after his return to England may provide a clue to the nucleus of truth which gave rise to the fiction. In describing the 'somewhat sentimental form of cannibalism' prevalent on the Upper Cross River Johnston remarked, 'Here they have the practice of killing all the old people of the tribe when they become toothless and useless . . . and the relatives of the deceased partake of the corpse, which is generally smoke-dried, friturated, and mixed with a hot mixture of red peppers and palm-oil. . . . It is the greatest compliment to offer a dish of this kind to a stranger; indeed, some two or three years ago a trader going up the Cross River on a pioneer expedition was asked to partake of a palm-oil stew of this description.'[2]

'Sprung from so little', as Johnston himself had said when comparing the development of the human race to that of the scriptural mustard-seed! And yet, when surrounded by beautiful and well-born women in search of sensation, it must have been tempting to embroider. A young man making his way was after all expected to give good value. Certainly political hostesses enjoyed his epigrams about the nutritive value of 'chopped Chancellor and potted Premier', and the enthusiastic contemporaries of Gilbert and Sullivan applauded his verses entitled 'A Cannibal's Ode to his Aunt'.

> *Search through the crowded market,*
> *Visit each cannibal feast,*
> *Where will you meet*
> *With a corpse so sweet*
> *As that of the dear deceased?*
>
> *Juicy she was and tender,*
> *And little did we discern*
> *The good we should reap*
> *From the cost of her keep:*
> *She has made us a noble return.*

[1] Alex Johnston: *op. cit.*, p. 107.
[2] Memorandum by Vice-Consul Johnston on the British Protectorate of the Oil Rivers 24.vii.88, *F.O.84.1882.*

Beauty we scarce remember,
Virtues we soon forget,
But the taste of our Aunt Eliza
Clings, clings, to my palate yet.[1]

The Johnston of 1888 was becoming a little too outrageous to be any longer *persona grata* in the drawing-rooms of the Baroness Burdett-Coutts. And yet it was only his social stock-in-trade, which overlay a deep seriousness concerning the subject of his jests. Perhaps it was just the Foreign Office manner. Certainly it is a remarkable fact that men like Wylde and Lister, whose whole working lives were preoccupied with the national assault on the African slave trade, habitually talked of 'savages', wrote humorous minutes about missionaries and cannibals, and missed no opportunity of sneering at the non-professional humanitarians whose interests were so close to their own. Johnston did not even sneer at the missionaries. His views about them were scarcely orthodox, and his style of propaganda would neither have inspired many vocations nor brought many new subscribers on to the societies' lists: it was none the less persistent and serious. His final action at Opobo before leaving the West Coast had been to accompany Archdeacon Crowther, the son of the famous negro Bishop of the Niger, on an expedition to negotiate sites for mission-stations, which Ja Ja had hitherto refused to permit. His account of the Cross River had concluded with the observation that 'With such of these cannibal tribes as have placed themselves under British protection, I have naturally warned them, before they concluded their treaties, that a continuance of these disgusting practices might bring down on them condign punishment from our Government, and the Chiefs have promised to use their influence with the people to abolish cannibalism; but the practice is so rooted in their customs and religious rites that it may be some time before the spread of civilization and the influence of the missionaries finally eradicate it, as it has similarly been eradicated in Old Calabar, Bonny and Brass, in which places some forty years ago human flesh might be seen for sale in the market-places.[2]

Again, in 1887 he had published in the *Nineteenth Century* magazine an article on 'British Missions in Africa' which, while fearless in criticism, showed an insight into the part of

---

[1] Alex Johnston, *op. cit.*, p. 108. The final verse was contributed to the author from memory by Sir Harry Johnston's sister, Mrs Henderson.

[2] Memorandum by Vice-Consul Johnston on the British Protectorate of the Oil Rivers 24.vii.88, *F.O.84.1882.*

the Christian Church in the whole historical process of the
European penetration of Africa quite astonishing for the time
at which it was written. He described his approach as an
East African traveller, weary and footsore after a journey in
the interior, to a typical Protestant mission-station situated a
few marches from the coast, his feelings of admiration as he
entered an oasis of civilization in the desert of savagery, his
wonder at the trim houses and gardens of the mission village
and at the clothed and prosperous condition of the inhabitants,
his gratitude for the kindly welcome of the missionary and the
motherly attentions of his gallant wife. He praised the ordered
life, lived in the midst of so many difficulties and imposed with
outward success upon a native community to whom his ideals
were utterly foreign. But, he added, 'It is just as well not to
stop too long: you will admire the missionary more, but his
converts less.' Judged from a purely Christian point of view
the East African missions had not been successful: in many
important districts where they had been at work for twenty
years, they could scarcely number in honest statistics, twenty
sincere Christians.

Then switching to his experience of the West Coast, where
large numbers of nominal Christians already existed, he
asserted roundly that their religion was discredited by numbering among its adherents all the drunkards, liars, rogues and
unclean livers of the coastal region. 'I regret to say, with a
very few real exceptions, those native African pastors, teachers
and catechists whom I have met with have been all more or
less bad men. They attempted to veil an unbridled immorality
with an unblushing hypocrisy and a profane display of mouth-
religion, which in an honest mind seemed even more disgusting
than the immorality itself. While it was apparent that not one
particle of true religion had made its way into their gross
minds, it was also evident that the spirit of sturdy manliness
which was present in their savage forefathers found no place
in their false, cowardly natures.' At the same time, with great
balance and objectivity, he recorded that some of the finest
missionaries he had encountered had been among the coloured
West Indians in the employ of the Baptist Mission in the
Cameroons. The fact was, he suggested, that it took at least
three generations before 'any clear appreciation of the
principles of morality, truth, gratitude and honour can
penetrate the intellect and curb the instincts of a negro',
and the same would hold of a Red Indian, a Polynesian or a
Papuan. Meanwhile, he concluded, in perhaps the most

massive tribute that has even been paid to Christianity by an
unbeliever:

> Is it of no account do you think, is it productive of no good
> effect in the present state of Africa, that certain of our fellow-
> countrymen, men and women, possessed of at least an elementary
> education, and impelled by no greed of gain or unworthy motive,
> should voluntarily locate themselves in the wild parts of this
> undeveloped quarter of the globe, and, by the very fact that they
> live in a European manner, in a house of European style, sur-
> rounded by European implements, products and adornments,
> should open the eyes of the brutish savage to the existence of a
> higher state of culture and prepare them for the approach of
> civilization? I am sure my readers will agree with me, it is as
> the preparers of the white man's advent, as the mediator between
> the barbarian native and the invading race of rulers, colonists
> or traders, that the missionary earns his chief right to our con-
> sideration and support. He constitutes himself informally the
> tribune of the weaker race, and though he may sometimes be
> open to the charges of indiscretion, exaggeration and partiality
> in his support of his dusky-skinned clients' claims, yet without
> doubt he has rendered real service to humanity in drawing
> extra-colonial attention to many a cruel abuse of power, and by
> checking the ruthless proceedings of the unscrupulous pioneers
> of the white invaders. . . .[1]

> Indeed [he wrote in his final report on the Oil Rivers], though
> the converted negroes may afterwards think the singing of hymns
> monotonous, and attending church a wearisome mortification
> of the flesh, no one can deny that they have been very greatly
> benefitted by their studies at the mission. No doubt if the great
> missionary propaganda of Britain confined itself to being a
> kind of school-board for savages, it would save time and money
> spent in instilling into these stunted minds dogmas and doctrines
> which they are incapable of understanding or appreciating, or
> turning to the practical purposes of life; but inasmuch as that
> is the original motive power of Christian missions, and one must
> utilize forces as one finds them, we must be prepared to let the
> missionaries dogmatize without let or hindrance, on account of
> the education and civilization which they laterally introduce.
> . . . They do an amount of good that has never been sufficiently
> appreciated either by the Government or the people of England.[2]

Johnston was hoping to return to the Niger Delta. Hewett
was reaching pensionable age, and had made no secret of his
intention to retire after one more term of service in a part of
Africa which had already ruined his health. Johnston hoped to

---

[1] *The Nineteenth Century*, Vol. 22, July-December 1887.
[2] Johnston to Salisbury 1.xii.88, *F.O.84.1882*.

E

succeed him as Consul—indeed, since the system of one-man consular rule could not conceivably last much longer, he hoped to have the founding of a regular administration throughout the whole of the Oil Rivers district, with the title of Imperial Commissioner and a salary and status equivalent to that of a Colonial Office governor. Apart from one brief holiday with his father in Hampshire, therefore, he spent the whole summer and autumn of 1888 in or near Downing Street, writing voluminous reports on the condition and prospects of the Niger Delta, framing schemes for its future government under the Foreign Office, and in particular using all his influence against the only possible alternative to an official administration, namely the extension of the Niger Company's Charter to include the Oil Rivers coast as well as the main river.

Such a move was all too likely, for during the very months while Johnston was in London, the Royal Niger Company and the member firms of the African Association were at last composing their differences, and in October and November agreements were signed under which the African Association undertook to support the Niger Company's application for an extension of its Charter. To a Conservative Ministry, dependent for its Parliamentary majority on the support of defectors from the Liberal Party who still felt obliged to defend Gladstonian principles on most matters other than Irish Home Rule, this solution had the great attraction that it could be carried through without asking Parliament for money and so without exposing their Liberal Unionist flank to the uncertainties of a controversial debate. Thus far the situation was identical with that in Northern Rhodesia and Nyasaland, in which Johnston, along with Rhodes and the British South Africa Company, was to be deeply concerned during the following year. In the case of the Niger and the Oil Rivers, however, there were arguments on the other side. In the first place the volume of trade was such that, even if customs duties were the only practicable source of revenue for some time to come, the prospects of establishing a self-supporting administration were bright: in other words, grants-in-aid could be small and of a very temporary nature. In the second place the Oil Rivers ports were easily accessible from the sea; Great Britain was committed under the Berlin Act to keeping them as a free-trade area; the monopolistic policy pursued by the Niger Company on the main river was already producing embarrassing diplomatic pressure from foreign governments, and there was the certainty that the number of incidents would greatly increase if the Oil Rivers came under the same exclusionist control.

Thus, while it would be idle to deny Johnston's personal interest in the outcome, his reasons for opposing the Niger Company were sound; and certainly, in view of his later relations with Rhodes, they are of very great interest. It was not, he said, his object especially to attack the Niger Company: he had been in favour of the granting of the Charter; he had regarded it as a *pis aller*, 'as the only alternative to surrendering the Niger and the Benue to a scramble between France and Germany, inasmuch as our own Government shrank from the responsibility of bringing the country under a direct form of British administration'. But he had also supported it because he had believed that once the Charter was granted, the Company would look for its own profits, as the Borneo Company had done, not so much from trading on its own account as from the increased revenue to be derived from competent administration. If the country had been opened up by a cadre of well-educated executive and judicial officials, the trade in dutiable imports and exports would have vastly increased, and it would have proved to the interest of the governing company to encourage the entry of traders of every nationality. Instead, 'a well-nigh Chinese policy of exclusion, mystery and deceitfulness has been followed and it may almost be said that a measure of the misfortune which has befallen the Nile has descended upon the Niger. . . . Whole districts once perfectly friendly towards Europeans are now impassable.' It is possible that in one respect Johnston was unfair to the Company, in that profits on government were explicitly forbidden by the Berlin West Africa Treaty. Chartered Companies were only allowed to levy duties sufficient to cover the cost price of administrative services. It may be that this miserly provision allowed no alternative to a monopolistic policy. Yet Johnston was not advocating the withdrawal of the existing Charter, he was merely recommending that it should not be extended to a district where monopolistic practices would attract much more attention.

There were, Johnston said, two other possible ways of administering the Oil Rivers: one was to amalgamate it, or a part of it, with the neighbouring Colony and Protectorate of Lagos, which was already under the direction of the Colonial Office; the other was to administer it directly as a separate Protectorate under the Foreign Office. The objection to the first of these alternatives was that the Oil Rivers, being subject to the special conditions of the Berlin Act, would prove an awkward enclave within the Lagos administration. Besides, he somewhat disingenuously argued, 'the extension of territory which the prosperity and good government of Lagos so richly deserved would more naturally take place in the direction of Porto Novo, Dahomey, Grand Popo and the Gold Coast, when that much to be desired arrangement with the French Government takes place, and in exchange for the now useless Gambia we clear the French off the Guinea Coast'. There remained the alternative of direct administration by the Foreign Office under an Imperial Commissioner, who could also be charged with exercising a judicious supervision and control over the Niger Company's operations within the sphere of its Charter. The cost of this Commissioner, assisted by four consular Residents and a small force of Hausa troops, Johnston estimated at £28,000 a year, the whole of which could be locally raised. 'I do earnestly hope', he concluded, 'that our responsibility towards these people is going to be recognized. . . . Considering what very slight benefit has as yet accrued to them from our rule, it is surprising what loyalty the Chiefs of the Oil Rivers have shown towards the British Government.

In spite of all temptations
To belong to other nations,

they have invariably inclined towards an English rule, even when our policy was most unsympathetic and vacillating. They have been cheated by British merchants, bombarded by British Captains and fined by British Consuls and yet they like us and stick by us and are proud of being "all same Ingilis man" and of speaking our language fluently if un-classically.'[1]

The British Government followed Johnston's recommendations about the Oil Rivers Protectorate. Exactly how it came to do so is a long and complex story, in which German pressure against the infringement by the Royal Niger Company of the free-trade provisions of the Berlin Treaty is probably the most important item. As the result of German complaints, an Imperial Commissioner was appointed to investigate the whole question of the Company's administration, and in particular to inquire whether chartered company rule should be extended to the Oil Rivers or not. The Commissioner,

[1] Memorandum on the British Protectorate of the Oil Rivers 24.vii.88 *F.O.84.1882.*

Major (later Sir Claude) Macdonald, paid his first visit to West Africa early in 1889, and on the basis of his report a separate administration was definitely established in the Oil Rivers over which, after Hewett's retirement in 1891, Macdonald reigned as the first Commissioner and Consul-General. In 1893 the region was renamed the Niger Coast Protectorate; in 1900 it became the Protectorate of Southern Nigeria. Johnston meanwhile had found other fields of work. He never ceased to regret his transfer from the West Coast: indeed, he carried his suspicions of the power and malignity of the Miller interest to rather absurd lengths. He had committed himself to such definite views on the government of the Delta that it would have been farcical for the Foreign Office to appoint him to carry out the independent inquiry committed to Macdonald, nor could it either have hastened Hewett's retirement or have appointed Johnston Commissioner over his head. Moreover, his new appointment, when it came, was the very opposite of a slight or a set-back: it carried him to a position far greater than any which he could have made for himself in Nigeria; it was in a very real sense a mark of the new confidence which he had inspired in the Prime Minister of England.

Johnston's relations with Lord Salisbury will always remain something of a mystery. Salisbury, it has been seen, had throughout viewed the conduct of the Ja Ja affair with an extremely critical eye, and however far he may have revised his opinions of Johnston, he never changed his mind about this issue. When it was brought to his notice by Macdonald in the middle of 1889 that Ja Ja's health was suffering in his West Indian exile, he commented, 'Ja Ja's death would be an extreme embarrassment. It would induce a close inquiry into the circumstances of his deportation, which cannot be defended according to European notions of good faith.' And yet when Johnston had been summoned a few days after his return to England in July 1888 to give a personal account of the episode, the interview had been followed after a few days more by an invitation from Lady Salisbury to spend a week-end at Hatfield 'House. How rare an honour this was may be glimpsed from a jealous outburst, which Johnston remembered to the end of his life, by Clement Hill, then the senior clerk in the African Department, who was responsible for the drafting of a substantial proportion of the outgoing despatches. He had been in the Foreign Office, he said, since 1871, 'and will you believe me, Lord Salisbury has never once asked to see me, and wouldn't know me if we met in the street'.[1]

In his novel *The Gay-Dombeys*, published many years later, Johnston was still able to describe with feeling the exquisite torture of his first big encounter with the socially great: the freezing scrutiny of monocle and lorgnette which turned upon the unknown outsider of meagre physical appearance as he took his place in the special saloon coach which conveyed the house-party from King's Cross to Hatfield Station; his rescue from discomfiture and his walk across the park to the house with a character, known to all the other guests as Poo-ey, who turned out to be Lady Salisbury's unmarried sister; the disarming welcome of Lady Salisbury, who placed him next to herself at drawing-room tea; a sudden encounter with the Prime Minister and Sir Robert Morier, Ambassador at St Petersburg and formerly Minister at Lisbon, terminating as abruptly with a direction to the billiard-room, where various young male Cecils were waiting to discuss cannibalism with the visitor from Africa; all the gay ceremony of dinner accomplished to the muted strains of galleried musicians, and afterwards charades organized by Lady Gwendolen, disguised in a vast moustache as Lord Randolph Churchill. Johnston remembered himself as part of a whale and also as a Moorish slave-dealer in charge of a crew of very large, unwieldy female slaves. On Sunday morning, church; and after lunch a long walk through the park with Salisbury and Morier.

And now [says the Lord Wiltshire of *The Gay-Dombeys*], now that I am tolerably out of the hearing of my excellent tenantry —though so quaint is our national education that I might shout out strings of African names and they would be not a bit the wiser—now let us settle the fate of the Niger. It is, I may observe, a curious anomaly that the future weal or woe of millions of black and brown people—should you call the Fulahs brown?— well then of millions of black and brown people is being determined in a Hertfordshire beech avenue in latitude 51 something North, where there hasn't been the ghost of a palm for—what shall we say: you Evolutionists are so liberal in time—two million years. I suppose it is all due in some way to the glacial periods, which made us what we are, able to lay down the law to the coloured peoples, who kept snug in the tropics while we were battling against the cold. And now to business. We've settled more or less our frontier with the Cameroons, and as regards the French . . .[2]

[1] *The Story*, p. 217.   [2] *The Gay-Dombeys*, pp. 188-9.

As regards the French, the letters exchanged between Salisbury and Johnston in September and October show clearly that the conversation in Hatfield park was concerned not merely with that section of the Niger occupied by the Chartered Company, but with the whole question of consolidating the British and French spheres in West Africa along the lines recommended by Johnston in his long letter to Anderson from Mondole in 1886. Johnston sent detailed maps illustrating the recent French annexations in the Ivory Coast and Dahomey, and urged in the most persuasive terms the importance of acquiring them in exchange for the Gambia. With characteristic ingenuity he even managed to present a vast extension of empire in the guise of a long-overdue measure of economy. Although two-thirds of the coastline between Sierra Leone and the Cameroons was in British hands, the existence in between the British colonies of little wedges of foreign territory meant that there could be no consistent, profitable fiscal policy, and no successful efforts to limit the importation of fire-arms, gunpowder and alcohol. Further, Johnston argued, 'these little wedges of foreign territory serve as bases from which the French and Germans can penetrate into the interior at the back of our colonies, and keep the colonial governments perpetually in a state of anxiety by their intrigues with the border tribes, and in many cases force our hands by compelling us to advance further still into the interior in order to forestall them from cutting off our sources of trade. Now if we closed up the gaps in the coast-line between Sierra Leone and the German boundary at the Rio del Rey, we could just sit down comfortably and develop our coast possessions and slowly permeate the interior with our civilising influence.' Eliminate foreign competition from the Guinea coast, he concluded, and nothing could prevent the emergence of 'a great British Niger Empire, which will rival India in its wealth of products and its teeming, industrious population. . . . Not only would all the Conservatives and Unionists have to support the Government's policy in this question, but a good proportion of the Gladstonians—perhaps even Mr Gladstone himself—would have to do the same, because the idea would be so enthusiastically received and supported by our great manufacturing and commercial centres that the pressure brought to bear by their constituents on their parliamentary representatives would compel the latter—whether Gladstonian, Radical, Non-Interventionist or Sentimentalist—to support the Government in this matter. I could promise your Lordship the concurrence of all the great missionary societies, of the steamship companies, of the various trading corporations, and emphatically of the Press. The *Daily News* might whine a little gently to itself, but every other journal of importance would be compelled . . . to acclaim and approve this movement. . . . The foundation of our West African Empire would be a splendid stroke of policy, which the nation would not readily forget, and which it would associate with that jealous care of Imperial interests for which your Lordship's administration has always been distinguished.'[1]

The crux of the plan was, of course, the cession of the Gambia. A proposal to take powers for that purpose had, Lord Salisbury explained, been made as long ago as 1876, 'But the House, a much more Conservative House than the present, would not hear of it: and Lord Carnarvon had to withdraw it. We may have an opportunity of trying again— but the obstruction of the Irish would probably make it impossible.' He thanked Johnston, however, for sending two maps which would enable him 'to do what can be done without the help of an Act of Parliament'. A month later, in writing to thank him for more maps, he added, 'The difficulties of the question are enormous. An agreement with France is necessary, and an assent from the British House of Commons: and neither the French Government nor the House of Commons are in a condition to give a fair hearing to any external question.'[2]

In retrospect it may be doubted whether Salisbury was justified in placing so much responsibility on Parliament for the confusion of territories on the West African Coast. It would seem that he was indeed using political difficulties as a screen behind which to hide a growing hesitancy on his own part about the wisdom of pursuing a strong policy in West Africa. All the indications are that the year 1888 marked a sharp turning-point in Salisbury's thought about British aims in Africa, and that the general effect of the change was a shift in emphasis from the west towards the east and the south. There is no question but that Salisbury's primary interest in Africa was Egypt. That in itself meant the conciliation, not only in Africa but in all parts of the world, of France and Germany, who as Egypt's chief creditors were in a position to make England's administration there a constant burden. England could rule Egypt without interference only in so

---

[1] Johnston to Salisbury 25.ix.88, 29.ix.88, 24.x.88, *Salisbury Papers*.
[2] Salisbury to Johnston 26.ix.88 and 25.x.88, *Johnston Papers*.

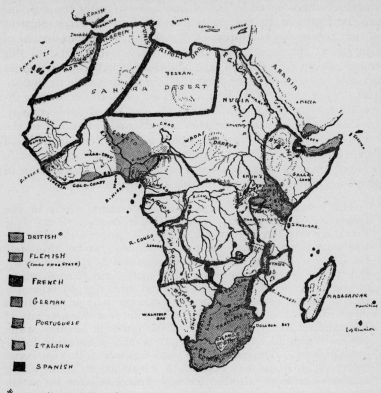

MAP of AFRICA
AS
APPORTIONED AMONG THE DIFFERENT EUROPEAN STATES
ACCORDING TO
THEIR PRESENT CLAIMS, ASPIRATIONS, OR LOCAL INTERESTS.

6. HOW AFRICA SHOULD BE DIVIDED—1888

From the original drawing by Sir Harry Johnston.
Johnston to Salisbury 25.ix.88, *Salisbury Papers.*

E*

far as she could make Egypt financially solvent. That is why England's first action in Egypt had been to order the evacuation by Egypt of the Sudanese garrisons and the abandonment of that country to the forces of the Mahdi: the encirclement of Gordon at Khartoum had been a disaster incidental to this retreat. From 1885 till 1887 the Mahdist forces had been mainly occupied in consolidating their position in the southern Sudan, and during these years it had seemed that the economy intended by the evacuation would be possible of achievement. In 1888, however, the dervishes turned their attention to the north in a series of attacks upon the southern frontier of Egypt and upon the Red Sea port of Suakin; and it immediately became apparent that even an evacuated Sudan was going to prove an intolerable drain on the Treasury of Egypt.

> The dervish attacks [says Lady Gwendolen Cecil in the biography of her father] brought the reconquest of the Nile Provinces into the foreground of Lord Salisbury's thought. He had recognized it from the first as an issue to be ultimately faced in the interests alike of humanity and Egyptian security. But it now became a central episode in his calculated prevision of events. It would have to be deferred until Egypt's economic revival should make her able to bear her part in the strain involved . . . [but] we find that from this date the necessity of safeguarding the Nile Valley from the intrusion of other white powers begins to appear as a separate and dominating factor in his policy. . . . During the nine years that were still to intervene before the reconquest of Khartoum, his resolve to eliminate all auxiliary occasions of difference with France affected his action consciously in every quarter of the globe.[1]

It was this growing conviction that the successful government of Egypt must in time involve the whole Nile Valley which made Salisbury almost wish to encourage French expansion in West Africa to an extent which would allow of the encirclement by France of the four British territories scattered along the Coast. 'The association of her new-born colonial enthusiasm with projects of empire in those regions presented the most tangible hope of detaching her from her Egyptian dream.'[2] At the same time his concentration upon the Nile Valley, coupled with the recognition that this must involve a passive policy in West Africa, made him look, in a way he had not done before, to the east and the south as the best

---

[1] Lady Gwendolen Cecil: *Life of Robert, Marquis of Salisbury*, Vol. IV, pp. 135-40.
[2] *Ibid.*, p. 252.

directions in which to press Great Britain's remaining claims
for her share in the total partition. From 1888 onwards he
took a far more lively interest in the sphere of influence which
he had negotiated two years previously with Germany for the
Imperial British East Africa Company. He joined, as a
politique de présence, in the German blockade of the East African
coast during the Arab rebellion of that year. He became
seriously and lastingly interested in Uganda, as commanding
both the headquarters of the Nile and the back door to Egypt.
He began to connect in his own mind, significantly even if
mistakenly, the outbreaks of East African Arab hostility to
European commercial and missionary penetration around
Lakes Nyasa, Tanganyika and Victoria with the activity of
the dervishes in the Sudan. He initiated the calling of the
international Anti-Slavery Conference, which met at Brussels
in 1889, and the main recommendation of which so far as
Great Britain was concerned was the building of a strategic
railway from Mombasa to Lake Victoria to enable the campaign against the Arab slave trade to be carried effectively
into the far interior.

By the summer of 1888, therefore, Salisbury was already
beginning to set the stage for his great East African settlement
with Germany, accomplished in 1890. But he was also, and
this was an even more radical departure, contemplating a
settlement with Portugal in south-central Africa by which the
territories already settled by British missions to the west of
Lake Nyasa and the south of Lake Tanganyika should be
connected with the British possessions further south. Bechuanaland, the Suez Canal of the Cape Colony as Rhodes had called
it, had been annexed in 1884, in order to forestall the physical
junction and the possible amalgamation of the German
Protectorate in South-West Africa and the still independent
Boer republics of the Orange Free State and the Transvaal.
In February 1888, following on reports that Boer concession-
hunters were active in Matabeleland, Sir Hercules Robinson,
the High Commissioner at the Cape, had sent J. S. Moffat
to conclude a treaty of perpetual amity with Lobengula, the
paramount chief of the Matebele, whereby he undertook not
to part with any of his land or to sign treaties with any other
power without the sanction of the British Government. Now
in the summer of 1888 Salisbury was considering the formal
declaration of a British sphere of influence stretching, not only
up to, but across, the Central Zambezi between the Portuguese
colonies of Angola and Mozambique. Hence the presence at

Hatfield of Morier, the prime architect of the abortive Anglo-
Portuguese treaty of 1884.

It was, however, a problem which involved more than
diplomacy. The sphere of influence declared, how was it to
be governed? In East Africa there was at least a Chartered
Company ready to assume the responsibilities which there
was as yet no chance of Parliament allowing the Government
to undertake. Deeply as Salisbury distrusted the capacity of
the promoters—they had, he drily observed, no energy for
anything except quarrelling with Germans[1]—the Chairman,
Sir William Mackinnon, was at least, as the founder of the
British India Steam Navigation Company, a person of some
substance in the City. But in Central Africa the position looked
much worse. South of the Zambezi, in Matabeleland, there
were said to be some speculators from the Cape—Salisbury
had not yet got the measure, possibly had not yet heard the
name, of Cecil Rhodes—who had made inquiries about
the possibility of a Charter, while to the north, engaged in
mortal combat with the Arab slave-traders in the Lake Nyasa
region, there was the African Lakes Company, a twopenny-
halfpenny Glasgow firm, whose pretensions to the dignity and
responsibility of a Royal Charter were contemptible. So that
here, the Prime Minister concluded, was Great Britain, for
so many years the leading power in African affairs, doomed
by the state of public opinion and the parsimony of Parliament
to stand at the critical moment inactive while the other
powers of Europe closed in upon the prize. 'What a pity it is
no one could put the whole African question lucidly before
the public—in some newspaper article I mean.' 'I had a sort
of feeling', wrote Johnston, 'that his eye rested upon me for a
moment before it looked ahead. At any rate this feeling
implanted in me the sudden desire to present the reading
public with a sketch of what I assumed to be our legitimate
ambitions. I thought to myself that night, after I had retired
to my bedroom, of the points in the conversation along the
avenues; I jotted them down and took them away in my
suitcase.'[2]

On August 22nd, 1888, there appeared on the centre page
of *The Times* newspaper an article of three columns entitled
'Great Britain's Policy in Africa, by an African Explorer'.
It was perhaps the ablest, certainly the most direct and
concise, piece of argument that Johnston ever wrote. It

[1] Lady Gwendolen Cecil: *Life of Robert, Marquis of Salisbury*, Vol. IV, p. 232.
[2] *Story*, p. 221.

outshone by many times any of the summaries of outstanding problems periodically prepared for Ministers by the officials of the Foreign Office Africa Department. In its practical vision and comprehensive grasp it streamed far ahead of any contemporary, or near contemporary, pronouncement of Lugard on the one hand or of Rhodes on the other. It may perhaps be regarded as the clearest surviving exposition of Salisbury's African policy, and yet it is too individual and characteristic a composition to be merely the pickings of another man's brain. However slight their acquaintance, however brief their meetings in the flesh, it is the voice of Salisbury's adviser as well as of his confidant. Africa, said Johnston, was the New World of the nineteenth century: what America had been to Europe in the sixteenth century, Africa had now become. 'This great tropical continent must inevitably be exploited by the white races as the other quarters of the globe have been; perhaps not to the same exclusive degree as America and Australia, but certainly to a greater extent than Asia, which possesses a latent and reviving civilization of its own.' During the first half of the nineteenth century England had had almost a monopoly of interest in Africa, but especially during the decade since Stanley had discovered the course of the Congo the interest of Europe had been aroused with a suddenness which had taken England by surprise. The hour of partition was approaching: England must lose no time in making up her mind what she wanted. If free trade were a universally accepted principle, it would perhaps matter little if the new markets of Africa came to be governed by other nations, but in as much as protectionist powers might, and actually were, possessing themselves of new tracts of Africa, it became a necessity for England to look to her own economic defences, not to impose protection herself, but to ensure the existence of markets free from the protectionist policies of others. From this introduction Johnston proceeded to survey the four quarters of Africa, north, east, south and west, and to examine on the basis of current happenings, where the opportunities for the future chiefly lay. The analysis was masterly:

> In Morocco and the Barbary States we can never hope—indeed I can see no reason why we should hope—to be rulers. They are the natural spheres of influence of the Mediterranean nations—Spain, France and Italy. In Algeria and Tunis France is already established, and indeed for the excellent work she has done there in the cause of civilization she deserves the cordial

thanks of Europe. Tripoli and Barca are the natural heritage of Italy, who, when she takes or receives them from the relaxing grasp of Turkey, will certainly restore them to the prosperity and fertility they enjoyed under the rule of Rome and Byzantium. Morocco will no doubt become an appanage of Spain, though it is probable that the consent of France to this arrangement will only be secured by permitting the latter power to advance its frontier westward to the River Muluya and to include the Oasis of Figig within its Algerian possessions. The only immediate interest that England has in these changes is that, by reconciling herself to them and even advancing them by her good will, she may secure the friendship of Spain and cheaply gratify Italy, while by making concessions to France in eastern Morocco and according a more complete recognition to French rule in Tunis she may the more readily induce that Government to acquiesce in a British protectorate over Egypt. The valley of the Nile indeed is the only part of Northern Africa where we have permanent interests. Egypt proper—Arabic Egypt that is to say—should become a vassal state under British hegemony, while Nubia, the Suakin district, Darfur and the Egyptian Sudan will no doubt be eventually administered directly or indirectly by us, either through some great chartered trading company, or by establishing British Residents at the courts of those native rulers who will be encouraged and perhaps assisted by us to establish themselves on the ruins of the Mahdi's collapsing power. . . .

For West Africa Johnston's proposals were the same as those he had developed many times before: French and British spheres should be divided by the Niger and by an imaginary prolongation of its upper course to the Atlantic sea-board; the Gambia should be exchanged for the abandonment of French claims in the Ivory Coast and Dahomey; the British enclave in German South-West Africa at Walvis Bay should be exchanged for the German enclave in Togoland. In relation to East and South-East Africa, however, his thoughts showed a great development from his position of 1886. England, he said, needed the northern part of Somaliland as a feeding-ground for Aden. Further down the coast the sphere of the Imperial British East Africa Company should be rounded off —as it was in fact to be in 1890—by the transfer from German protection of the small Sultanate of Witu.

South of Witu we have already secured, thanks to Sir John Kirk, the coast between the River Tana and the Umba and a wedge stretching inland as far as the Victoria Nyanza, which in the not far distant future may become united to Emin Pasha's province in the Sudan. The western shore of Lake Tanganyika nominally belongs to the Congo Free State; the eastern shore of the Lake should be secured by England, whose interests are solely (among European powers) represented there at present by missionaries and traders, who navigate Tanganyika by their steamers and have connected it with Lake Nyasa by a road. . . . From this western shore of Lake Nyasa, along the course of the Loangwa River, through a country rich in gold, tin and iron, we may eventually extend our rule over the relatively short distance which at present separates our recently acquired protectorate over the middle Zambezi from the British settlements on Lake Nyasa. Thus, if our Government only grants some measure of support to the British agencies, commercial and evangelical, which have obtained such a footing in the Lake region, our possessions in South Africa may be linked some day to our sphere of influence in Eastern Africa and the Egyptian Sudan by a continuous band of British dominion. The day will come, let us hope, when the African Lakes Company will shake hands with the British East Africa Company on the northern shores of Tanganyika; and Emin Pasha will rule in England's name and for the interests of civilization on the Albert Nyanza and the White Nile.

Here then, in August 1888, was the idea of the 'Cape to Cairo' route, which was to exercise so profound an influence on British destinies in Africa, emanating, not from Rhodes, but from an official of the British Foreign Office, who put it before the public on a hint from the British Prime Minister. Five years later, after Rhodes and Johnston had met and worked together and then quarrelled, Johnston was to remind him that the Cape to Cairo idea, which Rhodes was by then claiming as his own, had been introduced to him by Johnston; and *The Times* article published while Rhodes was still but little known outside South Africa is the best proof of this assertion.

Meanwhile the 'African Explorer' had to meet the accusing glances of his colleagues in Whitehall. Clement Hill sent for him and asked him point blank if he was the author of the article. Johnston replied that he was, but that he had reason to believe that Lord Salisbury knew of it and did not disapprove. 'Well: all I can say is, it is a very extraordinary proceeding, and I must make further inquiries.'[1] No more was heard of the episode, and the Vice-Consul Cameroons, keeping studiously out of the way of great persons, worked on at his Niger reports. Two months later Hill himself drafted a minute suggesting that, while it would be dangerous to create precedents for 'literary consuls', Johnston's services had been

[1] *Story*, p. 222.

so considerable that, although he had returned from West Africa in June, his period of leave on full pay should be dated from October 23rd.[1] In January 1889 he received his new appointment as British Consul at Mozambique, with a salary of £800 a year and expenses.[2]

On paper it was not such a great honour. It was in fact only the post that he had unsuccessfully applied for on entering the service three and a half years before, and Johnston's first reaction to it was to assume that Salisbury had not by any means rewarded him according to his deserts. 'I am prepared to go anywhere and attempt anything that is dangerous or difficult,' he wrote on receipt of the first unofficial tidings of the appointment, 'provided that in so doing I am placed in a position to especially carry out *your* policy and to be of real service to *you*. If you desired me to go to Khartoum, or Mecca, or Hlasa, I should start without demur. . . . But insomuch as I entered the Consular Service much more for the sake of an interesting career than for the need of a livelihood, I confess I am not attracted by the simple proposal of expatriating myself to a lonely part of Africa, with little opportunity afforded me of making my mark and of effecting some good to my country.' He went on to suggest that, if it really must be Mozambique, then Lord Salisbury might at least accord him a practical demonstration of his confidence by converting the post into a Consulate-General with supervisory powers over all the consular posts in Portuguese East Africa and also over the Consulate on Lake Nyasa.[3]

There is no reply to this letter to be found among the Johnston Papers. Nevertheless, there exists in the Foreign Office archives a whole chain of evidence to show that Lord Salisbury was well aware that the Mozambique Consulate in 1889 was potentially a more interesting post than its name and salary implied. He saw on the one hand that the thrust of British South African interests from Bechuanaland northwards into Matabeleland and Mashonaland, the present Southern Rhodesia, had stimulated a revival of what he was accustomed to describe as 'the archaeological claims of Portugal' to the same region. He knew on the other hand that it was through the province of Mozambique, up the Zambezi and its northern tributary the Shire, that there ran the main

[1] F.O. to Johnston 15.x.88, *F.O.84.1882.*
[2] F.O. to Johnston 28.i.89, *F.O.84.1968.*
[3] Johnston to Salisbury 5.xii.88, *Salisbury Papers.*

line of communication with Lakes Nyasa and Tanganyika, and to the sphere of operations of the four British Missions and the one British commercial company which operated round their shores.

Salisbury knew well that these interests had been subjected, ever since their entry in the late 'seventies, to a mounting hostility on the part of the slave-trading Arabs from the Zanzibar coast, who had rightly interpreted the coming of Europeans as a threat to their own means of livelihood. Tension had grown until in 1887 the African Lakes Company had found itself in a state of regular war with the Arabs and their African partners in the slave and ivory trade, who had attacked their station at the north end of Lake Nyasa and cut their caravan route from there to Lake Tanganyika. The Lakes Company, with the support of the Missions, had thereupon started a vigorous political campaign in the United Kingdom for the declaration of a British sphere of influence with itself as the Chartered governing authority, and had as an immediate step raised by private subscription a Fighting Fund with which to recruit and equip the nucleus of a Defence Force. A number of volunteers had been found up and down the East Coast, including one, Captain Lugard, whose name was to be writ large upon later pages of African history; and a small cannon and other arms had been sent out, which were intended to be conveyed to the Lake by the Zambezi route. The volunteers got through, organized native forces and fought not without effect for the best part of a year, but the arms which would have made their presence decisive were delayed month upon month by the Portuguese authorities in the Zambezi delta; and by the end of 1888 it was becoming clear from the reports of the Minister in Lisbon as well as from consular and private sources of information in East Africa that the obstruction on the Zambezi was merely the prelude to a concerted plan for asserting Portuguese sovereignty round Lake Nyasa. A scientific expedition was being prepared under the command of the explorer Serpa Pinto of such dimensions that its real object could only be political, and British suspicions were not dispelled by the equivocal assurances of Portuguese diplomatists.

Johnston's appointment, therefore, came at a significant moment, when it was obvious that a definition of spheres between Great Britain and Portugal could not be delayed for much longer, and when it was necessary that the Foreign Office should be represented in South-East Africa by someone who was well primed in all the wider issues which were involved. That it was more of a special mission than a routine posting is confirmed by the cryptic nature of the correspondence which survives in the Foreign Office archives. Contrary to the usual procedure, most of his instructions were evidently communicated verbally through Anderson or Lister. It was only in response to Johnston's specific requests for written authorization of plans that would involve extraordinary expenditure that his seniors committed themselves to paper, and even then their phrases were studiously vague. In the middle of February he was told that when he arrived at his post he was to 'proceed up the Zambezi and report on the extent of Portuguese rule in the vicinity of that river'. He was authorized before leaving to follow his own suggestion and place himself in communication with the Colonial Office about his plans, though Salisbury added the following revealing comment to the draft: 'I quite agree, but if he means to keep his secret he had better not consult too many departments.'[1] Again, at the end of March a letter was addressed to him approving a plan to secure conditional treaties with tribes beyond the region of Portuguese jurisdiction—treaties, that is to say, which while not committing the British Government to declare protectorates gave it, as it were, the right of first refusal by binding the signatories not to accept the protection of any other power without the Queen's consent.[2]

Meanwhile on March 14th a still more unusual proceeding had occurred in the Foreign Office. Johnston, his bags packed and his heavy luggage already at the docks, called to take leave of the permanent officials. Lord Salisbury, it turned out, had seen the Portuguese Minister, d'Antas, on the previous day, and Lister therefore went in to ask whether there were any last-minute instructions for the Mozambique Consul before he left. Five minutes later Johnston was alone with the Prime Minister.

Since we last met, he said, there has been a change in the affairs of Nyasaland, both for the better and the worse. The Portuguese seem more determined to push the matter forward to settlement north of the Zambezi, either by taking as much as they can get or coming to terms with us over Nyasaland. D'Antas was here yesterday—he says by the bye you can talk Portuguese? I suggested to him I might send you over to Lisbon to talk the question over with their ministers—Barros Gomez for example —and see whether it is possible to come to an understanding

[1] F.O. to Johnston 13.ii.89, *F.O.84.1968.*
[2] F.O. to Johnston 30.iii.89, *ibid.*

about frontiers which would keep the Portuguese out of the Shire Highlands and Central Zambezia. Of course if we could come to any arrangement of that kind it would be a capital thing. Do you think you would like to go there and try?[1]

The account is from *The Story of My Life*, written thirty-three years later, but it is borne out by a note of Lister's, written, obviously in some surprise, the same afternoon. 'Mr Johnston informs me that he has received verbal instructions to go to Lisbon to discuss East African boundaries. It will be necessary that he should have written orders for this journey and possibly even written instructions as to the language he should hold.' Salisbury did not disclaim Johnston's account of the interview, though he was not prepared to have so much written into an official letter. 'Draft instructions to him', he replied, 'to go to Lisbon and inform himself by conference with ministers of the intentions of Portugal with respect to British interests in the region under his charge. Give him past correspondence and instruct him to use similar language so far as he has to speak of the views of H.M.G.' The draft was prepared by Clement Hill, to whose orthodox mind it must have appeared even more extraordinary to send a junior Consul to conduct discussions with a foreign government over the head of the resident Minister than to encourage him to write articles on foreign policy for *The Times*. 'You are to bear in mind', he quite gratuitously concluded, 'that the object of your visit to Lisbon is to acquire and not to impart information.' Salisbury scratched out the offensive phrase and substituted 'principally to acquire information'.[2]

Needless to say, such a mysterious assignment was very much to Johnston's taste. He travelled overland to Portugal, carrying despatches to Queen Victoria at San Sebastian and to the embassy at Madrid. Reaching Lisbon at the end of March, he installed himself at the Hotel Braganza and waited upon the British Minister. Mr Petre, it seems, did not resent his presence. Perhaps the occasion for offence was so obvious as to call out even Johnston's none too ready tact. Perhaps Petre was relieved to have a new approach to a long-standing problem opened by someone with a more expert knowledge of African geography than himself. At all events the introductions to ministers were furnished and the talks began in an atmosphere of great cordiality. 'As to my amiability here,' he told Lister

---

[1] *Story*, p. 131.
[2] Lister to Salisbury and Salisbury to Lister 14.iii.89, and F.O. to Johnston 15.iii.89, *F.O.84.1968*.

after the first week, 'it knows no bounds. I ought to get a special allowance for such expenditure of sweetness from the Chief Clerk. I smile widely on an average for eight hours a day—so that I have lost all control over the muscles at the corners of my mouth. I extol everything Portuguese—the sky, the public gardens, the local opera, the novels, the wines, the recent realistic fiction, the colonial administration, the language, the history, the army, navy and police, and anything else Lusitanian on which my opinion is asked. I also paint Lord Salisbury as a raging lion where his least little tiny bit of British interests is concerned. The joint effect of these two phases seems to have made a good impression on the Portuguese.'

At the end of nine days he had agreed with Barros Gomez, the Foreign Minister, the basis of a settlement. The scheme, as he set it out for the Foreign Office, was simple, and very seductive. It was built around the principle that Great Britain should have 'an uninterrupted connection between her protectorates south of the Zambezi and her missionary and commercial settlements on the west of Lake Nyasa and the south of Lake Tanganyika'. Portugal therefore abandoned her claim to connect by a belt across the continent her settlements in Angola with those in Mozambique. In exchange for this concession Great Britain would recognize Portuguese influence both further east and further west than she had yet done, providing that there was free navigation on the Zambezi; free, or almost free, transit of merchandise through Portuguese territory; rights for the importation and transit of arms under reasonable conditions; a Commercial Treaty fixing low tariffs for fifteen years in the newly recognized territory; and a provision for permanent freedom of religious teaching in the same area. If a Convention on these lines were once signed, the Portuguese Government would further be prepared to grant important concessions to British companies for railway-building and other similar activities, for which two definite proposals lay at that moment in Barros Gomez's desk.[1]

It was, so Johnston later, and perhaps rather insincerely, described it, a plan of 'conciliation and concession to the Portuguese in East Africa in the belief that in return we should obtain material advantages and really be able to secure the development of the Portuguese dominions in East Africa to British subjects under the thin guise of Portuguese suzerainty'.[2]

---

[1] Memorandum on talks with the Ministers of Foreign Affairs, Marine and Colonies. Enclosed in Petre to Salisbury 9.iv.89, *F.O.84.1965*.
[2] Johnston to Salisbury 28.vi.90, *F.O.84.2052*.

The real question, however, was how much, territorially, could be conceded to the Portuguese, and where. Johnston had secured the abandonment by Portugal of her claims to a band across Africa. South of the Zambezi he had secured her abandonment of all claims to Matabeleland and Mashonaland. North of the Zambezi he had secured a British corridor from the Zambezi to Lake Tanganyika which took in the northern half of the west shore of Lake Nyasa. But he had conceded in exchange the Shire Highlands and the southern half of Lake Nyasa, and this was a point on which all previous British negotiators had been adamant. The area in question was not large, but it contained the headquarters of the African Lakes Company and almost the entire field of action of the Nyasa Mission of the established Church of Scotland. And the political influence at Westminster of these two organizations was great—so great that even Johnston realized that Lord Salisbury would probably prefer to lose the corridor across the Zambezi than the Shire Highlands.

> The uttermost concession I have been able to get from Gomez [he wrote in a private letter to Lister] involves not only the cession of the Shire, but even of a part of the western shore of Nyasa, of course under the most favourable terms as regards the commercial and evangelical interests there. But in return we get what to *my* thinking is so important, an uninterrupted though narrow belt of British influence from the Zambezi to the main spheres of activity of the African Lakes Company on Nyasa and Tanganyika. . . . All this belt of country is more and more attaching itself to British South Africa and seeking its base of supplies in that direction rather than on the East Coast, from which it is and will for a long time be cut off by this uprising of the Arab element. I cannot bear the idea of our making the Zambezi a hard and fast limit to British enterprise in Southern Africa and of wilfully and almost carelessly chucking away our last chance of securing to our grandchildren an open way between Tanganyika and the South African colonies, which may some day serve as a link between Egypt and the Cape. . . . I do earnestly hope that Lord Salisbury will approve of what I have done and back me up. . . .
> [Then, somewhat disingenuously, he continued] The Cape people care very little about what happens to Blantyre, but they care much (sentimentally, no doubt) about being limited northwards by the Zambezi. It is all very well to say that we should come to an understanding with the Portuguese about free transit; we should know by this time how our enterprise in foreign territory can be hampered and restricted by a jealous, spiteful little power like Portugal. No, let us keep open a belt of free

British (not neutral—God forbid—schemes of neutralization are the most hopeless solutions that despairing statesmen could devise) territory, sphere of influence or whatever you like to call it, so that it be coloured pink, between Tanganyika and the Zambezi. The Portuguese are now in a mood to grant this, so let us secure it while we can. It would involve the Government in no expense or responsibility, any more than the recent assumptions of protectorates over Matebele—and Mashonaland have done. . . .[1]

So much for Johnston's faith in 'the best terms for commercial and evangelical interests' which he had himself negotiated, and about which he was prepared in other company to be so optimistic. Petre, however, thought that the plan as a whole was a good one. 'The main object of Mr Johnston's visit being, I presume, to ascertain precisely whether it is possible for us to agree with Portugal upon some general acceptable basis of arrangement in regard to the questions which divide the two countries in East Africa. . . . I think that he has been eminently successful.' It was true that the scheme involved a concession which all his own instructions in the past had precluded him from making, but he had all along been of opinion that the only real, insurmountable obstacle to an understanding had been the unwillingness of the British Government to allow the Blantyre settlements to pass under Portuguese influence. The value attached by the Portuguese to this region could be measured by the sacrifices they were prepared to make to obtain it. Lister, too, was strongly in favour of acceptance. The Portuguese, he reminded Lord Salisbury, had one expedition on the spot under Cardozo and another on its way out under Serpa Pinto; the company and the missions would be at their mercy; the British Government could neither send a single man to defend them, nor plead the slightest claim to the territory. 'I am convinced', he said, 'that the plan proposed offers a very good basis for a settlement of our disputes with Portugal in Africa, and that it would be a great pity to reject it in order to please one very shaky company and a few missionaries.'[2]

Salisbury, as a politician, thought differently. He knew very well that he would rather face the wrath of Portugal than that of Scotland. He made no adverse reflections on Johnston's conduct of the negotiations, but he recalled him to London, and meanwhile set in motion a slow and elaborately

---

[1] Johnston to Lister from Lisbon 5.iv.89, *F.O.84.1969.*
[2] Petre to Salisbury 9.iv.89, with Minute by Lister, *F.O.84.1965.*

staged demonstration of British public opinion. The Scottish
interests were summoned to London and shown the Anglo-
Portuguese boundary which Johnston proposed to draw. It
was regretted that the African Lakes Company was not yet
financially in a position to assume the responsibilities of
governing Nyasaland under a Royal Charter. It was discreetly
hinted that the Government might be able to do more for a
reorganized company with wider support. Johnston, when he
returned, was sent up to Scotland to interview the Foreign
Missions Committees of the Church of Scotland and the
Free Church, and to plead for the peaceful acceptance of his
proposals. Lord Balfour of Burleigh acted as the spokesman
of both the commercial and the religious pressure groups.
On May 2nd he presided over a meeting in Glasgow of 'a
large number of the most solid and influential men in the
west of Scotland', at which it was unanimously agreed to
form an extended company 'to take over under Royal Charter
the administration and development of Nyasaland'.[1] Again,
the day after Johnston had talked to the missionaries Balfour
sat down beside Salisbury in the House of Lords. 'My Scottish
friends don't like the Portuguese terms,' he said. 'Neither do
I,' was the reply. 'I don't want your Scottish friends to accept
them. I want the Portuguese to know that I too have a strong
public opinion behind me, and I am sending their Government
a warning that they must not go too far.'[2] Balfour's answer
was ready. A memorial calling the Government's attention
to Portuguese designs in the land of Dr Livingstone had been
circulating in Scotland since before Easter. The first copies
were forwarded to the Foreign Office early in May: they had
been signed by 11,000 ministers and elders of the established
Church.[3]

The negotiations with Portugal were at an end: once more
Johnston returned to his packing. It was still, however, far
from clear what he was to do upon his arrival in Mozambique.
The Foreign Office had approved his plans to travel up the
Zambezi and ascertain the exact extent of Portuguese jurisdiction in the interior. It had also empowered him to make
conditional treaties with the independent tribes beyond the
sphere of Portuguese control. But the precise area in which

[1] William Ewing to F.O. 3.v.89, *F.O.84.1974.*
[2] This story comes from a biography of the Church of Scotland missionary,
Alexander Hetherwick, entitled *A Prince of Missionaries,* by W. P. Livingstone,
pp. 48-52.
[3] Balfour of Burleigh to Sir Philip Currie 5.v.89, *F.O.84.1994.*

these treaties was to be made had never been stated, and it would seem that the actual performance of any part of the programme was still dependent upon whether the Treasury could be persuaded to advance the expenses of the journey and the cost of the presents which would have to be given in exchange for the treaties. The Chancellor of the Exchequer, Mr Goschen, was an ex-Liberal and an outspoken opponent of expansionist policies in Africa. In his autobiography Johnston described a fruitless visit which he had been instructed to pay in the spring of 1889 to Goschen's private secretary, Mr Clinton Dawkins, in the hope of enlisting his support for the allocation of a treaty-making fund.[1] Up to the very eve of his departure in May the situation at the Treasury remained unaltered. Then suddenly there occurred a chance event, which Johnston was to regard as a turning-point in his own life and a landmark in the history of the British Empire. He was invited, a few days before he left, to an evening party by the Reverend John Verschoyle, the assistant editor of the *Fortnightly Review*. 'You will meet', Verschoyle had said, 'an extraordinary fellow over from South Africa, Cecil Rhodes.'

The company, as Johnston remembered it, was a brilliant one. Walter Pater was there; so was Frank Harris. But the existence of the other guests faded from his consciousness when, after hesitating for a quarter of an hour over oysters and soup, he fell into conversation with Rhodes. At midnight they were still talking on a dusty window-seat, when Verschoyle came to them across the emptying room and pointedly asked if he should call a cab. They drove together to Rhodes's suite at the Westminster Palace Hotel, and there the conversation continued until daylight. 'We settled as we thought the immediate line of action in South and Central Africa. I jotted down on paper the heads of the scheme I was to propose to Lord Salisbury, and the particulars of Rhodes's references— the Rothschild firm especially.' As the traffic of a May morning began to rumble outside in the Broadway, Rhodes went to his despatch-box and wrote Johnston a cheque for two thousand pounds—the expenses for his treaty-making expedition. Still in evening-dress, they breakfasted. Then Johnston slipped away to Queen Anne's Mansions to bathe and change. His first call was upon Sir Percy Anderson at the Foreign Office: Lord Salisbury, it was arranged, would see him at five. Next he went to deposit Rhodes's cheque. The rest of

[1] *Story*, p. 230.

the day he spent at the Army and Navy Stores, at Silver's in Cornhill and at Liberty's in Regent Street, buying camp equipment and presents for native chiefs—'confident by now that the great journey to Nyasa and Tanganyika was coming off'.[1]

The Nyasa-Tanganyika journey, however, had been but a detail of the all-night session. Describing his morning call upon Sir Percy Anderson, Johnston in his autobiography wrote: 'His was fortunately one of those dispositions not easily upset by unexpected news. . . . Here was *his* scheme—as it had been since our first meeting in the winter of 1883—rendered possible apparently from the money point of view. A man had come forward offering virtually to let us take over any degree of Central Africa between the Zambezi and the White Nile, and find the money to run it, at any rate until such time as the British public should awaken to its value. And he gave the Rothschild firm as his guarantee.'[2] Again, writing to Rhodes after a serious quarrel in October 1893, Johnston said:

I believe from such sources of knowledge as are at my disposal that you have been the direct means of saving for the British Empire all the territories stretching between the north of the Transvaal and the basin of the Congo, in addition to having given a valuable impetus to the growing idea among the British people that we should not abandon our control over Egypt, but that we should rather seek to open up a continuous chain of Empire from the Cape to Cairo. This last expression, 'From the Cape to Cairo', though often credited to you, is of my invention and was one of the first phrases I uttered on the earliest occasion of my meeting you in 1889 which attracted your attention. At that time affairs in what is now called British Central Africa were rather at a deadlock. The Foreign Office and the Colonial Office then and now entertained much the same ideas that you and I held about the necessity of extending the British Empire within reasonable limits over countries not yet taken up by other European powers, to provide new markets for our manufactures and afford further scope for British enterprise. But the permanent officials of the Treasury held opinions . . . exactly the reverse and hold them still. . . . If I am right, you are the more to be lauded, inasmuch as, at the juncture already referred to, when the Government, though wishing to save this country from the Portuguese and the Germans and secure it for England, yet had not a penny to spend on it, you stepped forward and said 'Make this extension of British supremacy, and I will find the money to

[1] *Ibid*, pp. 234-8. In a letter to Rhodes dated 13.x.90, to be found in the *Rhodes Papers*, Johnston enclosed a full account of how the £2,000 had been spent. The first item reads: 'May 31st 1889 Presents for native chiefs purchased in London before starting . . . £247.8.6d.'
[2] *Story*, p. 238.

administer the new territories.' It seemed to me as though this offer on your part changed the situation at once. . . . Within a week of its being made new instructions were drawn up for me at the Foreign Office, and an entirely new scheme of policy developed of which the direct result has been the establishment of British supremacy over British Central Africa. . . . In addition you sent (at my advice) agents to the Barotse country to conclude treaties which would secure British supremacy in that part, whilst you placed under my control the sum of £2,000 . . . [to be used] . . . in securing other claims to the British South Africa Company between Lake Nyasa and the Barotse country. . . . Some of this money also was spent in attempting to obtain a foothold at the north end of Lake Tanganyika . . . which was nullified by the conclusion of the Anglo-German convention.[1]

In other words, the scheme which Johnston put to Lord Salisbury at five o'clock that afternoon was nothing less than the ultimate extension of chartered company government from the Zambezi northwards to Lake Tanganyika, and possibly from Lake Tanganyika northwards to Uganda. Rhodes had already on April 30th applied for a Royal Charter, extending from Bechuanaland to the Zambezi, for the syndicate which was to become the British South Africa Company. But since the protectorates to the south of the Zambezi came under the purview of the High Commissioner at the Cape, the application had been sent to the Colonial office and not to the Foreign Office. Moreover, the application had been made in the name of Lord Gifford and the Exploring Company, an unimportant concern with a capital of only £50,000 which had just been bought up by Rhodes, Beit and Rudd representing a capital of £13,000,000. The papers had been forwarded to Salisbury by the Colonial Secretary, Lord Knutsford, on May 16th with the curious proposal that the Company might be 'required' to include within its sphere 'such portion of territory north of the Zambezi as it may be important to control with a view to security of communications with the Shire and Lake Nyasa and the protection of British missionary settlements'.[2]

There is no record of the exact date of Johnston's meeting with Salisbury. Most probably it was a few days before May 16th, but even if it was a day or two later, it is quite possible, since Rhodes was concealing himself behind Lord Gifford, that Salisbury had scarcely heard of him, and that his first question was literally, as Johnston reported it, 'Who *is* Mr

[1] Johnston to Rhodes 8.x.93, enclosed in Johnston to Rosebery 8.x.93, *F.O.2.55.*
[2] C.O. to F.O. 16.v.89, *F.O.84.1995.*

Rhodes? Rather a pro-Boer M.P. in South Africa I fancy.'
We do not know the details of the wider scheme which
Johnston was commissioned to unfold. Presumably Rhodes
had told him of his intention to acquire an interest in the
Africa Lakes Company, which had been fighting the Arabs
on Lake Nyasa. Possibly he had mentioned the project for a
trans-African telegraph, running from Bechuanaland to Lake
Nyasa and thence up Lake Tanganyika to Uganda and the
Sudan. He may even have adumbrated the question of an
ultimate fusion with the Imperial British East Africa Company.
At all events it was a proposition to be taken seriously, as
was the Rothschild reference, which Anderson had already
checked. And the immediate issue which, in view of the
Portuguese expedition under Serpa Pinto, could not wait
upon the result of the prolonged negotiations involved in
obtaining a Royal Charter, was whether Johnston might not
be allowed to conclude the necessary treaties at Rhodes's
expense, on the understanding that the areas so ceded would
be included with the sphere of the Company's charter. It
was a momentous decision, but Salisbury took it without
hesitation. 'It would be preferable,' he said, 'that the Foreign
Office should pay your travelling and treaty-making expenses
in Nyasaland, as we do not want to commit ourselves to
handing over that region to a Chartered Company. Outside
its limits I see no objection to Mr Rhodes paying your expenses and meeting the cost of negotiations.'[1]

In the very few days that remained before Johnston left
England there occurred two incidents, each in its way of
significance for his future. First he was sent to explain his
mission to Chamberlain, who, it was feared, was intending
to ask some embarrassing questions in the House of Commons.
The questions were quelled, but the interview was clearly
not a success. 'Mr Chamberlain', said Johnston, 'was very
quizzical.' The maps in his library were of the 1862-7 period
and contained no details at all of the great rivers and lakes of
the African interior. One suspects that Johnston's efforts to
rectify them then and there, efforts which would have delighted
Lord Salisbury if it had been the Hatfield maps which were
at fault, were regarded by Chamberlain as somewhat im-
pertinent. Frigid politenesses were exchanged and Johnston
departed feeling snubbed as never before. In the so-called
novels of his later life, if there is one character painted with

[1] *Story*, p. 238.

more venom than the Mr Bennett Molyneux who stands for
Clement Hill, it is 'the great Choselwhit, the mysterious idol
before whose non-committal eye-glass so much imperial
incense was then burnt'. The second experience was happier.
He spent his last week-end in England with the Percy Andersons at Hedsor Wharfe, near Maidenhead, and there first met
his future wife Winifred Irby, then a slender girl of seventeen,
who was a daughter of Lady Anderson's previous marriage
with the fifth Lord Boston.

Then, in the last week of May he was off—by train to
Brindisi, and thence by steamers to Port Said, Aden and
Zanzibar, where a gunboat, the *Stork*, was waiting by Lord
Salisbury's request to take him on to Mozambique. At Zanzibar
he obtained letters from the Sultan to the Arabs at the north
end of Lake Nyasa, commanding them to make peace with
the Queen's representative. He also engaged an able assistant
in William Churchill, who was to take charge of the
Mozambique Consulate during his absence in the interior.
Churchill was appointed without pay by the Foreign Office
as a Vice-Consul, and paid out of the fund placed at Johnston's
disposal by Rhodes.[1] The *Stork* reached Mozambique on July
9th, and then, while Johnston was introducing himself to the
Portuguese authorities, sailed on to investigate the newly
discovered Chinde mouth of the Zambezi, which was alleged
to be deep enough for an ocean-going vessel of moderate
draught. On the 20th she was back with the news that the
Chinde bar could be crossed without breaking bulk or landing
men. At once Johnston telegraphed for, and obtained, permission to begin his journey into the interior in the gunboat.

It was the first occasion on which the theoretical right of
free navigation on the Zambezi was able to be practically
asserted. Previously all traffic for the Zambezi and its tributaries had entered the river by Quelimane and the Kwa Kwa
mouth, which became unnavigable some forty miles from the
sea. From this point a land porterage of four miles had to be
made to the main stream at Vicente. All the steamers plying
on the Zambezi, Shire and Lake Nyasa had had to be dis-
mantled and reassembled at this stage, and all the cargoes
which they subsequently carried had to pass through the
Portuguese custom-houses. Now, on July 28th, 1889, the

---

[1] Johnston to Salisbury 20.vii.89, *F.O.84.1969*. The account enclosed in
Johnston to Rhodes 13.x.90 contains the following entry: '1st February 1890,
Half Years salary to W. A. Churchill, my *remplacement* at Mozambique . . .
£100.' There follows a note to the effect that the Foreign Office had agreed to be
responsible for this allowance as from 1.i.90.

Stork, with Johnston on board, crossed the Chinde bar and successfully gained the main river above the Delta. Next day the gunboat was moored in midstream a few miles below Vicente. The party transferred to the steam cutter, and on August 2nd encountered the African Lakes Company's steamer, the *James Stevenson*, which was refuelling at Morumbala on the Lower Shire. 'The end of my journey in the *Stork* has been accomplished', wrote Johnston triumphantly. 'In two or three more days I shall have reached the Ruo . . . and if at least one bank of the Shire beyond the Ruo is secured—as I hope to secure it—to England, our Nyasaland will become a kind of African Servia or Paraguay, an inland state with direct fluvial communications with the sea.'[1]

Johnston now joined the *James Stevenson*. But before he could reach the Ruo and start his treaty-making, he had to try conclusions with the mysterious expedition under Serpa Pinto, the despatch of which had prompted his mission to Lisbon three months before. Its destination had then been unknown, but the British Government had since been informed that its purpose was to explore the central region of the Zambezi and the Loangwa tributary. At Mozambique the authorities had been quite silent on the subject. Now messengers arrived saying that Serpa Pinto was encamped between Morumbala and the Ruo confluence, and requesting from Johnston the favour of a visit. The Scottish missionaries who were his fellow-passengers on the *James Stevenson* counselled him against walking into a trap, and indeed the scene for a Central African Fashoda seemed well set. Johnston had a few lightly armed porters. Serpa Pinto had an army of seven hundred men, of whom four hundred were equipped with breech-loading rifles. Moreover, when Johnston confronted him face to face, the pretence of a scientific purpose was soon discarded. Serpa Pinto said that he was on his way to visit the 'Portuguese chief' Mponda, whose town lay on the right bank of the Shire near its exit from Lake Nyasa. He was just then held up by the hostility of the Makololo chiefs of the Shire valley, incited, so he claimed, by the local manager of the African Lakes Company, Mr John Moir. He would prefer a peaceful transit if Johnston could arrange it, but he was ready in the last resort for war.

I stated that I felt sure the Makololo would never consent to the passage of such a large, armed expedition . . . that war

[1] Johnston to Salisbury from Morumbala 4.viii.89, *F.O.84.1969.*

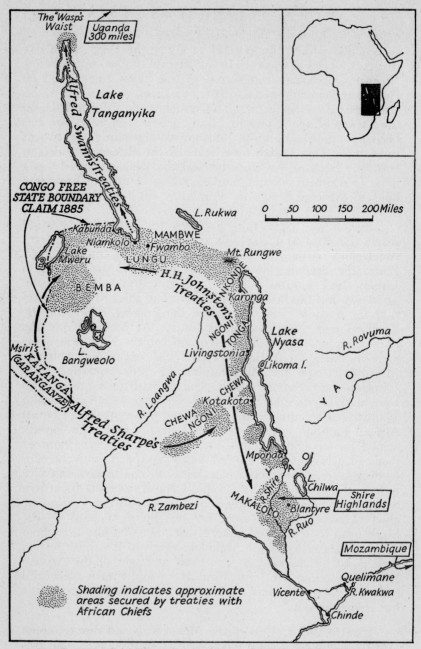

The "Wasp's Waist

Uganda 300 miles

Lake Tanganyika

Alfred Swann's Treaties

CONGO FREE STATE BOUNDARY CLAIM 1885

Kabundu

Niamkolo

Lake Mweru

BEMBA

LUNGU

MAMBWE

•Fwambo

L. Rukwa

Mt. Rungwe

H.H. Johnston's Treaties

NKONDE

Karonga

Msiri's KATANGA (GARANGANZE)

Alfred Sharpe's Treaties

L. Bangweolo

R. Loangwa

NGONI

TONGA

Livingstonia

Lake Nyasa

R. Rovuma

©Likoma I.

Y A O

CHEWA

Kotakota

CHEWA NGONI

Mponda

Y A O

L. Chilwa

Shire Highlands

MAKALOLO

R. Shire

Blantyre

R. Ruo

R. Zambezi

Mozambique

0   50   100   150   200 Miles

Shading indicates approximate areas secured by treaties with African Chiefs

Quelimane

Vicente

R. Kwakwa

Chinde

7. THE NYASA-TANGANYIKA JOURNEY OF 1889-90

between the Portuguese and the Makololo would close the Shire and jeopardize the lives of British subjects in the Shire Highlands . . . and might seriously affect relations between England and Portugal. . . . I reminded him that his Government had assured ours that his mission was not to the Nyasa territories but to the River Loangwa and the upper Zambezi. Serpa Pinto admitted that was his original aim, but that owing to troubles and insurrections in the Makanga country he had thought of going to the Loangwa by Lake Nyasa. 'Besides,' he innocently added, 'I wish to make treaties along the upper part of the Loangwa and west of Lake Nyasa'. This information of his plans was not without interest to me but I accepted it without comment. I only added that if he wished to reach Mponda's, his best and quickest route would be eastward by the River Ruo. . . . He admitted this, and said that if I would assure him in writing of my strong objections to his forcing his way through the Makololo country, he would endeavour—though not promise —to take another route. . . . In further conversation the scientific fiction gradually disappeared and gave place to a frank intention of extending Portuguese influence north to Lake Bangweolo and westward across the continent.[1]

Faced by the threat of war with England, Serpa Pinto halted his army short of the Ruo confluence and soon afterwards returned himself to the coast to consult his superiors. Johnston travelled on up the Shire to forestall his rival. A day or two later, while the *James Stevenson* was stopped to refuel, he went on shore with his rifle and sketch-book. He heard shots and presently tripped over the carcase of a magnificent waterbuck. He settled down to sketch it until a crackling in the reeds announced the approach of the owner. It was in these unusual circumstances that he first met Alfred Sharpe, who was to be his principal assistant in Nyasaland for the next seven years, and who was to succeed him first as Commissioner and then as Governor, from 1897 till 1912. Sharpe, on failing to secure an appointment in the Colonial Service in Fiji in 1887, had come to south-east Africa to shoot game. With Lugard he had joined the African Lakes Company's Defence Force at the north end of Lake Nyasa. He had been wounded in one of the early skirmishes and had gone to recuperate in Natal. Now he was back on the Shire, making an income, if not a fortune, out of ivory. Johnston engaged him on the spot as a temporary Vice-Consul, and a few days later despatched him from Blantyre on a treaty-making expedition westwards from the Shire Highlands to the upper

[1] Johnston to Salisbury from Mandala 26.viii.89, *F.O.84.1969.*

Loangwa. 'Mr Sharpe was intending to shoot big game there,' he explained to the Foreign Office, 'and bears all the expenses of his expedition. I merely pay for the presents . . . to the value of £100.' Johnston himself spent about a fortnight making treaties with the Makololo chiefs of the Shire valley and with the Yao of the highlands round Blantyre, and then set off for the Lake.[1]

The treaties signed by Johnston on this expedition are still filed with his despatches in the Foreign Office records. They are simple documents, all following a single printed form, by which the signatory declared himself at peace with the Queen of England, agreed to admit British subjects to his country and to submit all disputes in which they became involved to the decision of Her Majesty's representative. He undertook, finally, to make no cessions of territory to other powers without the consent of the British Government. The treaties did not confer protection, nor did they commit the signatory to accepting it at any future time. Their primary purpose was to prove at the council tables of Europe the priority of British interests over those of other powers in the regions to which they referred. As such, it was not necessary, nor was it possible, to cover the whole of Nyasaland and North-Eastern Rhodesia with a complete network of treaties. Johnston and Sharpe merely pushed out their treaty-lines in two long arms, one to the west, the other to the north, trusting to luck that no European rival would be able to make a better showing in the middle. Moreover, even on their lines of march, if any particular chief refused to sign a treaty, they simply moved on, leaving, as it were, a gap in the chain. When the Protectorate was later established, it was done by proclamation without reference to the treaties, and it applied equally to those groups which had signed and to those which had not.

Nevertheless, the treaties negotiated by Johnston were not, like their counterparts in so many other regions of Africa, mere meaningless scraps of paper signed in exchange for bottles of brandy by bogus chiefs who had no idea of what they were doing. Right along his route Johnston had the good fortune to be passing through country which had been

---

[1] *Ibid.* The account enclosed in Johnston to Rhodes 13.x.90 contains the following entries: '26th August 1889, Stores and presents purchased from African Lakes Co on behalf of Sharpe's expedition to Undi . . . £83.1.6d. Honorarium to Sharpe for journey to Undi . . . £100. 15th January 1890, Honorarium to Sharpe for journey to Mpezeni and Mwasi Kasungu . . . £100.' A note reads: 'After this I engaged him for the B.S.A. Co. at £500 p.a. plus £100 expenses. . . . His agreement terminates 17.ii.91.'

CECIL RHODES

LORD
SALISBURY
IN OLD AGE

MARIBU STORK IN FLIGHT

occupied for ten to fifteen years by English and Scottish missionaries, and he had the good sense to solicit their aid. The ex-missionary planter, John Buchanan, who was the Acting-Consul for Lake Nyasa, helped him with his treaties in the Shire Highlands. On the Lake the great Chauncey Maples of the Universities' Mission and the even greater Robert Laws of Livingstonia guided him to some of the Chewa and Tonga chiefs and acted as his interpreters and sponsors with the people. In these circumstances the much-quoted passage in his autobiography,[1] in which he asserted that the tribal sections with whose chiefs he signed treaties in 1889 were also those who later accepted peacefully the establishment of the Protectorate administration, should not perhaps be taken as too universal a judgment on the virtues of treaty-making. No doubt he was leaning more than he cared to admit upon the good-will, slowly and painfully built up by the missionaries. But the fact remains that his journey of 1889-90 was not just a necessary farce, but a real and useful prelude to his later administrative work.

There were, however, two treaties which differed materially from the rest, in that they were directed to the immediate local situation and not to the contingencies of competition among the European powers. These were the treaties which Johnston signed with the Arabs, with Jumbe Kisutu of Kotakota, half-way up the western side of the Lake, and with Mlozi and his colleagues who had been fighting with the African Lakes Company at the southern end of the Nyasa-Tanganyika plateau. Jumbe was a veteran of the lake regions, 'the third or fourth of a line of Swahili merchant princes, who, as quasi-viceroys of the Sultan of Zanzibar, have gradually made themselves masters of the country of Marimba'. Kotakota had grown up as an important collecting-point in the slave trade, the western terminal of a ferry service across the lake, an inland base at which caravans bound for Lake Bangweolo and the Katanga regrouped and took on supplies. Like Ujiji on Lake Tanganyika it was an Arab metropolis in central Africa with mosques and mullahs as well as store-houses and traders. Jumbe, however, was an astute diplomatist. With the coming of travellers, missionaries and consuls in the 'sixties and 'seventies, he had taken care to keep on good terms with the white men. The evidences of his past connexion with the slave trade were gradually suppressed, and by the time of Johnston's visit his wealth was derived mainly from

[1] *Story*, p. 277.

F

ivory. His native hunters ranged over the country in all directions; and Johnston, ascertaining that direct communication was open between his capital and the important state of Garanganze in the Katanga, sent a letter to Mr Arnot, a missionary in that place, informing him that a two months' journey from his remote settlement on the southern Congo watershed would bring him within sight of British steamers on Lake Nyasa.'

Nevertheless, though professing neutrality, Jumbe had been quietly aiding the North Nyasa Arabs with arms and supplies in their struggle with the Company, and it was clear that if he ever judged the moment ripe for more open collaboration, the Company and the missions could easily be driven from the Lake. A firm agreement with Jumbe was therefore an indispensable preliminary to peace further north. Johnston saw the situation and met it with a characteristic independence of higher authority. In the Shire Highlands he had merely authorized the Acting-Consul, Buchanan, to declare a British Protectorate if the Portuguese crossed the Ruo frontier. At Kotakota, so he informed Lord Salisbury, circumstances compelled him to negotiate a treaty 'which somewhat exceeds the extent of the agreements I was directed to draw up'. So convincing was the account which he gave of the extent and seriousness of the European scramble for Africa, so telling his comparison of the Queen's rule with that of the King of Portugal and the Emperor of Germany, that Jumbe accepted the offer of British protection, agreed to a generous definition of his territories, and promised to follow the advice of Her Majesty's representative. Simultaneously he signed an agreement with the African Lakes Company by which he accepted a subsidy of three thousand rupees a year in lieu of the customs and taxes which he had formerly levied on the ivory which passed through his dominions. Fortunately for Johnston, the despatch enclosing the treaty took more than three months to reach the Foreign Office, and by that time relations with both Portugal and Germany had reached a stage at which his action appeared not merely acceptable but timely.[1]

With Jumbe's treaty in his pocket, Johnston proceeded in the little steamer of the Universities' Mission to the village of Karonga's at the north end of the Lake, where the African Lakes Company had a trading-post, which had also in former years been the point of departure for their caravan-route to Lake Tanganyika. Some ivory had passed out by this route,

[1] Johnston to Salisbury from Karonga's 16.x.89, *F.O.84.1969.*

but mainly it had been maintained as a supply-line to the stations of the London Missionary Society, whose agents had been settled since 1879 at various points around the Tanganyika lake. Since 1887, however, communications had been cut by a gang of Zanzibar Arabs—Mlozi and Kopakopa, Msalema and Bwana Omari—who had selected the district round Karonga's, the home of the peace-loving and prolific Nkonde tribe, as the theatre for a campaign of slave-raiding and conquest. With the help of armed native levies from the country to the north-east of the lake they had swooped upon village after village, killing the male inhabitants, burning the villages and carrying off the women and children. The Company's station at Karonga's had become, first, the rallying-point for Nkonde refugees, and then the main target of the Arabs' attacks. Pending the arrival of help from headquarters, the Company's two European employees, Fotheringham and Nicoll, had been forced to abandon their base, but they had retreated into the hills with their Nkonde allies and there trained them as the nucleus of a defence force. They had been joined in due course by Tonga levies from the Livingstonia Mission, and by European volunteers, including Lugard, Sharpe and Johnston's predecessor, Consul O'Neill from Mozambique. Gallantly, in the course of 1888 the 'Defence Force' had fought its way back to Karonga's and had even under Lugard's leadership delivered counter-attacks against the stockaded encampments of the Arabs. But, owing partly to the feeble resources of the Company and partly to the activities of the Portuguese officials at the Zambezi mouth, arms and ammunition had been kept too short to enable the war to be carried to a successful conclusion. The Arabs had lost much of their considerable wealth in ivory, but they had not been driven from the country, and as the European and African volunteers had drifted away to their several avocations, the situation had become a stalemate.[1]

In these circumstances Johnston's only course was to negotiate a truce which would reopen the communications with the stations of the London Missionary Society and enable him to pursue his treaty-making mission between the two Lakes. There was of course no question, as with Jumbe, of a treaty with the Arabs which would recognize their *de facto* sovereignty over any piece of territory, but only of an agreement between the Arabs and the Company, by which each side called an end to reprisals and agreed to go their own ways

[1] Cf. Johnston to Salisbury 17.iii.90, *F.O.84.2051.*

for the future. The Arabs agreed to build no stockades within three miles of the Company's caravan-routes and to carry out no more attacks upon tribes which were in treaty relations with the Queen. It was not a victory. It was only an uneasy truce; but though Lugard, who was now in England trying to raise fresh supplies, was bitterly critical, the three Europeans who were with Johnston at Karonga's were unanimously in support of his action.[1] The despatch in which he described the concluding ceremonies of the negotiation conveys well the sinister atmosphere of the whole episode.

> The Arabs signed the treaty and we did likewise. Then the Arabs arose from their mats and walking around the half-circle of white men solemnly shook hands with each of us—their followers doing the same with our followers—and then returned to their mats, where they prayed aloud for a few minutes that Allah would help them to keep the treaty and that an unbroken peace should henceforth reign between them and the people of the Queen. After this milk was poured out by them and handed to us to drink, and we reciprocally filled and returned the cup to them. A bullock was killed—the loud sighs of its death agony and the gurgling of its spurting veins coming as a curious second to the Arabs' prayers and being the only sound which accompanied the intoning of their guttural Arabic phrases, and its meat was divided up among the wild-looking savages who represented the bodyguards of the White Men and Arabs. Then with the sweetest compliments and most graceful phrases which the Swahili tongue can frame the Arabs bade us adieu, and we severally returned to our towns, where for two days, amid a continual firing of guns, feasting and dancing was kept up. Three days after the signing of the peace the Arabs paid me a ceremonial visit at Karonga's. We ate together, exchanged presents and polite but vapid compliments, and afterwards I called together all the native chiefs who had suffered by the war, and had the treaty translated and read to them in the Arabs' presence. Then Mlozi, the chief Arab, addressed a few words to them, telling them they might return to their villages without fear, as the Arabs would never again attack the friends of the Englishmen. On each side a spear was broken as a sign that the war was over, and the broken fragments were exchanged. All the minor leaders of the native soldiery then stepped forward and shook hands, and the day ended in a riot of noisy friendship which was most fatiguing.[2]

Johnston concluded his business at Karonga's on October 26th, and the following day left with Nicoll for Lake

[1] Rev. D. Kerr Cross to F.O. 18.iv.90, *F.O.84.2080*.
[2] Johnston to Salisbury from Karonga's 26.x.89, *F.O.84.1969*.

Tanganyika. The Portuguese danger was far behind. His purpose now was to secure a chain of treaties across the plateau to be used as bargaining counters in the delineation of a frontier between German East and British Central Africa. His obvious line of march would have been by the so-called Stevenson Road, a rough track cleared by the African Lakes Company when moving the London Missionary Society's steamer in sections to Lake Tanganyika in 1881-2, which had been ever since the route between the two lakes. But Johnston's instincts both as a traveller and an empire-builder always urged him to range to the furthest limit of what could be justified to his superiors, and, encouraged by Dr Kerr Cross, the representative of the Livingstonia Mission at Karonga's, he struck north instead of north-west and made his first treaties with the Bandali people of Mount Rungwe. From there he dropped down to the basin of Lake Rukwa, which he described as a terrestrial hell, where the thermometer rarely fell below ninety-eight degrees even at night, where all the water was brackish, and where the inhabitants were fierce and treacherous. 'Under these circumstances,' he explained to Lord Salisbury, 'I thought we might well leave Rukwa to German enterprise: so I again ascended the Tanganyika plateau and hurried to the south-east corner of that lake, carrying some much-needed stores to the London Missionary Society's agents at Fwambo.'[1]

There is no doubt that he enjoyed every minute of this trip. The keen highland air sharpened every sense, and with the help of a couple of Nyamwezi donkeys he and Nicoll covered thirty and forty miles a day. At the northern edge of the plateau, with the incomparable spectacle of Lake Tanganyika contained within its encircling mountains, its waters sparkling blue three thousand feet below, he decided that his camping-place should one day be a town, the headquarters of the Tanganyika district in the British Central Africa of his dreams. He bought the site and named it Abercorn, after the Chairman of the British South Africa Company.[2] From his camp he sent messengers down to the mission stations below, and followed them himself next day. First, Fwambo, where he found Mr and Mrs Jones, Dr Mather and Mr Wright 'a little cast down and despondent'. They had been without supplies from Europe for more than a year, and a feud between two chiefs in the locality had deprived them for the moment even

[1] Johnston to Salisbury from Mozambique 1.ii.90, *F.O.84.2051.*
[2] *Story*, p. 271.

of their servants and labourers. 'Mr Jones, a most tender-hearted man, who would hesitate to crush a worm, had himself to kill, skin and cut up their last sheep for our dinner.'[1] The supplies were delivered, the chiefs were interviewed, the servants returned; and Johnston had his reward when, on the succeeding days, Mr Jones pulled out one after another his language notebooks compiled in a series of posts around the west and south of the lake. They were 'discerning studies', and in the *Comparative Study of the Bantu Languages* they were to fill what would otherwise have been a serious gap.

From Fwambo he moved on to Niamkolo, the lakeside headquarters of 'Captain' Swann, formerly an officer in the P. & O. Company, now a lay missionary in charge of the London Missionary Society's communications on the Lake. Like his even more remarkable predecessor, E. C. Hore, who had just retired after eleven years' service, he was accompanied not only by his wife but by a young family. Johnston took to him at once and found a valuable informant on the political situation. From Swann in particular he learned to look on the activities of at least some of the Arabs in a new light. The treaty with Kotakota proved in the event to be a lasting alliance, but in its inception it had been a calculated move to divide Jumbe from his compatriots in the north. The peace at Karonga's had been a cynical compact which would last just as long as Mlozi conceived the rival forces to be evenly balanced. But round Tanganyika Johnston found Arabs like Tafuma at the south-east and Kabunda at the south-west corner of the lake whose days of brigandage were over, and who had woven themselves by marriage as well as by might into the very fabric of Lungu chieftainship—to such an extent that the indigenous ruling families would do nothing without their advice. Swann directed him to these men as an essential preliminary to treaty-making and also taught him that the slave-trader turned colonist could even be a beneficent influence. If the natives submitted without much resistance to being made his subjects, then the conditions of that patch of country became a distinct improvement on the average native kingdom. There was more security for life and property, more attention to agriculture and cultivation, and useful trees and plants and domestic animals were introduced from the coast. 'The Arabs have had their little wars,' he concluded, 'but were not in so doing much wickeder than we have been in many of our acquirements of territory. . . . The scheme

[1] Johnston to Salisbury 17.iii.90, *F.O.84.2051.*

professed by some enthusiasts of starting crusades and driving
the Arabs from Central Africa is about as easy of accomplishment as that of driving the Turks from Europe and Palestine
. . . and would be about as futile to our interests as the last-
named project.'[1]

At Kabunda's village Johnston treated himself to a week's
holiday, a week which to the attentive reader of his autobiography stands out as perhaps the most consciously enjoyed
moment of his life. He had come far and done much. He was
in superb health. He had accomplished one dramatic mission
which was of his own devising, and of which he never doubted
the historical significance. There was the prospect of an even
more dramatic and significant sequel at the north end of the
lake, by which he would secure to the Empire at least the
beginnings of another treaty-chain leading onwards to Lake
Victoria—the 'wasp's waist' between German East Africa and
the Congo state, joining the British spheres in the east and the
south. In such a heady moment of seeming fulfilment it was
delightful to pause at the back of beyond, to lay aside briefly
the course of action and to exercise in unparalleled circumstances his talents as an artist and a naturalist. Kabunda's
guest-house was clean and commodious. His Baluchi wife
could contrive an excellent curry, and between frequent and
ample repasts Johnston would wander with his sketch-book
to the reed-fringed estuary of the Lofu River, which was the
refuge of every wild bird from the windswept waters of the
lake itself. Thirty-five years later he could still recapture the
scene in every detail.

> Gazing westwards one had before the eyes a remarkable
> conjunction of mountain, river, marsh, estuary, sand-spit and
> open lake scenery; and in the immediate foreground, on the
> water and the clean sand, such a variety and congeries of bird
> life as was rare even in tropical Africa. . . . There were pelicans
> of grey, white and salmon-pink, with yellow pouches, riding the
> water like swans, replete with fish and idly floating. Egyptian
> geese, fawn-coloured, white and green-bronze; spur-winged
> geese, bronze-green, red-faced, white-shouldered, white-flecked;
> African teal coloured much like those found in England; a
> small jet-black pochard with a black crest and yellow eyes;
> whistling tree-duck either chestnut and white or black and white,
> zebra-barred. . . . Farthest away of all the bird assemblages
> would be a long file of rosy flamingoes sifting the water for small
> fish and molluscs. They were so far off that their movements
> were scarcely perceptible; against the green background of the

[1] *Ibid.*

marsh they looked like a vast fringe of pale pink flowers in full bloom. Small bronze-green cormorants were plunging into the water for fish. . . . On the sandspit two dainty crowned cranes were pacing the sand and the scattered, wiry grass, looking for locusts. . . . Add to the foregoing stilt-plovers of black and white with exceedingly long, slate-grey legs; spur-winged plovers with yellow wattles; curlew; sandpipers; crimson-beaked pratincoles; sacred ibis, iridescent blue, green and red-bronze; verditer-blue, red-beaked gallinules; black water-rails with lemon beaks and white pencillings; black coots; other rails that were blue and green with turned-up white tails; squacco herons, white and fawn-coloured; large grey herons; purple-slate-coloured herons; bluish grey egrets; small, white egrets, with yellow beaks, or large with feathery plumes; Goliath herons, nut-brown, black-streaked, yellow and pinkish grey; small black storks with open and serrated beaks; monstrous, bare-headed marabu storks; and dainty lily-trotters, black and white, golden yellow and chocolate-brown. . . . Every now and then a disturbance would occur. I might cough and they would be recalled to my presence; or one of Kabunda's children would come down to the bank and tell me a meal was ready. Then the ducks would scatter over the surface or the geese rise with a clamour for a circling flight.[1]

The northward adventure, however, was not to be. Towards the middle of December his peace was disturbed by a runner carrying mails from the Shire Highlands—the first he had received since leaving Blantyre at the end of August. From them he learnt that, following a skirmish between the Portuguese and the Makololo on the Ruo frontier in September, Consul Buchanan had declared a formal protectorate over the Makololo and Yao Districts; and next that in November Lieutenant Coutinho with a largely augmented Portuguese force had crossed the Ruo, hauled down the British flag at Katunga's, the port of Blantyre, and given notice of his intention to occupy the Shire Highlands. Of the repercussions of the situation in Europe Johnston was still ignorant, and it seemed clear to him that he must return at once to the scene of action. He tried hard to persuade Swann to act in his place at the north end of Lake Tanganyika, but that officer, though he was quite prepared to place the mission transport at Johnston's disposal and to assist him as interpreter, was forbidden by the rules of his Society to engage directly in political affairs. A breach of these rules would be the harder to justify in that Johnston had no written mandate for any part of his programme, and more especially in that Lake

---

[1] *Story*, pp. 273-5. See Plate 7, facing p. 161.

Tanganyika was traditionally if not by definition the concern of the Consul-General at Zanzibar. The best he could do, therefore, was to obtain from Swann a promise to consider with his colleagues any more authoritative request that he might be able to send him from the coast; and with that he set off southwards with all speed.

The two hundred and forty miles to Karonga's he covered in nine days. There the African Lakes Company's steamer was waiting to take him in five days more to the south end of Lake Nyasa. He made a treaty with the important Yao chief, Mponda, who had declined to meet him on his northward journey, and then hurried on to Blantyre. To his surprise all was peaceful. He rode on to Katunga's to catch the steamer for the Lower Shire and Zambezi: still there were no Portuguese. Only at the Ruo was he met by Coutinho, who from a fortified camp on the British side of the river handed him his mails together with a fine present of food and wine, and informed him that the frontier question was under discussion between their respective governments.[1] He reached Mozambique on January 30th, 1890, and five days later received a telegram from the Foreign Office informing him that the Portuguese Government had in consequence of representations engaged not to settle any territorial questions by acts of force, and to instruct the authorities in Mozambique to withdraw their troops from the Shire and Makololo districts.[2]

Lord Salisbury had already acted with vigour, on the basis of a telegram received in mid-December from Consul-General Euan-Smith at Zanzibar reporting the arrival from Lake Nyasa of Bishop Smythies of the Universities' Mission and of a French traveller, Captain Trivier. Both had given accounts of the Portuguese movements on the Shire. The Bishop had actually seen a written warning to British settlers in the Blantyre district that they must either place themselves under Portuguese protection or take the consequences.[3] From other sources there had been information of three Portuguese gunboats being sent to the Zambezi, and also of the embarkation of troops at Goa for Mozambique.[4] Energetic protests had immediately been lodged at Lisbon, culminating in one ultimatum delivered on January 2nd and another on the 11th.

[1] *Ibid.*, p. 276.
[2] F.O. to Johnston 4.ii.90, *F.O.84.2050.*
[3] Euan-Smith to Salisbury 16.xii.89, *F.O.84.1982.*
[4] E.g. Sir William Mackinnon to F.O. 21.xii.89, *F.O.84.2009.*

F*

The Portuguese ministry had first yielded and then resigned. Salisbury's outward attitude after his coup was one of inflexible contempt. 'Since there is no shame in the surrender of impotence,' he told his parliamentary critics, 'the weaker of two widely unequal powers enters upon a dispute with the stronger consciously immune from ultimate catastrophe and proportionately reckless.'[1] In private, however, no one knew better how far-reaching might be the effect on his relations with other powers, and the still imprecisely known activities of Johnston in the rear of both German East Africa and the Congo State became temporarily a source of real anxiety. Johnston had inevitably achieved a certain international notoriety as the target of Portuguese Anglophobia—he had been described in the Lisbon papers as a 'slippery individual, mellifluous and insinuating'[2]—and now, most unfortunately, rumours of his treaty-making on the Nyasa-Tanganyika plateau had leaked out through the same Captain Trivier who had reported on the Portuguese in the Shire Highlands.[3] At the height of the Lisbon crisis Salisbury had paused to send a repudiation of the putative treaties to the German Government[4]; and in anticipation of Johnston's return he had telegraphed to Mozambique ordering him to maintain absolute secrecy about his activities in the interior.[5]

It is in the light of this situation that Salisbury's otherwise ambiguous comments of the next few months need to be viewed. His reply to Johnston's telegraphic account of his proceedings received on January 30th reveals a friendly complicity. 'Lord Salisbury entirely approves your action so far as the territory south of latitude 11° South is concerned. North of that line a mutual agreement was come to between the German Government and H.M.G. in the course of last summer that no steps should be taken on either side without previous communication. Treaties to the north would be invalidated by this, and you should refrain from any public statement with regard to it.'[6] After ten days more, which had been occupied by Johnston in pestering for a gunboat in which to visit the outlying portions of his consular district, Salisbury's tolerance grew more humorous and more caustic. The Admiralty's

[1] G. Cecil: *Robert, Marquis of Salisbury*, Vol. IV, p. 257.
[2] Petre to Salisbury 19.xii.89, *F.O.63.1215*.
[3] Euan-Smith to Salisbury 14.xii.89 *F.O.84.1982*.
[4] F.O. to Sir E. Malet 17.xii.89, 18.xii.89, 19.xii.89, *F.O.64.1215*.
[5] F.O. to Johnston 26.i.90, *F.O.84.2050*.
[6] Johnston to Salisbury 30.i.90, *F.O.84.2051*; F.O. to Johnston 31.i.90, *F.O.84.2050*.

concurrence had been secured with some difficulty, and the Permanent Under-Secretary, Sir Philip Currie, inquired 'Should Johnston be told? If no limitation is put on his power of requisitioning the gunboat, he will send for it at once and perhaps make more use of it than is desirable.' 'He will be worse on land than at sea,' was Salisbury's reply. 'Let him have it.'[1] And again a week later, when a reorganization of the African Consulates was suggested by Sir Percy Anderson, under which Johnston would be transferred from Mozambique to Nyasaland with a larger salary, Salisbury commented, 'I doubt about giving the Bull a consulship in the China shop.'[2]

Nevertheless, as the Portuguese storm died down, so Salisbury's apprehension about his impetuous subordinate faded also. At the end of March he telegraphed that he had read with much interest Johnston's account of his journey and work in the Lake Districts and that he was gratified by the energy and courage of which he had given proof.[3] In April he sanctioned without a trace of irritation his request for home-leave in order to recruit his health, though it came after less than a year's service at his post. Johnston meanwhile had availed himself of the gunboat to go to Zanzibar and to enter, with Consul Euan-Smith's connivance, into further extensive negotiations, for which he not only had no mandate, but which seemed on the surface to have been in direct disobedience to the Foreign Office instructions. He reported at the end of April that his purpose had been to consult Euan-Smith about the Arab problem, to secure the Sultan of Zanzibar's recognition of the new protectorates around Lake Nyasa. An emissary had accordingly been despatched overland, carrying a present from the Queen to Jumbe of Kotakota and letters from the Sultan commanding his subjects in the Lake region to respect the treaties made with the Queen's representative.[4] What Johnston did not reveal was that the same emissary carried a letter, with treaty-forms and a supply of presents paid for out of Rhodes's fund, to the London Missionary Society's agent Alfred Swann, begging him to carry out the mission to the north end of Lake Tanganyika which they had already discussed. 'Show my handwriting to no one, but go. . . . The North End is the highway to the Equatorial Regions, and the Germans have despatched

---

[1] F.O. to Admiralty 11.ii.90, *F.O.84.2074*.
[2] Treasury to F.O. 17.ii.90, *F.O.84.2075*.
[3] F.O. to Johnston, 29.iii.90, *F.O.84.2050*.
[4] Johnston to Salisbury 21.iv.90, *F.O.84.2051*.

Emin Pasha to take it over and so close the door to Britain. Go at once. I ask you because there is no one else who can assist me in this crisis, and I trust your connection with the London Missionary Society will prove no hindrance.'[1]

Truly, as Salisbury was to remark on a later occasion, Johnston was not accustomed to 'minimize any discretion allowed him'. And yet, it was Salisbury's genius to recognize that such a man had his uses. When the story reached the Foreign Office six months later in the shape of a vigorous protest from the Directors of the London Missionary Society, even Sir Percy Anderson was scandalized. 'Treaty-making by a missionary apparently in the always acknowledged German hinterland. There must be some mistake. Send to Mr Johnston for explanations.' Three days later Johnston, apparently unabashed, produced the treaties. 'This', wrote Anderson, 'is the proceeding respecting which we have had the warm remonstrance of the L.M.S. and may have a still warmer one from the Germans. It is so remarkable that it is difficult to comment on it.' Salisbury, on the other hand, showed no trace of surprise, no inclination whatever to reproach. 'Johnston was of course acting beyond his instructions. But it was not acknowledged hinterland. It was the "wasp's waist". . . . All Johnston's irregular proceedings were covered by a disclaimer we sent to Berlin about a year ago. This should be cited.'[2] By the time these words were written Johnston was a C.B. and Commissioner and Consul-General designate for Mozambique, Nyasaland and the British sphere north of the Zambezi.

[1] Johnston to Swann, quoted in Swann to Thompson 2.viii.90, L.M.S. Archives, cited by A. J. Hanna: *Nyasaland and North-Eastern Rhodesia*, p. 161. The account enclosed in Johnston to Rhodes 13.x.90 reads: '26th April 1890, North end Tanganyika, Secret Expedition to secure, Sums left behind at Mozambique to meet cost of: Honorarium for Alfred Swann . . . £100; Salary for Kiongwe for 1 year . . . £100; Do for Kiongwe's 2 assistants . . . £20; Kiongwe's travelling expenses . . . £70; Presents for native chiefs . . . £100; Food and expenses for 2 assistants . . . £30.' An accompanying note reads: 'This was hurriedly got up after consultation with Euan-Smith, and in order to counteract object of Emin Pasha's new expedition. I intended thereby to secure the North End of Tanganyika and the Wasp's Waist. Alfred Swann who was to lead it was already on Tanganyika. . . . He was only to go as far as the north end of the Lake, and my excellent Kiongwe (well supplied with flags and treaties) was to do the rest, and to go if possible as far as the Victoria Nyanza. Alas, now I have had to recall them owing to Lord Salisbury's German agreement, and your £420 will have been spent somewhat in vain. I am very sorry.'

[2] L.M.S. to F.O. 2.xii.90, *F.O.84.2096*; Johnston to Salisbury 5.xii.90, *F.O.84.2052*, with minutes.

Chapter 6

A FRIGHTFUL MENAGERIE

WHEN Johnston left Mozambique at the end of April
1890, he travelled first to Port Elizabeth and thence
overland to Kimberley, in order to pay a brief visit to Rhodes.
His own mission apart, much had happened since their
previous meeting in London almost exactly a year before to
turn the bold projects they had then discussed into accomplished facts. First and foremost the British South Africa
Company had been formally incorporated under a Royal
Charter signed by the Queen in Council on October 29th,
1889. Its field of operations had been rather loosely defined as
all South Africa north of the Crown Colony of Bechuanaland,
and the Transvaal, and west of the Portuguese possessions in
East Africa. Northwards the Company's sphere was limited
temporarily by the Zambezi, but it was tacitly understood
that even to the north of that river the Charter would be
extended in so far as effective occupation was achieved through
the Company's agency. Rhodes, therefore, at the time of
Johnston's visit was busily engaged in staking out the widest
possible claims for the frontiers of his new dominion. Jameson
was already at Bulawayo with Lobengula, the paramount
chief of the Matabele, preparing him with gifts and soft words
for the forthcoming entry of Rhodes's pioneers into near-
by Mashonaland to the south and east. Colquhoun, the
Administrator-Designate of Mashonaland, was Johnston's
fellow-guest in Rhodes's house. North of the Zambezi Rhodes
had been negotiating for nearly a year for an amalgamation
with the African Lakes Company which would give him the
undisputed claim to Nyasaland. The Scotsmen had proved
hard to woo, but they had accepted £20,000 against shares
in their Company and an annual subsidy of £9,000 which
had enabled them to keep open their communications with
Lake Tanganyika.[1] John Moir, their African manager, who
was just then returning from Nyasaland to be the Company's

---

[1] It cannot be a coincidence that this was the exact sum offered by Rhodes to
Lugard for the putting down of the slave trade in Nyasaland at an interview
which took place in July 1889. This verbal offer was subsequently dishonoured
by Rhodes—see M. Perham: *Lugard: The Years of Adventure*, pp. 150-2.

Secretary in Glasgow, was also in Kimberley with Johnston. For the region west of Nyasaland Rhodes had with him the celebrated explorer Joseph Thomson, and J. A. Grant, a son of Speke's companion, who were about to depart and complete Sharpe's treaty work north of the middle Zambezi. Another agent, Lochner, had already left for Barotseland in the far north-west.

Theoretically Rhodes was only the Chairman of the South African Board of the Company, responsible merely for the handling of local details. The main Board sat in London under the Chairmanship of the Duke of Abercorn, with others such as the Duke of Fife and Albert (later Earl) Grey, who were considered by the Government 'safe men', and whose appointment and entrenched position constituted the principal security for the Company's good conduct. In practice, Rhodes at Kimberley had things pretty much his own way. He acted first and reported to London, if at all, afterwards. With his great political influence at the Cape, he could usually count on the support of the High Commissioner, Sir Henry Loch, and thus he could spike any guns that might be trained on him from the Colonial Office. There was, however, one serious weakness in his position. In so far as the territory north of the Zambezi was concerned, as also in all matters involving the boundaries of the Company's sphere with the colonies of foreign powers, the responsible department of State was the Foreign Office, which had no local representative corresponding to the High Commissioner, and which always dealt directly with the London Board. The London Directors, moreover, did not share Rhodes's insatiable territorial ambitions. They believed in his central thesis that the copper belt of the Katanga must be connected with the Witwatersrand by a reef of mineral wealth running north and south through Mashonaland and across the central Zambezi. They approved his plan for securing this territory by the enlistment of a force of pioneers who would be rewarded for their military services by substantial grants of land. They were prepared to support his further contention that such a colony, once settled in Mashonaland, must have an outlet to the sea through the Portuguese dominions on the east coast, thus saving the long haul through Bechuanaland and round the Transvaal from the south. But this did not imply to them, as it did to Rhodes, the squeezing out of the Portuguese along the whole eastern frontier of the chartered territory south of the Zambezi; to the north of it they were comparatively uninterested in the

acquisition by the Company even of Nyasaland and Barotseland, and totally indifferent to any wider enthusiasms for a
Cape to Cairo route.[1]

In May 1890, therefore, Rhodes was deeply concerned to
strengthen his representation with the Imperial Government
independently of his London directors. His handsome subscription to the Irish party at Westminster was paying an
immediate dividend in that his former Secretary, Rochfort
Maguire, was returning to sit in Parliament as a Parnellite
nominee. In Johnston he hoped to find a henchman within
the Foreign Office citadel who would forward his schemes
with all the blind devotion which he was accustomed to
receive from his friends and supporters.

It is unlikely that Johnston ever visualized himself as cast
for precisely such a rôle. Direct contact with Rhodes always
produced an effect upon him; but it is remarkable that the
overmastering personality which caused many stronger men
to bend and to admire provoked Johnston to imitation rather
than servility. In a curious way he regarded himself as
Rhodes's equal. His letters to Rhodes are tinged with a
megalomania which he did not often display. They show an
intense and revealing reaction to Rhodes, but it is not the
reaction of a creature. 'You are a greater man than I, as you
have immense resources at your command. I have only a pen
and a tongue. I can scream and write frantic articles, but you
move on with your armies and your gold with all the quick,
majestic, resistless advance of an elephant through brushwood.
I am content to carry my clamour and watch how you do it,
and perhaps carry my fussy little ways to other parts of the
continent where as yet there are no resistless British elephants.
We shall meet again some day. . . . I think we shall arrive at
the same goal, but you will get there first. But so long as the
British South Africa Company subserves the interest of the
British Empire, it may count on me for the same zealous,
disinterested support which I accord to all the factors in the
scheme of a universal British dominion.'[2]

There survives a telegram, dated May 2nd, 1890, from
Rhodes to his London Office reading 'Station named Abercorn
firmly established south end Tanganyika, another midway
between lakes. This highway must remain English. I will not
work for Germans.'[3] Otherwise there are no direct records of

---

[1] E.g. Cawston to Rhodes from St Moritz 3.ix.90, *Rhodes Papers*, Vol. 3A, No. 38.
[2] Johnston to Rhodes from London 13.x.90, *Rhodes Papers*, Vol. 3A, No. 52.
[3] Enclosed in Fife to Currie 28.v.90, *F.O.84.2082.*

these Kimberley talks. Rhodes was not only an infrequent and terse correspondent himself, but an uncertain preserver of incoming letters. A long memorandum addressed to him by Johnston from St Helena shortly after the meeting has most unfortunately perished. From oblique references in later documents, however, it seems clear enough that Johnston was prepared at this time to recommend that the whole British sphere north of the Zambezi, Nyasaland included, should be placed under the Company's Charter providing that the administration was committed to him as a servant of the Imperial Government. 'On points of detail,' he wrote to Rhodes three years later, 'I have often differed from you, and have by no means tamely surrendered my opinions, some of which I have been enabled to maintain to this day through your expressed policy of not quarrelling about details so long as the main object you had at heart was secured. That main object reduced to its simplest expression, I always understood between us, was nothing but the extension of the British Empire from the Cape to Cairo. To attain this end I little cared whether it was done in British Central Africa under the guise of a Chartered Company or under that of an Imperial Protectorate, so long as the country was made British and the work was entrusted to myself at any rate to initiate.'[1] It goes without saying that Johnston was prepared to use all his influence for the widest extension of this northern sphere against German claims in the north-east, Belgian claims in the north, and Portuguese claims in the north-west. But, immediately, Rhodes was even more deeply interested in the Anglo-Portuguese frontier to the south of the Zambezi; it is evident that he looked for Johnston's strongest support in this field, and that the first of many misunderstandings arose from what he regarded as Johnston's defection from his cause.

I cannot congratulate you on your work in England [he wrote three months after the Kimberley conference]. It is true you have got a C.B., but I trace your hand all through the Portuguese treaty. It is a disgraceful treaty and I will have nothing to do with it. You have given away the whole west, including half the Barotse just ceded to me, and the whole of Manicaland and Gazaland, and we have got nothing which we had not already got. I can only express my opinion that you ought to be thoroughly ashamed of your work, but in spite of your desertion I shall go on fighting, and I have not the slightest intention of giving way

[1] Johnston to Rhodes from Zomba 8.x.93, encl. in Johnston to Rosebery of the same date, *F.O.2.55.*

to the Portuguese. . . . I am now occupying Manica, and I do
not think even you and the Portuguese combined will turn me
out. The least I can ask you to do is to repair the mischief you
have done by getting the Portuguese treaty dropped.[1]

How unjustified were these suspicions appears clearly from
Johnston's correspondence during the same three months. He
travelled home from the Cape in close company with Rhodes's
intimate friend, Rochfort Maguire. A gigantic turtle, acquired
in Ascension and presented to Lady Salisbury on arrival,
secured him an invitation to join in its consumption at a
dinner at Arlington Street on June 11th. The Anglo-German
Agreement, which was to be signed on July 2nd, was just then
in the final stages of negotiation. The proposal to cede
Heligoland, which had been suddenly introduced by Salisbury
to the German Ambassador on May 13th, had worked wonders
at Berlin; it was now known that in exchange for it the Germans
were prepared to cede their enclave on the East African coast
at Witu, to recognize a British protectorate in Zanzibar and a
British sphere of influence in Uganda, and also to draw the
boundary between German East and British Central Africa to
the east of the Stevenson Road. At the dinner Salisbury gave
Johnston the welcome news that he could now ratify his
treaties on the Nyasa-Tanganyika plateau. He showed, however, no disposition to talk about the Portuguese, and steered
the conversation quickly on to West African affairs. At the
Foreign Office, so Johnston told Rhodes, he was 'consulted
to a certain extent about the Anglo-German Agreement, but
directly I began to find fault with it, Anderson and Currie
said it was too late to effect any change, and the only modifica-
tion I in any way brought about was to carry up the North
Nyasa boundary to the Songwe. And to obtain this we had to
give Germany Mafia Island off the mouth of the River Rufiji.
. . . I also proposed the exchange of Zanzibar (which I don't
think is of such immense importance to us as Mombasa) for
German South-West Africa, but the Germans scouted the
very idea.'[2]

Only when the German agreement was settled did Salisbury
switch his attention to the Portuguese. Johnston was asked
for a memorandum, and at the end of June submitted one
which so far reflected Rhodes's attitude to the problem that
it did him little credit in the eyes of his superiors. He reminded
Lord Salisbury that before going out to Mozambique the

[1] Rhodes to Johnston 22.ix.90, *Johnston Papers.*
[2] Johnston to Rhodes 13.x.90, *op. cit.*

previous year he had advocated a policy of conciliation and
concession to the Portuguese in East Africa. His subsequent
experience in Portuguese East Africa had led him to believe
that it was 'all over with any chance of Portugal voluntarily
assenting to an arrangement which shall be in accord with our
largely extended claims and interests in the countries lying to
the west of the East African seaboard'. The only alternative
was, 'to put it plainly, to help ourselves'. The substance of
his plea was that what is now Southern Rhodesia should have
a common frontier with Nyasaland along the stretch of the
Zambezi between Zumbo and Tete. 'The Zambezi railway'
he argued, with one of those flights of fancy to which he was
always prone, 'is making surprising progress. . . . It is possible
that in three or four years it may reach the Zambezi near
Tete, in which direction it is aiming. Do not let us therefore
allow the Portuguese to drive in a wedge of their obstructive
rule between our Shire Highlands and our Mashonaland.'
If, as he feared, Lord Salisbury had already admitted the
Portuguese position at Zumbo, let them be confined there to
a small circle twenty miles in diameter. 'The British South
Africa Company confidently expects to be established in
northern Mashonaland by next September. They then intend
to open up direct communications across the Zambezi with
the Lakes Company in the Shire. Their local forces will be
quite sufficient to tackle anything the Portuguese can bring
against them. It would then be unfair both to the Portuguese
and to the British pioneers if your Lordship allowed the former
to believe that you recognized their rule along the Zambezi
past Tete, except in the patch round Zumbo, where they
might eventually be bought out.'[1]

It is true that Rhodes, at the same time, was holding views
even more extreme. In a letter transmitted to the Foreign
Office by the Duke of Abercorn in the middle of July, which
evoked from Salisbury the comment 'They are quite hopeless',
Rhodes advocated that the Portuguese should be confined to
a coastal fringe ten miles deep, and suggested that it was not
impossible that they might be pushed right out of Africa.
'They are a bad race, and have had three hundred years on
the coast, and all they have done is to be a curse to any place
they have occupied. . . . It is quite possible that the mad
folly of the Portuguese may lead to a collision with us, ending
in our taking over Delagoa Bay to the Rovuma, but my whole
contention is that now Germany has been settled with, we

[1] Johnston to Salisbury from Queen Anne's Mansions 28.vi.90, *F.O.84.2052.*

can afford to show a bold front and not claim any further definition of boundaries.'[1]

Nevertheless, if Johnston's views were moderate in comparison, they were still extreme enough to secure his exclusion from all further consultation at the Foreign Office until the Anglo-Portuguese Agreement was in draft. Indeed, so he informed Rhodes, the first he knew of its existence was on taking up a copy of *The Times* in bed on the morning of July 21st. He called at the Foreign Office to protest, only to be told that he was being 'plus royaliste que le roi', in that the London Directors of the Company had seen and agreed to the terms of the treaty. He described the situation to Rhodes in one of his most brilliant feats of characterization. Cawston, the London Secretary of the Company, could think only about 'the Pungwe valley railway from Mashonaland to Sofala. *That* was all right, so the Agreement generally was very good. The Duke of Abercorn quite agreed with Cawston. The Duke of Fife's princess had had a miscarriage and he could not give any attention to African affairs. Albert Grey thought all was for the best in the best of all possible worlds, that Rhodes was a fine fellow and that there was a great future before South Africa. Beit did not think very well of the Agreement, but agreed with me it would be a comfort to get something settled and get to work at the real development of the country. I believe there were some other reasoning beings who were directors of the Company, but no one took any more account of them than we do of six of Christ's twelve apostles.' Realizing that he could not carry on such a one-sided battle, he had proposed two major modifications in the agreement, first that Portugal should undertake never to cede any East African territory to any power but Great Britain and, second, that she would grant the permanent lease of a landing-strip at the Chinde mouth of the Zambezi[2]; and having secured the acceptance of these two points, he undertook to use his influence to get Rhodes to accept the treaty. 'I have now done all I can for you,' he concluded, 'believing that in so doing I have served the cause of the Empire. I have got you Nyasa, Tanganyika and Mweru. I shall get you Garanganze (Katanga) and other things if you show some sign of caring for them. At the same time it is very

[1] Duke of Abercorn to Sir Philip Currie 16.vii.90, enclosing Rhodes to Abercorn from Cape Town 25.vi.90, *F.O.84.2086*.

[2] Johnston to Rhodes 13.x.90, *op. cit.*; cf. Johnston to Currie 21.vii.90, *F.O.84.2052*.

disheartening and puzzling when you don't answer any of
my letters and telegrams. I have not the least idea how far
you go with me.'[1]

Rhodes, however, had seemingly lost all interest in the
North, and was intent only on bludgeoning his way through
Manicaland to the sea at Beira. When the Portuguese Cortes
refused to ratify the treaty and the ministry resigned, he
cabled to the London Board saying he hoped the Foreign
Office would take the opportunity to drop the whole matter.
'I am sorry to say', wrote Salisbury on the communication,
'that Portugal is playing Rhodes's game.'[2] A few weeks later
the Duke of Fife formulated on Rhodes's behalf a thoroughly
cold-blooded attempt at blackmail. Lord Salisbury, he argued,
would appreciate that it was impossible to prevent the
migration of European South Africans into adjoining territories
where they believed a profit could be made. Portugal would
be powerless to oppose them and her authority would not
be recognized by English-speaking settlers. If, therefore, by
reason of any unfortunate treaty England's hands were tied,
the establishment of some new and independent Government
would seem inevitable. 'An insolent letter,' reads Salisbury's
minute, 'Simply acknowledge.'[3]

These then were the circumstances in which Rhodes's
accusations of desertion reached Johnston in London, and it
says much for his character that, without any protestations of
loyalty and without committing himself in any way to Rhodes's
side for the future, he yet replied with dignity and good temper.
Writing in red ink at the head of the paper 'Read this before
you chuck it into the wastepaper basket', he rehearsed all the
circumstances of his connexion with the Anglo-German and
Anglo-Portuguese Agreements. Then adjuring his correspondent to 'reflect a little over this, light a fresh pipe and go
on', he read him a little lecture in *Realpolitik*.

Say we want to annex Egypt. So and So and Somebody Else
have started a Sudan Company and maintain we can't get on
without annexing Egypt. We rather want to do so, not only
because we don't like to offend So and So, but because the
project tickles the Jingo spirit at home. However we hesitate. A
complete annexation may mean war with France, and all Europe
won't exactly approve. H'm. What shall we do? In its present
loosely-knit, unorganized condition the Empire would hardly
stand a war with France merely on account of the interests

[1] Johnston to Rhodes 25.vii.90, *Rhodes Papers*, Vol. 3A, No. 18.
[2] Weatherley to Currie 19.ix.90, enclosing telegrams from Rhodes, *F.O.84.2090*.
[3] Fife to Salisbury 7.xi.90, *F.O.84.2094*.

of the Sudan Company? No, well, let's try safe half-measures. Let's get Egypt to cede us all the country south of Wady Halfa and give us Suakin as a port? We do so. Europe says it's a reasonable solution. As a result we soon become emphatically masters of the Egyptian Sudan. By and by France gets involved in a war, or some other troubled water comes before us, from which we quietly fish out and annex Egypt. Having already got her Hinterland, nobody raises much objection. . . .

You seem to think [he concluded] that the making of the treaty lay in my hands. You forget that I am only a poor little Consul occasionally permitted through the amused tolerance of Lord Salisbury to make remarks and suggestions on African affairs. . . . Lord Salisbury would not come to any decision unless we had first tried to make terms with the Portuguese. . . . The Queen was partly at the back of this conciliatory policy. . . . You only think of Africa south of the Zambezi: I not only consider our interests throughout Africa, but our imperial interests throughout the world.[1]

As with the Portuguese treaty, so with plans for the administration of the sphere north of the Zambezi, the poor little Consul was prepared to show a mind of his own. Indeed in this field, and more especially in relation to Nyasaland, his attitude was, and remained, almost proprietory. If British Central Africa could be ruled to his own satisfaction under the aegis of the British South Africa Company, well and good; if not, then he was free to try and negotiate better terms with the Treasury, or else to seek a compromise between direct Imperial and Chartered Company government. A few weeks after his return to England in June 1890 he submitted to the London Board of the South Africa Company a scheme for the exploitation of the whole region by a Supreme Administrator with forty-two European assistants and 150 Indian troops. To begin with, the administrative department of six, and the troops with their five European officers were to be deployed along a single line of garrisoned stations stretching from the Shire Highlands to Lake Tanganyika. Within this administered strip there were to be a Chief Justice and clerk, a medical officer and two nurses, a director of public works, a mining engineer, two builders, two roadmakers and two horticulturalists. Trade was to be carried on under the direct control of the Administrator by twelve commercial agents and water communications were to be maintained by a

---

[1] Johnston to Rhodes 13.x.90, *op. cit.*

steamer flotilla with five European engineers. Beyond the 'Pale', four Residents—'more or less pioneering men'—were to make their headquarters at the courts of semi-independent, native chiefs and 'pave the way for the opening up of new countries'. The scheme was prepared in consultation with Sir George Goldie and was based upon the organization of the Royal Niger Company, but in Nyasaland, in contrast with the Muhammedan north of Nigeria, Johnston recommended that missionaries should be encouraged to the uttermost. 'As their immediate object is not profit, they can afford to reside at places till they become profitable. They strengthen our hold over the country, they spread the use of the English language, they induct the natives into the best kind of civilization and in fact each mission station is an essay in colonization. So far from being jeered at or reproved for marrying a white wife and taking her with him into the wilderness, the missionary should be encouraged to do so and to beget as many children as possible, because in this way each couple sows the spores of future colonies.' The suggested expenditure—£32,000 a year—would, he warned the Directors, take their breath away, but the system would in a short time pay for itself and in ten to twenty years would show a profit.[1] 'What I feel earnestly', he wrote in his accompanying letter to Cawston, 'is that the matter should soon be brought to a decisive issue; that you should make up your minds speedily as to your willingness and power to administer British Central Africa, and then apply to the Government for powers to do so.'[2]

Johnston soon began to realize, however, that not only was the British South Africa Company unwilling for the moment to spend more than the minimum necessary to maintain its claim to the sphere north of the Zambezi,[3] but also that the long-projected absorption of the African Lakes Company, which was the indispensable preliminary to the extension of the Charter to Nyasaland, had made but little real progress since Rhodes's visit to England in the summer of 1889. The directors of the Lakes Company had pursued a tortuous course,

[1] Johnston to British South Africa Co. 17.vii.90. Printed copies in *F.O.84.2052*.
[2] Johnston to Cawston 18.vii.90, *Cawston Papers*, Vol. II.
[3] On receipt of Johnston's scheme, Rhodes, it seems, cabled his London Office, offering to spend £25,000 a year on putting it into practice, provided that Nyasaland, was included in the Company's sphere. 'Lord Salisbury', says Johnston, 'was tempted, but the Foreign Office had already made half-promises to the Mission. Moreover the Company, when sounded, were not really sure that they *could* find £25,000 a year for a guaranteed term of years.' Johnston to Rhodes from Chinde 7.vi.93, *B.S.A.C. Papers*. See also a memorandum by Cawston dated 3.xi.90 in *Cawston Papers*, Vol. II.

including at one stage a parallel set of negotiations with Sir William Mackinnon and the Imperial British East Africa Company.[1] Foiled in this manœuvre by the Anglo-German settlement, and pressed by the large body of their shareholders who were also supporters of the two Scottish missions, they were now fighting for a form of merger with the South Africa Company which would still leave the effective control of Nyasaland affairs in the hands of a sub-committee of Glasgow shareholders. Though Johnston did not know it, the South Africa Company had conceded in principle this very important point. By an agreement between the two companies of April 29th, 1890, amalgamation was postponed until such time as it should be acceptable to the Lakes Company's shareholders. Meantime the South Africa Company would allow the Lakes Company £9,000 a year for maintaining law and order in Nyasaland. When the amalgamation was finally completed, control of the Chartered Company's policy in Nyasaland would be formally vested in a Glasgow Board which would be chosen from among the former shareholders of the Lakes Company.[2]

Johnston did not know the details, but his well-founded suspicions led him in the course of the summer of 1890 into spirited exchanges with the South Africa Company. For on one point his mind was made up. He would under no circumstances undertake to develop Nyasaland under the aegis of the Lakes Company. For Rhodes to step in where the Imperial Government was hesitating was one thing; but for Rhodes to delegate his responsibilities to 'a miserly, fanatical, uncultured set of Glasgow merchants', whose total assets in the region amounted to £30,000, and who for all their undeniable connexion as individuals with the splendid work of the Scottish missions had no very enviable reputation in government circles for straightforward dealing in their capacity as a commercial company, was to his mind insufferable. 'There must be no one-horse business,' he warned Cawston in July. 'The Glasgow board are not capable of administering British Central Africa.' In August he drew Cawston's attention to the

[1] See an interesting minute by Anderson dated 25.x.89 in *F.O.84.2005*: 'I asked him (William Ewing, Secretary of the Lakes Company) how the two companies were to join hands. He said, as far as he understood, each was to push into Tanganyika, one from the north, the other from the south, and so get behind the Germans.'

[2] Copies of the most important letters which passed between the two companies are enclosed in Ewing to Salisbury 14.iv.90, *F.O.84.2079*. A copy of the Memorandum of Agreement of 29.iv.90 is enclosed with a Memorandum by Anderson dated 1.xi.90 in *F.O.84.2094*.

activities of speculators who were already busy seeking concessions from Nyasaland chiefs with a view to blackmailing the
administering authority at a later date. 'Now are you going to
let Nyasaland slip through your hands? It looks like it. After all
our worry and trouble in making arrangements with Germany
and Portugal, we shall find nearly all the soil of Nyasaland
bought up by Sharrer and Bowler and others of that sort. And
this is mainly because you are content to leave the management
of these parts in the hands of the Glasgow people.' By October
he was positively threatening. 'Why don't you make haste and
swallow up, digest, deglute the African Lakes Company? . . .
As long as from scruples of over-kindly good nature or from
the dread of spending money you allow the A.L. Co. to maintain an independent existence you have no claim to be
consulted in Nyasaland matters. I judge the A.L. Co. utterly
unfitted to be entrusted with governing powers, so unless and
until the South Africa Company has followed it up, and has
sat in its place and calls to me from Nyasaland "Here I am
where once the A.L. Co. was," I shall devote my attention
wholly to seeing in what way this country can be rescued from
anarchy and its affairs controlled by the Imperial Government.'[1]

Johnston was not alone in his opinions. On November 1st,
1890, Rhodes's solicitor, Hawkesley, called at the Foreign
Office to discuss the extension of the Charter to the sphere
north of the Zambezi. He produced for the first time a copy
of the April agreement with the Lakes Company, and on
reading it through Sir Percy Anderson at once pointed out
that the £9,000 subsidy 'for administrative purposes' was
quite illegal, since the Lakes Company was an unchartered
trading association with no administrative rights or powers,
and that both British settlers and natives in Nyasaland had
persistently objected to their past attempts to exercise such
powers. The proper course, he said, would be for the British
South Africa Company to carry through the amalgamation
first, and apply for an extension of the Charter afterwards.
Hawkesley then remarked that if the alternative were Consular
Administration, he did not think the South Africa Company
would object. They would confine themselves to trade and
save the £9,000 a year. But Anderson was not susceptible to
the threat. He replied that Consular Administration would
not relieve the traders of the task of defending their stations,

---

[1] Johnston to Cawston 18.vii.90, 5.viii.90, 8.x.90 and 13.x.90, all in *Cawston
Papers*, Vol. II.

protecting their caravans and opening trade-roads, which might be considered some part of the objects for which the payment was to provide.[1] And with that Hawkesley withdrew.

What Consular Administration, on the scale on which the Imperial Government was prepared to provide it, would have implied, appears all too clearly from a desperate appeal which Johnston addressed to Lord Salisbury's Private Secretary, Eric Barrington, some six weeks later. His leave was running out, and since the question of amalgamation had got no further, he had been told to prepare to return and rule British Central Africa somehow with the assistance of one Vice-Consul.

A province of some 400,000 square miles [he wrote], about 840 miles from east to west and 560 miles from north to south, in South Central Africa has got to be kept in some kind of loose order by somebody. That is to say, more and more Englishmen—traders, miners, missionaries, sportsmen—are flocking in yearly. We can't keep them out, and we should be a disgustingly degenerate lot of Britons if we wished to, for we may well exult in the reckless spirit of adventure which prompts our countrymen (actuated by every variety of stimulus from the cold zeal of spreading Presbyterian principles to the greedy craving for gold) to settle in these new lands. Happy indeed would France and Germany, and Belgium and Portugal be if they had the like disposable quantity of raw colonizing material to spread over their African possessions. However, as I have said, somebody has got to keep order in this chaos of old-established savagery and new-born civilization; otherwise we shall have Arab wars and native wars, and white 'atrocities' and savage reprisals. Civil war among the savages must be checked, so that something like settled cultivation and the rearing of flocks and herds may begin. Arab aggression and the slave trade must be put a stop to. Unscrupulous men must be restrained from defrauding or maltreating the natives, and the natives must not be allowed to whip a missionary naked because they think the Germans or Portuguese are taking too strong a hand with a section of their tribe 100 miles distant. . . . At first I believed that Her Majesty's Government could subscribe no funds towards the administration of this country, so I, as a *pis aller*, looked to the British South Africa Company to take it up. They were, as you know, willing enough to do so, but it was not thought advisable to extend their Charter beyond the Zambezi as there were conflicting interests in Nyasaland. . . . With the policy of a direct Imperial administration of Nyasaland I have always been in agreement. . . . Still the numerous British

[1] Memorandum by H. P. Anderson 1.xi.90, *F.O.84.2094*.

settlers and the neighbouring governments of Germany, Belgium and Portugal will look to us to keep up some degree of order within our sphere of influence, and this I fear cannot be adequately done by two Imperial officers . . . two lone men, giving out a *vox et praeterea nihil*. At the same time we cannot, no we cannot permit the African Lakes Company to maintain a police force and settle its own quarrels. If we do, the Commissioner will become a miserable, powerless cypher, and we may have at any time another Arab war to settle, which began in a dispute about land, or the price of ivory. The same principle applies to the general idea, which I think was entertained at one time, that the question of security for life and property should be met by each resident there being allowed to take up arms to defend himself. This would never do. There are many unscrupulous Europeans already in that country who would regard as acts of self-defence measures which we should certainly qualify as deeds of offence.

His most urgent needs, he concluded, were one government horticulturist and botanist for thorough examination of useful products, salary and allowances £500; one practical engineer for surveying and road-making, £500; pay, passage-money, uniforms, arms, food, of fifty Sikh policemen with white officer, £5,000; purchase of sites for government buildings, donations to native chiefs, cost of barracks, porters, horses, donkeys, £1,000; total £7,000—'outside the cost of myself and Vice-Consul, which I believe has already been provided for. Could not the Treasury be asked for a grant of £10,000 whilst you were about it?'[1]

It was in all conscience a modest enough demand. Yet according to the principles of public finance then prevailing he might as well have asked for the moon. Anderson admitted that he had stated his case well and fairly, but told him firmly that there was no chance of inducing the Treasury 'to get a grant for incidental expenditure in Nyasaland'.[2] Nevertheless Johnston's letter had been a warning which Anderson could not ignore, and two days after receiving it he introduced a fresh approach into his dealings with the Company. 'I have been thinking over our yesterday's conversation,' he wrote to Cawston, 'and am disposed to think that the question of administration is a serious obstacle to your pecuniary arrangements with the Lakes Company, as, put it how you may, you are giving £9,000 a year for the maintenance of law and order which cannot be so used by the recipient. On the other hand it might be employed to useful purpose by the real administrat-

[1] Johnston to Barrington 15.xiii.90, *F.O.84.2052.*
[2] Anderson to Johnston 22.xii.90, *F.O.84.2050.*

ing body, the Government, who might not find it easy to get a grant from the House of Commons. If you should be disposed to follow this train of thought and could see your way to working it into a proposal, I think that Lord Salisbury should have the chance of considering it; what his view might be I, of course, cannot at present say.'[1]

The idea was one which had already occurred to the British South Africa Company's directors as a possible way out of their difficulties with the Glasgow men.[2] Early in November they had asked Johnston whether he would be free, as an imperial officer, to accept an appointment as the Company's administrator north of the Zambezi, with control over the expenditure of the £9,000 subsidy. Johnston had expressed his personal willingness, providing that the Foreign Office would allow him to be at one and the same time 'a sort of Consul-General for South East Africa and (temporarily) an Administrator for the British South Africa Company'. Lord Salisbury, however, had not reacted favourably to the plan. The Company's Charter did not yet extend to the north of the Zambezi: for political reasons it could not be so extended until the difficulty with the Lakes Company had been resolved. Yet in the absence of Charter powers neither Johnston nor anyone else could legally act as the Company's administrator.[3] Reluctantly, therefore, Abercorn and his colleagues on the London board had fallen back upon the idea of a partition, by which Nyasaland proper, the sphere of the Glasgow company, should be annexed and administered directly by the Imperial Government, while the South Africa Company merely sought an extension of its Charter in the unclaimed regions to the west. Under such an arrangement there need be no further

---

[1] Anderson to Cawston 17.xii.90, *Cawston Papers*, Vol. II.

[2] Albert Grey to Cawston 29.xi.90, *ibid*. 'The difficulties of the situation in Nyasaland because of Scotch jealousies and cussedness, make it in my opinion most desirable that we should support Bruce's proposal to facilitate the Govt taking over Nyasaland by paying over to the Govt the £9,000 a year we now pay the Lakes. If the Govt would consent, this course apparently gets us out of all our difficulties. It rids us of all necessity of amalgamating with the Lakes. It reduces the Lakes to nothing bigger than a small trading concern, and it enables us to look forward to the profitable inheritance of Trans-Zambezia without the incubus of a Scotch Director. For if in the course of time it should appear that the Govt were in need of a larger annual subsidy than £9,000 in order to enable justice to be done in Nyasaland, it would always be open to us to make the offer that we would find the monies required if we were allowed to add Nyasaland to Charter Land, and this, I think is the answer to your objection that if the Govt assumes the administration of Nyasaland, one of the principal parts of our great idea when we first embarked on the Charter would be destroyed.'

[3] Cawston to Johnston 3.xi.90; Johnston to Cawston 3.xi.90, *Cawston Papers*, Vol. II.

delay in extending the Charter, the £9,000 subsidy could be withdrawn from the Lakes Company and offered directly to the Imperial Government as an inducement for it to undertake the responsibility for Nyasaland, and Johnston as the Imperial Commissioner in Nyasaland could also become at least in name the Company's administrator within the chartered sphere. Strange as it may seem that it should be in the interests of a commercial company to carve a piece out of its intended sphere and then subsidize the British Government to administer it, it was nevertheless in the circumstances a strictly business proposition. The British South Africa Company would lose Nyasaland, but in exchange it would gain an immediate title to the rest of northern Zambezia. It would subsidize Johnston in Nyasaland, but it would gain a settled administration on its eastern border which could be extended in name, if not in practice, to its own sphere until such time as it was in a financial position to assume the reins itself.[1]

No doubt the Company's views were already privately known to Anderson when he addressed his exploratory letter to Cawston on December 17th. Certainly he knew that Rhodes was due to pay a short visit to London at the end of January 1891 in order to discuss the final version of the Anglo-Portuguese Convention. There was thus the opportunity for a quick deal on the extension of the Charter which would settle Johnston's position one way or the other before he returned to his post. How far the negotiations progressed before Rhodes's arrival, the records do not show. Probably the whole transaction was sufficiently remarkable to make both sides hesitant to commit their views to paper. Nevertheless, these few slight clues, gleaned mostly from the papers of George Cawston, serve to illuminate what would otherwise appear an inexplicably sudden turn in Johnston's affairs, which sent him back to Nyasaland no longer, as he had feared, a mere voice, but a ruler with force at his command.

Johnston's third set of meetings with Rhodes occurred early in February 1891. It is understandable that they were not at first too friendly. They had not corresponded since their angry exchange over the first Anglo-Portuguese convention in September. Moreover, even though the idea of partition had emanated from the British South Africa Company, the necessity for it was a bitter disappointment to Rhodes. 'If I am not assuming too high a rôle,' Johnston later wrote of this period, 'I may say that I acted as go-between between yourself

<hr />

[1] Abercorn to Cawston 30.xi.90, *Cawston Papers*, Vol. II.

and the Foreign Office. The Foreign Office may have been somewhat cautious in their views, and you may have been rather extreme in yours. I know for myself that at that time I held this opinion privately, that it would be better either to turn the whole thing into a Protectorate, or place the whole of it under the Company's Charter. But a compromise had to be arrived at. In attempting to suggest a basis for this compromise I was again subjected to a good deal of intemperate language on your part, and once or twice accused of "treachery", which meant, I suppose, that I had failed to act according to your opinion as an uncompromising partisan of the British South Africa Company.'[1]

Nevertheless, Rhodes understood hard bargaining, and during a three-hour session on either February 8th or 9th, the main lines of an agreement were hammered out. A boundary was drawn following the western watershed of Lake Nyasa from the Anglo-Portuguese frontier in the south to the tenth parallel of south latitude in the north; from this point the boundary was to turn to the north-west and run parallel to the Stevenson Road as far as the Lofu River, whence it would follow the Tanganyika watershed to the Congo frontier. All the British territory to the east of this boundary was to be a Protectorate administered directly by the Foreign Office; all British territory to the west of it was to be brought under the South Africa Company's Charter and distinguished from the Protectorate as the Company's 'sphere of influence'. For a period of ten years, however, the supreme political control even within the Company's sphere was to be vested in the Commissioner for the Protectorate, who was to supervise the actions of all the Company's servants in matters relating to peace and order, and who was to have the absolute disposal of all armed forces and police. For the latter an annual credit of at least £10,000 was to be provided by the Company, which was to be spent by the Commissioner at his own discretion. If he chose to concentrate the whole force within the borders of the Protectorate he was free to do so. The Company would also delegate to the Commissioner any rights it might have acquired by its investments and subsidies to make use of the steamers and the stocks of arms and ammunition of the African Lakes Company.[2]

From this agreement between Johnston and Rhodes, reported in a private letter from Johnston to the Permanent

---

[1] Johnston to Rhodes 8.x.93, *op. cit.*
[2] Johnston to Currie 9.ii.91, *F.O.84.2114.*

Under-Secretary of State, Sir Philip Currie, on February 9th, the formal arrangements between the Foreign Office and the Company followed with astonishing speed. It is significant that the only amendment imposed by the Foreign Office was the reduction of the size of the Protectorate by the exclusion from it, for technical reasons arising from the Berlin Act, of the strip connecting Lake Nyasa and Lake Tanganyika.[1] The only significant amendment proposed by the Company was that the term of the agreement should be reduced from ten years to three; this was accepted by the Foreign Office, subject to the right of the Secretary of State to prolong it at his own discretion for a further two years from January 1st, 1894.[2] On February 13th the Company signified its willingness to appoint Johnston as Administrator within its sphere.[3] On the 14th Johnston received from the Foreign Office his formal appointment as 'Commissioner and Consul-General for the territories under British influence to the north of the Zambezi' in addition to his existing post as Consul at Mozambique. His salary was raised from £800 to £1,200 a year, his allowances from £200 to £600.[4] Minor negotiations between the Foreign Office and the Company continued through March, and the extension of the Charter was finally executed by an exchange of letters dated April 2nd and 29th.[5]

And so, after nearly a year of diplomacy and negotiation in London, Johnston prepared for another spell of active work in Africa. Of how he had spent his leisure during that year neither his own autobiography nor his brother's *Life and Letters* afford the slightest evidence. His private papers are hardly more illuminating. There is a long statement by a well-known palmist, Emma Richardson, who read his hand on the journey from South Africa to England in May 1890, which Johnston himself thought of sufficient interest to copy verbatim and to keep it for the rest of his life. Viewed as a whole, it is a commonplace document, full of silly platitudes and scarcely concealed inconsistencies. Only here and there does a passage suggest that occult powers may have been fortified by the shrewd and curious observation of a fellow-passenger. 'You are methodical and tidy, but intensely im-

[1] Memo by H. P. Anderson 12.ii.91, *F.O.84.2156.*
[2] F.O. to B.S.A.C. 11.ii.91, *F.O.84.2156*; Memo by Currie of 26.ii.91, *F.O.84.2157*; F.O. to B.S.A.C. 3.iii.91 and B.S.A.C. to F.O. 5.iii.91, *F.O.84.2158.*
[3] B.S.A.C. to F.O. 13.ii.91, *F.O.84.2156.*
[4] F.O. to Johnston 14.ii.91, *F.O.84.2118.*
[5] F.O. to B.S.A.C. 2.iv.91, *F.O.84.2161.*

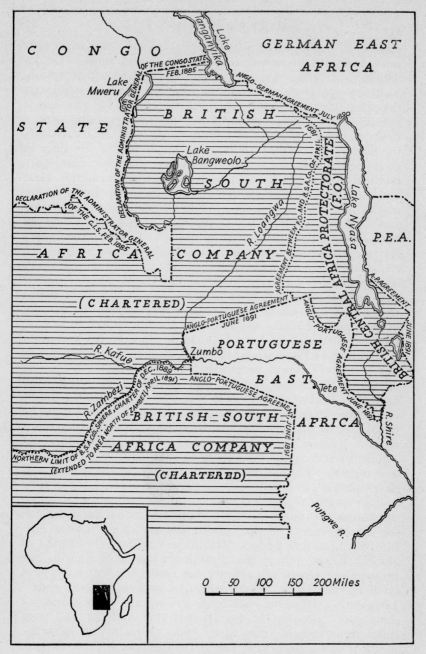

8. BRITISH CENTRAL AFRICA:
Protectorate and Charter Sphere.

patient of restraint; imaginative by nature, but with your fancy somewhat controlled by a keen and critical faculty which to a certain extent guards you against self-deception. You are not truthful by nature—on the contrary distinctly deceitful—but the critical faculty above alluded to, and a certain striving after impartiality, together perhaps with a desire to be well thought of and not frowned at, have decidedly modified this tendency of late—as I can see by the lines in your right hand—so that I should say you were now more truthful and exact in your statements than formerly. Your untruthfulness also does not spring from an intention to maliciously deceive, but rather from an exuberant imagination and an optimistic tendency to represent things not as they are but as they should be in your opinion. . . .' After the palmist's statement we have only an invitation from Lady Salisbury, a charming letter from Dorothy Tennant in reply to Johnston's congratulations on her engagement to H. M. Stanley, and a curiously assorted collection of acknowledgments of presentation copies of a life of Livingstone written during the autumn of 1890 and the spring of 1891, from the Queen and Salisbury, General Roberts and Lord Knutsford, the Colonial Secretary.

It would be fascinating to speculate on the reactions of any one of these eminent persons to what must certainly be one of the strangest biographies ever published in the English language. Johnston, needless to say, was an unfeigned admirer of Dr Livingstone, but characteristically the highest tribute he could pay to his memory was to bedeck the Christian saint with a halo of evolutionary theory. Two remarkable, but utterly irrelevant, chapters set forth first the 'Natural History' and then the 'Human History' of Central Africa. 'Progress in development', we learn, 'is by no means uniform, whether it be in man and the things of men or in the mute, stupid, blundering operations of Nature. . . . So perhaps a hundred years sufficed for the emergence of the Hamite savages of the Lower Nile into the historical period, into the astonishing civilization of ancient Egypt; just as the same short course of time in this unsurpassed nineteenth century has raised the higher types of civilized man into beings with the power of demi-gods.'[1] Livingstone, it seems, belonged by nature to the order of demi-gods. 'Brought up in different surroundings, and with different influences reacting on him, or rather no influence at all, it seems likely that David Livingstone, with his intense

[1] H. H. Johnston: *Livingstone and the Exploration of Central Africa*, London 1891, pp. 25-8.

MOZAMBIQUE: AN OLD PORTUGUESE HOUSE

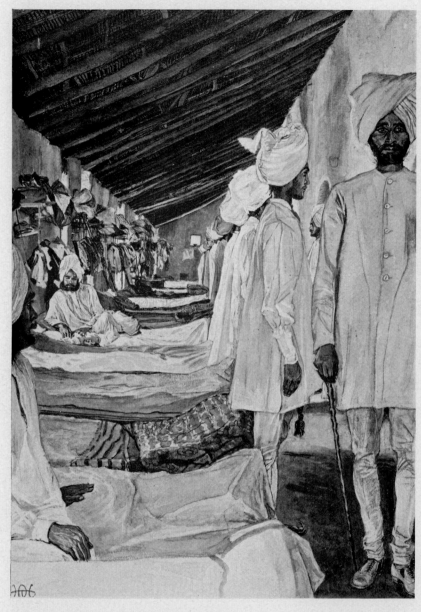

ZOMBA: THE SIKHS IN THEIR QUARTERS

love of nature . . . and his tendency to reason and theorize from his observations might have become a second Darwin; but it would seem as though the pressure brought to bear on him by his father's teaching and preaching succeeded in giving his mind just a sufficient religious warp to make him a missionary of religion instead of an emissary of science.'[1]

Still, even as a missionary of religion, Livingstone proved himself a good evolutionist, for he saw plainly that it would take several generations to implant 'real sound civilization and Christianity in the negro race'. And, however far the precepts of the New Testament might fall short of those of pure Science, Johnston was in no doubt that they represented a distinct advance on those of primitive animism. No doubt the observance of the Sabbath had been elevated among the modern Bechuana into a disagreeable dogma, surpassing in importance any other detail of religion. 'But this is counter-balanced by the more organized industry which is displayed on the six working days of the week, and by the contrast which the harmless, decent excesses in singing, praying and preaching their emotional Christianity offer to the beastly, degrading orgies of drunkenness and debauchery which formerly accompanied such feeble worship of ghosts and demons, such superstitious rain-making and witch-finding as they practised in their old heathen days. . . . Now they put up prayers for rain just like the Archbishop of Canterbury.'[2]

Johnston was still the *enfant terrible* of the Foreign Office, and not only in his metaphysical lucubrations. In discussions of African politics in the public press and at social gatherings it was still his wont to show less than the usual degree of reticence expected of officials; and not infrequently these indiscretions rebounded upon him from embarrassing heights. There survives, for example an autograph letter from King Leopold to Lord Salisbury, dated July 1890, which might well have proved detrimental to the career of a lesser man. 'Sir John Kirk,' wrote His Majesty, 'aura sans doute mis de ma part sous les yeux de votre Seigneurie une carte du *Graphic* qui enlève à l'Etat du Congo la majeure partie du Katanga. On dit cette carte l'oeuvre de M. H. H. Johnston, Consul britannique à Mozambique. J'ai prié Lord Vivian de signaler à votre Seigneurie que Monsieur Johnston aurait avoué dernièrement à Londres à une personne qui me l'a répété, qu'à la fin de 1889 il aurait fait des traités avec plusieurs chefs de l'Itawa (côte sud-ouest du lac Tanganyika), traités

---

[1] *Ibid.*, pp. 58-9.   [2] *Ibid.*, pp. 93-4.

politiques en vue d'enlever des territoires à l'Etat Independent, jugeant, a-t-il ajouté, le moment bon pour prendre le plus possible à l'Etat du Congo. . . . Je redoute des complications et je suis obligé de prendre des mesures conservataires.' There was no denying the accuracy of the King's information, and it took all the drafting experience of Sir Percy Anderson to frame a soothing reply.[1]

Nevertheless, when Leopold visited England in the spring of 1891, he was still on the warpath. 'He spoke to me at length about Johnston, to whom he ascribes infinite enormities in the way of map-making and article-writing,' Salisbury scribbled. 'I did my best to reassure him.'[2] King Leopold, it seems, would have spared no effort to prevent Johnston's appointment to the charge of the vast territories on his southern boundary. In interviews with Sir Philip Currie and Sir Percy Anderson he returned to the attack. But Salisbury, though he was prepared to give the King advance assurances that no infringements of Congo Free State territories would be countenanced in London, stuck by his man. Unlike some of the permanent officials he never faltered in his recognition of the fact that Johnston, by virtue of his peculiar relationship with Rhodes, occupied a special position which entitled him to be ridden with a looser rein than other servants of the Crown. He had allowed Rhodes

---

[1] King Leopold to Lord Salisbury from Ostende 12.vii.90; Salisbury to Leopold 18.vii.90, both in *F.O.84.2086*.

[2] Memorandum by H. P. Anderson with minute by Salisbury 21.iii.91, *F.O.84.2159*. In the previous August Johnston had addressed a passionate appeal to Salisbury on the subject of King Leopold's Katanga claims: 'I have reason to believe that the King of the Belgians wants to chase us out of an important piece of territory which we need to complete the new province of British Central Africa. This territory is Garanganze. It is ruled by an important chief called Msiri, who is decidedly friendly to the British and by messengers sent to me last January on Lake Nyasa . . . has expressed himself ready to place his territories under H.M.'s protection. Encouraged by this friendliness, I sent him to Mr Alfred Sharpe to conclude a treaty. Mr Sharpe will probably have reached his dominions about last June or July. . . . Garanganze, called by the Swahili Arabs Katanga, is the richest country in minerals (gold and copper) in all Central Africa. It is fairly healthy and has a fertile soil. Its people are peaceful and industrious. The King of the Belgians has no right to it. On the official maps of the C.F.S. territory issued by him after the Berlin Congress he does not even include it in his dominions. Of late through the indulgent carelessness of British mapmakers it has been allotted to the C.F.S. on the map, and now the King . . . is about to despatch a strong expedition there under M. Delcommune . . . to endeavour to collar Garanganze either by cajolery or force. . . . I don't see why the King of the Belgians should be treated any more generously or sentimentally than France, Germany or Portugal. From a Belgian point of view he is an admirable patriot, who has by many a hook and crook, by many a wile and intrigue, by much expenditure of his own and not a little of that subscribed by the rich English people whom he bamboozled, created a fine African Empire for little Belgium. But why his enterprise should be viewed by *us* . . . with indulgence . . . I cannot conceive.' Johnston to Salisbury 25.viii.90, *Salisbury Papers*.

to finance a part of Johnston's Nyasa-Tanganyika expedition and the associated expeditions of Alfred Sharpe to the Mweru region, expeditions in which the disputed treaties had been made. He was now allowing the South Africa Company to pay for the police force which was to defend both the new Protectorate and the Company's sphere. In Johnston he had found a man, as he believed, ready and able for the difficult task of serving two masters. He was prepared to disavow his actions, but not to throw him overboard or even unduly to limit his freedom.

Johnston's position was indeed one both of extraordinary responsibility and of extraordinary licence. He had to govern a territory the size of England and France together on an income which to many of his contemporaries would have seemed barely sufficient for the upkeep of an English country house. He could afford at the start just a hundred and fifty armed men, seventy Sikhs and eighty Zanzibaris. If this tiny force should be overpowered, as it easily might be in a single ambush or in an encounter with one Arab slave-trading caravan, he could expect no support either from the Treasury or from British garrisons overseas. The British Government was committed financially only to two consular salaries. On the other hand his revenue, if meagre, was almost entirely under his own personal control. The South Africa Company had agreed to ask no questions about expenditure up to £10,000 a year. There was no imperial grant-in-aid, therefore he was free from Treasury leading-strings. The police force was recruited by him on his own conditions and terms of service. It was commanded by officers who were given long periods of unpaid leave from their regiments in order to engage in the service of his administration. If he wished to engage civil officials, administrators, customs officers, accountants, engineers, surveyors, he was free to do so providing that he could pay them. If he could raise a local revenue from taxation he could spend the proceeds on additional staff. Within the limits imposed by Parliament and Treasury, the Foreign Office would help him all it could. It asked the Government of India to recruit his Sikhs. It persuaded the War Office to arm them free of charge. The Admiralty, which had already placed two gunboats on the Zambezi, sent a ship to meet him at Zanzibar in May, to convey him, with his recruits and with 100 tons of ammunition, stores and building material, first to Mozambique and then to Chinde. There the two gunboats were awaiting him with the African Lakes Company's steamer, the *James*

Stevenson, and a fleet of canoes in tow. On July 14th, 1891, perhaps the strangest expedition that ever set out to administer a British possession weighed anchor and steamed off up the Zambezi. 'You must be careful not to exceed your estimate,' wrote Rhodes from Cape Town. 'You seem to have a frightful menagerie with you. They will cost something to keep, between whites, Indians, Zanzibaris and Somalis. P.S. When you next write, please grumble less.'[1]

[1] Rhodes to Johnston from Cape Town, undated, but about July 1891, *Johnston Papers*.

Chapter 7

KING JOHNSTON OVER THE ZAMBEZI

DESPITE the weight of his new responsibilities, Johnston arrived in Central Africa in a characteristically ebullient mood. He had adorned his sailor's straw hat with a white, yellow and black band to symbolize the co-operation between the European, Asian and African races upon which his régime was to be built. He had also provided himself with ample supplies of stiff, foolscap paper edged with the same daring tricolor, upon which he began without delay to report his actions and to convey his thoughts with a buoyant enthusiasm and an unprecedented freedom of expression to the Foreign Office, to Rhodes and to the London directorate of the South Africa Company. His verbal output was always immense. In later years it was to be sustained by the habit of dictation, carried out at high speed, often while painting a picture, and always while sucking innumerable sweets. 'You thought I was going to reply to the Treasury despatch by a minute, did you?' he wrote to a correspondent in 1896. 'Ha! Ha! Why, I never reply to anything in less than two volumes octavo.'[1] In 1891 he was still writing all his despatches by hand, but even so he had frequently to express compassion for his readers. 'I hope', he wrote to the London Secretary, 'the British South Africa Company has given you an office chair of ivory, ebony and gold, and three assistant secretaries to enable you to cope with . . . H. H. J.'[2]

His first care was naturally for his communications with the sea and the outside world. He had spent the first fortnight of July at the mouth of the Zambezi, marking out on the Chinde bar a site for the British concession, provided for in the Anglo-Portuguese Convention, at which passengers and freight could be trans-shipped from ocean steamers to river vessels without the tedious assistance of Portuguese officialdom. Johnston's persuasive pen could invest even a barren sand-bank on the shores of the Indian Ocean with a certain interest. He sent home immaculate drawings, illustrating his arrangements for

[1] Johnston to Farnall 9.ix.96, *F.O.2.107.*
[2] Johnston to Weatherley from Zomba 16.xii.91, *B.S.A.C. Papers.*

a coaling-station, a consular house, a post-office and bonded warehouse, a shipping agency, a hotel, a club, a lawn-tennis court, a botanical garden and paddocks for horses and cattle.[1] He had already been urging Mackinnon to apply for a subsidy for a monthly steamship service to Chinde, he now suggested that Mackinnon might be interested in the formation of a Zambezi Flotilla Company. 'I hope you will get your railway out of the stingy Imperial Parliament,' he concluded. 'The Mombasa-Victoria Nyanza railway and the Nyasa-Shire-Zambezi waterway should . . . effectually kill caravans passing overland from Tanganyika and Nyasa.'[2]

Communications also formed the main theme of his early correspondence with the South Africa Company. The local representatives of the African Lakes Company had denied all knowledge of the arrangement with Rhodes whereby they were to provide him with free transport for his administrative stores. They charged him exorbitant prices and they kept him waiting month upon month for delivery. Government transport apart, Johnston believed with some reason that their management was inefficient and that their general trading activities amounted to but a tithe of what was possible. In this fact he was directly concerned, both because the development of legitimate trade was necessary to compete with the slave trade, and because legitimate trade, unlike the slave caravans, would flow in and out through his custom houses and so contribute to his revenue. He therefore used every effort to get the South Africa Company to start a trading department, if need be in competition with that of Glasgow. He offered to contribute out of his small subsidy to the cost of steamers. He even offered in his enthusiasm to direct the trading operations himself.

There is nothing for it. You must make up your minds to trust me, for say one year, with the supreme direction of all things in British Central Africa. I must be able to say to one of your trading agents 'build a store here', 'Give six and threepence a pound for ivory', 'You are selling that cloth too dear', 'You must send an indent for twelve gross of brass pans', 'Supply Crawshay instantly with one dozen child's tops, 26 wax dolls, 3,000 yards of cotton, 30 packets of fancy stationery, five bales of imitation cashmere shawls, and send them off to Lake Mweru tomorrow'. I know as much about your African trade as your Moirs and your Ewings. It is twelve years ago to-day since I landed in Tunis and I have studied Africa ever since. Besides,

---

[1] Johnston to Salisbury from Chinde 28.vi.91, *F.O.84.2114.*
[2] Johnston to Mackinnon from Chinde 7.vii.91, *Mackinnon Papers.*

3. FACSIMILE LETTER FROM JOHNSTON TO SIR WILLIAM MACKINNON
From the original letter in the *Mackinnon Papers*, School of Oriental and African Studies, London.

for the first year or two in my great task of bringing five hundred thousand square miles of Central Africa under British control, the shop is only second to the sword. But it is a shop which must be wisely and judiciously managed, and its shopboys must not be allowed to baulk my efforts by cheating an African chief over damaged jam or pretending that half a crown and a rupee are just the same value. In plain words the African Lakes Company is loathed by everyone in the land. Its policy has been idiotic because its silly little frauds have not even profited it. However enough on this score. If you start your Trading Department in the way I have sketched out, send out, with public or private instructions to work under my direction in all things, two good men of the accountant type, and for a change, just for a change, send Englishmen.[1]

To the Foreign Office Johnston had already depicted a different facet of the same problem. In what Lister described as 'a horribly rhetorical despatch' written two days after landing in Central Africa he had described the broad strategy he intended to pursue. The greatest cause of unrest both in the Protectorate and in the Company's sphere was the trade—not only the simple trade in slaves, but also the import trade in arms and powder and the export trade in ivory, in both of which slaves were used as porters—flowing along a multitude of east-west caravan-routes between the Indian Ocean and the far interior. If the British Central Africa Administration could put up an effective barrier to this trade by maintaining a single chain of armed posts running north and south along its eastern frontier, then not only would the slave trade be checked but the largest part of the problem of law and order would be solved. The legitimate commerce in ivory and other products would be forced into the Nyasa-Shire-Zambezi waterway, where mechanical transport could largely relieve the necessity for human porterage; the revenue would benefit from the customs duties; the up-country tribes would be brought into direct contact with European trading organizations, and the way would be prepared for the extension of civilized government.

Needless to say, a force of seventy men could not by itself maintain such a barrier. It might perhaps hold the relatively open highland country between the limits of gunboat navigation on the lower Shire and the south end of Lake Nyasa. But that would at best only divert the more southerly traffic to swell the already established routes crossing the lake itself. On

[1] Johnston to Weatherley from Zomba 16.xii.91, *B.S.A.C. Papers*.

the Lake Johnston had only one uncertain ally in the Arab Jumbe of Kotakota, with whom he had made a treaty during his expedition of 1889. Elsewhere and particularly towards the southern end of the Lake, both shores were held by Yao chiefs, like Mponda and Makanjira, long connected with the slave trade, ensconced in a hundred well-concealed hide-outs, possessed of sailing-dhows and scores of large canoes, with a mobility and organization which Johnston with his tiny land forces could not hope to overcome. His proposal was, therefore, that the Admiralty should be persuaded to constitute an Inner Africa Flotilla by adding two gunboats, one for Nyasa and one for Tanganyika, to the two already operating on the Zambezi and Lower Shire. 'If you prevent the Arab and Black Portuguese slave-raiders from crossing the Central African Lakes and rivers and the necks of land between by your water and land police you simply cut off all communication between the slave purchasers and their markets or hunting-grounds. This is an infinitely better and more effective way of stopping the Slave Trade than chasing Arab slave dhows in the Indian Ocean. . . . It is here in the centre of this Dark Continent only, that one realizes to the full the indignation with which slave-raiding and trading inspired the soul of Livingstone. Here where one sees hundreds of square miles without a human inhabitant, without a vestige of cultivation other than the grass-grown furrows of a former plantation; here, where a three months' raid by Arabs or Black Portuguese will wipe out a whole tribe and reduce a fertile, fruitful tract of country to the old, hopeless African wilderness.'

Moreover, as Johnston remarked with his irrepressible gusto, his plan was one which needed no appeal to the Treasury —'a Department without bowels of compassion or a throb of imperial feeling'. It could be carried through Parliament on the Slave Trade vote, or even by reducing 'the extravagant bounties by which we induce our naval forces on the East Coast of Africa to bestir themselves and chase slave dhows. . . . I am told that in good slave-catching seasons this perquisite has added £2,000 to the Admiral's yearly income. I am not aware, however, that wretched, blood-stained, ravaged, famine-stricken Central Africa has profited one jot or tittle by this enrichment of an already well-paid official. In fact the more Central Africa is deprived of its peoples, the more profitable to our navy on the East Coast of Africa does slave-catching become.'

Lord Salisbury was impressed by the argument. Perhaps he

G*

was not even above enjoying the rhetoric. 'An expurgated edition of this despatch might be usefully laid before Parliament,' he wrote, 'but it would be wiser to leave out his strictures against the various Departments of the Government.'[1] An expurgated edition was sent also to the Admiralty for their Lordships' observations.[2] It received no reply. Johnston was to get his gunboats, but only in 1893, after his arguments had been reinforced by disaster. Meantime the communications which reached England in large batches, but at long intervals, suggested that Johnston was successfully and happily established in his dominion, and that he would perhaps after all survive without the assistance of the Royal Navy. He painted a blissful picture of his bachelor domesticity at Zomba, where the Residency estate was being reconstructed and embellished by his official horticulturalist, Alexander Whyte, an already elderly gentleman who had spent most of his life as a planter in Ceylon, but who was to remain with Johnston throughout his term in Nyasaland and to follow him in 1899 to Uganda. 'You could not have a lovelier place to live in: magnificent scenery, fertile soil, cool climate, a mountain torrent tumbling through the grounds, hanging forests, mighty grey crags, green lawns, sleeping cattle, and Whyte's kitchen gardens, plantations and wheatfields.' He told the South Africa Company that if they sent commercial agents they must be 'spruce, temperate, clean and pleasant-mannered, struggling with me to keep up a higher tone of society in this embryo colony by dressing for dinner in nice, white dinner jackets and behaving like quiet, low-voiced gentlemen'.[3] Yet to the missionaries, traders and coffee-planters who walked the forty miles from Blantyre to do their business with him, the impression cannot have been entirely one of stuffy Victorian conventionality. The Residency had been enlarged with outbuildings, forming a square for defence in time of trouble; and these back premises were occupied, not altogether silently or even self-containedly, by 'the pets'—baboons, wild pig, serval cats, and even a young leopard which 'though perfectly good-tempered was apt to be a little rough, especially with guests'. Besides the two large aviaries, from which some fifteen hundred presentations were made at different times to the Natural History Museum, the gardens were patrolled by gorgeous crested cranes, and a particularly tame guinea-hen watched by the Commissioner's

---

[1] Johnston to Salisbury from Chiromo 18.vii.91, *F.O.84.2114.*
[2] F.O. to Admiralty 11.ix.91, *F.O.84.2174.*
[3] Johnston to Weatherley 16.xii.91, *op. cit.*

chair while he worked, accompanied him on his walks and chattered noisily at his feet while he inspected the troops.[1]

For two years administration was practically confined to a narrow strip of country on each side of the Shire from the Portuguese frontier to the Lake. The main body of the sepoys was stationed with the commandant, Cecil Maguire, at Zomba, ready at all times to sally forth in lightning attacks on any band of Yao marauders who ventured to trouble the settled area. The remaining members of the government service were few in number and widely spaced. A subaltern seconded from the Royal Engineers, B. L. Sclater—a relation of Johnston's old patron Philip Sclater, the Secretary of the London Zoo—worked with three English N.C.O.s and a small Zanzibari labour force to realign and make carriageable the vital, strategic road connecting the Lower and the Upper Shire. Sharpe, the Vice-Consul and Deputy Commissioner, had his official residence at Blantyre, but was frequently away on long tours in the north, serving on boundary commissions, treaty-making and settling urgent disputes. The routine administration of the Blantyre district, the court and police work, the issuing of trading and other licences, the registration and verification of land claims, the forwarding of administration stores and mails, was performed by John Buchanan, a former lay member of the Church of Scotland mission, now a coffee-planter on his own account, who had however virtually laid aside his private business to serve the embryo state for a pittance of £350 a year. Down-river, at the Lower Shire ports of Chiromo and Port Herald, Johnston employed two former servants of the African Lakes Company as general administrators, postmasters and collectors of customs. On the Lake and beyond it there was no attempt to govern, but two more ex-employees of the Lakes Company, Nicoll and Kydd, performed duties of a consular nature; while far away to the north-west, on the shores of Lake Mweru, a former white hunter, Richard Crawshay, was enlisted to open a small station known as Rhodesia, the primary purpose of which was to maintain the claims of the South Africa Company against possible incursions from the Congo State.[2]

In the formal letter of instructions following his appointment Johnston had been charged with four duties, which proved in practice neither as simple nor as distinct the one

[1] Johnston: *Story*, pp. 292-3. See Plates 10 and 11, facing pp. 224 and 225.
[2] Cf. Johnston to Salisbury 5.xii.91, *F.O.84.2114*.

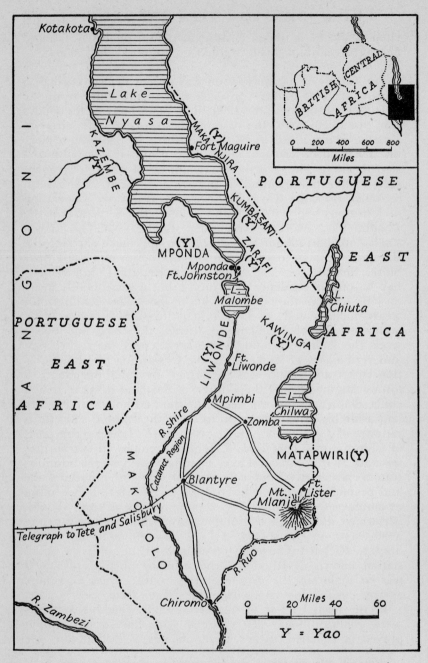

9. THE SHIRE HIGHLANDS AND LAKE NYASA

from the other as they had no doubt appeared to the mind of the drafting official seated at his desk in the Foreign Office. He was 'to consolidate the protectorate of Her Majesty over the native chiefs; to advise these chiefs on their external relations with each other and with foreigners, not interfering unduly with their internal administration; to secure peace and order; and by every legitimate means . . . to check the slave trade.'[1] Needless to say, the Whitehall idea of a collection of self-contained tribes, neatly organized under easily identifiable hierarchies of chiefs, was as far as possible from the realities of the situation in Central Africa. Within the area of the Protectorate the social organization of the indigenous peoples —Chewa and related tribes in the south, Tonga and Tumbuka in the north—had during the course of the nineteenth century become increasingly overlaid by that of immigrant, conquering groups. The whole strip of territory to the west of the Shire valley and right up the western watershed of the Lake had fallen under the dominion of the Ngoni, a warlike group of Zulu race, whose leaders had swept up from the south in a great migration of rapine and conquest during the third, fourth and fifth decades of the century and were now settled as the overlords of the indigenous Chewa in three or four loose principalities stretching along the high pasture-lands separating the Protectorate from the Company's sphere. East of the Shire and all round the south end of the Lake, Yao from Portuguese East Africa formed a similarly intrusive element. In their homelands around the sources of the Rovuma and Lujenda rivers the Yao had long been associated as middlemen with the Arab and Swahili slave-traders of Ibo and Kilwa. Their hunting-grounds had always been among the weaker, less organized and worse-armed peoples of the lake shores and the Shire valley; and as the search for ivory had spread to the west, Yao war-lords with their escorts had moved down from the hills and built towns in the slave country, whose people they now dominated in semi-feudal fashion. Yao state warred with Yao state, each seeking to enslave the subjects of the other, each competing with the other for control of the caravan-routes to the west. In the already devastated Shire Highlands refugee groups of the indigenous Manganja had settled round the stations of the Church of Scotland mission and the African Lakes Company. Further south again in the lower Shire valley similar groups had consolidated themselves round the Makololo followers of Livingstone who had settled there in the 'sixties.

[1] F.O. to Johnston 24.iii.91, *F.O.84.2113*.

But north of the Highlands, between Zomba and the Lake, and athwart the main line of steamer communications on the upper river, the Yao states continued their predatory activities unchecked.

This then was the situation with which Johnston had to deal in the spirit of his instructions from the Foreign Office. The Makololo, who had appealed for British protection against the Portuguese, and the Manganja groups of the Highlands, presented no problem. A series of simple agreements negotiated by Buchanan between December 1891 and February 1892 provided for the cession of all sovereign rights and for the acceptance of such laws and regulations as might from time to time be imposed by the Queen's representative.[1] The Ngoni in the western hills could for the time being be ignored. In all his dealings with them Johnston emphasized that so long as they ruled themselves and their subjects in peace and refrained from molesting others he would not interfere in their affairs. The Yao, however, were a more urgent and more difficult problem. It is significant that Johnston, though he missed no opportunity of claiming in his despatches that he had no quarrel with the people of the country and that he was dealing only with a minority of immigrant ruffians and slave-traders, was nevertheless anxious to preserve the Yao chieftaincies throughout the northern half of the Shire Province. No doubt it was because they provided him with a ready-made chain of command, a manageable number of local government units in place of the plethora of village heads with whom the administration would have to deal if the Yao were driven out or demoted. He hoped to incorporate them formally in the Protectorate by a series of agreements by which they would cede their sovereign rights to the Queen, forswear the slave trade, and agree to collect from their subjects taxes sufficient for the maintenance of an armed garrison in their midst. He realized clearly, however, that no such solution was possible without an initial demonstration of force.

> Wherever it was possible by means of peaceable and friendly negotiations to induce a Chieftain to renounce the slave trade, I have used such means in preference to a recourse to force; and in this way a considerable number of the lesser Potentates of Nyasaland have been brought to agree to give up adjusting their internecine quarrels by resort to arms, to cease selling their subjects into slavery, and to close their territories to the passage of slaves and slave-traders. Their agreement was, however, in

[1] Examples in Johnston to Salisbury 7.iii.92, *F.O.84.2197.*

most cases a sullen one, and their eyes were turned instinctively to the nearest 'big' Chief to see in what way he was dealt with. If he too accepted this distasteful gospel of peace and good will towards men, they were then ready enough to adhere to their own compacts . . . but if the powerful Potentate—the champion man of war in the district—held aloof from the new Protectorate, massed his forces in the strongholds, and preserved a watchful or menacing attitude towards the Administration . . . then the little Chieftains began to relax in their good behaviour of a month's or a week's duration, once more to capture and sell their neighbour's subjects, or to smuggle through their by-paths a coast-caravan with its troop of slaves bound for Kilwa, Ibo or Quilimane.[1]

Accordingly, on September 30th, 1891, Johnston set out from Zomba on his first military expedition. Now, as on all foreseeably serious occasions in Central Africa, he accompanied the troops himself, marching, and when need be fighting, under a white umbrella which was never lowered. He took with him Maguire, sixty-eight sepoys with their Parsee doctor Sorabji Boyce, ten Zanzibaris and some fifty Makua mercenaries from Mozambique. The African Lakes Company provided two steel barges for supply work on the Upper Shire, and their steamer, the *Domira*, for transport on the Lake. His destination was the country of Makanjira, the most powerful of the Nyasaland Yao, whose main base was on the south-east side of the Lake, but who had been engaged for some years in conquering the country of a fellow Yao, Mpemba, on the opposite shore. First, however, it was necessary to come to terms with Mponda, whose town on the right bank of the Shire near its exit from the Lake dominated the main line of land communication between the eastern and the western shores. Marching up the left bank of the Shire from Mpimbi, the port of Zomba, the police force encamped opposite Mponda's town on October 7th, and immediately set about the construction of Fort Johnston. 'In six days,' he wrote, 'our position was admirably defended by a fort, designed by Captain Maguire, and constructed by the Indian soldiers, the Zanzibaris and Makuas. This place, to which they were good enough to attach my name, was a circular redoubt with a diameter inside of 90 feet. The centre was occupied by a low circular house used as a provision store and cooking place. Round this focus our tents were pitched; and on the side of the fort nearest the river was a magazine dug partly underground and protected by a strong platform of earth heaped over a stout wooden framework. On this platform,

---

[1] Johnston to Salisbury 24.xi.91, *F.O.84.2114.*

which was about eight feet above the level of the fort, a sentry stationed night and day could look over an immense stretch of perfectly flat plain to the verge of Lake Nyasa. The fort was defended by a rampart of bamboos, inclined outward at a slight angle, and supporting about three feet of sand thrown up against it from the outside. Below the sand rampart was a counterscarp or level ledge, and below this again a deep ditch four feet broad with perpendicular sides. Across the ditch, there was a glacis of sand.[1]

While Mponda hesitated between peace and war, Maguire sallied out to rescue two Swahili messengers who had been imprisoned by the Makandanji clan, the Yao barons of the east bank; and during his absence Johnston, who had remained in the fort with twenty-four men, was horrified to observe a force of two thousand men ferrying across the Shire from Mponda's. They were not however coming to attack him, but only to take advantage of the Makandanjis' preoccupation to conduct a slave-raid into their country. The male subjects of the Makandanji were away from their villages fighting Maguire, so Mponda was seizing the opportunity to carry off the women and children. With his puny force Johnston had to remain a passive witness of these proceedings, but when Maguire returned he made them the subject of an ultimatum. Mponda was given three days in which to return the slaves, and when he failed to do so incendiary shells were fired across the river from the fort. The following morning the whole garrison, with Johnston and Maguire, crossed the river and after two or three sharp tussles with the defenders burnt the whole town and destroyed the stockades. In subsequent operations 270 slaves were freed, and on October 24th Mponda came over to the fort and signed a treaty of peace. The Makandanji chiefs, Zarafi, Chindamba and Mkata, followed suit on November 7th, and three others, Liwonde, Chikusi and Chingwalu, were added on the 13th and 14th. All these treaties ceded full sovereign rights, with powers of jurisdiction over all foreigners; they declared the slave trade to be abolished; and all but the first established the right of the Protectorate Administration to levy a tax of six shillings a hut. In the case of Mponda, the tax was 'to be computed according to the resources of the country'. To Mponda and the Makandanji modest subsidies were guaranteed out of the proceeds of taxation.

Meanwhile, after Mponda's surrender, Johnston had carried out a daring but inconclusive naval raid upon Makanjira.

[1] See Plate 12, facing p. 256.

Approaching his principal town in the *Domira* on October 29th, he had been met by hostile demonstrations and prolonged rifle-fire. So, while Maguire shelled the town from the steamer with a seven-pounder mountain-gun, Johnston led a landing party which encountered heavy resistance but, having been relieved by Maguire, stayed ashore long enough to burn a dhow and capture two cannon. The following day they landed again, Maguire with the Indians, Johnston with the Zanzibaris and Makua. They burned two more dhows and destroyed most of the town. Johnston's party located Makanjira's house and carried off six cases of letters written in Swahili and Arabic. But Makanjira himself, with most of his people, had already made good his escape to the high hills behind the coastal plain. To pursue him with fifty men was unthinkable.[1] And so, after a brief attempt to find Makanjira's two remaining dhows, the expedition returned to Fort Johnston and thence, leaving a Sikh sergeant with twenty sepoys and fifty Makua as garrison, to Zomba. The Upper Shire Yao had been pacified, and would remain so at the cost of a continuing commitment at Fort Johnston. Makanjira had suffered a setback, but would in the absence of further measures return to dominate the southern half of the Lake.

At Zomba Johnston devoted himself during the last two months of 1891 to questions of customs and revenue, and to the ever-mounting problem of European settlers and their land claims. He also found himself deeply involved in almost every detail of his policy with the gentlemen of the Church of Scotland mission at Blantyre. It is probable that in nearly every part of the colonial world there has at some time been friction between the secular officials of government, who in the absence of democratic control have regarded their powers as absolute and unquestionable, and missionaries, who in the absence of the same controls have assumed that they held a divine mandate to check the exercise of arbitrary power, to uphold the weak and to represent the interests of the in-articulate. In Nyasaland there were many special reasons for such friction. The Church of Scotland Mission had been established in the country since 1876. It had survived without the protection of a European government for fifteen years. Indeed, having gathered nearly all its converts from the refugees from the Yao raids, who lived in 'mission villages', worked on the mission estates and looked to the missionaries

[1] Johnston to Salisbury 24.xi.91, 10.xii.91, *F.O.84.2114.*

for the administration of internal justice and the provision of external defence, it had become in some sense a government in itself. The Scottish missionaries had learned the habit of command, and it is understandable that they did not find it easy to surrender it overnight in favour of an upstart Administration directed by a notorious and outspoken unbeliever, who was known to have been prepared two years previously to abandon the Shire Highlands to the Portuguese, and who was now suspected of wishing to sell the whole region into bondage under the British South Africa Company. No doubt Johnston would have been wiser to have spent more time at Blantyre and to have eliminated all possibility of misunderstanding as to the nature of his commission and the purposes of his policy.

Still, neither the history of the mission nor Johnston's own lack of caution can be held to excuse the mean and pharisaical persecution, set in motion within a few weeks of his arrival and relentlessly pursued by men who had travelled far from their homes to heal the sick, redeem the captive and preach Christ to the heathen. As an emissary to their Committee in Edinburgh they were content to employ one Eugene Scharrer a naturalized German, twice bankrupted in his earlier commercial dealings in Zanzibar, who arrived in London in November 1891 to push preposterous claims to land in the Shire valley, and whose importunities on his own account did small credit to his professions of philanthropy.[1] Nevertheless, after consultations with Scharrer, the Church of Scotland Foreign Missions Committee gravely informed Lord Salisbury that Johnston had instituted 'what may be called a reign of terror', in which every kind of fault had been immediately punished by war. They requested that no direct taxation should be levied from the natives for at least three years, and they concluded with a catalogue of odious insinuations against the private lives of every single member of the Administration except Johnston, Maguire and Sclater.[2] A month or two later a deputation called at the Foreign Office, was reminded by Lord Salisbury that the slave trade could not be put down with rose water, and retreated, as Lister described it, 'with their tails between their legs'.

Still, the correspondence from Edinburgh continued to flow in, the enclosures from Blantyre showing an astonishing degree of frustrated imperiousness, ignorance and misunderstanding. 'I cannot see how Johnston has authority to force the people and Chiefs to pay taxes,' reads one typical example from the

---

[1] Emmanuel and Simmonds to F.O., 24.xi.91 and 16.xii.91, with enclosures, F.O.84.2179 and 2181.   [2] Dr McMurtrie to Salisbury 24.iii.92, F.O.84.2245.

Reverend W. A. Scott. 'Paid servant of a Company which has no Charter for this part of Africa, and Commissioner at the same time.' 'Is the native to pay taxes, or is he not?' inquired Mr Hetherwick of his Mission Committee. 'Kindly find from the Government and let us know the answer. The native comes to us to ask what he is to do. What answer are we to give? The demand is most unjust and fated to do much harm. Are we to advise Native to comply with it?' Or again, 'Johnston's forces raided on Chiradzulu, looting Mitoche's village, burning houses, forcing taxes. Question Government. Has Johnston such power as Commissioner or as Rhodes's agent? Wire reply. Another village and grain burned because one man refused summons to Court. Injustice unbearable.' 'What then is the outcome?' demanded Mr Scott. 'Just what any single British citizen has a right to demand for himself and his fellow-citizens, viz. (1) that he shall not be taxed in the interest of any private Company; (2) that if any Company has administrative powers granted to it, the rights of others in the country shall be safeguarded by an independent Commissioner who has no interest in that Company; (3) that Government officials shall have no trade connection (e.g. Johnston, Commissioner from Her Majesty's Government and Rhodes's paid servant at the same time. Buchanan, planter, Native Magistrate, and tax collector, all in one. Johnston lifts ivory and taxes on behalf of the British South Africa Company, and Buchanan cuts down native crops to force the natives to hoe his coffee.'[1] In Blantyre itself the mission newspaper *Life and Work* published monthly attacks, as full of wilful distortion and unfounded hearsay as were the assertions that the Commissioner was receiving a private salary from Rhodes and looting ivory in order to swell the Company's profits.

In the face of such self-convicting records of arrogance and hysteria it is tempting to conclude that all the right was on Johnston's side. Certainly his patient investigation and rebuttal of most of the charges against his subordinates lends weight to this view. He did not confine himself, like Lister, to the comment that 'a duty on missionaries would be useful—Scotch ones to pay double, with an extra tax for Presbyterians in any form'[2]; and even in counter-attack his shafts went nearer the mark than those of his opponents.

The only persons who object to the collection of the native tax are the Blantyre missionaries and Mr Scharrer. In both

[1] McMurtrie to Salisbury 29.viii.92, with enclosures, *F.O.84.2257.*
[2] Lister to Johnston (private), cited in Alex Johnston, p. 141.

cases the objection arises from the fact that they consider the natives dwelling on their estates to be in some measure their feudal retainers—allowed to dwell on the soil, cultivate a proportion of it, but required to work for the proprietor when called upon to do so. Becoming gradually accustomed to look upon these people as their serfs, they resent any direct dealings between them and the Government, and fear that if the native workers are called upon to pay taxes, they may inquire why they are made, in the first place, to hoe the plantations and carry the loads of the white man who claims to have bought the tribal lands on which they dwell. On the demeanour of the Blantyre missionaries, their attempts to carry on a sort of administration of justice of their own, and to set themselves up as superior to the local Administration, I may yet have to address your Lordship. A case which occurred the other day at Blantyre, where seventeen mission-boys headed by the organist and armed with sticks, went out to arrest a man charged with some offence, and to bring him up before the Head of the Mission for examination, ended in broken heads and a riot which brought all parties concerned into the Consular Court. I have however written privately to the Heads of the Mission at home in the hope that a little conciliatory advice, and even pleading on my part may rectify the hostile attitude which has been taken up by this Mission against the Administration in Nyasaland. . . . I am extremely anxious to be on friendly terms with all the foreign settlers here, and as the missionaries make admirable colonists, I desire to help them and conciliate them to the best of my ability.[1]

And yet, if their attitude had been more responsible and more constructive, there is little doubt that the Blantyre missionaries could have pointed out and helped in the solution of some real injustice in the operation of the new régime. The surviving evidence is too slight to permit of any certain judgment, but it is difficult to resist the conclusion that Johnston's system of taxation must have borne hardly upon the native inhabitants of the settled area round Blantyre, who were alone within the effective reach of the tax-collector. Elsewhere in the Shire province it seems that the tax was in practice a very moderate tribute levied in ivory and foodstuffs on the chiefs in annual commutation of the nominal poll-tax. Outside the Shire province no taxes at all were levied and it was therefore idle in Johnston to argue that he had received no complaints from the other missions working in the country. Again, there is little doubt that the practice of sending small expeditions of Zanzibari and Makua soldiery to punish highway robberies

---

[1] Johnston to Salisbury 10.iii.92, *F.O.84.2197.*

and similar misdemeanours by the burning of huts and the confiscation of grain and livestock must have involved considerable injustice to individuals. Such injustices were of course almost inevitable where a foreign government was still engaged in securing the basic recognition of its subjects, and where there was not, and could not be, any regular machinery for the detection and prosecution of crime. Nevertheless, the Blantyre mission, if it had been out to help and not to hinder, could have mitigated many of these wrongs in the areas where it was closely in touch with the people. Instead, the missionaries failed to realize that the rough justice, which prevailed all over Africa during the early years of the European occupation, was a consequence of too little force and not of too much. They spent their energies in seeking to curb the powers of an unwilling tyrant who would paradoxically have been less tyrannical in proportion as he had been more powerful. If their co-operation in a sensible fiscal policy had aided him to escape from his penury, and so from his impotence, they could even have helped to free him from his dependence on the South Africa Company which was the greatest cause of their distrust.

Indeed, before the year was out a disaster on Lake Nyasa had demonstrated all too realistically the limits of Johnston's power. Information having reached Zomba early in December that Makanjira was preparing an expedition against Fort Johnston, Maguire was sent down with such reinforcements as could be spared. While there he received a letter from Kazembe, a Yao ally of the Administration on the western side of the Lake, offering to guide him to the hiding-place of Makanjira's two remaining dhows, some ten miles north of the town which had been destroyed in October. Maguire chartered the *Domira* and set out with thirty sepoys. The weather was rough and the approach to the dhows was through a tortuous reed-fringed channel. Maguire landed his men in a steel barge, but met with a hot fire from prepared positions in the reeds. He reached the dhows and destroyed them, but on returning to the beach found the barge torn from its moorings and dashed to pieces by heavy waves. While a smaller boat was being launched from the *Domira*, he lost three sepoys by rifle-fire, and in swimming out to the steamer he was himself shot dead by a bullet in the neck. The *Domira* had meanwhile grounded, and remained so for six awful days, during which the crew and the surviving troops struggled to refloat her under continuous fire from the shore. On the third day the defenders proposed a truce in exchange for sixty bales of cloth, and MacEwan, the chief engineer, and Boyce, the Parsee doctor, went ashore with six unarmed followers to try and recover the bodies of Maguire and the three sepoys. They were lured out of sight and murdered by Makanjira's command.

The news reached Johnston at Zomba on Christmas Eve. Maguire had become his close and valued friend, and this was the promised day of his return. He had spent it writing an immense despatch on the Yao campaigns of the autumn, and between the paragraphs he had wandered out repeatedly on to the balcony of his study on the upper floor of the Residency to scan the road from the Shire valley where it came into view winding round the mountain side. At last towards evening he sighted a lonely runner. Suspecting the worst, he rushed out to intercept him lest panic should spread among the garrison. On hearing the man's report he made immediate arrangements to start for Blantyre, and he walked the forty miles through the night with a bare hour's rest half-way. He sent runners down the Shire with telegrams for London and Calcutta, and an urgent entreaty to Captain Keane of the Zambezi flotilla. He broke the news to the European community, which had gathered from outlying parts for the feast. He asked for volunteer officers to lead the troops, and made emergency arrangements for supplies. He then set out for Fort Johnston to take command of the garrison himself.[1]

The immediate danger was not so much from Makanjira as from the Yao of the upper Shire, who might be inspired by the events on the Lake to make a united onslaught on the Fort. It was essential to show activity, to consolidate the friendly, to deter the waverers. The garrison Johnston found in good heart, anxious only to renew the attack on Makanjira and to revenge the lives of their commander and comrades. That, however, could not be contemplated. Johnston was clear in his mind that he could take no further action on the Lake until he was supported with an armed steamer. Till then all efforts must be concentrated on holding the Shire province. Mponda, it was gratifying to find, had remained loyal to his treaty. He had sent three hundred men to assist in the defence of the Fort, and he had kept the Indian garrison plentifully supplied with food. Likewise from the south-western shores of the Lake, which were now threatened with a renewal of Makanjira's transpontine attacks, Jumbe and Kazembe had sent in tributes of ivory and produce. It was among the Yao states to the east

[1] H. H. Johnston: *British Central Africa*, London 1897, p. 105; *Story*, pp. 298-9.

and south-east of the Fort that Makanjira's victory had had its
deepest effect, and it was against these, headed by Zarafi,
Msamara, Mkata and Likoro, that Johnston directed during
January and February a series of small campaigns. His proceedings were cautious, and were limited to destroying a
number of villages in the Shire plain, the inhabitants of which
had been interfering with his water transport. He did not
attempt to pursue the fugitives or contact the main forces in
their hill fastnesses further to the east.[1] Unfortunately his
prudence was not imitated by his subordinates when he
returned to Zomba in the middle of February. Less than a
fortnight after his departure King and Watson at the Fort
received an offer of help from Chikusi, the Ngoni chief to the
west of the river, and forthwith embarked upon a major
expedition against Zarafi. On February 24th they walked into
a trap in Zarafi's main village and only narrowly escaped
total annihilation. As it was, six sepoys and three Zanzibaris
were killed, King was very severely wounded, and the seven-
pounder mountain-gun, the Administration's sole piece of
artillery, had to be abandoned in the bush.[2]

The situation, as he confessed to Lord Salisbury, was not a
happy one. From the Lakes Company's agents, as also from
Jumbe of Kotakota, he was receiving plain warnings that the
Arabs at the north end of the Lake were piling up arms and
ammunition, the possession of which would make the suppression of their activities in the slave trade yearly more difficult to
carry out.[3] And yet in his preliminary and still inconclusive
efforts in the south he had already lost Maguire and eighteen
of his seventy-one sepoys, ten killed and eight severely wounded
or incapacitated by sickness. The Government of India would
hardly be enthusiastic in replacing them. He had further been
responsible for the damaging of the *Domira* and the death of
her chief engineer. He could scarcely count upon the Lakes
Company's assistance in any more warlike operations. Even
on the civil side his predicament was severe. Sharpe and
Nicoll had been on leave in England since his own arrival
in the country and would not be back until the summer.
Buchanan, the mainstay of his administration in the Highlands,
had broken down in health and was about to return to Scotland. Communications on the lower Shire and Zambezi were
erratic. He had been without mails for two months, and had

[1] Johnston to Salisbury from Zomba 16.ii.92, *F.O.84.2197.*
[2] Johnston to Salisbury 25.ii.92, *ibid.*
[3] Johnston to Salisbury 20.ii.90, *ibid.*

had to despatch Sclater to the coast to recruit more European assistants and to hasten the passage of supplies. And in these exacting circumstances he was having to deal with intricate land questions, in which settlers threatened him with appeals and legal proceedings if he failed to certify their frequently outrageous claims. He had single-handed to 'keep the Consular and Administration accounts, try cases in the Consular Court, administer dead men's property, and conduct a huge correspondence, local and foreign; and every now and then perform fatiguing and anxious journeys of forty, fifty or sixty miles on foot to set matters right where they ought never to have gone wrong.'[1]

It was the nadir of his fortunes, and at this most critical moment the South Africa Company did nothing to help him. With Rhodes, in default of replies to his earlier letters, he had ceased to correspond. The London office of the Company, advised by Kirk, who in his retirement had grown quite the cautious business man, had been busy ever since the news of Maguire's death in disclaiming responsibility for Johnston's 'war policy'. They were as a matter of fact in a curious dilemma, for, as Kirk pointed out, the dual nature of Johnston's appointment would be subject to additional strains the moment the Government and the Treasury were involved in expenditure to prosecute war against the slave trade inland. 'I think the sooner you have some understanding with the F.O. the better, as to any overdrafts H. H. J. may make on his allowance. . . . If the Treasury pays they may expect you to have a back seat.'[2] Nevertheless, the risk of Treasury openhandedness was taken, and in March the Company simply informed the Foreign Office that it would not hold itself liable for any expenditure by Johnston in excess of the guaranteed £10,000.[3]

From the Imperial Government Johnston received more sympathetic treatment. Salisbury was as unwilling as ever to go to Parliament for new money, but he was now prepared to use the whole weight of his influence, as Prime Minister as well as Foreign Secretary, to secure that Johnston should have whatever could be supplied in services or kind from other departments and from existing Votes. A reluctant Admiralty was bullied into ordering two gunboats for the Lake, manning

[1] Johnston to Salisbury 25.ii.92, *F.O.84.2197*.
[2] Kirk to Cawston 14.i.92, 17.i.92, 8.ii.92, *Cawston Papers*, Vol. IV.
[3] B.S.A.C. to F.O. 25.iii.92, *F.O.84.2245*.

them with blue-jackets, and even, to its great indignation, paying to the Central Africa Administration the considerable cost of their overland transport from the Lower to the Upper Shire.[1] A more urbane but also more dilatory War Office was persuaded to make available guns and shells, rifles and bullets, uniforms, tents and other military equipment, though it flatly refused to arrange for their transport.[2] The India Office was successfully pressed to allow the recruitment of more Sikhs and the secondment of Indian Army officers, though Johnston was forced after a long tussle to accept responsibility for family and disablement pensions.[3] Even the stern and supercilious Treasury was driven, protesting the unprecedented irregularity of the various proceedings, into making one or two small grants for unforeseen contingencies.[4]

However, all these measures, valuable as they were, took time to achieve, and still more time before their effects could be felt thousands of miles away in Nyasaland. The gunboats were completed by July 1892 and delivered at the Chinde mouth in October, but it took until the following summer to bring them up the Shire, to carry them in sections round the rapids, to reassemble and launch them on the Lake. Captain C. E. Johnson arrived from India to take command of the police force in June 1892, bringing with him replacements for the Sikh casualties; but it was not until April 1893, when the survivors of the original seventy-one were almost due for repatriation, that Lt. Edwards was able to bring over the big reinforcement of a hundred new men.

Meantime Johnston had to keep the flag flying by his own efforts, and to build up the civil side of his administration to a stage of self-support in which it would be possible to spend the whole of the South Africa Company's subsidy on the augmented police force. To do this he had to gamble heavily on the taxable capacity of his infant colony. During the first nine months of his rule his only revenue from customs had been an export duty of a shilling a pound on ivory. From April 1892 he was permitted, by the international ratification of an amendment to the Berlin Act, to impose an *ad valorem* duty of five per cent on imports. He had in addition his poll-tax agreements

[1] Salisbury to Johnston (teleg.) 7.v.92, *F.O.84.2198*; Admiralty to F.O. 12.vii.92, *F.O.84.2253*; A to F.O. 19.viii.92, *F.O.84.2257*; F.O. to A. 20.ix.92, *F.O.84.2259*; A. to F.O. 14.x.92, *F.O.84.2261*; F.O. to Treasury 24.x.92, *F.O. 84.2262*.

[2] F.O. to W.O. 11.viii.92, *F.O.84.2256*; W.O. to F.O. 14.x.92, *F.O.84.2261*.

[3] F.O. to I.O. 22.viii.92, *F.O.84.2257*; I.O. to F.O. 9.viii.92, *F.O.84.2256*; F.O. to Johnston 12.viii.92, *F.O.84.2196*; F.O. to I.O. 29.xii.92, *F.O.84.2266*.

[4] E.g. Treasury to F.O. 29.xi.92, *F.O.84.2264*.

with the native chiefs of the Shire province. But without a
larger cadre of officials revenue, however legal, could not in
practice be collected. 'Collectors', if they could cover the cost
of their own salaries by their activities as tax-gatherers, might
have time over to devote to the administration of justice and
the supervision of public works. But with so little force behind
them they might fail to cover their expenses. Taxation in the
early days of a colonial administration represented a nice
calculation, different for every district, of the ability of the
inhabitants to pay and of their very real powers of resistance.
Any one of Johnston's Collectors might in a tactless moment
precipitate a conflict with their highly armed and unpoliced
subjects which would involve the government in costly reprisals. And then he would have an overdraft. He must have
spent many a midnight hour pondering on the consequences of
an overdraft. How long would the Company let it run before
they stopped supplies? And what would happen then? Would
the Treasury come to his rescue? Or would he be held personally
liable, would he be bankrupted, recalled in disgrace, forced to
dismiss people who had left other employment and in some
cases travelled far to serve him?

Still, the risk had to be taken. At the height of the crisis
caused by Maguire's death he sent Sclater down to the coast
to seek recruits. An Accountant was among the first to come
up—an ex-purser from the Union Steamship line. Others
came as Collectors. One was an experienced customs man.
Two more were qualified surveyors. And at last there came
from England a Private Secretary, J. F. Cunningham, later
Secretary to the Administration, who with the Accountant
made the nucleus of a headquarters staff.[1]   In September
1892 Johnston informed the Foreign Office that he was employing twenty-seven Europeans in eleven administrative and
fiscal districts. His custom-houses at Chiromo and Fort
Johnston were taking £300 a month, while another £200 a
month was coming from native taxation—'nominally six
shillings a head per adult male, really not more at present
than a shilling a head, since we take payment in produce more
than in money, and do not press for the full tax'. The total
revenue he estimated at £6,000 a year, his pay-roll, apart
from the police, at £5,500.[2]

Both figures proved in the event to be optimistic. Yet the
conclusion is irresistible that, so far as the Shire province was

[1] H. H. Johnston: *British Central Africa*, pp. 107-8, 117.
[2] Johnston to Salisbury from Chiromo 6.ix.92, *F.O.84.2197*.

concerned, it was the gamble on civilian staff that turned the
tide in the Administration's favour. 'It should be borne in
mind', he wrote to Salisbury in May 1892, 'that we are striving
to protect three-quarters of Nyasaland against the attacks of
the remaining quarter; and that we are not only doing so by
the interposition of our own pitiably small though gallant
police force, but by teaching the Nyasalanders how to resist the
attacks of the Eastern Yaos and the coast Arabs who have
hitherto attempted to dominate the country. That I am giving
a truthful picture of the situation is evident from the fact that
I am here to give it. If we had not had the bulk of the Nyasaland people on our side, instead of finding help to the extent
of several thousand men and generous supplies of food, we
should have been overwhelmed after the reverses following the
death of Captain Maguire, and either swamped in a general
uprising or starved for want of supplies.'[1] In the major calculation he was undoubtedly right. It was a situation in which the
momentum of the new government had at all costs to be
maintained.

Second only to the problem of law and order and of the
basic sources of revenue necessary to maintain and extend it
was the problem of land. To some extent this had occupied
Johnston's time and thoughts ever since he had arrived in the
country, but it was above all during the last half of 1892 and the
first quarter of 1893 that he turned his whole attention to its
solution. The policy which he evolved is of great interest, and it
is significant that it owed nothing to direction from the Foreign
Office, which allowed him a free hand, and to which he merely
reported for final approval a series of *faits accomplis*. In judging
it one must remember that he was acting under the same
limitations of money, and so of power, that were conditioning
his assumption of administrative functions. He literally could
not have afforded the time necessary to master the indigenous
conceptions of land ownership. Still less, if he had done so,
could he have afforded to operate a policy which took them
fully into account.

Land clearly was the country's greatest economic asset. It
was from the land that the indigenous inhabitants drew their
livelihood, and it would be from the meagre surplus of their
harvests that the majority of them would always make their
contribution to the revenue. At the same time the land was
far from fully occupied; and it was one of Johnston's basic
assumptions in Nyasaland, as later in Uganda, that some land

[1] Johnston to Salisbury from Zomba 10.v.92, *ibid*.

should be made available for immigrants, whether European or Asian, who would contribute to the economy by growing tropical produce for export. He had stricter views than most of his generation about the prevention of speculation and about the alienation of permanent freehold title. His long-term settlement policy was to grant only leasehold tenure to non-African immigrants. But before this happy position could be reached, he had first to establish Crown ownership of the land to be leased. In many colonies this was effected by a simple proclamation that all vacant land belonged to the Crown, the underlying theory being that where there was no cultivation there had been no previous ownership. But in Nyasaland Johnston's whole theory of sovereignty rested upon the doctrine that sovereign rights had to be ceded to the Crown by the native chiefs, whether under pressure or by their own free will; and it seemed to him a logical deduction that the ownership of vacant land resided in the nearest chief and was transferable by him to others. That meant on the one hand that ownership of the land could be ceded, along with sovereign rights, to the Crown. On the other hand it meant that Johnston had to come to terms with those who claimed to have bought land from native chiefs prior to his own treaties with them.

As regards the disposal of Crown land within this Protectorate [he wrote to Lord Rosebery, who had succeeded Lord Salisbury at the Foreign Office in July 1892], I am usually averse to doing so . . . believing that it is a bad policy for the Crown to lose hold of lands which at present will fetch only a poor selling price, and which in time may become very valuable. I therefore prefer to lease Crown land at a very low rent for fourteen or twenty-one years, at the expiration of which dates the Crown can re-enter into the possession of valuable properties. . . . I have only made land grants or agreed to sell land as a method of settling outstanding claims where a compromise with the Crown has been arrived at. . . . That the lines on which I am settling the land question in Nyasaland are such as to meet with general approval is a statement I cannot make with any assurance. There are claimants whose demands it would be impossible for me to satisfy to the full unless I handed over to them thirty, forty or fifty square miles of territory, with all the native inhabitants as their serfs, with exclusive mining rights, road-making rights, and in some cases a 'right to exclude all other Europeans from the land'. Men who make claims like these have in most cases come up to Nyasaland rich only in their aspirations, have started with a few pounds' worth of inferior trade goods—flint-lock guns, gunpowder and cloth—and with these have induced some heedless young Chief or silly old savage to put his mark on a

paper conferring vast territories and sovereign rights on the
needy pioneer; and when it is necessary to reduce this pioneer's
claim to reasonable proportions (in relation to the amount paid
and to other and conflicting claims) he usually treats me to a
series of abusive letters, threatens me with a full exposure of my
tyrannical proceedings in *Truth*, and no doubt forwards to the
Foreign Office a highly coloured version of his own views of the
case.[1]

So far as the Shire Province was concerned, Johnston's
method of land settlement consisted of a visit to the site of
each claim, an inquiry into the price paid for the land, an
interrogation of the chief who had sold it to ascertain whether
he had realized what he was doing, followed by a process
of informal bargaining between the Commissioner and the
claimant, in which the former offered security of title in the
shape of an official 'Certificate of Claim' in exchange for such
modifications of the original demands as the case seemed to
require. If the price paid did not match the area claimed, then
either the one had to be increased or the other reduced in proportion. Even at the strictly realistic valuation of land at a
penny to threepence an acre, such a condition was sufficient to
bring the majority of claimants to reason. It was an invariable
condition that all land occupied by native villages or plantations was excluded from the claims, and where he thought it
necessary Johnston took pains to inform the inhabitants of such
villages that they were under no obligation to pay rent or
render service to the adjacent European landlord. All certifi-
cates of claim provided that the Crown should receive a five
per cent royalty on minerals, and that the Crown could re-
claim land subsequently needed for roads, railways and other
public utilities. Johnston never sent away a genuine pioneer
empty-handed. Even where flagrant deception had been
attempted, whether upon a Chief or upon the Administration,
he always provided land somewhere on easy terms for a man
who meant to develop it. Only his hand was heavy on the
absentee speculator. One claimant who had bought a concession
to trade on the possessions of a certain chief, and who returned
from a lengthy holiday in England to find that the chief in
question had in the meantime disposed of his land, was curtly
told that if he wished to avoid prosecution for trespass he would
have to trade from a balloon.

Such methods sufficed for the small men of the Shire Highlands, the Buchanans and Pettits, the Simpsons and Bradshaws

---

[1] Johnston to Rosebery 13.x.92, *F.O.84.2197.*

the Browns and the Lindsays. They sufficed also for the Missions, most of which claimed, and received, considerable grants of freehold land. But there were two groups of claims of a completely different order from the rest, which formed a part of Johnston's land settlement and which require entirely separate consideration. The first was the gigantic claim of the British South Africa Company, based on the treaties of Thomson, Grant, Sharpe and Lochner, to exclusive mineral rights and to rights of pre-emption over all the land in the Charter sphere, and also to parts of central and southern Angoniland which lay within the boundaries of the Protectorate and which amounted to something like two-fifths of the Protectorate's land area. The second was that of the African Lakes Company, which claimed to have acquired by purchase and treaty at various dates from 1885 onwards vast areas of land in the Shire Highlands, in the Upper Shire plain, along the western shores of Lake Nyasa and along the whole length of the Nyasa-Tanganyika plateau. In so far as it had already acquired a large interest in the Lakes Company, and in so far as a complete amalgamation of the two companies was in prospect, the South Africa Company was a party to the second group of claims as well as to the first.

In theory Johnston's frequently enunciated principle was that all claims to land within the Protectorate must be judged by exactly the same criteria. In practice he could hardly avoid favouring the cause of his paymaster. In the south, indeed, he made a bold start in his handling of the claims of the Lakes Company, which proved to be the most fraudulent of any which were presented to him. He forwarded to Lord Rosebery a copy of one document purporting to convey 140,000 acres for a consideration of £2, 13s. distributed among four persons who were not in any sense the chiefs of the district. By the investigation of this and similar proceedings he whittled down the claims of the Company in the Shire Highlands to a series of estates totalling 55,000 acres. Other still more numinous claims in the upper Shire plain were written off in exchange for building and harbour sites in the neighbourhood of Fort Johnston. The West Nyasa claims he refused to countenance at all. For all these activities he was to incur the anger of Rhodes. But there remained in the north-western corner of the Protectorate a compact territory of 20,000 square miles, where the Lakes Company's treaties had been more carefully made, and where, despite the grossly inadequate consideration paid, the chiefs did not deny what they had done. This claim, subject to

the usual condition that villages and cultivated land were excluded, Johnston was prepared to confirm. He was also ready to
sanction the South Africa Company's claim to pre-emption and
mining rights in the west and south-west, and to justify the lack
of adequate consideration in both these claims by the rough
calculation that the South Africa Company must have spent
about £50,000 in treaty-making and in subsidies to his
Administration.[1]

It was a generous assessment, prompted perhaps by a slight
feeling of guilt because he had been obliged to spend the whole
of the Company's subsidy on the Protectorate to the exclusion
of the Company's sphere, and also no doubt by a growing
certainty that he would soon have to go to Rhodes for still more
money. In December 1892 Sharpe had returned from a long
tour in the north-eastern region of the Company's sphere with
intelligence of conditions there which justified no complacency
about the continuing lack of any administration. All the way
from Nyasa to Tanganyika, and thence westwards to Mweru
and Bangweolo, the safety of Europeans depended on their
abstaining absolutely from any interference with a thriving
slave trade. The utmost that Sharpe as the Queen's representative had thought it prudent to suggest to the Arabs who
dominated the district between Tanganyika and Mweru was
that they should avoid in their raids the villages actually
situated along the supply-route to the 'Rhodesia' station.[2] So
much for the state of 'effective occupation' which had been
designed to block the encroachments of the Congo Free State.
Johnston knew well that this region had only recently been
traversed by King Leopold's expedition under Captain Stairs
to Katanga, and that conditions there would be fully reported
in Brussels.

More immediately, he was being troubled by a large expedition under von Wissmann, which had come to begin the
occupation of the German territory on his eastern frontier. In
the interests of international comity, all his own acute problems
of supply had to wait while he found thousands of porters for
the transit of the Germans with their steamer through the
Shire Highlands and on to the Lake. 'It seems impossible to a
German to deal decently and kindly with savages,' he grumbled

[1] The most important despatches on land policy are Johnston to Rosebery
13.x.92, *op. cit.*, and Johnston to Rosebery 14.x.93, *F.O.2.55*. But see also Johnston
to Salisbury 5.xii.91, *F.O.84.2114*, and Johnston to Rosebery 18.x.92, *F.O.84.2197*.
[2] Sharpe to Johnston 17.xii.92, enclosed in Johnston to Rosebery 2.i.93,
F.O.2.54.

to Sir Percy Anderson. 'Everything must be done in a bluster-
ing, bullying manner, and with a meanness and lack of
honesty which I am beginning to think must be special Teutonic
qualities since they are so prominent in the Germans and the
Lowland Scotch.'[1] More pertinently he feared, and not
altogether without reason, that Wissmann's arrival at his
destination, far from contributing to law and order, would be
the signal for serious Arab troubles in the north of the Protectorate and the adjacent parts of the Company's sphere. In
February 1893, at the very time when the Germans were his
unwelcome guests, he had to deal with a revolt by the Yao
chief Liwonde in the Upper Shire plain less than fifty miles
from Zomba, which looked so threatening that he was obliged
to call upon the Lower Shire gunboats for an emergency
reinforcement of blue-jackets. The campaign was brief and
successful, but he felt it necessary to follow up his victory with
a new fort and garrison at Liwonde's.[2] It was plain that even
when his new Sikh detachment arrived he was not going to
have sufficient force left over from his existing commitments to
tackle even Makanjira with safety.

In a long letter to Anderson at the end of March he raised
yet again the question of a Treasury grant-in-aid. 'I feel very
much at this juncture my dependence for supplies on the
British South Africa Company. I feel it in this way: that I am
compelled through force of circumstances to expend almost
the whole of the £10,000 a year on the Protectorate and not in
the Company's sphere beyond, and yet in the Protectorate I
cannot favour the Company in any way.' The land claims of the
Lakes Company were inferior from a legal point of view to the
most spurious claims of the private settlers. The extension of
the South Africa Company's Charter to the Protectorate was as
strongly opposed as ever by missionaries and settlers alike. 'It
therefore becomes increasingly unfair to go on using the
British South Africa Company's money for the defence and
development of the Protectorate,' he told Anderson. 'And yet
what am I to do? If I remove the police force from Nyasaland
to the Company's sphere, the whole country would be swamped
at once by the descent of the slave-trading Yaos.' Significantly,
since he invariably underestimated expenditure, he remarked
that an imperial grant-in-aid for the Protectorate alone would
need to be of the order of £20,000 a year. Since he was writing
privately to his chief Johnston referred according to his

ZOMBA: THE LEOPARD'S DRINKING PLACE

CRESTED CRANES

custom to many other matters, mixing the serious with the playful in a measure which he knew would be appreciated. And as usual his 'strictures on the various departments of the government' flowed fast and furiously.

> The delight of the General Post Office in London is to shoot all our mail into Zanzibar, where . . . the Goanese postmaster . . . is not well acquainted with our geography. . . . The General Post Office appears totally to forget that it exists solely for the benefit and convenience of the public and British Empire, and it has no business to have those silly little fits of official dignity which manifest themselves in refusing to recognize the existence of new places. I wish you would solve the matter *more Africano* by just having the Postmaster-General exposed in chains for three days at the main entrance to the Foreign Office. This is the way in which we do NOT treat natives out here. In the middle of this barbarism I feel that we cannot be too fastidiously correct in our legal procedure, and so the *Habeas Corpus* Act flourishes, but I often think a rougher procedure would do a great deal of good in England. If you could arm your young men of the Africa Department and launch them suddenly in a raid on the Treasury, the higher officials of which being hunted from room to room at the point of the bayonet, I feel sure a much happier result would be obtained, and for months after every suggestion of the Foreign Office as to expenditure on British interests abroad would be willingly, even slavishly, carried out.[1]

It was not the habit of British Governments of either party during the late nineteenth century to face the financial implications of imperial extension before they had to, and Johnston's appeal was, as he must have realized, a forlorn hope. 'It may be useful', Anderson commented, 'to note that Johnston considers that if he lost Rhodes' money he would require £20,000 a year from the Treasury.' Rosebery appended his initial. Salisbury, had he been in office, would doubtless have enriched the public records with one of his delightful essays in understatement—'It would be impracticable, I fear, for us to adopt *all* Mr Johnston's suggestions'—but he could hardly have done more. Johnston's only real chance of saving the solvency of his Administration, therefore, lay in a fresh approach to Rhodes, and that, as he well knew, meant the abandonment of the thesis that his subsidy was a mere retaining fee paid for the maintenance of the Company's claim to its chartered sphere pending its readiness to go in and develop it by itself.

It is doubtful how far Rhodes would ever have subscribed to

---

[1] Johnston to Anderson from Zomba 23.iii.93, *F.O.2.54.*

such an interpretation of the 1891 agreement, but certainly by 1893 his attitude was hardening along very different lines. Johnston confessed to him in January 1893 his need of another £5,000 a year, and Rhodes in reply laid claim to the reversionary rights to the land and minerals, not merely of the Company's sphere but of the whole of the Protectorate as well. 'We pay £10,000 a year for the maintenance of government there, and sooner or later our shareholders will ask me what return either present or prospective they are to get for their money. Until this question is settled it is useless to discuss the various financial questions you bring forward in your letter, and they must stand over until we can come to some agreement with the Foreign Office.' In a letter to Rosebery, drafted at the same time, he said, 'We have been and are still paying £10,000 a year for nothing. We have not even got control of our expenditure, and we are quite willing to go on doing this: but in justice to our own shareholders we must have secured to us the reversion of the land and minerals so soon as civilization is sufficiently established to render them available. . . . We claim, and I think we have a right to claim, that in consideration of our subsidy no concession acquired by anyone except ourselves will be recognized, and that this stipulation may be made generally known as an instruction to Mr Johnston and a contract with the British South Africa Company.' Significantly, this letter was never sent. Perhaps Rhodes realized that the legend of the disinterested apostle of Empire might suffer by so frank a declaration of the business side of the exercise. Perhaps he feared that even a Liberal ministry might be provoked to defy so obvious an ultimatum by providing an imperial grant-in-aid. Perhaps he decided on reflection that pressure could be more effectively brought to bear indirectly, through Johnston.[1]

The revolt on the Upper Shire had prevented Johnston from keeping a rendezvous at Chinde with Rhodes, who was returning from England by the East Coast route in February 1893; but in March he telegraphed proposing a visit to Cape Town in May. In April Rhodes set out in two long letters the terms he was prepared to discuss. They were based, not on the agreement of February 1891, but on a doubtful analogy with an understanding between the South Africa Company and the Colonial Office relating to railway development in Bechuana-

---

[1] The three letters quoted in this paragraph are from the Cape Town (Kimberley Office) records of the British South Africa Company, now in the Central African Archives at Salisbury. They are Johnston to Rhodes 20.i.93, Rhodes to Johnston (undated) and Rhodes to Rosebery (undated and not sent). The first is now largely illegible, but its contents are clearly deducible from the last two.

land. In this territory, Rhodes argued, the Imperial Government, though shouldering the entire cost of administration, had given to the South Africa Company the sole right to obtain land and mining concessions from the native chiefs as a reward for the services rendered in building the trunk railway line from Kimberley to the north. It was therefore clear that in Nyasaland, where the Company carried the whole cost of government, it should be entitled to the same monopoly. I note what you say as to your pressing need of an extra subsidy of £5,000 a year, and on behalf of the Chartered Company I am prepared to grant this . . . provided you agree to the principle . . . that we are to have the preferent rights to the land and minerals both in the Protectorate and in the sphere without. . . . I do not object to the land grants you have already made, for they are in favour of men who are residents and who have expended already considerable sums in beneficial occupation of the soil and their presence in the country is distinctly an advantage, but for the future remember that the Chartered Company alone has the right to acquire . . . concessions of land and minerals. I would point out to you that the Crown cannot take land to its own benefit within the Protectorate, but with the relationship existing between us as described by me, you can acquire land for the British South Africa Company and apply the proceeds to the administration of the territory—therefore you should make the grants of land to the African Lakes Company, now held by us, as large as possible, for you and your Administration benefit most by so doing.'[1] In the second letter Rhodes expressed his willingness to raise the subsidy even to £7,500 a year, and to provide an additional sum of £1,500 towards a steamer for Lake Tanganyika—he was anxious, he said, to provide as quickly as possible a means of communication with Uganda[2]—but 'in the event of the principle I am contending for not being agreed to by Her Majesty's Government, I must in justice to my shareholders request that our subsidy of £10,000 be devoted entirely to the

[1] Rhodes to Johnston from Cape Town 4.iv.93, *B.S.A.C. Papers*.

[2] But compare with this statement the following exchange of telegrams in *Cawston Papers*, Vol. IV: (i) Cawston to Rhodes 19.v.93: 'I.B.E.A. Co. at General Meeting of Shareholders May 29th. They will receive powers enable British Government absorb all their territory under Zanzibar Protectorate. Kirk, Mackenzie, privately express opinion, if we offer take over territory, arrangements can be made. They say they would require guarantee £20,000 annually five years. Think half enough. Do you approve of approach them? Wire views. Maguire Cawston meet Kirk next week.' (ii) Rhodes to Cawston 20.v.93: 'Have quite enough on hand. It strengthens whole English position Africa if British Government assumes responsibility I.B.E.A. Co.'

development of the sphere outside the Protectorate, leaving you to raise, with the assistance of the Imperial Treasury and the resident planters, the necessary for the administration of the Protectorate'.[1]

Had Johnston not had an actual and prospective deficit, he could of course have repudiated Rhodes's proposition root and branch. By the terms of the 1891 agreement he could have held the Company to their £10,000 subsidy without any conditions until the end of 1895. He could probably have held them to a further £2,500 a year in respect of their undertaking to provide him with free transport. As he was later to remind Rhodes, it was not even true that the Company was carrying the whole or even the major part of the expenses of the Protectorate. Besides the two consular salaries, the Imperial Exchequer had provided in all four gunboats and their crews, arms and ammunition to the value of £9,200 and about £6,000 for various contingencies against the Company's total of £29,000.[2] But the Administration was in debt and in danger. It had no security on which to borrow. It had to realize its only assets, which were its somewhat tenuous rights in the land. Undeveloped land, without communications, without settled government, was not worth much. Rhodes's terms might seem extortionate; but it is doubtful whether anyone in the City of London would have offered better. Subject to the British Government's ratification, therefore, Johnston had no option but to accept them in principle. The most that he could hope to achieve in Cape Town was Rhodes's agreement to some minor modifications—an extended term for the increased subsidy, some safeguards for the natives on their occupied land, an assurance that the proceeds of land sales would be applied to the development of the country, a provision whereby the Administration could retain such plots of land as it needed for its own stations, ports and other installations. His Cape Town journey was a mission to the pawnbroker, but to such shifts did Victorian England, at the height of its material prosperity and power, reduce the architects of its overseas greatness.

Johnston stayed with Rhodes a fortnight at his country house at Rondebosch. He found him a changed man both in appearance and character from the healthy masterful personality he had admired in 1889 and 1890. 'His manner had become much more sombre; he had long fits of sulky silence,

---

[1] Rhodes to Johnston 30.iv.93, *B.S.A.C. Papers*.
[2] Johnston to Rhodes from Chinde 7.vi.93, *ibid*.

alternating with rapid conversation, so full of great propositions backed by monetary proposals, that one almost felt obliged to ask him to pause while a notebook and pencil could be fetched.' He was complaining of the after-effects of a fall from his horse some weeks previously, and to Johnston it often seemed as though he was under the influence of drugs—a possibility which Jameson in later years did not deny. Sometimes Rhodes would drive him into Cape Town for official luncheons and would watch sardonically his astonishment at the prevailing midday drunkenness. On other days they made expeditions to a little seaside bay, during which no word would be exchanged between setting out and coming home. Johnston remembered long, silent dinners, when Rhodes, eating little himself, would rebuke him for his enormous appetite.[1] Between the silences, however, there were sudden bursts of irritable invective. 'I enjoyed my stay at the Cape immensely,' Johnston wrote when it was all over, 'except when you used to get cross of an evening and abuse me like anything over the drawing-room fire when we dined alone.'[2] Four months later he was to express it differently: 'The only acknowledgment of the efforts I had made both to meet your views and to carry out my duty were accusations of disloyalty, untrustworthiness, etc., etc., all the more difficult to answer because made to me in your own house.'[3]

Certainly the visit was no honeymoon between like-minded protagonists of Empire. Johnston described in his autobiography how on the evening when their bargain took its final shape, Rhodes had him fetched out of bed at midnight and invited him to keep careful notes, remarking offensively that he could not always be returning to the same subject. And certainly the draft agreement which Johnston prepared next day was couched in bold and almost hostile terms. The subsidy was to be increased to £17,500 a year and its term was to be five years, from April 1893 till April 1898; Rhodes was to find in addition £3,000 for one steamer on Lake Nyasa and £1,500 for another on Lake Tanganyika. 'To come somewhat abruptly to the point,' the strange document goes on, 'your price for executing this very liberal arrangement is this': transfer of all Crown land to the Company; settlement on the Company of pre-emptive and mineral rights over all the rest of the land, except that already granted to missions and private settlers,

[1] Johnston: *Story*, pp. 302-4.
[2] Johnston to Rhodes from Chinde 7.vi.93, *B.S.A.C. Papers*.
[3] Johnston to Rhodes 8.x.93, *F.O.2.55*.

subject only to the provisions that native villages and plantations were not to be disturbed, and that in exercising the right
of pre-emption a fair price, to be assessed by the Commissioner,
should be paid to the native communities involved. The
agreement, which took the form of a letter from Johnston to
Rhodes dated Cape Town, May 3rd, 1893, was endorsed 'I
approve of and accept this letter with its conditions—C. J.
Rhodes.' The original was filed in the offices of the British
South Africa Company at Cape Town. A copy was forwarded
by Johnston to the Foreign Office with the request that it
should be ratified by cable.[1]

And yet, despite the quarrelling, and the strained language
of the 'Cape Town agreement', the two men were still prepared
to trust each other a long way. Within the agreement Rhodes
did nothing to circumscribe Johnston's independence and
discretion as the Commissioner appointed by the Imperial
Government. And outside the written document he did two
things of more positive import. He promised to pay the increased subsidy for one year even if the Foreign Office should
refuse to ratify the agreement. And he made Johnston an
outright grant of £10,000, to be paid if need be from his
private fortune, for the complete subjugation of Makanjira and
the recovery of the remains of Captain Maguire and his fellow
casualties.[2] On the strength of these two verbal undertakings
Johnston, before he left South Africa, engaged additional
hands for his civilian administration, and telegraphed to the
Adjutant-General in India for a fresh contingent of 100 Sikhs.
What deeper understanding may have underlain these arrangements we do not know. There are hints in Johnston's writings
that they were connected not only with Makanjira but with
plans for a large advance by the Administration into the north-
eastern part of the Company's sphere. But, as it happened,
before even the defeat of Makanjira, the agreement had mis-
carried and the basis of all further mutual trust had been
destroyed for ever.

From Cape Town Johnston made a wintry journey by coach
through the Orange Free State and down into Natal. At
Durban, where a gunboat was waiting to take him back to the

---

[1] Johnston to Rhodes, Cape Town, 3.v.93, *B.S.A.C. Papers*, enclosed also in
Johnston to Rosebery 3.v.93, *F.O.2.54*.
[2] The written evidence of this verbal understanding is in Johnston to Rhodes
8.x.93, *F.O.2.55*. Johnston's account was never denied by Rhodes, although he knew
that copies of the correspondence had been sent to the Foreign Office and the
British South Africa Company.

Zambezi, he was carried on board delirious, with blackwater fever. At Delagoa Bay he was so ill that he had to be landed and nursed for a week in the house of the British Consul. But his recovery was speedy, and on this as on all other occasions he experienced afterwards a period of physical and mental energy which, even by his exacting standards, was extraordinary. His first concern was to mobilize his military and naval forces for the coming struggle with Makanjira. On his way up the Zambezi he recruited 400 Makua for service as auxiliaries and carriers for the new Sikh force which was due to arrive from Bombay in August. Back at Zomba there were new quarters to be built and fresh problems of supply to be solved. At Mpimbi on the Upper Shire the assembly of the two lake gunboats, the *Pioneer* and the *Adventure*, and a steel lighter, the *Dove*, was proceeding under the supervision of Commander Hope Robertson with the assistance of artisans from England and Indian riveters from Zanzibar. The new waggon-road from the Lower to the Upper Shire was already completed, with a branch from Blantyre to Zomba. But Johnston was determined that the advance against Makanjira, by which he intended to bring the whole of the western shore of the Lake under the effective control of his administration, must be made from a base in the Shire province which was really secure. He had to strengthen his line of forts, now four in number, which guarded the dangerous country between Mpimbi and Fort Johnston. And he had to establish two new ones, named after Anderson and Lister, one to the north and one to the south of Mlanje mountain, to protect the eastern frontier of the Shire Highlands from the Yao raiders who had their bases in Portuguese territory beyond. His standing garrisons now accounted for a hundred Sikhs with native auxiliaries. Thanks to Rhodes's special fund, he had a hundred more available for the advance.

The Shire Province was now definitely demarcated into eight administrative districts, and Johnston at last felt strong enough to impose, in place of the hitherto almost nominal poll-tax, a hut tax of three shillings upon all natives living within the administered area, payable in money, in produce or in labour.[1] To this extent police expenditure was yielding a dividend. There was beginning to be a distant prospect of internal solvency. But Johnston had no doubts at all about the wisdom of his negotiations at Cape Town, and after six weeks had gone by without the expected ratification from London he

[1] Johnston to Rosebery 1.vi.93, *F.O.2.54*.

wrote to Anderson in stronger terms than he had ever used to
him before.

The alternative is for the Imperial Treasury to grant a
minimum £15,000 a year towards the administration of the
Protectorate, and for the South Africa Company henceforward
to devote all its £10,000 a year to its own sphere. One or other
course must quickly be decided on, and the resulting measures
be frankly and explicitly set forth, so that we are not for ever
obliged to shroud our status here in vague statements and feeble
disclaimers. In short the Government must be honest. In this
world you get nothing for nothing. Already, no doubt, you
think the £10,000 a year subsidy of the British South Africa
Company dearly purchased by the lien which it gives them over
British Central Africa. Well, you have only the —— —— ——
Treasury to thank for the awkwardness of the situation. Had not
this odious, short-sighted, soulless miser in 1890-91 refused
resolutely to entertain the idea of a subsidy to start the new
Protectorate, you would not have had to appeal, as a last chance
of saving the country for Great Britain, to the generosity of a
Chartered Company. I, personally, am quite indifferent as to
who provides the money . . . but . . . money, I am afraid I must
have. You can't buy customs duties without building custom-
houses, can you? We must open up the country with roads, and
here and there construct a bridge or two. We must erect healthy
and comfortable dwellings for our employés. To be well or
ill-housed out here means almost the difference between living
and dying. We must stake the bank of the Shire here, build a
jetty there, and drain a swamp in another place. Much of this
expenditure is speculative; that is to say, we make the outlay
with the ultimate hope of recovering it some day by the increased
value of the property.[1]

It is most unlikely that Johnston, in mentioning the alternative of a Treasury grant, had any serious hopes that this course
would be adopted. But even if he had, it would not have
been in any way dishonourable, for the text of the Cape Town
agreement had specifically mentioned this course as an alternative which would be acceptable to Rhodes. It is certain, beyond
a shadow of doubt, that Johnston was doing nothing at all to
tamper behind Rhodes's back with the agreed conditions of the
increased subsidy. It was therefore a stupefying experience
when, in the second week of October, with the Makanjira
expedition mounted and ready to start, he opened a letter from
Rhodes in Durban, enclosing a telegram from the Cape Town
Secretary of the South Africa Company, Dr Rutheroord Harris.

[1] Johnston to Anderson from Chiromo 20.vi.93, *F.O.2.54.*

'Draft Agreement with Colonial Office and Foreign Office supposed to represent H. H. J. Agreement with C. J. Rhodes has arrived. It is a pure mockery, and as Maguire says, we really get nothing and are at H. H.'s mercy. I think he must have written privately and hope you will at once notify him by letter that the extra £7,500 is at once stopped, as Agreement is so utterly in opposition to what was agreed here as to render chance of accord from your point of view impossible.' It is a remarkable fact that a man of Rhodes's stature was prepared to take violent, impulsive action, which might have endangered his whole position north of the Zambezi, on the advice, quite unsupported by any evidence, of a man like Harris, of whose limitations he must have been very well aware. 'I have just received,' he wrote to Johnston, 'on my way to Mashonaland, the enclosed telegram from Dr Harris. It speaks for itself. I have of course stopped at once your extra amount, and shall arrange as soon as possible to spend the whole of our subsidy north of the Zambezi in our own territories by someone in whom I can place confidence. What I feel deeply is your disloyalty, though it was not altogether unexpected. . . . It is clear that you must have written privately, and in a perfectly different style to the basis agreed between us at Cape Town.'[1]

The formal agreement presented by the Foreign Office to the British South Africa Company on August 24th, to which Harris's telegram referred, had indeed differed in two important points from the draft signed by Rhodes and Johnston in Cape Town. It had been provided that the increased subsidy should be paid for ten years instead of five, and that the whole of it should be expended within the Protectorate.[2] The second point had been due to a simple misunderstanding. The first, as the Foreign Office records make perfectly clear, had been introduced at the suggestion, not of Johnston, but of the Colonial Office, which had entirely repudiated the analogy with Bechuanaland, and which had analysed the Cape Town agreement in a memorandum so pungent and realistic that it should stand as a classic document in the history of imperialism in this extraordinary period.

The bargain offered appears to be that the Chartered Company should be allowed to acquire all the Crown lands, and all the land that Mr Johnston can influence the natives to cede, in return for £87,500, paid towards the support of the administra-

[1] Full copies both of Harris's telegram and of Rhodes's letter are included in Johnston to Rhodes 8.x.93, enclosed in Johnston to Rosebery 8.x.93, *F.O.2.55*.
[2] F.O. to B.S.A.C. 24.viii.93. *F.O.83.1242*; cf. F.O. to C.O. 4.viii.93, *F.O.83.1241*.

H*

tion in five annual instalments. At the end of the five years, the Crown will apparently be destitute of any territorial estate in this country, and will have no adequate subsidy at its command with which to maintain law and order, and unless the Chartered Company chooses of its own free will, and as an act of policy or generosity, to renew the subsidy, there will apparently be no device but (1) to ask Parliament for a grant-in-aid, (2) to cede the direct administration of the country to the Chartered Company, or (3) to abandon it. If the first of the above alternatives is considered to be the only practicable one in the event contemplated, then it would appear *prima facie* to Lord Ripon more prudent to ask Parliament for a grant-in-aid at once than to sell the whole reversionary interest of Great Britain in the land for a five years' subsidy, for five years is but a brief space in the history of a dependency. But his Lordship recognizes that there are practical objections to multiplying grants-in-aid for the purposes of Imperial development; and assuming that this is also the opinion of Lord Rosebery and of Her Majesty's Commissioner, Lord Ripon can only express his admiration of the ability and tact which Mr Johnston has displayed in negotiating on behalf of Her Majesty's Government with Mr Rhodes. . . . But Lord Ripon . . . considers the proposed period of subsidy too short, and would suggest that an effort might be made to induce the Chartered Company to guarantee the continuance of the subsidy for ten years, or, at all event, for some longer period than five.[1]

The Foreign Office had taken Lord Ripon's advice, with the result that Johnston had been accused of treachery. 'Rhodes', wrote Anderson, when the papers came before him, 'has treated Johnston brutally.'[2] It was not too hard a judgment. It is related of Johnston by one who knew him intimately that in later life he would never discuss his personal relations with Rhodes. Normally a genial and uninhibited talker, at the mention of Rhodes's name he would become suddenly and impenetrably silent. In the text of his autobiography the Cape Town agreement is cursorily mentioned, but there is no reference to the subsequent quarrel. Only in an appendix did he respond to a request for more information made by those to whom he had showed the proofs, and there he told a brief and muddled story. Rhodes, he said, had cabled asking him to join a section of his police force in Southern Rhodesia in attacking the Portuguese and driving them down to the coast of Manicaland. He had replied that such action was impossible without the direct orders of the Foreign Office, whereupon Rhodes

[1] C.O. to F.O. 24.vi.93, *F.O.83.1240.*
[2] Minute on Johnston to Rosebery 8.x.93, *F.O.2.55.*

'repudiated the new agreement I had entered into at Cape Town and revoked all further monetary assistance. I was therefore threatened with a complete loss of revenue and was compelled to lay the whole situation before the Foreign Office early in 1894.'[1] The Portuguese incident here mentioned cannot be identified with certainty. Probably Johnston's memory was telescoping two quite separate issues. What can be definitely established from the contemporary documents is that it was the misunderstanding over the Cape Town agreement which opened the breach between the two men, and that it was on Johnston's side that the breakdown in confidence was at first the more decisive. Rhodes was no doubt accustomed to fling about taunts of treachery and desertion. It was a part of the strong man's stock in trade, and such is human nature that it usually achieved its object. But with Johnston in 1893 he used it once too often. He provoked a reaction which he had probably never bargained for.

Whoever states that I wrote privately or publicly, or expressed in conversation, or in any way made a communication to anyone in authority or not, intended to modify the purport of my letter to you of the 3rd May, or indeed any statement in any way disloyal to yourself, utters an unqualified lie. . . . I have done yeoman service for the British South Africa Company. As far as it was honest to go I have gone in helping them to substantiate their claims, and in the advancement of their interests. I have spared neither the risk of my own life, the abandonment of all ideas of comfort, nor the right to rest at times like other people. I do not recollect having spent one single day as a holiday during the two years and a half which I have worked in Central Africa. Sundays and week-days, mornings and evenings, I am to be found either slaving at my desk, or tearing about the country on horseback, or trudging 20 miles a day on foot, or sweltering in boats, or being horribly sea-sick on Lake Nyasa steamers. I have to carry on in my office, myself, a most onerous correspondence in Swahili, which I have to write in the Arabic character, in Portuguese, in French, and in English. I have had to acquire a certain mastery over Hindustani to deal with the Indian troops. I have learnt three native languages besides Swahili in order to talk straight to the people. I have undertaken grave responsibilities, and I have devoted myself to the most wearisome and niggling of tasks. One day I am working out a survey which has to be of scrupulous accuracy, and another day I am doing what a few years ago I never thought I should be called upon to do —undertaking the whole responsibility of directing military operations. I have even had myself taught to fire Maxim guns

[1] Johnston: *Story*, p. 497.

and seven pounder cannon, I, who detest loud noises and have a horror of explosives. This catalogue of small accomplishments is petty compared to the average qualifications of an ordinarily good Anglo-Indian official, but the Anglo-Indian official, to begin with, is much better paid, he leads a far more comfortable life, he has not such a crushing sense of responsibility, and, above all, he does not have to serve two masters and please them both. I was willing to endure all these miseries so long as I felt that I was really doing a good work in Africa, and that that work was being appreciated by the Foreign Office which employs me and the British South Africa Company which finds the funds for my administration; but the position has now become too intolerable to be further supported.

Either, he told Rhodes, he must make inquiries at the Foreign Office and from independent sources as to his *bona fides*, and on the basis of such information write him a sincere apology for his allegations, or he, Johnston, must inform the Secretary of State of the impossibility of his working further with the Company. The inquiry would take time, and meanwhile events in Central Africa could not be brought to a standstill. He gave Rhodes, therefore, until the spring of 1894, when he hoped to return to England on leave, to make his retractation. Meantime he proposed to hold him to his promise of the Makanjira grant. The expenditure had been embarked on. The additional troops had reached the country. He was not going to send them back until he had carried the campaign to a successful conclusion. If Rhodes dared to dishonour his drafts, he could do so.[1]

While this formidable missive—it ran to nearly 4,000 words and included a full recital of the relations between Rhodes and Johnston since their first meeting in 1889—was on its way in triplicate to Cape Town, to Downing Street, and to the London Office of the British South Africa Company, the new telegraph line between Cape Town and Salisbury was humming with mutually inflammatory interchanges between Harris and Rhodes, showing just how far they, for their part, had departed from the Cape Town agreement, which they were purporting to defend. They were discussing how to brief Rochfort Maguire, who was handling the negotiations with the Foreign Office in London. 'I am not going to create with my funds an independent King Johnston over the Zambezi,' Rhodes began. 'Pay not a penny more than £10,000 a year, and let Foreign Office know that we have paid the extra money in belief that they would carry out agreement made with Johnston in Cape Town.' 'I quite under-

---

[1] Johnston to Rhodes 8.x.93. Copy in Johnston to Rosebery 8.x.93, *F.O.2.55*.

stand,' replied Harris, 'and wrote to Johnston at once cutting off all supplies I possibly could, and also charging his last year's overdraft against his current £10,000 so that he has not much to go on with.' The thumbscrews, then, were on.

'Of course,' mused Rhodes, 'the difficulty is that Johnston, as Imperial officer and paid by the Imperial Government, should be a servant of the Company. Up to the present he has been a servant of the Home Government in the Protectorate, and a servant of ours in the sphere north of the Zambezi. In the proposed settlement I see he tried to get the Sphere added to the Protectorate and to be independent of us in both. We understood the agreement to be that the Protectorate should be added to the Sphere, and that he should be under us in both. The difficulty is that he is an imperial officer, but still we will see what they say to my demands.' So it was not only land claims in Nyasaland that Rhodes was after. 'We shall win the sentiment of the planters in the Protectorate in the future with our telegraph, and if we grant them the introduction of their coffee into our territories free of duty, they will then be only too ready to come under our government. . . . In fact to sum up, the whole of the Sphere must be under us, and as to the Protectorate we concede *temporarily* to be under Her Majesty's representative, but in return for our payment for good government we should have the exclusive right to concessions.'

By the word *temporarily* Rhodes presumably meant that he was prepared to wait until the increased subsidy, proved insufficient, as he knew it would. Then, having already gained possession of the land, an offer to take over the government of the Protectorate would scarcely be resisted by the English Cabinet. So, at least, it would seem to have been understood by Harris, who was busy adding conditions of his own which would hasten the date of the foreclosure. 'Your summing up', he said, 'is much the best solution. . . . Temporarily in the Protectorate we leave H. H. Johnston as imperial servant, but subject to your consultative consent in all matters, but outside the Protectorate and within the sphere he remains solely under Company and is not imperial. Added to this . . . my proviso of £7,500 per annum of subsidy to be spent entirely in the Sphere, including Barotse, we having the right to increase this as our funds permit, but not to increase the Protectorate subsidy . . . failing which we take Sphere and pay for it; Johnston takes Protectorate and finds his subsidy from the three liberal gentlemen whom he describes as being at head of Treasury.' The most telling epitaph on these proceedings was perhaps supplied by Maguire, Rhodes's former secretary, to whom the telegrams had been repeated. 'Fear', he cabled, 'can do no more than secure conditions Cape Town correspondence Commissioner H. H. Johnston. Your telegrams go further.'[1]

On the shores of Lake Nyasa Johnston was in the meanwhile conducting amphibious warfare on a considerable scale. The naval gunboats were by now in fighting trim, and both of the African Lakes Company's steamers had been hired as transports for 130 Sikhs, with two of the three Indian Army officers, Major Johnson and Captain Edwards. The expedition started from Fort Johnston on November 5th, and made first for Kotakota, where Chiwaura, one of Jumbe's principal sub-chiefs, had joined the Makanjira faction. Chiwaura was attacked and routed on the 8th, and Jumbe, now thoroughly reinstated in control of his district, was able to provide a force of two thousand irregulars for the succeeding operations against the Rifu district further to the south, which was Makanjira's main stronghold on the western shore of the Lake.[2] The irregulars were despatched overland under Sharpe; Johnston and the Sikhs followed by water on the 13th. A week's campaign sufficed for the defeat and capture of Makanjira's colonists and for the restoration of the friendly Yao chief, Kazembe, who had signed a treaty in 1891.

On the 19th the expedition moved across to Makanjira's home towns, which were strung out along thirty-six miles of the south-east shore. The ships sailed through the night and arrived at dawn, achieving complete surprise. Landings were successfully made opposite the principal town, which had been rebuilt a mile further inland than the one which Johnston had destroyed in 1891. Opposition was attempted, but a continuous bombardment from the ships prevented any strong concentration of defenders from reaching the Sikhs, who were able to fire the town, and, following in the path of the flames, to sweep it clear of its inhabitants. On the 22nd Johnston began the construction of a fort, named after Cecil Maguire, on the site of the earlier disaster. Next he installed a female pretender to Makanjira's chiefdom, by name Kumbasani, round whom he endeavoured to rally the subject Nyanja population of the district. Makanjira, needless to say, was not permanently defeated by these brief

[1] Telegrams Harris (Cape Town) to Rhodes (Salisbury) 14.x.93, Rhodes to Harris 16.x.93; telegraphic conversation between Harris and Rhodes 16.x.93; telegram Maguire (London) to Harris 20.x.93. All in *B.S.A.C. Cape Town Papers*, Central African Archives.
[2] See Plate 13, facing p. 257.

operations. His people had been cleared from the western side of the Lake, and from the lakeside villages on the east. His dhows had been captured, and the gunboats would ensure that they were not again replaced. Johnston hoped that once driven out of business as the principal ferryman to the slave trade on Lake Nyasa, he would be unable to buy more arms and ammunition and that he would gradually decline into insignificance. In the long term he was right. But meantime he was compelled, on his return to Zomba in December, to leave a garrison of seventy Sikhs at Fort Maguire. He had carried his administration to all but the extreme north of the Lake, but at the cost not merely of a single expensive expedition but of a considerable addition to recurrent expenditure.[1]

Johnston, however, had returned from the campaign in a militant mood. He was determined that the advance, so long prepared, should not be abandoned while he remained in charge of the administration. He was equally determined that the additional funds which he now required must be obtained without slipping further into the clutches of the South Africa Company. He had decided that his forthcoming leave in England should be devoted to the pursuit of a Treasury grant-in-aid. If he failed to get it, he would not return. Meantime, his ultimatum to Rhodes had been serious, and he did not mean to soften it by modifying his expenditure of the monies which had been promised him unconditionally for the current year. At Zomba he found a collection of sly and supercilious letters from Rutherfoord Harris, on the one hand urging him to push the Company's claims with the Foreign Office, on the other hand threatening him in terms of scarcely veiled malice in case he should fail to toe the line. 'We can get much further with the Foreign Office—*quorum pars magna fuisti*—hence I enclose for your private perusal a copy of the cable sent by me at Mr Rhodes's request to Maguire. . . . If you do not secure for the Company the minimum mentioned by Mr Rhodes you can read from his wire to me . . . what he intends to do for the future. . . . All your letters have been carefully read and studied. . . . If you want peace with Mr Rhodes, you can only obtain it by giving, or rather more correctly, by not withholding from him and his Company their just dues and position in British Central Africa.'[2] There was more in the same vein, and there survives among the Company's papers an unpleasant correspondence between Harris and Rhodes's bank manager, Lewis

[1] Johnston to Rosebery 9.xii.93, *F.O.2.55.*
[2] Harris to Johnston from Cape Town 27.x.93, *B.S.A.C. Papers.*

Michell, to whom Johnston's letters had been passed, which shows with how much real ill-will the magnate's henchmen were pursuing 'the little, prancing Proconsul'.[1] Time was when Johnston would have replied to such bullying with lengthy protestations and elaborate expositions of his policy and the philosophy of empire which lay behind it. But desperation had given him a new dignity and a new strength. He flatly refused to make any representations to the Foreign Office before his return to England in the spring of 1894. And in a series of coldly defiant despatches he stated his intention to hold Rhodes rigidly to his financial promises.

> Inasmuch as it would be a serious matter for this Protectorate and for British Central Africa generally that the war with the eastern Yaos should be recurrent, I have determined by means of the special grant made by Mr Rhodes to conquer the eastern Yaos once and for all, even though this action should result in the spending of the whole of the grant of £10,000. . . . Putting aside, however, the Makanjira fund of £10,000, there will remain a sum total of £17,500 which I assume the right to spend if necessary before the 31st of March 1894. . . . I refuse to reduce my expenditure to the £10,000 limit for the year ending March 31st next, because I was distinctly promised by Mr Rhodes that whatever was the reply of the Foreign Office he would guarantee me that subsidy for twelve months in order to enable me to go ahead in the interior. . . . If you decide that from the 1st April next the Company will only and solely be responsible for the payment of £10,000 a year to my Administration, you can then instruct me formally to withdraw all officers of the British South Africa Company whose maintenance is incompatible with the fixed limit of £10,000 a year paid for the maintenance of a police force. Before taking this step, however, I would advise you to consider the serious consequences which would result from retrograde action on the upper Congo and the south end of Tanganyika, all the money which you have up to date invested in those parts for the creation of buildings and the development of the country will be thrown away, and the natives whom we have now accustomed to look to us for protection will be thrown once more on the tender mercies of the Arabs or the Belgians.[2]

By holding Rhodes to his undertakings Johnston thus secured for the year 1893-4 a total subsidy of £27,500, which, with the local revenue of £7,000, was just sufficient for his needs. But with the Makanjira fund exhausted and the Company's subsidy reduced once more to £10,000, his prospective

[1] Michell to Harris 21.xi.93 and 22.xi.93, *B.S.A.C. Papers.*
[2] Johnston to Harris from Zomba 9.xii.93, *ibid.*

deficit for the following year would be nearly £20,000. And so in December 1893 he began to prepare the Foreign Office for the now inevitable tussle with the Treasury. He listed the twelve stations already existing and found that with the salaries of their European magistrates and the small forces of native constabulary, varying from thirty to sixty, required for their everyday protection, the cost of their maintenance was £20,000 a year. The Indian troops with their three British officers cost £7,500, transport and passages a further £5,000. The administration of the Protectorate and of the two occupied districts of the Company's sphere was costing, he reckoned, £35,000, excluding the gunboats and their crews, which he estimated at a further £25,000.

That the expenditure had risen so high he ascribed uniquely to the slave trade, which had involved him in continuous warfare. That so much had already been done to put it down was due mainly to the generosity of the Company, which could not, however, be expected for the future to shoulder responsibilities which belonged properly to the Imperial Government as a signatory of the Brussels Act. His proposal was now that the Company should be asked to contribute £7,500 for the two administered districts of its sphere, and a further £7,500 towards the defence of the Protectorate in which it enjoyed such large concessions; that the imperial Exchequer should provide the balance of £20,000 (£45,000 with the gunboats); and that Government and Company should recoup themselves by dividing the slowly mounting revenue in the proportion of four to three until the debt was paid off. The alternative was to abandon the struggle with the slave trade and all attempts to check the importation of guns and powder, to abolish the stations at Deep Bay, Fort Johnston, Liwonde and Forts Anderson and Lister, to reduce the police force to 100 Sikhs and 100 Makua, and to employ half this force in the settled district of the Shire Highlands and half in defending one or two points north of Lake Nyasa where the Company had special interests at stake.[1]

The new plan, regarded as a purely financial proposition, was by no means an unfair one for the Company, and Johnston did not hesitate to communicate it to Herbert Canning, the Secretary of the London Board, through whom it must have passed in due course back to Cape Town. But taken in conjunction with his simultaneous defiance of Harris, it must have been well calculated to rouse still further the wrath of Rhodes.

[1] Johnston to Rosebery 16.xii.93, *F.O.2.55.*

For Rhodes was interested in control and not in mere investment. He did not want the Imperial Government to increase its
financial stake in Central Africa. He wanted a puppet, not a
king, over the Zambezi. It is therefore the more remarkable
that correspondence from Cape Town to Zomba had never
been more conciliatory than during the first quarter of 1894.
'Mr Rhodes', wrote Harris, without the hint of a jeer or a
threat, 'notes that you have drawn on him for the whole sum of
£10,000 for the Makanjira expedition and he is glad to hear
from you that the campaign has had a beneficial effect on the
country. . . . As you have very truly observed, our energies are
still being severely taxed to meet the many calls upon the purse
of the Company, and for this reason we shall be glad if you will
draw upon us for as small sums as possible, and rather run your
accounts to a close margin with the banks for this year. At the
same time Mr Rhodes has no wish to abandon what you have
already done around the region of Lake Mweru, and while
maintaining that, trusts to you to remember the financial
obligations the Company has already incurred. Once, however,
that we show a production of gold from Mashonaland or
Matabeleland, as we hope to do this year, our financial burdens
as a Company would be greatly lightened, and we could then
well afford to let you bring this region around Lake Mweru and
the Luapula into much closer touch with your Administration
at Zomba.'[1]

Strength respects strength. The earlier tactics of Rhodes and
Harris had rested on the assumption that the Imperial Government would not pay. At the mere suggestion that this assumption might be unfounded they were prepared to overlook
defiance and to throw out hints of larger subsidies for the north,
now that the Matabele war was over. There was however
another, additional explanation for their change of tone.
Rhodes had run into a difficulty with his trans-Africa telegraph,
the Salisbury-Blantyre section of which was to cut in a straight
line across the neck of Portuguese territory separating Southern
Rhodesia from Nyasaland. The overall responsibility for the
construction of the line from Blantyre to Tete, as also the
handling of relations with the Portuguese authorities at
Mozambique, had been entrusted by Rhodes to Johnston at
the time of their Cape Town discussions. The right to carry the
line across Portuguese territory had already been established, so
the Company contended, by the terms of the Anglo-Portuguese
Convention of 1891, and Johnston on his way back from Cape

[1] Harris to Johnston 10.iii.94, *B.S.A.C. Papers*.

Town to Zomba had drafted along with the Portuguese acting-governor an agreement which, taking the right for granted, merely set out the conditions under which the line when built would be operated. There was little, however, in the name of Rhodes to inspire affection in Portugal, and upon receiving the draft the Lisbon Government had immediately denounced it, recalled the official who had signed it, and stated that it would meet its obligations under the Convention by giving the contract for the Portuguese section of the line to a rival company.

Johnston meantime had moved fast. By December 1893 the track for the line had been cut all the way from Blantyre to Tete, and poles and wires were on their way up the Zambezi, some of them on board the naval gunboats. In these circumstances Johnston's own policy was clear. He would press on the construction until some action which could be construed as forceful opposition was offered by the Portuguese. He would then desist under protest and enter a claim for damages on the Company's behalf. This position was in fact reached on February 19th, 1894, when the Portuguese Commandant at Tete gave notice that he would oppose the erection of a telegraph pole on an island in the middle of the Zambezi. On receiving the news at Zomba on the 26th, Johnston instructed the gunboat commander to send a formal intimation to the Commandant that he yielded to force and would leave the matter to be settled by the British Government.[1]

Rhodes was less closely in touch with the situation. He was acting under a misapprehension about what had really happened on February 19th, for the first rumour to reach the outside world had been to the effect that there had been a clash between British and Portuguese gunboats in the neighbourhood of Tete.[2] As soon as he heard this report on March 8th, Rhodes despatched a characteristic telegram to Johnston. 'Am very pleased to hear that you are protecting our property and not allowing the telegraph line to be wantonly destroyed. . . . Let me know if you want any help. Meantime hold the fort.' On the same day he sent another to Duncan at Salisbury: 'We hear Portuguese have attacked our telegraph people at Tete. . . . Where is Spreckley? Could he lay his hand on fifty men at Umtali? This thing may develop, and he may have to look to the protection of our interests at Beira.'[3] It was two days after

[1] Johnston to Rosebery from Zomba 25.ii.94, enclosing Bowhill to Johnston from Tete 19.ii.94 and Johnston to Commander Carr 26.ii.94, *F.O.2.66*.
[2] Cf. Macdonell to Rosebery from Lisbon 26.ii.94, *F.O.63.1272*; Loch to Ripon from Cape Town 8.iii.94 and 16.iii.94, in C.O. to F.O. 8.iii.94 and 17.iii.94.
[3] Rhodes to Johnston 8.iii.94, Rhodes to Duncan 8.iii.94, *B.S.A.C. Papers*.

this, on the 10th, that Harris had drafted his very complaisant letter about Johnston's expenditure. 'Mr Rhodes feels sure,' that letter had concluded, 'that the Home Government prefer that we should take decided action rather than ask their permission to do so, and thinks they are inclined to support you if you will insist upon it, in all matters connected with the telegraph construction in British Central Africa.'[1]

Most probably this was the incident to which Johnston was referring in the mysterious passage in the epilogue to his autobiography.[2] If so, he was not far wrong in the intentions which he there ascribed to Rhodes. Only his memory was playing him false in suggesting that it was the prime cause of their estrangement. That estrangement, it has been seen, had its origins in the amendment by the Foreign Office of the Cape Town agreement to which Rhodes mistakenly believed that Johnston had been a party. Rhodes's accusations of treachery and his attempt to cut off the promised funds had antagonized Johnston far more permanently than Rhodes had been antagonized by his own suspicions. Whether as a result of Johnston's *apologia* or whether through the intervention of Maguire in London, Rhodes must have come to realize that his suspicions were unfounded. On his return from Matabeleland in February 1894 he came as near as he ever did to making an apology. 'Dear Johnston,' he wrote, 'all writing does harm when two friends have differed. You had better as soon as possible come and see me on your road home. We have completely beaten the Matebele and should be through to you at the end of year with telegraph. Yours C. J. Rhodes.'[3] It was Johnston who at this stage was implacable. There is no record that he even replied to the invitation. Certainly he did not go. Surely it was his rejection of this approach and not his impeccable handling of the Tete situation which earned him Rhodes's undying hatred. The last straw to an imperious nature like Rhodes is when an imagined client turns to another and more powerful patron. Rhodes had set his heart on the acquisition of Nyasaland for the British South Africa Company. He had planted there, as he supposed, the one man in the imperial employ who would play into his hands. And now that man, ignoring his summons, was going to discuss the future of Nyasaland in London without reference to himself. It was Johnston's contempt that was unforgivable.

[1] Harris to Johnston 10.iii.94, *B.S.A.C. Papers.*
[2] *Supra*, pp. 234-5.
[3] Rhodes to Johnston from Cape Town 6.ii.94, *Johnston Papers.*

Chapter 8

A MOST VALUABLE LIFE

ON a superficial view nothing is more paradoxical than the resignation with which the imperial government, after so many past refusals and hesitations, finally accepted responsibility first for Johnston's debts and then for his proposed grant-in-aid. Yet upon further analysis the revolution is not so inexplicable. Johnston's appeal was made in 1894 to a Liberal and traditionally anti-expansionist ministry, on an issue in which it had nothing to fear from a Conservative and expansionist Opposition in Parliament. It was made, moreover, to a Liberal ministry which had just faced a similar issue in Uganda, and from which Mr Gladstone, the principal representative of traditional attitudes within the Cabinet, had since resigned and made way for Lord Rosebery, the leader of the innovators. Among the rank and file of party members the doubtful could be rallied, as they had been rallied over Uganda, by the assurance that the Government was not initiating a new policy, but that it was merely the victim of circumstances created by its predecessors, from which there was no longer any avenue of escape. By 1894, in fact, Nyasaland had served its novitiate on the undefined perimeter of imperial responsibility. So far as English politics were concerned, the temporary partnership with the Chartered Company established by the five-year agreement of February 1891 had served its purpose. With a history of three years of British administration, and with a steadily mounting deficit, the Protectorate could be represented as a commitment to be recognized, and no longer as an option to be taken or left.

All these considerations must have occurred to Sir Percy Anderson, now the Assistant Under-Secretary of State at the Foreign Office, when, at the end of February 1894, he composed a fighting memorandum on Johnston's disclosure of the financial position of the Protectorate. 'Nyasaland cannot be abandoned,' he wrote, echoing almost the very phrases of Sir Gerald Portal's account of his mission to Uganda. 'The Arabs, hard pressed by the German and Congo State forces, would make it their stronghold. The consequences would be disastrous. If Great Britain is not prepared to undertake the obligations, they must be made over to Germany, the Congo

State or Portugal, or transferred to the Chartered Company. Under the exceptional conditions of this lake district, subjection to the Company would be almost as distasteful to the settlers and missionaries, who command widespread sympathy in England and Scotland, as the rule of Germany or the Free State. . . . From the Imperial point of view there would be danger in the supremacy of a body which would be reckless as to entangling Great Britain in international complications. Nyasaland is in contact with Germany and Portugal, and contiguous to the Congo State. Frontier questions, certain to arise with each of these countries, might be handled with a reckless disregard of consequences. If direct control is retained, the conclusion seems unavoidable that some contribution will have to be made from the Exchequer. . . .'

Indeed, the only parts of Johnston's statement to which Anderson took exception were his references to the past generosity and philanthropy of the Company and his suggestion that the Imperial Government should merely join the Company as a co-subscriber to his administration. The Company, Anderson reminded the Cabinet, paid its subsidy as a condition of its Charter, and, moreover, it got a full return for its money. It was bound to administer its territory, north as well as south of the Zambezi. But in the north it had required time. The south had to be brought under settled rule before the north could be undertaken. No cheaper method could have been devised than that of placing the north temporarily under the Commissioner of the neighbouring Protectorate. It had cost the Company less than £15,000 a year, a sum which the Directors, if administering with their own officers, would have found utterly insufficient. The bargain was complete in itself: there was nothing philanthropic about it. So much for the past. For the future, Anderson remarked, Johnston seemed to contemplate subsidies made over to him by the Government and the Company forming a revenue, supplemented by local resources, with which he would deal in his present autocratic fashion. But this was impossible. 'At present he practically takes his orders from Mr Rhodes—when he takes any orders. He reports to the Foreign Office, but chiefly complains of our dilatoriness and obstructiveness and of the niggardliness of the Treasury. He is nominally serving two masters, in practice scarcely serving either. . . . Financial help will entail an alteration in the Commissioner's position. He must be in fact, and not in name only, a servant of the Government.'[1]

---

[1] Memorandum by H. P. Anderson, dated 26.ii.94, *F.O.2.66.*

Anderson's phrases were tart. Perhaps they had been sharpened by the first misleading reports of the telegraph incident at Tete, which suggested that Johnston and Rhodes might have mended their differences in a joint conspiracy against the Portuguese on the Zambezi. Other and grimmer comments were penned in Whitehall when Johnston confessed, on the eve of his return to England, that his deficit was of the order of £20,000 and that it was increasing at the rate of £1,450 a month. 'A pleasant prospect!' wrote Lord Kimberley, the new Secretary of State. 'Send to Lord Rosebery and the Chancellor of the Exchequer.' 'Yes indeed,' echoed Harcourt, 'they are the natural fruits of Jingoism.'[1] Yet neither then nor later was there any suggestion that the Government might repudiate the debt, or even that it should dispense with the services of the official who had incurred it. On the contrary, when it was discovered on his return that Johnston had been obliged to deposit the whole of his small private fortune as security for the drafts on his Administration, the Treasury was at once asked to take steps to set him free. In respect of the existing deficit, a committee was set up in July 1894 to disentangle the accounts of the Protectorate from those of the Company's sphere; and in August Johnston was invited to submit estimates for the year 1894-5 on the understanding that the Treasury would be responsible for arrears totalling £23,000 and for a grant-in-aid of £12,000 for the current year for the Protectorate alone. In signifying their preparedness to invite Parliament to vote the sum of £35,000 their Lordships felt bound to remark in their avuncular way that to have incurred these arrears 'throughout a period of three years without the cognizance of this Department was a financial irregularity of very grave character. The position however in which the British Commissioner was placed was no doubt most exceptional, and my Lords understood that the Secretary of State is of opinion that special indulgence may fairly be extended to Mr Johnston in this matter.'[2]

No formal decision had yet been taken about the administrative separation of the Protectorate from the Sphere, and it was assumed throughout the negotiations with the Treasury that the Company's police subsidy, as also its contribution for water transport, would continue until January 1896. But the settlement of the deficit had acted as an effective catalytic for other problems also. The debt had been accepted as a debt of the Protectorate. The grant-in-aid had been given on condition

[1] Johnston to B.S.A.C. from Zomba 10.iii.94. F.O. copy in *F.O.2.66*.
[2] Treasury to F.O. 16.vii.94.

that the finances of the Protectorate should in future be subject to Treasury control and audit. Under Treasury control, the civil officials of the Protectorate became established and pensionable servants of the Crown and no longer merely the temporary employees of Johnston's Administration: they could no longer be moved about from the Protectorate to the Sphere and vice versa.[1] Again, with the emergence of a recognized parliamentary grant for the Protectorate, it was no longer necessary to conceal the expenditure, mainly on gunboats and military stores, which the Exchequer was already contributing. The Admiralty agreed to keep the Nyasa gunboats on the Navy Vote for one more year, while the deficit was being paid off, but it was provided that in the estimates for 1895-6 they should be transferred to the Protectorate grant-in-aid. Finally, and above all, a Treasury thus openly committed to such considerable expenditure was awake, as it had not previously been, to the argument that it was wiser to spend a little more on defence and police forces at once than to risk the much greater expense of an expeditionary force to quell an Arab or native rebellion at a later date. On public works, as on most branches of civil expenditure, Treasury control was strict; but on his estimates for the year 1895-6 Johnston was permitted to increase very considerably his expenditure on the military side. Arrangements were made for him to visit India at the end of his leave, to plan the recruitment of Sikhs for Central Africa on a semi-permanent basis, and to engage two additional Indian Army officers for the training of regular and irregular forces of Makua and Tonga tribesmen. For 1895-6 the grant proposed in October 1894 was £28,000, more than double the grant for current expenditure for the previous year.

Thus when Rhodes reached London in November 1894 to discuss the future of Central Africa, the position of the Protectorate was already established upon a long-term basis and on a scale which was lavish in comparison with any sums that the Company had ever proposed to spend north of the Zambezi. It had never been true, as Rhodes had so frequently claimed, that the Company had carried the whole expense of administering the Protectorate. In one way and another the Imperial Exchequer had probably contributed as much as the Company. But under the new dispensation the Treasury grant-in-aid for the Protectorate alone was to be nearly three times the Company's police subsidy for Protectorate and Sphere combined. Even assuming that the whole of the subsidy would be in

[1] Cf. Johnston to Kimberley 22.x.94, Inclosure 2, *F.O.2.67.*

practice spent on the Protectorate, it now formed only one-fifth of the Protectorate's total revenue. It was inconceivable that the Imperial Government having committed itself so far, would be tempted by the approaching expiry of the 1891 agreement to contemplate retreat.

Rhodes was too good a business man to attempt to gainsay these facts. In a three-hour interview with Anderson on November 19th he said he would frankly confess that he had always understood the 1891 agreement to mean that he was to pay the expenses and to have the reversion of the Nyasaland Protectorate. But he would not go further into the question. He recognized that the United Kingdom's interest in Nyasaland had been steadily growing, that 'the Scotchmen had got a hold on it', and that the expenditure had been far higher than had been anticipated. All this had paved the way for the Parliamentary grant, and he saw that his dream could not be realized. He was disappointed, but accepted the fact.

The conversation then turned to Johnston. Rhodes, it seems, made no reference to any past differences, but produced a letter addressed by Johnston to the Company on October 17th, 1894, the full text of which has unfortunately not survived. To judge from Anderson's account, it was a foolish, self-important letter, couched no doubt in the grandiose style which Johnston was wont to affect in his, fortunately, rare attempts at formality. It informed the Company as from Her Majesty's Government that its Sphere would continue to be administered by himself until the end of 1895, after which period the question of whether the Charter should be renewed would have to be carefully reconsidered. It was a letter which can only be explained in terms of Johnston's intense emotional involvement in the issues at stake—by the still rankling sense of his ill-treatment at Rhodes's hands, by his exultation at having won his independence and by a streak of spite which was certainly the weakest element in his character. It is an interesting commentary on Rhodes's own emotional involvement that he did not treat the letter as merely contemptible. It had made him, Anderson said, very angry. 'I told him that, as regards his arrangements with the Government, he might forget it, for not only was it entirely unauthorized, but I had done my best to explain to Johnston the position almost in the very terms he had used. I got him to understand this, but he said that it was impossible for him to continue to employ Johnston; that he could not trust him nor accept him in his employment. He was ready at once to undertake the administration of the Chartered territory, and would send Dr Jameson to select a post outside Nyasaland. He begged therefore that Government would allow him to do this. I said I would submit his proposal, but that we must hold him to his police subsidy of £10,000 to the end of 1895. This he accepted.'[1]

Five days later, on November 24th, Anderson on behalf of the Government and Rhodes on behalf of the South Africa Company signed a memorandum of agreement supplementary to the agreement of February 1891. It provided that the Company should assume administrative responsibility for its own sphere by a date not later than June 30th, 1895; that it should continue to pay the police subsidy until December 1895; that the outstanding accounts between the Company and the Protectorate should be regulated by the accountants of the Foreign Office and the Company on the basis that the Company was liable for the annual police subsidies of £10,000, a special grant of £5,000 given in 1891 for expenditure in raising the police force, for expenditure on steam transport on the Lake for administrative purposes, and for such amounts as could be shown to have been expended for the benefit of the Chartered territory as opposed to the Protectorate. It was further agreed that the unexpended balance, if any, of Rhodes's private donation of £10,000 for the Makanjira campaign should be returned to him; that the Company's treaties within the Chartered sphere should be sanctioned, as also its claims to mining rights in the western districts of the Protectorate; and that the claims to land and mining rights in the North Nyasa district would be sanctioned subject to a further investigation of the validity of the title.[2] These terms were so far satisfactory to Rhodes that he consented before his return to South Africa to a surface reconciliation with Johnston, engineered by his co-director, Albert Grey. 'But', wrote Johnston, 'even at that meeting he said he never wished to see me again—and he never did'.[3]

To all in Foreign or Colonial Office circles the permanence of the breach must have been apparent. Yet it did not seem to have done Johnston any harm: rather the reverse. It eliminated a constant source of suspicion of his motives and actions, which had tended to become more dangerous the longer he had been away from London. It brought into sharper relief the difficulties under which he had been working. The slipshod accounting

[1] Memorandum by H. P. Anderson 19.xi.94, *F.O.83.1315*.
[2] Memorandum of Agreement with British South Africa Company respecting British Central Africa, supplementary to the Agreement of February 1891, 24.xi.94, *F.O.83.1315*.
[3] Johnston: *Story*, p. 497.

of the past three years was forgiven. The real administrative ability of his plans and estimates for the future of the Protectorate was seen and recognized. More than this, people from a wider circle who distrusted Rhodes and all that he stood for in the way of a ruthless, materialistic approach to Empire, turned to Johnston, as they would later turn to Lugard, as the exponent of a gentler, more rational creed of European expansion in the tropics. The period of international snatch and grab was drawing to a close: even those who had been most opposed to British participation in it were bound to recognize that the problem of administration remained and could not be ignored. There were those, on the Conservative as well as on the Liberal side of English politics, who were searching for a practicable alternative to the system of government by Chartered Company, a method of ruling primitive peoples living in the tropics, which would be responsible and yet cheaper and less elaborate than anything yet evolved by the Colonial Office. To such people Johnston's 'Report of the First Three Years' Administration of the Eastern Portion of British Central Africa', which was presented to Parliament as a Command Paper in August 1894, came as something of a revelation. The Stationery Office was besieged with orders, and several reprintings were necessary.

It was not for any recital of his administrative achievements that this document was remarkable among State Papers, but rather for the detached and thought-provoking discussion of the problems of pioneer colonization. In it Johnston assumed successfully the rôle of a man of science writing informally and quite artlessly to his friends at home. He discoursed brilliantly, and for once succinctly, on the climate, the geology, the botany, the zoology and the native races of his tropical colony. He told the story of the coffee-tree, imported by Mr John Buchanan from the botanical garden in Edinburgh, which had become the progenitor of two million trees now growing in the Shire Highlands, and also that of the *dub* grass, which had arrived accidentally in a packet of seeds from Ceylon, and which was now spreading as luxuriant pastures over the Residency grounds at Zomba. 'Perhaps', he wrote in a typically confidential aside, 'it may not be uninteresting to mention that the only pleasurable side of my life here during these last three years has been the formation of large aviaries and zoological gardens. . . . I succeeded in getting nine European fowls up to Zomba, but they have not been a great success. Muscovy ducks very well. European geese do not suffer in apparent health, but cease to breed. Turkeys are moderately successful. This is the

4. JOHNSTON'S PALLAH

From the original drawing by Sir Harry Johnston in the
possession of Mr J. B. Henderson.

native country of the guinea fowl. They can be readily
tamed, and perhaps it is not sufficiently known what admirable
gardeners they are, spending all the day-time hunting for grubs
amongst the vegetables and flowers.' There was a change from
Rhodes in all this; and yet none could say that the matters
treated were unimportant.

In dealing with law and order and native administration he
struck a similarly sympathetic note. He was adept by now at
pointing the contrast between the desperate minority of Arab
slave-traders and militant Yao chieftains, who opposed the
establishment of civilized rule, and the suffering masses of the
population, who looked to the Administration as their pro-
tector, and longed only to live in peace and prosperity under
the Union Jack. But he did not descend into cheap heroics or
sentimental paternalism. He denied that his action against the
slave trade had been of the nature of a perpetual crusade. He
had not gone out of his way to attack every small injustice that
was committed in remote areas, but only to assert his authority
in the settled districts and along the main lines of communication. Many native communities were, he said, 'very unreason-
able in their demands on us for protection'. But his own policy
was not to interfere unnecessarily with the rule of native chiefs.
To those of their subjects who wished for a more civilized
form of government he would say, 'Why not come and
settle in the vicinity of one of our forts?' The function of the
Administration was not to destroy tribal life, but to keep the
peace and to provide, by a judicious immigration policy, a few
growing-points round which individuals who wished to adopt a
new way of life might do so. Intelligent natives, he remarked,
had already been stimulated by European settlement to a
desire for personal property. This tendency he proposed to
encourage. 'At least one, a man named Kumtaja, at Blantyre,
and another called Nyama, at Zomba, have started coffee-
planting, wheat growing and other enterprises, much more like
the occupation of a European than the hand-to-mouth existence
of a savage.' At the end of his report Johnston returned again
to the fundamental facts of climate. Two and a half per cent
of the European population died of malaria every year.

> The practical conclusion to which we may arrive is that
> whilst the European has a great rôle to perform in Central Africa
> as ruler and teacher, it is probable that between the Zambezi
> and the Upper Nile he will be numbered by hundreds of thousands
> and not by millions at any rate for the next two or three hundred
> years. After that man may have acquired such control over

Nature that the making of a climate healthy or the adapting of the system to an unhealthy climate will be a mere matter of Physics. . . . Awaiting that development, we must at present devote ourselves to reclaiming Africa from the unintelligent rule of Nature by educating the Black Man and introducing the Yellow Man, and establishing ourselves in sufficient numbers in the more healthy districts so that we may direct these operations *in situ*. . . . The immigration of the docile, kindly, thrifty, industrious, clever-fingered, sharp-witted Indian [he remarked in a contemporary article in the *New Review*], will furnish us with the solid core of our armed forces in that continent, and will supply us with the telegraphic clerks, the petty shopkeepers, the skilled artisans, the cooks, the minor employés, the clerks and the railways officials needed in the civilized administration of Tropical Africa. The Indian, liked by Black and White, will serve as a link between these two divergent races. Moreover Africa, in opening this vast field to the enterprise and overflow of the Yellow Races of the Indian Empire, will direct a large current of wealth to the impoverished peninsula, and afford space for the reception in not far distant homes of the surplus population of Southern Asia.[1]

It was a stimulating contribution, and men in public life began to be aware of its thirty-six-year-old author, no longer as an African official in some way connected with Rhodes, but as an authority in his own right. It was not that Johnston himself had changed fundamentally either in temperament or habits of thought. As a very young man he had been phenomenally mature in some ways, and even in late middle age he was to remain as phenomenally immature in others. Certainly in 1894 his puckish sense of fun was cascading as irrepressibly as ever in caricature and light verse. It is possible that the lines he wrote in celebration of the introduction of female typists into the Foreign Office never came into the hands of any of the doubtless eminently respectable ladies who assisted Sir Clement Hill with his correspondence. If so, it was perhaps as well:

> *Did you not know that Spicer kept a home,*
> *Finished and furnished in 1894,*
> *Whereto the Damsels of the Street might come,*
> *Worn with Love's War?*
>
> *There to repose, re-paint, recuperate,*
> *There to renew their fascinating ways,*
> *Gratis their lodging and the food they ate*
> *For seven days.*

[1] Enclosed in Johnston to Kimberley 31.iii.94, *F.O.2.66*; cf. *Review of Reviews*, Vol. X, p. 37.

Did you not know?

Here none without encouragement are left
Who wish to seek an honest livelihood,
Whose looks are unimpaired, whose hands are deft,
Whose manners good.

For such as these our Spicer holds in view
Employment; and the Foreign Office aids
By letting him engage a chosen few
As waiting maids.

Here in grim Downing Street's Quadrangle, they
Attain respectability at last.
The Genius Loci in its lofty way
Ignores their past.

One houri brings E. Walrond Clarke his lunch;
Two houris on Sir Clement's wishes wait;
Three houris ply with sandwiches and punch
The Secretary of State.[1]

There is also record of a charming little water-colour in which members of the Africa Department were represented in the guise of birds, headed by a large and solemn-looking pelican labelled *Hillia Clemens*. Its circulation gave much pleasure and was long remembered in Downing Street, but it is known to have caused prolonged resentment in one spectator, whose voice was to become increasingly powerful in the disposal of Foreign Office patronage. In other ways, too, Johnston still gave plenty of scope to would-be critics, for he was, and remained, magnificently indiscreet. Very senior eyebrows indeed were raised, for example, when it was observed from *The Times* of November 7th, 1894, that in a single public speech at Liverpool he had referred to slave-dhows flying the French flag in the Indian Ocean, to slave-owning by Portuguese colonists in Central Zambezia and to a remarkable revival of the slave trade in German East Africa. Even Anderson was stirred to wrath. 'We cannot control Johnston. . . . He has reproduced on the platform what we cut out of his Parliamentary Paper.' A reprimand, the sterner for being unofficial, was despatched to Newcastle, where the misdemeanour was likely to be repeated on the following evening, only to receive the pained reply that 'I was very hard on the ancient Egyptians and somewhat downright in my remarks on the Arabs, but I was particularly careful to say nothing that might embarrass H.M.G.' He had cancelled,

[1] Cited Alex Johnston: *op. cit.*, pp. 117-18.

however, a round of similar engagements which had been due to follow in Scotland, and with this gesture Anderson had perforce to be mollified.[1]

Such episodes, needless to say, caused nothing more than occasional interludes in the otherwise steady stream of official commendation which flowed down upon Johnston at this time. Apart from a month's coaching tour in Switzerland with three of his sisters, he had been unremittingly at work, since his return to England, in his flat in Queen Anne's Mansions. Army officers desiring a taste of active service, civil officials of all kinds, steamer mechanics and other technicians had been interviewed and engaged. A whole host of legislative matters, of small biographical interest but great intrinsic importance, Customs schedules, Township regulations, Labour ordinances, Conditions of Service for all grades in the Administration, had been drafted and revised in consultation with the Crown lawyers. Besides the tedious correspondence about past accounts and future estimates, there had been a vast amount of work best classified under the heading of Supply. The Foreign Office Protectorates were not served as yet by the Crown Agents for the Colonies. Johnston had to place his own orders for civil, military and naval stores, for building-materials and for every single piece of machinery and equipment, furniture and stationery, required for the conduct of government. Since there were few contractors or merchants in Central Africa, the African and Indian employees of the Administration had to be paid in kind. This meant orders for calico by the thousand bales and for glass beads by the ton. Even for its European officials the government had to act as grocer, haberdasher, wine merchant, chemist and ironmonger. All these things had called for the Commissioner's attention during the brief period of his leave. And, above all, there had been the preparations for the final military pacification of the country, of which his forthcoming visit to India was to be the last and least burdensome engagement.

Indeed, when he sailed from Liverpool at the beginning of the great frost of 1895, it was for the best enjoyed and most stimulating holiday of his life. He was accompanied, as a real Commissioner should be, by a Military Adviser, an officer seconded for two years from the Grenadier Guards, who was doubtless adept at all those little attentions and matters of protocol which make up the qualifications of a good aide-de-

[1] Anderson to Johnston 7.xi.94, *F.O.2.65*; Johnston to Anderson 8.xi.94, *F.O.2.68.*

FORT JOHNSTON, LAKE NYASA
The Sikh uniform of black, yellow and white was designed by Johnston
to symbolize harmonious race relations

AFTER THE BATTLE, NEAR KOTAKOTA, LAKE NYASA

This Ngoni warrior, though lying as if dead, in fact recovered and later joined the regular forces of the Protectorate camp. At Cairo he was the guest of Kitchener; and Baring, now Lord Cromer, was distinctly more welcoming than he had been at their first meeting eleven years before. At Bombay he was joined by Major Edwards, his able Commandant from Nyasaland, and with this fitting retinue he journeyed on to Calcutta to experience the delectable hospitality of Government House —'a bedroom which might have been allotted to a sultan, a sitting-room out of the Arabian Nights, and ante-chambers and verandahs with exquisite flowers'.

The diplomatic side of his mission was successfully completed in less than a week. The Government of India's decision to allow no more Sikhs to go to Central Africa had been rescinded. The Adjutant-General and the Military Member of Council had agreed to the recruitment of two hundred fully trained volunteers from the best Indian regiments on three-year contracts and had undertaken to replace them at the end of that term. And so, without waiting for the Viceroy's merely formal confirmation, Johnston and his staff set off on a tour of Sikh and Punjabi regimental centres. They established a depot at Agra, then travelled on through Lahore and as far as Peshawar. While his *aides* did the routine work, Johnston devoted himself to mollifying colonels, visiting the relations of the Sikhs already in Central Africa, and preaching everywhere his message of a promised land beyond the Ocean for would-be agricultural settlers, traders and artisans. In the intervals of business he found a week in which to gaze at the high Himalayas from Dalhousie, and he spent happy days painting the Moghul monuments of Lahore from the back seat of a hired landau. At last, towards the end of March, his little army was ready and equipped, and he moved it down to Bombay and aboard the steamer *Madura*, chartered from the British India line for the voyage to Zanzibar and Chinde.[1] The embarkation must have been picturesque, for after the Sikhs, resplendent, with their towering turbans and crisp curly beards, in the white, yellow and black dress uniforms designed by Johnston, there mounted the gangway a strange procession, the personal property of the Commissioner, of buffalo, sheep and goats, peacocks, Chinese geese, ducks, turkeys and blossom-headed parakeets, the victims of a well-intentioned but ill-fated attempt to enrich the zoological resources of Africa.

There can be little doubt that India appealed to the more superficial side of Johnston's imperialism. By nature an ascetic man, he yet loved the panoply of power with which British

[1] Johnston to Kimberley 12.iv.95 and 19.iv.95, *F.O.2.88*.

I

Indian officialdom was surrounded. He liked to be a great lord, and to ride out to dinner on an elephant. But coming at the end of his relationship with Rhodes, India gave him also the vision of an Empire squarely controlled by the administrator and the soldier, the representatives of a creative, unmercenary oligarchy rather than of a master race, men who came to rule and not to exploit, men who could be trusted to see justice done between black and yellow and white. His visit to India made Johnston far more uncompromisingly the official in his attitude to imperial problems. He continued to advocate European and Indian settlement in tropical Africa, but only for functional reasons. European settlers could contribute to the economy of an imperial colony, but their attitude to the native inhabitants was indefensible: they must be governed and not left in control. White colonists, he never tired of telling the Foreign Office, would, left to themselves, re-establish slavery in their own favour. Similarly, from the time of his visit to India, he indulged in no more wild talk about tropical Africa as the America of the Hindu. The Sikh soldier was functional—'far superior to the impossible, perspiring, beef-fed British soldier or sailor'. The Indian peasant farmer or small trader, if equipped with a little capital, was functional too; but Johnston was clear now that he did not want, by assisted emigration, to encourage 'the riff raff of India'.[1] As for the negro, Johnston was still too fundamentally an Evolutionist to believe in the possibility of any startlingly rapid progress through education.

Central Africa [he wrote in 1897] is probably as remote from self government or representative institutions as is the case with India. It can only be administered under the benevolent despotism of the Imperial Government, though in the future and developed administration there is no reason to believe that black men may not serve as officials in common with white men and yellow men. . . . It is the mission of an impartial administration to adopt a mean course between the extreme of sentiment and the extreme of selfishness. It must realize that but for the enterprise and capital of these much-criticized, rough and ready pioneers Central Africa would be of no value and the natives would receive no payment for the products of their land, would in fact relapse into their almost ape-like existence of fighting, feeding and breeding. Therefore due encouragement must be shown to European planters, traders and miners, whose presence in the country is the figure before the ciphers. Yet it must be borne in mind that the negro is a man with man's rights; above all that he was the owner of the country before we came; and

[1] Johnston to Kimberley from Zanzibar 12.iv.95 and 1.vi.95, *F.O.2.88.*

deserves, nay, is entitled to, a share in the land commensurate
with his needs and numbers; that in numbers he will always
exceed the white man while he may some day come to rival him
in intelligence; and that finally if we do not use our power to
govern him with absolute justice the time will come sooner or
later when he will rise against us and expel us as the Egyptian
officials were expelled from the Sudan.[1]

More immediately, the recruiting tour, and perhaps especially the unusual circumstances of the journey across the Indian
Ocean and up the Zambezi in company with the Sikhs and
their European officers, served to build up a relationship of
intimacy and confidence with the members of this military
arm which was not the least remarkable achievement of a
Commissioner who was the least military of men. His relations
with the naval officers on the Zambezi and Lake Nyasa had
always been uncertain, and in Uganda he was to quarrel openly
with the military. He had no sympathy at all with men who
assumed the right to go shooting when there was important
work to be done. But with Edwards, as with Maguire and all
the Indian Army officers who served him in Central Africa,
many of them as volunteers on less than their service pay, he
never wavered in his admiration. 'Throughout all my survey
and experience of the world', he wrote at the end of his life, 'I
had never met their superiors in education, bravery or zeal.'[2]

It was as well, for on his return to Nyasaland in April 1895
there was much fighting to be done. During the year he had
been away Sharpe had kept, had even increased, the Administration's newly acquired hold over the shores of Lake Nyasa.
Fort Johnston had stood fast. Fort Maguire had been attacked
by Makanjira, who had succeeded in murdering the rival
chieftainess, Kumbasani, in her village near by; but the invaders had been driven out with heavy losess by the garrison,
which had since maintained an increasingly efficient surveil-
lance over the dhow traffic on the Lake.[3] At Kotakota, half-way
up the opposite shore, Johnston's ally the old Arab Jumbe had
died; his successor had been deported to Zanzibar for inciting a
number of murders among local notabilities; and an administrative station had been set up from which a European official
had begun to rule the Marimba district directly through a

[1] H. H. Johnston: *British Central Africa*, 1897, pp. 183-4.
[2] H. H. Johnston: *Story*, p. 320.
[3] Johnston to Rosebery 4.ii.94, Sharpe to Johnston 14.iii.94 in Johnston to
Rosebery 14.iii.94, *F.O.2.66*; Sharpe to Kimberley 21.xi.94, *F.O.2.68*.

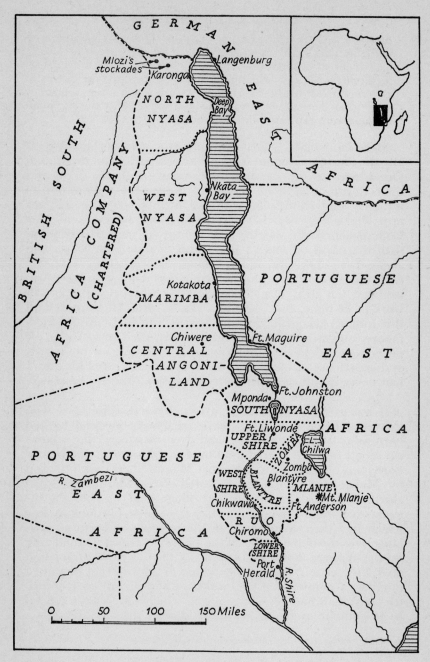

10. NYASALAND IN 1895

council of native headmen.[1] Further north, at Deep Bay, an able official, Mr Crawshay, had built a strongly fortified station commanding the most frequented of the ferry-routes across the northern section of the Lake.[2]

Still these were as yet precarious gains. South and east of the Lake Makanjira remained at large, and his allies among the eastern Yaos, Kawinga and Matapwiri, Zarafi and Liwonde, had mounted in February the most considerable insurrection that had yet taken place, in the Upper Shire plain between Fort Johnston and Zomba: they had been repulsed, but not subdued.[3] North of the Lake the situation was still more threatening. Mlozi and his compatriots from the East Coast had now had six years since the truce of 1889 in which to build up their arsenals and strengthen their stockaded towns. The Germans, desiring to keep the ivory trade from the far interior flowing through their ports had been less than scrupulous in controlling the importation of arms and powder, which were the ivory-merchant's most coveted currency.[4] The Bemba, to the west of the Stevenson Road, had thus become heavily armed, and communications with Lake Tanganyika were again becoming unsafe. Slave-raids were conducted almost within sight of Crawshay's station at Deep Bay and the Lakes Company's trading-post at Karonga's. Administrative reports referred to the Nyakusa tribe as Mlozi's subjects and recognized that the African population of a much wider area, inevitably seeking to ally themselves with the stronger of the two intrusive elements, were uncertain whether to look to Mlozi or the European government. While such a state of affairs endured, there could be no question of taxation or settled government beyond the immediate environs of the fortified posts.[5]

It was a situation which Johnston, now that he had the power, did not mean to endure for long. May and June he devoted to the strengthening of his African police. The Makua detachment was raised from seventy to a hundred, and Atonga irregulars from the West Nyasa district were recruited and trained to release, so far as possible, the Sikhs from garrison

---

[1] Sharpe to Kimberley 18.vii.94 and 2.viii.94, *F.O.2.67*; Edwards to Johnston 17.vii.94 in Johnston to F.O. 4.x.94, *F.O.2.67*; Sharpe to Kimberley 5.xii.94, *F.O.2.68*.
[2] Sharpe to Johnston 14.iii.94, *op. cit.*
[3] Sharpe to Kimberley 14.ii.95, 28.ii.95, 14.iii.95, *F.O.2.88*.
[4] Johnston to Rosebery 27.xii.93, *F.O.2.55*; Sharpe to Kimberley 11.vi.94 and 18.vi.94, *F.O.2.66*.
[5] Swann to Sharpe from Deep Bay 7.viii.94 in Johnston to Kimberley 15.x.94, *F.O.2.67*, and Marshall to Johnston from Abercorn 7.viii.94 in Johnston to Kimberley 19.xi.94, *F.O.2.68*.

work in the south. Among the immigrant community at Blantyre he introduced the first measure of municipal self-government—a 'Council of Advice' which agreed to levy rates totalling £425 for street-lighting and road-building.[1] In July he set out on a tour of inspection in the north. From Fort Johnston he went by gunboat to Fort Maguire and thence across the Lake to Kotakota, where he regulated by means of a new and excellently conceived form of treaty the administration which had been set up in Jumbe's former kingdom. By these treaties the chiefs and headmen of eight territorial sub-districts ceded their sovereign rights to the Queen of England, agreed to conform to the laws and regulations in force in the Protectorate, and promised to sever all connexion with the slave trade and to use their influence to bring about the extinction of the status of domestic slavery. In return all the land upon which they and their people possessed villages and plantations was confirmed to them in perpetuity: they would not be dispossessed save by their own consent and for an equivalent allotment elsewhere. Waste and unoccupied land on the other hand became the property of the Crown, to be alienated by the Commissioner at his discretion; but it was provided that a quarter of any selling-price or annual rent from the alienation of land should be paid over to the chief of the district, as also a quarter of any royalties accruing from mining rights and other privileges. In return for their assistance in the collection of hut-tax, ten per cent of any sums so collected was to be remitted to the chiefs concerned.[2]

The part of the Protectorate lying to the west of Lake Nyasa was already divided on paper into four administrative districts: Central Angoniland, Marimba, West Nyasa and North Nyasa. By his treaty-making at Kotakota Johnston was inaugurating something approaching effective occupation in the two central ones. Central Angoniland he proposed to add as a part of his programme of autumn campaigning. 'Several chiefs from this district', he informed Lord Kimberley, 'have offered to sign treaties; and other chiefs (the Yao immigrants) have of late assumed such an aggressive attitude and made such a determined attempt to renew the slave trade, that military expeditions will have to be sent against them this autumn, and either, amongst the terms of peace they will have to agree to the payment of taxes, or in the event of their not submitting . . . they will have to be expelled from the country as Makanjira has been, and the administration of their lands taken over by the

---

[1] Johnston to Kimberley 30.v.95, *F.O.2.98.*
[2] Inclosures 1 to 8 in Johnston to Kimberley 2.viii.95, *F.O.2.89.*

Crown. Consequently, by January 1st next I expect to be in a position to justify the imposition of taxes in the Central Angoniland district, and even amongst the Angoni dwelling there, for the latter, through their intestine quarrels, have frequently invoked our assistance recently, and we have intervened to preserve peace; but in making this intervention (with Chief Chifisi for instance) we have informed them that they will henceforth have to pay taxes. To this they have agreed, and in my Estimates for next year I have provided for the better administration of their country through European officials.' The North Nyasa district, on the other hand, though containing a population potentially friendlier than any other, could not be administered so long as the Arabs maintained their independence on its northern border. As a last endeavour to procure a peaceful settlement, Johnston in July sailed on from Kotakota to Karonga's and sent messengers to Mlozi, offering to meet him in parley alone and unarmed on the lake-shore. But Mlozi refused to leave his stockades, and war thus became inevitable.

It was not altogether that Johnston, having acquired new strength, had become more bellicose. There remained one important group of peoples in the Protectorate with whose independence he did not as yet propose to interfere. The northern Angoni chiefs dwelling in the high hinterland of the three northern districts were, he reported, very powerful 'and although at present evincing much friendliness towards the English, they are not sufficiently dependent on us to be subjected to taxation. On this point I have not changed the policy I have pursued from the commencement of my administration, which is, that where a district . . . does not continually seek our help in the management of its affairs, or does not assume an aggressive attitude towards the British Administration, I prefer to leave it untamed and ungoverned; but where for one cause or another I am obliged to place officials and erect stations, I think it is only right that the natives . . should contribute their reasonable share towards the expenses of administration.'[1]

Johnston had now made his plans; it remained only to await the dry season and then to carry them out. The ultimate outcome was perhaps a foregone conclusion. He had the trained troops and the arms of precision against which native forces, however superior numerically, could not stand and fight in open battle. But there were accidents in African warfare which could

[1] Johnston to Kimberley 2.viii.95, *F.O.2.89*; Johnston to Salisbury 15.xi.95, *F.O.2.89*.

not be foreseen, which might dangerously interrupt the momentum of his campaigns and still bring his Administration into great discredit. The country of the eastern Yaos was broken and mountainous, and adequate precautions against ambush were hard to contrive. Nyasa was prone to sudden and violent storms, and the lake gunboats were notoriously unseaworthy; the element of shipwreck had been a vital one in the Maguire disaster, and it could all too easily be repeated. With Mlozi especially, the possibility of heavy casualties was one which had to be seriously faced. His stockades would have to be breached by artillery and then taken by storm. Such operations might be an everyday occurrence on the north-west frontier of India, but an obscure African Protectorate could scarcely afford to leave twenty dead, even upon a victorious battlefield.

It must therefore have caused Johnston real relief to learn, early in August, of the Conservative victory at the June election, and of Lord Salisbury's return to the Foreign Office. The Liberals had paid his debts and found him a place on the Treasury alms-roll. With the Liberal Chancellor, Harcourt, he had even formed a personal friendship. But neither to Rosebery nor to Kimberley was Johnston much more than a name. 'Stupendously long' was about the most illuminating comment that Rosebery had ever written upon a despatch from Zomba. Kimberley had been fair and friendly, but just as profoundly uninterested. With Hill, now Head of the African Department, indifference might turn in a crisis to hostility. Indeed, Salisbury's first action in Nyasaland affairs after his return to office was to check both Hill and Anderson for a tendency to interfere too minutely in Johnston's proceedings. 'It seems to be a mistake to be constantly altering our Regulations as Mr Johnston wishes to do,' grumbled Hill on a matter of no importance. 'It is a mistake', replied Salisbury, 'to pull too much at Johnston's bit. Better let this pass.'[1]

Military operations began on September 28th with a week's campaign against the two most southerly Yao chiefs, Matapwiri and Mtiromanja, who had been proving themselves troublesome neighbours of the Shire Highlands by raiding and robbery conducted from bases in the hilly country between Mt. Mlanje and the Portuguese frontier. This, however, was but the dress rehearsal for the main expedition which left Zomba exactly a month later, cleared Zarafi from his mountain strongholds north of Mlanje, and then, marching straight on to Fort Johnston, conducted a lightning round-up of illicitly held guns

[1] Minutes on Johnston to Salisbury 2.ix.95, *F.O.2.89.*

and slaves in Mponda's country, and swept up overland through Makanjira's hill villages to Fort Maguire. Though this remarkable feat of human mobility was not carried through without fighting, its essential function was to demonstrate publicly to the inhabitants of the least accessible and most unruly portions of the Protectorate the force which the British administration could now deploy. Hitherto officials and garrisons had remained for the most part in their forts, situated, with two exceptions, along the Shire valley and round the Lake. Their policing activities had been confined to the interception of slave-caravans crossing the river valley and on their approach to the lake shore, and to trivial punitive expeditions against the more accessible villages of raiding chiefs. Nine times out of ten they had failed in their objectives, because the offenders had escaped to the hills, whither small detachments did not dare to follow them. Now, however, the hill-dwellers, most of whom had never seen a European or an Indian, were shown the spectacle of 350 fighting men and as many more porters, winding remorselessly up the mountain ridges, sweeping away all opposition to their progress, freeing slaves, intercepting and disarming fugitives, burning the villages of resisters and carrying off their stores of ivory and cloth, fire-arms and powder. The main body in twenty-eight days covered 459 miles, all on foot. The casualties were minute: one Sikh and one African soldier killed, two Sikhs and ten Africans wounded; the enemy losses were reckoned at ninety dead. More than a thousand slaves were released, many of them confined in slave-sticks and awaiting removal to Portuguese and German territory. At Mponda's alone 112 guns and 270 pounds of powder were captured from places within sight of Fort Johnston.

As was appropriate, but nonetheless admirable, Johnston accompanied the expedition himself throughout the greater part of its journey, marching in the centre of the column and organizing the vast retinue of native carriers, while Edwards directed the military operations. In the brief intervals between sleeping, marching and fighting he received the chiefs who wished to make their submission, encouraging them to move with their people from the hills down into the plains beneath, and explaining to them the conditions of peaceful co-existence with the Protectorate government. The bulk of the population, he explained to Lord Salisbury, was of Nyanja stock, and with all of these he had made peace, and they had come in to settle in their old homes. The ruling race, however, were Yao, and of these the majority had fled with their leaders, Zarafi and

I*

Makanjira, into the unadministered region of Portuguese East Africa around the headwaters of the Lujenda River, where they were receiving hospitality from Mtaka and Mtarika, the leading chiefs of the Yao homelands. He prophesied that they would probably not care to return under the very strict conditions of disarmament that he was imposing, but he added the warning that so long as Yaoland remained in its present condition of turbulence, totally uncontrolled by the Portuguese, so long would it be necessary to maintain an armed police force to guard the eastern land frontier from the attacks of slave-raiders. On this occasion at least Johnston's predictions were not unduly optimistic. Several years were still to pass before administration could become a reality in the south-eastern borderlands, but the period of constant anxiety was over. The military promenade had been a signal success.[1]

At Fort Maguire on November 23rd he received the first telegram to pass along the newly opened line from Cape Town to Blantyre. Hitherto it had taken at best a month to communicate with the Foreign Office and to obtain a reply by means of the submarine cable at Mozambique: now the operation had been reduced to a matter of hours. To Johnston himself the line was shortly to render one inestimable service; for his successors the convenience would be qualified by the experience that government from Whitehall had begun.

Meanwhile, the Commissioner was letting no grass grow under his feet. That night he returned in the gunboat *Adventure* to Fort Johnston. On the following day he re-embarked for the five-day journey to the north end of the Lake. The *Domira*, tightly packed with Sikhs and native troops, and escorted by the gunboat *Pioneer*, had already sailed. The *Herrmann von Wissmann*, hired from the German authorities at Langenburg, would follow on the 25th. On November 30th and December 1st, 398 riflemen and 36 gunners, with their officers, supplies and munitions of war, were disembarked at Karonga's. At nightfall half the force set out in pelting rain to place itself in position along the Rukuru River, between Mlozi's town and the German frontier. An hour before dawn the remainder began to move up the main Tanganyika road, dragging two seven-pounder mountain-guns, which at 7.30 opened fire at nine hundred yards' range upon the two subsidiary stockades of Msalema and Kopakopa. The surprise effect was complete. The inmates of both forts fled without resistance, some into the

[1] Johnston to Salisbury, 13.xi.95, *F.O.2.89*; and 6.i.96, *F.O.2.106*, enclosing military reports by C. A. Edwards.

arms of the Rukuru detachment, others to Mlozi's stockade. The two arms of the European force then closed in, and by early afternoon Mlozi's was completely invested.

Soon Johnston, who had been recruiting carriers from among his native allies at Karonga's, arrived with three more seven-pounders and two nine-pounders, and at 4.30 in the afternoon, the rain still pouring down, a steady bombardment was begun. During the night the besieged attempted two sorties, but were repelled. At daylight on the 3rd the guns were moved up to within 375 yards, which was near the limit of effective rifle-fire from the loopholes of the fort. Soon afterwards a white flag was raised within the fort and firing ceased. Mlozi came out and stood beneath the walls, and Johnston on his side approached within shouting distance. He promised Mlozi his life if he surrendered, but nothing more. Thereupon the flag of truce was lowered and the bombardment recommenced. By three o'clock two hundred and thirty shells had been expended, but although most of the houses in the centre of the town had been destroyed, the thick mud ramparts were little damaged, and it seemed to Edwards that the only course was to attempt a direct assault on the following day.

Johnston, however, had been interrogating a deserter and had discovered the exact location of Mlozi's own house. As a last endeavour a nine-pounder was trained upon it and two more shells were fired. The effect was instantaneous. At 5.15, with heavy supporting fire from the walls, a large body of the defenders streamed out of a gate on the east side just opposite Mlozi's house, and almost simultaneously another sortie was made from the north. The besieging forces countercharged, there was some desperate hand-to-hand fighting, and by 6.30 the town was theirs. Johnston had found himself in the thick of the mêlée, part fight and part flight, and remembered shooting through the head with his revolver an Arab who had run straight at him gun in hand.

In the two days' engagement Johnston had lost one Sikh and three Africans killed, and one European, six Sikhs and seven Africans wounded. Of Mlozi's supporters, mostly Nyamwezi soldiers of fortune from the central region of German East Africa, 216, including Kopakopa and three other Arabs, had been killed by the Protectorate forces, besides an unknown number of refugees pursued and cut off by the native Nkonde of the district, who had many years of oppression to avenge, and whose activities in the circumstances could not possibly be controlled. Nearly six hundred slaves were found cooped up in the town itself, as also the bodies of seventy Nkonde hostages who had been slaughtered at Mlozi's command. Of Mlozi himself there was at first no sign. He was brought in, however, some hours after dark by the sergeant-major of the Atonga troops, who had found him hiding in a carefully concealed cavity under the floor of his house. Next morning, since he was in the legal sense a native of East Africa and therefore justiciable only by a native court, he was put on trial before a hastily improvised bench of Nkonde chiefs, and charged with the murder of the hostages in his town. Eye-witnesses came forward in plenty from among the prisoners of war and the released slaves. Johnston exercised the only judicial power he as yet possessed in such cases by confirming the death sentence, and at one o'clock that afternoon Mlozi was hanged.[1]

At last the time had come when the expeditionary force could safely be divided. On December 5th a detachment of 190 men was detailed to complete the demolition of the Arab towns and to assist the District Collector, Mr Crawshay, in building a fortified station at Karonga's and another on the Tanganyika road at the frontier with the South Africa Company's sphere. Two days later the main body embarked for the south. A hundred and fifty of them travelled direct to Kotakota in the *Domira*, there to settle in collaboration with Mr Swann and a large force of local levies the outstanding accounts of the Administration on the western shores of the Lake.[2] The remainder, using the *Wissmann* and the two gunboats, sailed straight south to the Shire port at Liwonde's town and thence marched to Zomba. With them, perilously ill, went Johnston, a victim to his third attack of blackwater fever. A brief telegram was sent in his name to London, announcing the victory at Mlozi's, but nothing more: it was answered by Salisbury on January 1st, congratulating him on the award of a K.C.B. By the same courier there arrived at Zomba the first news of the Jameson Raid.

Poor Johnston. Though he cannot have seen it clearly, he must have sensed that the moment of his triumph was also the moment of his greatest danger. At thirty-seven the youngest member of any of the orders of knighthood, his battle with Rhodes brilliantly vindicated by Jameson's mad act, his latest illness was yet a portent which he could not ignore. This time there could be no question of a mere holiday at home. The

[1] Johnston to Salisbury 3.i.96, enclosing Edwards to Johnston 1.i.96, *F.O.2.106*.
[2] Johnston to Salisbury 24.i.96, *F.O.2.106*.

straight road to solid achievement which he had opened in
Nyasaland would have to be trodden by another. Unless he was
suicidally inclined, his career in the tropics was at an end. And
yet what work outside the tropics would he find? The older
established governorships in temperate regions belonged to the
Colonial Office and were now in the gift of Chamberlain. For
orthodox diplomacy he was scarcely fitted either by temperament or inclination. From Lugard, who wrote in pathetic terms
to congratulate him, he might well take warning—Lugard who
had founded the East African empire and had been for nearly
four years without recognition and without work.[1] As an
official of the Consular Service Johnston could at least count on
being provided for materially, perhaps with some post in a
pleasant but insignificant Mediterranean port, like his old
friend Sir Richard Burton. But to regain the work he loved and
did well, an administrative post of power and influence, he
would have to lie low and watch his opportunities, and perhaps
climb another and more frequented ladder to success in a world
that wanted no thrusting pioneers.

Had Johnston faced such considerations squarely, the second
half of his life would probably have been less unhappy than it
was. That they cannot altogether have escaped him is suggested
by the fact that he delayed nearly three weeks before confessing
his state of health to the Foreign Office. 'Have returned Zomba,
but have been very ill blackwater fever. Please ask Sharpe to be
back at post by beginning of April as my health is precarious.'
His superiors, hard men of the world as they were, were fully
seized of the danger and reacted instantly and with the utmost
sympathy. 'His life may depend on his getting away,' wrote
Anderson. 'His life', Salisbury reiterated, 'is most valuable and
it ought not to be risked more than we can possibly help.' And
with his own pen the Prime Minister redrafted in more urgent
tones the telegram of recall. 'Hope you will leave without
delay. . . . Immediate leave granted of course.'[2]

But Johnston did not come. In January he had a serious relapse, but February found him apparently recovered and
enjoying one of those periods of demonic energy which he had
experienced after both his previous attacks of blackwater. He
remained at Zomba dictating furiously, painting, interrogating
his multitudinous linguistic informants, overseeing the preparation of the magnificent collections of stuffed birds and mammals
which he would take home to the Natural History Museum.

---

[1] Lugard to Johnston 12.i.96, *Johnston Papers*.
[2] Johnston to Salisbury 26.xii.95, *F.O.2.89*; F.O. to Johnston 2.ii.96, *F.O.2.109*.

The administration of the Protectorate was not neglected amidst the pursuit of all these private interests. It was during these few months that the civil organization took steady and enduring shape. The accounts and estimates were presented with meticulous care. His annual report, in particular, was a masterpiece of knowledge, foresight and hard thinking. Now that the primary, military problems were settled, he was turning his attention seriously to the economic future of the country. He was preoccupied above all with the interacting problems of taxation, labour and production. Much of what he wrote had been written before by an earlier generation of imperial officials in South Africa and elsewhere, but through it all there ran a characteristic vein of optimism about the negro, of realism about his future in the tropical parts of the continent, which might, but for blackwater, have made Johnston's name as famous as Lugard's was to be in the field of tropical administration.

The native labour question is almost the most important question which can now claim the attention of those administering the Protectorate. . . . The cultivation of coffee would be a hundred times more extensive than it now is if there was an adequate labour supply. In like manner towns would be built, roads would be laid out, railways could be made, marshes could be drained, river channels could be straightened and deepened, and countless crops could be planted and weeded, if sufficient natives came forward to wield the spade and axe, and pick-axe and hoe. All that needs now to be done is for the Administration to act as friends of both sides, and introduce the native labourer to the European capitalist. A gentle insistence that the native should contribute his fair share to the revenue of the country by paying his hut-tax, is all that is necessary on our part to secure his taking that share of life's labour which no human being should evade. At the same time the Administration is bound to see that the native is fairly treated, that he is fairly paid, and that attention is given to his food and general welfare on the part of his European employer. . . . In no part of the world is honesty more obviously the best policy than in Africa in dealing with the negro, who has a very clear sense of justice. The news that such-and-such a man has been unfairly treated by his employer, and has brought back no wages after three months' work, will deter a whole district from furnishing further recruits for the labour market at Blantyre. Fortunately now the native begins to understand that, if his European employer does not treat him fairly, he has redress at the hands of the nearest official. . . .[1]

[1] Report on British Central Africa Protectorate from April 1st, 1895, to March 31st 1896, in Johnston to Salisbury from Zomba 29.iv.96, *F.O.2.106.*

Johnston estimated that the revenue of the Protectorate, which was approaching £20,000 a year, was derived, £6,000 from native taxation and £14,000 from duties on goods imported and exported by Europeans and Indians. Naturally in this circumstance he could not ignore the contribution of the foreign capitalist. He prophesied, however, that in ten years' time the figure would be £100,000 derived sixty per cent from direct native taxation and forty per cent from the indirect taxation of immigrant enterprise. In the still longer term he foretold an even more radical turning of the tables. 'Some native overseers (originally boys educated at the Missions) are now landowners and planters on their own account. I entertain great hopes of the intellectual development of the negro of Central Africa. I do not know whether he comes of a more intelligent stock than those West Coast tribes that have furnished the type found in many of the old American slaves from whom the ordinary idea of the negro is derived, but certainly it is encouraging to notice the rapid way in which our Central Africa natives are learning what the white man can teach them. . . . Our mission undoubtedly here is to raise the negro of Central Africa into a civilized nationality, for we can never hope to colonize the bulk of this country with the white race.'

In February 1896 Johnston, pondering on the significance of the Kaiser's telegram to Kruger, had written wildly of sticking to his post through the protracted war which he imagined was on the point of breaking out between England and Germany. He even outlined a plan to capture immediately the German Administration's steamer on Lake Nyasa. There was, as Salisbury drily observed, 'still a good deal of fever left'. By April, when the annual report was composed, he had fully recovered his mental balance, and it is obvious from the whole tone of that report that he was writing for his successors as well as for his employers. When he finally left, early in May, he must have known in his heart that he would not return.

Chapter 9

A LITTLE DISENCHANTED WITH IMPERIALISM

EARLY in July 1896, the night after his arrival in London, Johnston dined with the Andersons at their home in Eaton Square. It would be a fair conjecture, though nothing more, that earlier the same day young Sir Harry, dapper Sir Harry, had declared his love and proposed marriage to Winifred Irby, the daughter of the house. Of the history of their relationship we know little, except that it had begun in a remote kind of way in 1889. Since his English visit in 1894 Johnston had invariably concluded his semi-official letters to Anderson with an expression of regard for the family. Presumably there had also been a private correspondence of which no trace has survived. It was to be a lasting though a childless union; but it may be doubted whether they were ever a really well assorted couple, she twelve years younger and as tall as he was short, discreet, conventional, lady-like, ambitious like him, but perhaps more for position than achievement. Old Sir Percy, however, was delighted, and friendly as never before. A house of Lady Anderson's in the New Forest was to be put at Johnston's disposal for the summer, so that he could make a perfect recovery. After that, Sir Percy hinted, there might be a vacancy in the Legation at Brussels. Strange reports were beginning to circulate about the Congo Free State, and there would obviously be a strong case for appointing a Minister to the Belgian court who had a considerable experience of African administration.

A week later Anderson was dead, struck down by a sudden attack of thrombosis. Sir Philip Currie had already left the Foreign Office, and the new Permanent Under-Secretary, Sir Thomas Sanderson, though an able diplomat with a quick wit that responded perhaps more instantaneously than Anderson's to Johnston's lighter side, had no special knowledge of African problems, and was without a father-in-law's interest in helping him to surmount the obstacle that had arisen in his career. Leaving Lady Anderson and her daughter to their mourning, Johnston betook himself to a small country house near Wimborne, and settled down to close and careful work on his book on British Central Africa. There he was joined by his sisters, his friends from the Office, and in due course by his fiancée, and official cares and private sorrows were gradually submerged in the newly discovered joys of the safety bicycle, on which the members of the house-party disported themselves among the beauty-spots of Wiltshire, Hampshire and Dorset. Johnston was still in name the Commissioner for the Central African Protectorate, and in the intervals of hospitality, courting and authorship he composed memoranda of unprecedented length and outspokenness to lighten the vacation-tide labours of his colleagues in Whitehall.

Here [he wrote to the acting head of the African Department at the beginning of September] is my little note, and I have put into it the bitterness of years, and I have made it a Test Case. Either it will secure the budgets of B.C.A. past, present and to come, and there will ensue therefrom the Great Peace when the Johnston lamb will lie down and snuggle into the magnanimous Treasury lion: Or there will be a complete breach between the Treasury and myself. . . . Midnight drills in the Department (your Department I mean) . . . Morris tubes fitted up in the F.O. corridors . . . the venal messengers bought with Foreign Office stamps . . . a rush for Treasury Chambers at dawn . . . their Lordships under arrest . . . bombs . . . and we have seized the coffers of England, you, I and others . . . Africa is annexed from Cape Matapan to the Cape of Good Hope, from Cape Verde to Guardafui . . . War declared against all who object . . . Victory . . . Peace . . . and you retire to such principality as I may allot to you. . . . You know I do *really* want this Memorandum to be put before the Treasury. Will you see if it can be done?[1]

The memorandum in question was indeed something quite remarkable in the field of inter-departmental polemic. The immediate subject was an unexpected surplus in the Nyasaland accounts of some £7,000, which Johnston proposed to place towards the cost of a new and adequately powerful gunboat for Lake Nyasa, and which the Treasury argued should be deducted from the imperial grant-in-aid for the coming year. But Johnston made it the occasion for a general treatise on Treasury niggardliness towards what he described with some justification as 'the Cinderella of the Protectorates'. For the Treasury to allow him to spend his surplus would be, he contended, an act not of grace but of suitable penitence for past neglect. Thoroughly to regain his favour their Lordships would need in

[1] Johnston to Farnall 9.ix.96, *F.O.2.107.*

addition to provide the balance of £2,000 necessary to complete the purchase of his new gunboat. For it was of course their Lordships' fault that he required a new gunboat. He had been sent out in 1889 to organize the Protectorate and to put down the slave trade, but he had not been provided with any funds for the work. As a result he had had 'to truckle somewhat pitifully to a band of speculators', but not even by this means had he managed to acquire a gunboat. The consequence had been the deaths of Maguire, Boyce, McEwan and of three brave Indian soldiers. But still the Treasury had remained flint-hearted, and the gunboats had had to be bullied out of the Admiralty, a Department which had naturally omitted to consult him about the design. The Protectorate had been saddled with 'two poor little vessels as little capable of navigating Lake Nyasa in rough weather as two Thames steam-launches would be for the constant crossing of the English Channel'. Therefore in the Makanjira expedition of 1893 and again in the Arab war of 1895 he had been obliged to spend some thousands of pounds in hiring steamers from the African Lakes Company and the German Government. Anyone who followed his chain of reasoning would immediately perceive why it was the fault of the Treasury that he had now to construct and place on Lake Nyasa a new gunboat 'competent to police its waters efficiently and, if the sad need arose, to cope with the German power on that Lake'. But that was not all. It was high time that the Treasury learned to look upon Africa as an investment and not as an object of charity.

I say nothing about the sentimental aspect of the question suppressing the slave trade and so on—because I know we are a nation of hypocrites with philanthropy on our lips and a profit and loss account in our hearts. Mere sentimental considerations would have no weight with their Lordships in inducing them to divert Africa-wards a thin runnel of the pactolus-stream flowing through their hands. It is because, after sixteen years aquaintance with Africa, I firmly believe a large share of that continent to be needed for the due expansion of our commerce and our energies that I am so anxious to impress my views on the Treasury. . . . I do not expect for the British Central Africa Protectorate the same generosity which has been shown to Uganda—a district of much greater interest to the general public. I am so nearly in accord with the Treasury as to their fair contribution to the annual expenditure in Nyasaland that it seems a pity that my life should be made miserable by these elaborate disputes over the fringe of subsidies. . . . Both Mr Sharpe and I are agreed that looking back over our five years work in Central Africa the worries, troubles and anxieties caused by wars with the slave-traders, disputes with Germans, Portuguese and British South Africa Company, inefficient mail service, fevers, lawless Whites and turbulent Blacks are, united, as one pennyweight to the ton compared with what we have suffered over finance.

Altogether Johnston's little note must have made excellent after-dinner reading in the assembled company at the Farrs, Wimborne, Dorset. Perhaps in all fairness it should have been addressed not only to the Treasury but to the great British public as represented in the Parliament at Westminster. But there was at this period a certain smug superiority about the permanent advisors of the Chancellor, as if of the self-constituted guardians of a Gladstonian tradition that was politically outdated, which made the Foreign Office men, naughty as they knew it to be, not unwilling to forward the essay complete and unabridged. 'The Treasury certainly will not like it,' wrote Sanderson, 'but I think a private communication might be useful.'[1]

At the end of September the house-party broke up, and on October 15th Harry Johnston and Winifred Irby were married quietly at St Paul's, Knightsbridge. The honeymoon was spent in Italy, partly at Cadenabbia on Lake Como, partly in Rome as the guests of Sir Clare Ford, the British Ambassador. While there Johnston called on the Prefect of Propaganda, Cardinal Ledochovski, in order to clear up certain misunderstandings about Portuguese missionaries in Nyasaland, and was amused to discover that ignorance of African geography was not confined to secular statesmen. In 1889 he had found Chamberlain hazy as to the whereabouts of such major landmarks as the Zambezi and the Limpopo. When Kitchener had invited him to stay in Cairo in 1895, he had evidently been under the impression that it was Nyasaland and not Uganda which abutted on the southern frontier of the Sudan. And now the good Cardinal, who was renowned for his erudition in African matters, and who was personally directing one of the greatest forward movements in the history of the Christian Church, persisted in confusing the Shire tributary of the Zambezi with the Shari affluent of Lake Chad. It was no doubt scarcely less astonishing to the Cardinal Prefect that the distinguished English explorer and administrator, when asked what small service could be rendered to him in Rome, replied that he was a poor man and would appreciate nothing better than to be

[1] Memorandum by Sir H. Johnston on the Treasury and British Central Africa, *F.O.2.107*.

allowed to pay for his honeymoon by sketching and describing the Vatican Gardens for the London *Graphic*. Thereafter Johnston spent a wholly delightful week in daily visits to the Vatican precincts. 'Once,' he remembered, 'when we were in the Park, a quiet-looking brougham came to a stop, and an old man descended from it, either to visit a shrine or merely to see what we were up to. His kindly gaze embraced us; he re-entered his carriage and drove off; thus we saw Leo XIII after all.'[1]

In mid-November Johnston was back in England, looking for work. A visit to Lord Salisbury's Private Secretary, Mr Eric Barrington, revealed that while the Consul-Generalship of Norway could be his for the asking, the Prime Minister had strongly recommended him to Chamberlain as a possible successor to Sir Hercules Robinson, the retiring High Commissioner in South Africa. It was a hope beyond his wildest dreams, and so, as the Oslo post had to be filled without delay, he let it go. But it was a forlorn hope. In February 1897 Milner was appointed to Cape Town: it was the greatest disappointment of Johnston's life. In a mood of bitter chagrin he wrote privately to Lord Salisbury expressing his great desire for administrative as opposed to diplomatic work, and even threatening to return to Nyasaland if a healthier alternative could not be found. The reply was gentle but very firm.

> 20 ARLINGTON ST.
> 18.2.97
>
> DEAR SIR HARRY,
>   I feel that your letter has been written under the impression —a mistaken one—that I have at my disposal many posts similar to that which you now hold. . . . As a fact I have only two or three such posts and they are not now vacant. They come to me by accident. They naturally belong to the Colonial Office: but it is more convenient that the Foreign Office should keep certain newly settled or acquired territories until all controversial questions in respect to them with foreign states are settled. Hence it is that the F.O., which is not naturally an administrative Office, has a few of these embryo colonies under its care. You wrote as if you imagined that the High Commissionership and Governorship of the Cape was in my gift. It is not so. Being asked to recommend candidates, I mentioned your qualifications: but I had nothing whatever to do with the choice that was ultimately made. Unfortunately I mentioned to Barrington what I was stating about you, and he appears—most indiscreetly—to have told you . . . I should be very glad to utilize your great abilities in the public service if I had the opportunity, but I fear I am

[1] *Story*, p. 337.

unlikely to have it. I should be very sorry to hear that you had gone back to Nyasa, as I think it would certainly be fatal to you: but I have no alternative of active service to suggest. I understand from your letter and from Barrington that you have made up your mind against consular employment of the ordinary kind, with which it is in the regular position of the F.O. to deal. I am very sorry I can make no suggestion.

Believe me, Yours very truly,

SALISBURY[1]

The message conveyed between the lines of Salisbury's letter was perfectly plain. The Prime Minister had one opinion of Johnston's abilities, in which he did not falter. But the Colonial Secretary had quite another; and Salisbury, having made one unsuccessful recommendation, felt that he could trespass no further upon his colleague's undoubted prerogative. As a matter of fact, had it not been for Barrington's optimistic indiscretion, the situation was one which Johnston must surely have been able to assess for himself. Whatever Chamberlain's precise degree of complicity in the Jameson Raid, there was no doubting his very close connexion with Rhodes both before and afterwards. After the Raid, the natural and obvious course for any Colonial Secretary not deeply committed to the interests of the British South Africa Company and its founder would have been to have revoked the Company's Charter and to have entered upon the direct administration of all the chartered territories. To have done so would have been a far more convincing reply to international criticism than the inevitably half-hearted punishment of a few brave and patriotic, if also desperate, men. Parliament, which would certainly have shied at the expense of Imperial administration in 1889, would equally certainly not have withheld in 1896 funds necessary to save the national honour. But Chamberlain had not revoked the Charter. Against the Company as such he had taken only the one inescapable measure of requiring that it should for the future place its armed forces under the control of a military officer appointed by the Imperial Government.[2] Nominally Rhodes was in disgrace, having resigned both the Premiership of the Cape Colony and his place on the Board of his own Company; poor Jameson and his accomplices were serving time in Holloway Gaol; the name of so brilliant a civil servant as Edward Fairfield was being sacrificed before the Parliamentary Committee of Inquiry. But the real influence of Rhodes

---

[1] *Johnston Papers.*
[2] Colonial Office to Foreign Office 4.iv.96, *F.O.83.1443.*

was still strong enough to keep his private empire intact: quite certainly therefore it was strong enough to keep Johnston from high office in southern Africa, and indeed from any other important post in Chamberlain's gift.

Immediately he received Salisbury's letter Johnston capitulated. 'I will note what you say about Consulates,' the Prime Minister wrote two days later. 'I shall be very glad if a suitable vacancy should occur: for I look with great apprehension to the results which are too probable if you return to Nyasaland.'[1] In June came the offer of Tunis. It was a bitter pill, a fall in the official list from Commissioner to plain Consul-General, a drop in salary and allowances of nearly £500 a year. But he took it. And the Foreign Office, for its part, did its best to be kind. The Treasury was persuaded to add £100 to the salary and to make a special arrangement whereby his pension should not suffer from the move. Great consideration was shown to him in the matter of home leave in the hot weather. And, perhaps most soothing of all, Sanderson would occasionally abandon the official draft for a charming, private note, couched in the style of oriental diplomacy, 'to the Consul-General distinguished above other Consuls-General, the subjugator of the slave trade, shining like a star upon the North Coast of Africa: My illustrious Friend, when we received your letter dated from Malta on the 19th of December, and perceived that it might happen to you to eat the mince-pies of Christmas in the company of the Governor, our heart was cheered and our liver was expanded and we saw verily that the All-Merciful is able to turn to a beneficent purpose the machinations of the evil ones. And as for your letter, oh exalted and judicious one, we have read it, though it appears to be written with a pen supplied by the Stationery Office, of which it is not possible to speak without a breach of good manners—and have understood it. . . . Moreover the Government of the Queen, may God bless her, appreciate your wisdom and commend your zeal.'[2]

There were two official residences attached to the Tunis Consulate, one in the town, the other thirteen miles outside it, at La Marsa on the site of ancient Carthage. Johnston chose the country house, a former Beylical palace, standing in thirty acres of private grounds, with its home-farm, paddocks and orange-groves. The repairs and redecorations absorbed most of his savings from Central Africa, but the result was a way of life as nearly satisfying as was possible for an active and ambitious

---

[1] Salisbury to Johnston 20.ii.97, *Johnston Papers*.
[2] Sanderson to Johnston 7.i.99, *ibid*.

man forced at thirty-eight into what was virtually retirement. For Johnston was a quick worker, and there was in truth little work of real importance to be done. He had with him as his Private Secretary at La Marsa his youngest brother, Alex Johnston, nineteen years his junior, a good linguist and one of the few stenographers equal to the stunning speed of his dictation. In the town he had an able Vice-Consul, Gerald Lascelles, to look after the routine business of the office, which consisted mainly in looking after the interests of the considerable Maltese population of the Regency. And so there was plenty of leisure for managing a country estate, for riding, painting and botanizing, and above all for reading and writing.

It was during these two years at Tunis that Johnston became by temperament a scholar, and even something of a recluse. Throughout his younger life he had experienced more solitude than falls to the lot of most men, and he had learned to fill it with a staggering variety of interests and pursuits. But through it all he had retained a tremendous and unaffected love of society. During his visits to England his engagement-book had been full to overflowing. He had been famous as a diner-out, a raconteur, an enthusiast for party games and fancy dress. Now at Tunis he tended to leave all but the most important social duties to his wife and secretary. The British and diplomatic communities gathered regularly at La Marsa on Sunday afternoons to enjoy the excellent hospitality of the Consulate, but it was with difficulty that Sir Harry was extracted for twenty minutes from his upstairs study to bid his guests farewell. 'I am anything but disappointed with Tripoli,' wrote Eustace in Johnston's autobiographical novel *The Gay-Dombeys*. 'From the point of view of position and power it is a comedown after being a despot in Central Africa at £1,200 a year. But the climate is so good, and the peace and quiet are most welcome, and the residence—an enclosed Moorish palace between high walls with a secret garden—most delightful. For me especially, just a little disenchanted with imperialism, and tired of wars and conquests, it is ideal. I shall be able here to work assiduously at my accumulations of notes and studies and finish several big books on Africa which I have long had on hand.'[1]

One big book, *British Central Africa*, had appeared shortly before the move to Tunis in the summer of 1897. As in *The River Congo* and *The Kilimanjaro Expedition*, Johnston had brought together in a single volume the sum of his researches in ethnography, linguistics, botany and zoology, and to this solid

[1] *The Gay-Dombeys*, p. 269.

core he had added admirable chapters on history, government, Christian missions and European settlement. His earlier tendency to wild speculation had disappeared. The element of personal narrative, though it could not be entirely eliminated from a subject in which so much of the evidence rested upon his own direct experience, was marvellously disciplined into the appropriate channels of scientific expression. Even in the historical sections, in which he was of necessity describing his own achievements, the style was objective, unaffectedly modest, and without a trace of rancour or other personal feeling. It was not a book designed either to make money or to score a cheap success. Its composition had been on the contrary almost an act of religious duty. Where another man might have regarded himself as a servant of God as well as of his country, Johnston thought of himself, quite humbly and sincerely, as an emissary of Science as well as a patriot. To use the opportunities afforded by his employment in seeking out and recording scientific facts was his substitute for prayer. To make the results available for others, however imperfectly, was his act of public worship, the tribute of an evolutionist to the cause of Science.

In Tunis the situation was rather different. He was no longer on the battlefront of man's struggle with the blind and stupid forces of Nature, in the remote places of the earth where new facts could every day be captured from the realms of Darkness and old Night. His rôle must therefore change to that of an interpreter and publicist, surveying from a distance the whole field of Africa, and painting in their correct historical proportions the efforts that had been made to open it to the influences of Progress. In his study at La Marsa Johnston produced his first literary work based mainly on the researches of others. It was called *A History of the Colonization of Africa by Alien Races*, and the preface was dated Tunis, November 1898. For fifteen months spare-time work it was no mean achievement. After the briefest discussion of how Africa had come to be peopled by the so-called native races, he passed in rapid review the efforts of Phoenician, Greek, Roman, Byzantine and Arab immigrants to dominate the northern and eastern coastlines of the continent and to penetrate the deserts behind. The modern period he treated in a series of more or less synchronic essays on the achievements of the invading nations of Europe—Portuguese, Dutch, Spaniards, British, French, Belgians, Italians and Germans. These sections he interspersed with chapters on the slave trade, Christian missions, exploration and colonial adminis-tration, in which the broader continent-wide themes could be brought together and developed. When compared with the almost completely rewritten version of 1913, the 1899 edition of *The Colonization of Africa* seems but a rough and hasty sketch. Johnston knew so much of the indigenous Africa which had been invaded that it was disappointing how little of this peculiar knowledge had been used to illuminate the significance, for Africa, of the alien races and their doings. Here and there occurred a flash of insight prompted by first-hand experience, as in a turgid passage in which he compared the material benefits so far conferred on the African peoples by British and Portuguese.

These wonderful old Conquistadores may have been relentless and cruel in imposing their rule on the African and in enslaving him or Christianizing him, but they added enormously to his food supply and comfort. So early in the history of their African exploration that it is almost the first step they took, they brought from China, India and Malacca the orange-tree, the lemon and the lime, which, besides introducing into Europe (and Europe had only hitherto known the sour, wild orange brought by the Arabs), they planted in every part of East and West Africa where they touched. They likewise brought the sugar-cane from the East Indies and introduced it into various parts of Brazil and West Africa, especially into the islands of São Thome and Principe and the Congo and Angola countries. . . . From their great possession of Brazil . . . they brought into East and West Africa the Muscovy duck (which has penetrated far into the interior of Africa, if indeed it has not crossed the continent), chili peppers, maize (now grown all over Africa, and cultivated by many natives who had not yet even heard of the existence of white men), tobacco, the tomato, yam, pineapple, sweet potato, manioc, ginger and other less widely known forms of vegetable food. . . . The Englishman has brought with him the potato, and has introduced into most of his colonies the horse, and in places improved breeds of cattle, sheep and goats. [He has introduced] a good many European vegetables and fruit-trees; the tea-plant, the coffee-plant, and many shrubs and trees of special economic value. But what are these introductions— almost entirely for his own use—compared in value to the vast bounty of Portugal? Take away from the African's dietary of to-day the products that the Portuguese brought to him from the far East and the far West, and he would remain very insufficiently provided with necessities and simple luxuries.[1]

In general, the first edition of *The Colonization of Africa* was marred by being far too narrowly a report on the immense

[1] H. H. Johnston: *A History of the Colonization of Africa by Alien Races*, 1899, pp. 39-40.

course of reading to which Johnston subjected himself at La Marsa. It brought together a vast mass of mainly accurate fact, but the composition was hurried, and the judgments often hard and shallow. Its biographical significance is that during his leisure at Tunis he added to his already incomparable knowledge of contemporary African politics the firm foundation of wider historical knowledge that was to make him through-out his long retirement the foremost interpreter of Africa to Edwardian and early Georgian England.

Meantime, his stay at Tunis was not all leisure and learning. In November 1897 he set out on a month's tour of the Regency, visiting first his vice-consular agencies down the coast at Susa, Monastir, Mehdia, Sfax, Gabes and Jerba, and then striking on horseback across the northern edge of the Tunisian Sahara to the date-producing districts of Gafsa and the Jerid. Moving on through the remote, mountainous country along the Algerian border, he revisited the scenes of his earliest African adventures in the Mejerda range, and then returned by the now completed Bône railway to Tunis.[1] In an unofficial record of the trip, published along with many drawings in *The Graphic*, he gave the French full credit for the marvellous development of the country, both politically and economically, which had taken place since his visit of sixteen years before. To the Foreign Office he sent a comprehensive report on the actual state of British commerce in the Regency and on the opportunities still to be exploited, which earned him an interesting tribute from Sir William Harcourt. 'The insolent pretension that we alone have the right and the mission to promote civilization is one which it is not likely that the rest of the world will accept,' wrote the Liberal ex-Chancellor. 'I am always preaching here the lesson you read to British traders against the John Bullism of their "take it or leave it" system. We are falling back in the commercial race not principally from hostile tariffs but because our long monopoly has led us to despise the art of solicitation by making things which people want, offered to them in a language which they understand, at prices which suit their pockets. It is by these simple arts that the Germans win their way through all the hostile tariffs of other nations.'[2]

Johnston's admiration for French rule in North Africa was fortified by the warm personal friendship which he quickly developed with the Resident-General, M. René Millet, and

[1] Johnston to Salisbury 28.xii.97, *F.O.27.3345.*
[2] Harcourt to Johnston 18.iii.98, *Johnston Papers.*

which was strong enough to survive even the strains put upon
it by the Fashoda crisis. When he returned from his summer
leave in September 1898, it was to a Tunis where his correspondence was being opened, and where the majority of the
French officials did not seek to disguise their hostility. On
November 2nd he reported that secret orders had been transmitted to all French forces in the country to prepare for a
general mobilization on a war footing. For the rest of the year
he was busily engaged in collecting information through his
own network of secret agents about the military dispositions and
prepared defences of the Regency. In December he took his
findings in person to Malta, there to 'eat the mince-pies of
Christmas and concert his plans with the Governor.'[1]

The Cabinet in London made anxious inquiries about the
possibility of a French expedition against Egypt through
Tripoli. On this point, however, Johnston's reasoning and his
researches were equally definite. Such a march, he replied,
would take 50,000 men commanded by another Napoleon six
weeks to accomplish, and the desert would force them to follow
the coast all the way. 'After the outbreak of war, either France
would have lost command of the sea, and therefore would be
unable to send any more troops at all to Tunis, or else she would
have become for a time mistress of the Mediterranean, and then
would be able to send a naval expedition to Egypt.' So far as
Tunis was concerned, therefore, the boot was on the other foot.
So far from being a strong point for attack, it was on the
contrary a weak link in French defences. The military reports
all showed that the French were massing their forces against
an expected invasion in the north of the Protectorate. The
whole south of the country would be at the mercy of a force of
10,000 men landed somewhere between Gabes and Sfax. The
natives would certainly rise in support of an English invasion:
so also would the Arabs of Algeria. 'Naturally,' he added, 'a
British invasion of North Africa would upset for a time a great
deal of the civilizing work the French have initiated, as the
Arabs would commence a savage war of extermination against
the French colonists, who in the northern part of the Regency
have dispossessed them of their lands by the subtle chicanery of
law. But it would be the readiest way of striking at France on
land with any hope of a speedy and successful result.'[2]

Throughout all these alarms Johnston and Millet remained,
personally, on the best of terms. They were even agreed on

[1] Johnston to Salisbury 2.xi.98; F.O. to Johnston 8.xii.98, *F.O.27.3419.*
[2] Salisbury to Johnston 10.ii.99; Johnston to Salisbury 25.ii.99, *F.O.27.3467.*

the indefensibility of Tunis against a British attack, and at the height of the crisis they came to a mutual understanding whereby, if hostilities should break out, Johnston would occupy the Residency and protect its contents from looters, while Millet retreated by the railway towards the Algerian frontier. By April, however, the war scare was over. A great fancy-dress ball at La Marsa was attended by all the principal personages of the French community, and Johnston in official despatches was once more openly comparing Millet's work in Tunis to that of Lord Cromer in Egypt. Though the dominant spirit of French protectionist policy had compelled him in carrying out the directions of the Paris ministries to protect and foster French commerce in a way not pleasing to British ideas of free trade, Millet had nevertheless endeavoured 'to treat Tunisia, not as a conquered country to be wholly sacrificed to French interests, but as a state dependent on France for advice and protection, yet to be governed in such a manner as to insure in the first place the prosperity and happiness of its native population'.[1]

In May 1899 the resumption of good relations was sealed by a surprise visit from the Princess of Wales in the course of a Mediterranean tour with her two daughters, the Crown Princess Maud of Norway and Princess Victoria. Johnston's only previous contact with English royalty had been a sad fiasco three years earlier, when at his accolade the ageing Queen, imperfectly instructed by her secretaries, had bestowed on him a few brief words of condolence for the wounds he had suffered on the North-West Frontier of India. But this was as different as could be: a family party on holiday, eager for every kind of enjoyment and practising the utmost informality with all whom they met. Lady Johnston was in her element; Millet co-operated to the full. A colourful detachment of Spahis accompanied the party on several expeditions to view the local antiquities, for which Johnston was the perfect guide. The Princess was keenly interested in Nyasaland, a favourite godson, Lt. Edward Alston having been killed there in Johnston's last campaign. She knew his biography of Livingstone, and he shared her admiration for the works of her countryman, Hans Andersen, whose life she urged him to attempt.

His evident success with the royal visitors appeared to Mr Alex Johnston, who lived in his household, symptomatic of a new contentment with life which had grown steadily during his two years in Tunis. His health seemed to have quite recovered. His marriage was shaping well. For once he was not striving to

[1] Johnston to Salisbury 26.iv.99, *F.O.27.3467.*

maintain a superhuman activity. Having finished one book, he had even allowed eight months to go by without beginning another. Politically Tunis might be a backwater, but it was far from being the exile which he had once feared. His pictures hung annually in the Academy; his articles in *The Graphic* were noticed. He could be in England for two months of every year, and for another six he was excellently placed to offer Mediterranean hospitality. His private correspondents at this time—men like Curzon, Bryce and Harcourt—all mentioned their intention of calling in on him at La Marsa, and many others actually did so. Johnston at forty-one, the handicap of his stature relieved by a slight tendency to rotundity, with all his gifts and all his past achievements, was no back number, and, which was better, did not much care if he was.

And then, only a few days after Princess Alexandra's departure, came serious temptation in the shape of a telegram from Lord Salisbury, offering him for two years the post of Special Commissioner in Uganda at the fabulous salary of £2,800 a year. He was to be Commander-in-Chief as well as Commissioner, and he was to have a Private Secretary, a military adviser, and a doctor all attached to his personal staff.[1] It was a flattering offer, but it was one that should never have been made. A man who had suffered three attacks of blackwater fever, and who had been forced to abandon one important post for no other reason, should not have been enticed, for any exigency of the public service, back into the domain of the anopheles mosquito. Anxiously Johnston discussed the telegram with his wife. They knew that it would mean separation, and they did not underestimate the danger to his life and health. On the other hand they saw an opportunity which might not come again. The Commission would be Johnston's work *par excellence*, and the fact that the Foreign Office had offered such terms to get him amounted to an open recognition that he was the best man they had. If he could only survive his two years, surely a grateful Government would express its thanks by finding him an important post in a healthy climate. The Uganda mission, in fact, would be the means of overcoming the great obstacle that had arisen to his promotion. Through it he would pass at last from the backwaters of diplomacy to the coveted glories of an established colonial governorship. Not once, but twice, he would have demonstrated his administrative capacity: before such proof even the prejudice of a Chamberlain must melt away.

[1] F.O. to Johnston 8.vi.99, *F.O.2.221*.

There were other reasons which weighed too. There was his classificatory work on the Bantu languages, which had been going on steadily for seventeen years, and which had already led him to the conclusion that the dispersal area of the original Bantu-speakers who had colonized the whole of southern Africa must have been in the region north and west of Lake Victoria, a great part of which would come within the scope of his Commission. Perhaps he would find there, as Bleek had long ago predicted, living examples of the archaic, reduplicated prefix which would prove the substance of his grand hypothesis. At all events the North-Central Bantu languages remained the greatest gap in his now vast collection. Until that gap was filled he could not begin with any confidence his final and most serious work of analysis and comparison. 'I do not think for a moment', he wrote in his autobiography, 'that I contemplated refusing, much as I realized the risks of life and the possibility of failure. And although this tremendous journey—as it proved to be—brought to a close my public service, I still do not regret having quitted Tunis to make it.'[1]

And so in July 1899 the Johnstons packed up their furniture and made ready the La Marsa house for the occupation of Consul Ernest Berkeley, who, having been moved from Uganda, was to succeed them in Tunis. During that month and the next they spent what time they could spare from preparations for the Special Commission at a small hotel at Seaford on the Sussex coast. They exchanged letters with Lugard, who was resting in Cornwall before taking up his post as the first Governor of Northern Nigeria. 'I shall anxiously look out for the opinion you express on the country,' wrote Lugard, 'for my interest in it has never flagged and is centred there. I hope we may meet again a year or eighteen months hence in England, you from Uganda, I from Nigeria, and compare notes on our several tasks. . . . By that time the railway will have been completed, and you will be able to run home in a month.'[2] In September they moved for the last fortnight of their holiday to Venice, where they stayed with Lady Johnston's relations, the Bishop of Ely and Lady Alwyn Compton. They enjoyed a feast of beauty from which it was hard to tear themselves away—he to Marseilles and the Zanzibar steamer, she to await in England the news of his return.

[1] Johnston: *Story*, p. 361.
[2] Lugard to Johnston 3.ix.99, *Johnston Papers*.

Chapter 10

THE GOD-GIVEN TASK OF SUBDUING
THE EARTH

UGANDA, when Johnston assumed his Special Commission, was in its seventh year as a British Protectorate. With its eastern frontier running, as it then did, right through the middle of modern Kenya, along the eastern scarp of the Rift Valley, it was about three times the size of Nyasaland and had about two and a half times as many inhabitants. As in Nyasaland, the greater part of the area was still in practice unadministered. Garrisoned forts were strung out along the main lines of communication, along the caravan-route from the East Coast to Lake Victoria and on to Ruwenzori in the far west, and from Lake Albert down the Nile towards the recently reconquered Sudan. Real political control, however, was only exercised, and that cautiously, in the small area between Lakes Victoria, Edward and Albert which comprised the native kingdoms of Buganda, Toro and Bunyoro. Buganda had been since 1877 an important mission field of both the Anglican and the Roman Catholic Churches, and British political influence had inserted rather than imposed itself during a period of social revolution and civil war resulting from the conflicts between pagan, Muslim and Christian on the one hand, and between Roman Catholic and Protestant Christians on the other. Into this medley had come in 1889 the representatives of the Imperial British East Africa Company, first Jackson and then Lugard, who by astute diplomacy and by the judicious employment of a tiny force of independent troops had managed to hold the balance between the warring factions, and even in some measure to unite them under a coalition of Protestant and Catholic chiefs. The Imperial Government had stepped into the shoes of the financially ailing Chartered Company, in Uganda in 1893 and in Kenya—the East Africa Protectorate as it was then called—in 1895. Commissioners had been appointed, together with civil and military officers, and grants-in-aid had been voted on what was, by comparison with Nyasaland, the fairly liberal scale of about £50,000 a year for each Protectorate. Most important of all the building of a strategic railway from Mombasa to Lake Victoria had been set in train at an ultimate cost to the imperial Exchequer of some five and a half million pounds.

Nevertheless, the establishment of an Administration in Uganda had proved a more perilous, and a very much more expensive, undertaking than had been anticipated. The regular military force of the Protectorate, known since 1895 as the Uganda Rifles, had been built up mainly from the Sudanese followers of Emin Pasha in his retreat southwards from the Mahdi after the disaster to Gordon at Khartoum. Though numbering by 1897 some 1,600 men, nearly four times the regular force employed by Johnston in Nyasaland, the Uganda Rifles represented in real power but a feeble counterweight to the highly-armed populations of Buganda and Bunyoro. They had no leavening of first-class Indian troops. They were commanded by officers of the British Army, high-spirited and gallant men many of whom later achieved military distinction, but most of whom had come to Uganda for a brief spell of sport and adventure rather than to give the continuity of service needed to build up a sound military tradition. Above all, the Sudanese rank and file of the Uganda Rifles were disgracefully paid: privates received four rupees a month, paid in inferior trade-goods and frequently in arrears.

These facts considered, it was astonishing what had been achieved. While the railway crept slowly forward from Mombasa towards Nairobi, the supply-route across the Rift Valley, over the Mau escarpment and on through Kavirondo and Busoga had been kept open with only occasional disasters to caravans and mail-runners from the Masai and Nandi warriors. The kingdom of Buganda had been held steady under the Christian chiefs, despite the covert antipathy of the Kabaka Mwanga and of certain Roman Catholic and pagan leaders in the provinces. The neighbouring kingdom of Toro in the west had been reorganized under a confederation of chiefs friendly towards the Administration and supported in their authority by a small garrison at Fort Portal. The persistently hostile state of Bunyoro, lying along the north-western frontier of Buganda, had been invaded and occupied with the aid of large irregular forces of Baganda, glad to seize the opportunity of plundering the territories of their agelong enemy. Garrisons had been established far down the Nile at Wadelai and Nimule to forestall possible intrusions by Belgians and French in the tense international scramble preceding Fashoda.

Still, the result of all these efforts had been to stretch the regular forces of the Protectorate to the utmost limit. By 1896

DESIGN FOR POSTAGE STAMPS: NYASALAND
This design with two negro labourers bestriding Africa 'from the Cape
to Cairo' was used for the first engraved stamps of Nyasaland

A FORTIFIED VILLAGE IN THE TUNISIAN SAHARA

there was practically no central reserve force left in Buganda; and some of the wretched Sudanese detachments had been marched hundreds of miles from one campaign to another, from Bunyoro to the Nandi country, from Nandi right round Lake Victoria to Buddu, where Mwanga had staged an open revolt, and from thence back to the Mau summit, where they were required in September 1897 to accompany an expedition under Colonel Macdonald to an unknown destination in the far north. Faced by this last test of their endurance, they had mutinied, with results that could easily have proved fatal to the young Administration. The neighbouring East Africa Protectorate had sent what troops it could spare, and an expeditionary force had been despatched from India, taking inevitably some five and a half months to arrive. Mwanga, who had been deposed for his activities in 1897, had broken out of his refuge in German territory to the south of Buganda and had succeeded in joining the implacable Kabarega, Omukama of Bunyoro in the Lango country to the north of the Somerset Nile. Had the Sudanese garrisons in occupied Bunyoro declared for the mutineers, the situation might have been grave indeed.

In the event the worst had not happened, and the Indian contingent, when it arrived, had been able not merely to overcome the mutineers but finally to defeat and capture both Mwanga and Kabarega, thus bringing Uganda to approximately the same degree of internal security as Johnston had achieved in Nyasaland by the suppression of Makanjira and Mlozi. But the financial cost of these operations in Uganda had been about ten times the cost of those in Nyasaland. From 1897 to 1899 the imperial grants-in-aid had been driven up to £400,000 a year, a figure which, together with the expenditure on the railway, was capable of endangering the government in power in the United Kingdom. It was clear to the Foreign Office that fundamental reorganization was necessary, designed to reduce expenditure and to raise a local revenue. For measures in both these directions the approach of the railway and its accompanying telegraph to Lake Victoria seemed to offer a great opportunity. When news of a crisis could be telegraphed to London in a day, and when troops could be moved from Mombasa to Kampala in a week, it would be possible to reduce and concentrate the garrisons. Equally, when transport costs were decimated, and more, by railway and steamer communications, there was hope that trade would begin to flow, that revenue from customs would rise and that, with the introduc-

K

tion of an exchange economy, it would be possible to levy direct taxation.

There was one further reason why, on Commissioner Berkeley's withdrawal through illness in March 1899, the Foreign Office decided to send out in his place a high-ranking officer at double the usual salary. The arrival of the Indian contingent under Colonel Evatt had gravely upset the balance of civil and military officers: it had also introduced childish, but nevertheless serious, dissensions between the military themselves. Officers of the Indian Army were considered in the eighteen-nineties to belong to a socially inferior caste to officers of the British Army; and in Uganda subalterns from the Brigade of Guards and other fashionable regiments made objections to serving under Evatt and generally behaved with all the scandalous vulgarity of which the English upper classes were then capable. Though his personal sympathies lay with the British officers, Sir Clement Hill, who was still at the head of the African Department at the Foreign Office, apprehended that here was a situation which only a very senior official could control.

Great therefore was Hill's consternation when his political masters, Salisbury and St John Brodrick, decided that the important post which had been created at his suggestion was to be offered, not to 'a Major-General with administrative experience', nor to a similarly qualified 'Colonial or Indian civilian', but to Johnston, the outsider, the flashy favourite, whose nimble wit he did not appreciate, and which offended him the more in that he suspected it of occasionally exposing to ridicule his own ponderous professional competence.[1] Since Anderson's death, Hill had become accustomed to be very much the master in his own house. Sanderson, the Permanent Under-Secretary, did not interfere much in African questions. Brodrick, the Parliamentary Secretary, confined himself as a rule to House of Commons issues. Even Lord Salisbury was getting old and could no longer maintain that minute control over the civil servants in Whitehall which was the corollary of the wider discretion he allowed to his representatives in remote places. The terse comments in red ink on the incoming despatches, the careful emendation of the outgoing drafts, were now but a memory in the Office, and with their disappearance the professional hands had grown more assertive. The appointment of Johnston was Salisbury's last important intervention

---

[1] F.O. to Treasury 29.iv.99, *F.O.2.235*, with memoranda by Hill, Brodrick and Salisbury; F.O. to Johnston 1.vii.99, *F.O.2.200*: general instructions for Special Commission, drafted by Hill.

in East African affairs. Thereafter the reins passed to Hill, and the home background to all Johnston's work in Uganda was coloured by the nagging antagonism of his pompous and disapproving official superior.

Johnston, unlike Hill, did not regard his Special Commission as an unmerited piece of good fortune, to be atoned for by a self-effacing subordination to the dictates of Whitehall. He had taken a serious risk to life in accepting it. He understood clearly that, even if he survived, it would be his very last venture into the field of tropical administration. He was determined that it should be spectacular as well as a success. Not only would he revolutionize the political and economic condition of the Protectorate, but he would return with an encyclopaedic knowledge of the native peoples and their environment which would form the basis of British policy in East Africa for many years to come. His mission would be one of scientific inquiry as well as administrative action. It was of the essence of his plan that his own headquarters should be peripatetic, and that he should be assisted by a personal staff quite independent of the regular secretariat of the Administration. So much had indeed been implied in the terms of the offer sent to him at Tunis, which had provided for a private secretary, a military adviser and a doctor. Yet, when it came to the point, the doctor and the military adviser disappeared from the estimates; the private secretary's allowance paid the salary of J. F. Cunningham, his former assistant in Nyasaland, who was in fact if not in name Secretary to the Administration; and Johnston was left to defray out of his own pocket the pay and expenses of his real private secretary, his brother Alex, and of a natural history collector, Mr W. G. Doggett, who was the only other constant member of his personal staff. Hill even attempted to argue that since his was a *special* Commission, Johnston was not even entitled to the normal outfit allowance paid to all consular officials serving abroad. 'He has double that which any other Uganda Commissioner has had, and what he got in British Central Africa,' pencilled the jealous bureaucrat on the margin of the application.[1] It was to be a constant refrain, repeated upon every piece of correspondence about Johnston's personal affairs.[2]

The Special Commissioner's party reached Zanzibar on September 28th, 1899. There Johnston engaged as usual Ali

[1] Johnston to Sanderson 28.vii.99, *F.O.2.203*; Johnston to Salisbury 28.iv.oo *F.O.2.299*, etc.   [2] E.g. F.O. to Johnston 12.vii.oo, *F.O.2.296*.

Kiongwe, his faithful Swahili caravan leader and major domo on all his journeyings in eastern and central Africa since his Kilimanjaro expedition of 1884. Only on this occasion the caravan itself was unnecessary. On the 30th he was at Mombasa. On October 4th he was bowling in a first-class saloon coach through the thorn scrub of the Nyika desert, which he had last crossed by forced marches, with a raging fever and with all the anxiety of deserting porters trying to escape back to the coast with their as yet unearned advance of pay. Evening brought him to Makindu, which he dubbed the Bletchley of East Africa. Through the night the train rolled on towards Nairobi, the Swindon still very much in embryo.

As the dawn suffused itself over the Athi plains, we saw from the windows of the train a rare and beautiful sight. These immense, level stretches of grassland, reduced in the present drought to a uniform grey-yellow stubble, were literally covered by herds of game, individuals of which would approach quite close to the line, as though they had already lost all fear of the rushing, jointed monster with the smoking head. We saw zebras as close as one might see horses grazing in the meadows along an English railway, and gnus were to us as cattle, lazily flicking the flies off their haunches. Grant's gazelle and Thomson's gazelle would graze and merely lift their lovely heads as we rattled by. Hartebeests faced us and shook their horns in mock indignation. Three or four giraffes, even, could be discovered on the skyline, while pallah and oribi, warthogs and jackals were things of no account. . . . The whole hour's panorama of this wonderful Zoological Garden was like a sportsman's dream, but the fact was we had been crossing the Athi Game Reserve, where two years of strenuously enforced respect for the Game Regulations has brought about this wonderful collection of animals, so wonderfully growing in confidence . . . that herds of zebra frequently gallop like runaway horses through the sketched out township of Nairobi.[1]

Johnston did not stop in Nairobi, but travelled straight on to railhead, then at Naivasha and just within the frontiers of his own Protectorate, where a formidable collection of administrative questions awaited him. There was first the problem of transport between railhead and the Lake. Hitherto only a fraction of the caravan traffic to central Uganda had used the direct highland route with its wild pastoral inhabitants and its chronic shortage of food. Now that there remained only 250 miles of porterage from Naivasha to Kavirondo Bay, it was absurd that the bulk of the goods imported by traders continued

[1] Johnston to Salisbury from Naivasha 10.x.99, *F.O.2.204.*

to pass by the traditional 1,200-mile route through German East Africa, with the resultant prohibitive prices for the barest European needs like soap or kerosene oil. Johnston set himself with energy to tackle the problems of security and food supply which might induce a change. He prepared proposals for the fusion of the postal systems of the two Protectorates under a single self-supporting service. He dealt also with some of the myriad problems posed by the railway's advance. He interviewed Masai chiefs about land tenure. He encouraged the Indian shopkeepers who were moving up country in the wake of the first goods trains. He considered the questions of licences, of customs, of game preservation, of maintaining some framework of law and order among the unruly company of British engineers and their Indian labour force.[1]

I wonder [he wrote to the Foreign Office] if in England the importance of one aspect of this Railway construction has been realized? It means the driving of a wedge of India two miles broad right across East Africa from Mombasa to the Victoria Nyanza. Fifteen thousand coolies, some hundreds of Indian clerks, draughtsmen, mechanics, surveyors and policemen, are implementing the use of the Hindustani language, and carrying the Indian Penal Code, the Indian postal system, Indian coinage, Indian clothing, right across these wastes, deserts, forests and swamps, tenanted hitherto by wild native savages or wild beasts. . . . The coolie camps have seared the more populated districts with a fringe of prostitution. Masai women, Kikuyu women, Akamba women leave their rough and grudging spouses for a generous association with the kindly well-paid Indian workman. . . . I noticed little or no abuse of alcohol consequent on the projection of this Indian army, but . . . alcoholism was decidedly prominent as a vice among the British mechanics. . . . Those who do not leave England to travel in out of the way parts of the world, where men of the British workman class are employed as soldiers, sailors, artisans, machinists and such like, do not realize what a drunken nation we seem in the eyes of the Latin races and of subject peoples of black and yellow skin. It is whiskey, whiskey everywhere, and staggering men with dull, purple cheeks and glazed eyes reeling about the streets of African and Asiatic towns, sometimes half-naked . . . vomiting blasphemy and obscenity. . . .

Johnston, as always, was outspoken, though he did not lose his sense of proportion. The railway, he concluded, was 'one of those strong gouges which civilization employs to rough-hew her ends, a gouge which leaves a great clean track of good,

---

[1] Johnston to Salisbury from Naivasha 11.x.99, 13.x.99, *F.O.2.204.*

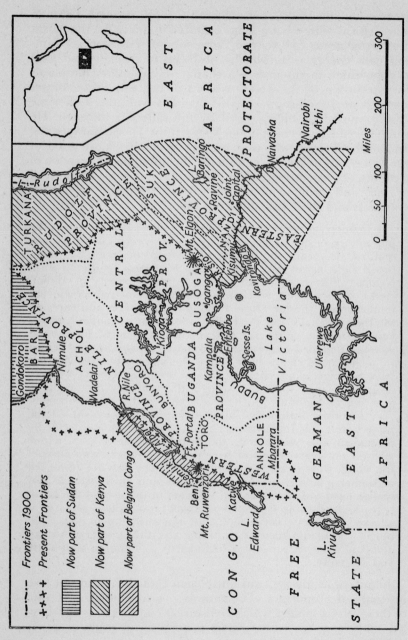

11. EAST AFRICA AND UGANDA

sprinkled at its edges with items of suffering, little deeds of harm, and unintentional injuries of atoms'. To the historian at least it was one of his finest despatches, casting a flood of light and meaning upon what still remains the most significant single development in the economic history of East Africa. But Hill was unimpressed. 'There is no new information in this,' he wrote, 'though it gives a satisfactory account of the work on the railway. It is more suited perhaps to a magazine article than a despatch.' Lord Salisbury, had he been given the opportunity, might well have disagreed; but, like many of the despatches written by Johnston during the next two years, it was not judged worthy of circulation.[1]

From Naivasha the Special Commission reverted to more old-fashioned methods of locomotion, on horseback and on foot, across the floor of the Rift Valley and up its western flank to the Eldama Ravine station, then the headquarters of Uganda's eastern province. Johnston still wore his straw boater with the white, yellow and black band. Somewhere in the caravan a porter carried on his head an ample supply of the old, tricoloured official stationery. And now each evening, when the camp was pitched, when Johnston had laid aside his painting or his language notes, and when Doggett had returned from his daily ramble with camera or calipers, the dressing-gong sounded and the Europeans retired to their tents to don dinner-jackets with yellow waistcoats designed still further to reinforce the symbolism of interracial harmony. The party stayed for most of November at the Ravine, while Johnston revised the estimates prepared by the Acting Commissioner, Colonel Ternan, reorganized the system of district administration in the eastern province, selected in accordance with his instructions the site for a future joint capital for the two East African Protectorates high up on the western side of the Mau range nearly 8,000 feet above sea-level, and established a new government station in the Suk country near Lake Baringo to bar the way to the illicit ivory-hunters who were just then carrying their ghastly work of extermination into the region round Lake Rudolf.[2] 'Even in regard to persons supposed to be sportsmen pure and simple,' he commented to Lord Salisbury, 'I would point out that behind their profession of sport there is often a very practical purpose lurking. Lord Delamere, for instance, left this part of the country last year with £14,000

[1] Johnston to Salisbury from Naivasha 10.x.99, *F.O.2.204*.
[2] Johnston to Salisbury, Eldama Ravine, 6.xi.99, 14.xi.99, 17.xi.99, *F.O.2.204*; and from Entebbe 18.ii.00, *F.O.2.297*.

worth of ivory, and his medical officer, Dr Atkinson, has been steadily shooting elephants ever since. . . . I really think the time has come to be severe on professional sportsmen whose devastations considerably affect the value of what may prove to be an important asset in the productions of this Protectorate.'[1]

At last towards the end of the month the expedition made its chilly way over the Mau summit and descended the long gently-sloping Nyando valley towards the great Lake nearly 5,000 feet below. They were passing now through the dangerous country of the Nandi and the Kipsigis, where raids on caravans were a monthly occurrence, and where the progress of the railway and telegraph were during the following year to neces-sitate considerable military operations. Johnston, however, came through without incident and made straight for the future terminus of the railway at Kisumu, where he made sensible arrangments, later obstructed by Hill, to speed the construction of the *William Mackinnon*, the lake steamer which was to be the last link in the chain of mechanical transport from Europe to the heart of Uganda.[2] Then, early in December, he began the last and longest stage of his march, round the northern shores of the Lake, through Kavirondo and Busoga, to Buganda. He was pleasantly conscious of being once more in the tropics. 'The traveller coming from the east,' he wrote, 'feels, when he crosses the Sio River and enters Busoga, that he has reached something like West Africa at last. Banana planta-tions grow everywhere in splendid luxuriance. Whatever is not cultivated field is tropical forest of grand appearance. The grey parrot of West Africa swarms in these woodlands, and fills the air with its shriekings and whistlings. . . . The magnificent blue plantain-eater, the violaceous plantain-eater . . . and large horn-bills with enormous white casques people these lofty trees, from which indiarubber lianas sway like the ropes to be used in moving stage scenery.'[3]

How deeply Johnston revelled in the birds and the flowers is suggested by the wonderful reproductions of his water-colour paintings that adorn the two volumes of his *Uganda Protectorate*. But he felt at home also with the people, the densely-settled, smiling Bantu peasants of the Lake Victoria Basin, so different from the graceful but reserved Nilo-Hamitic pastoralists of the highlands. Unlike many, perhaps most, Englishmen, he was a

[1] Johnston to Salisbury, Eldama Ravine, 21.xi.99, *F.O.2.204*.
[2] Johnston to Salisbury, Ugowe Bay, 1.xii.99, and Entebbe 22.i.00, *F.O.2.297*; F.O. to Johnston 31.i.00 and 21.ii.00, *F.O.2.295*.
[3] *Uganda Protectorate*, pp. 67-8.

consistent evolutionist. The true savage might be noble, at least in appearance, but he preferred those who were in economic and social development a stage nearer to himself. Among the Basoga he felt for the first time that here at last was something for civilization to work on. A C.M.S. missionary at Iganga in Busoga reported with evident satisfaction to his Society that the new Commissioner had made him his mouthpiece in speaking to the local people. 'He communicated to them his plans for their future government and when closing his remarks said: "Tell them how interested the Queen is in their welfare, how she wants them to improve themselves and their country" and added, "We were like you long years ago, going about naked like the Bakavirondo with our war paint on, but when we learnt Christianity from the Romans we changed and became great. We want you to learn Christianity and follow our steps and you too will be great." It was afterwards remarked to me by one of the natives that such words were never spoken to them at the Fort.'[1]

It was the people of Buganda itself, however, who overtopped all Johnston's expectations. He crossed the Nile near its outlet from Lake Victoria, and sensed himself immediately in another country, where the principle of authority, recognized by all classes in the community, offered, no matter how it had been abused in the past by bad and bloody tyrants, the first and surest foundation for future progress. In place of the twisting, ragged footpaths he had followed hitherto, broad straight roads climbed inexorably over the steep, flat-topped hills and crossed as undeviatingly the papyrus-filled swamps between. The great dark-green forests of Kyagwe fringed the horizon, but the immediate route was lined by neatly thatched, reed-fenced habitations, set each in its own banana grove, while along the roads and through the gardens moved the stately, unhurrying figures of the Baganda, draped, some still in stiff, brown barkcloth, but most already in spotless white gowns of imported calico. Johnston recalled an engraving, which had hung in his parents' home, of a painting by a long-forgotten, early Victorian artist entitled the Plains of Heaven. It exhibited, he said, 'a Turneresque landscape of untrue perspective, with those vague unclassified trees, so untruthful in drawing, to which Turner was addicted. Streams of water flowed without any regard to the law of gravity, and a Turneresque shimmer in the atmosphere disguised other faults in drawing. In and out of these bosky

---

[1] A. Wilson to C.M.S. from Iganga 21.xii.99, C.M.S. Archives, Uganda Mission 1900, No. 31.

K*

groves and hollows, and along the banks of the heavenly streams promenaded an innumerable company of the Blessed, as vague in drawing as the landscape, and chiefly characterized by long flowing garments of white which did away with the necessity for the correct delineation of any limbs.' In the Buganda scene he recognized a delicious travesty of the Plains of Heaven, with the Baganda processing like saints in long, trailing garments.

Among other marks of their redemption the Baganda, or at least their chiefs, already excelled in the art of making tea, and of providing it, charmingly served, for the weary European traveller at the thirstiest points along the road. Spacious, thatched rest-houses had often been constructed for the evening camp, and food for all the tired caravan appeared, as if by magic, at the appointed hour. Chiefs in Buganda never came to call at an inconvenient moment, nor outstayed their welcome when received. As guests their table manners were fastidious, and all of them could converse direct with Johnston in the Kiswahili tongue of the East Coast, which he had learned on Kilimanjaro and practised throughout his years in Nyasaland. As the expedition approached Kampala, the demonstrations increased both in frequency and formality. Messengers came running with the greetings of the infant Kabaka, of the three Regents, and of the great chiefs assembled at the capital. Finally, the Acting Commissioner, Colonel Ternan, marched out to welcome his new superior: in the town he had prepared all things with a sense of ceremony which the Baganda were quick to understand. And so, on December 20th, 1899, the Special Commissioner made a triumphal entry through decorated streets, marching straight to the council hall, where he received the Protectorate officials, the missionaries, the principal traders, and the highest-ranking chiefs, addressing them in turn in English, French and Kiswahili. In the evening a great dinner was held at Kampala Fort, while thousands of Baganda torch-bearers illuminated the streets and lanes of the surrounding hills.

It was indeed a royal ovation. Yet it did not take either this or the astounding spectacle of the Baganda streaming in their thousands up the mission hills of Namirembe, Rubaga and Nsambya to divine service on Christmas morning, to make Johnston realize that here in Buganda lay the crucial issue for the success or failure of his Special Commission. The primary task laid upon him in his official instructions was to set the Protectorate upon a course that would make it financially self-supporting at the earliest possible date. In his view this depended upon two things: the ability of the Administration to levy taxes, and its right to control the use of at least a proportion of the land. Buganda was economically the most advanced province of the Protectorate, therefore it was in Buganda that these reforms must be first introduced. Yet it was transparently clear that in Buganda, with its already partly westernized and politically-conscious ruling class, and with its very considerable power of armed resistance if this class were provoked, these two essential rights could only be exercised by prior negotiation and consent. Back at Naivasha in October, he had first hinted to the Foreign Office his intention to acquire land rights by treaty, and Hill had minuted: 'Sir H. Johnston's method is simple: treaty or compulsion, your money or your life. It answered well in Central Africa where all recalcitrant chiefs were improved away and where the area was comparatively small: but it was preceded by many small wars.'[1] It was an odious insinuation, untrue of all the Nyasaland agreements except the handful which had been imposed as terms of peace upon the Yao chiefs who had initiated hostilities against the Administration, and it was still wider of the mark in respect of the agreements which Johnston was to negotiate in Uganda. The Baganda in particular proved, as he himself admitted, 'hard and sagacious bargainers', and so far from imposing anything upon them, he met and remet them on their hesitations and amendments until at the end of nearly three months there emerged the most complex and far-reaching Agreement ever concluded between an African people and an occupying European power.

The proposition put by Johnston within a day or two of his arrival in Buganda to the three Regents and the other leading chiefs would seem from the limited evidence available to have been a simple one, following the lines of the agreements he had concluded with the chiefs of the West Nyasa district of Nyasaland in 1895: first, that in exchange for the confirmation of their rights in the land actually under cultivation, the Baganda should cede all waste and forested land in the country to the Crown; secondly, that they should agree to the imposition of a hut-tax of 3 rupees a year, out of the proceeds of which one-tenth should be retained by the chiefs collecting it, and out of which a further sum not exceeding £2,000 a year should be set aside for the Kabaka's Civil List. The Baganda chiefs were powerful, and their rule extended over about a million people.

[1] Johnston to Salisbury from Naivasha 13.x.99, *F.O.2.204.*

A tenth of the taxes collected would amount to a considerable sum, and Johnston, writing on Christmas Eve to the Foreign Office, said that although the chiefs had not yet given him their reply, he was confident that he had provided a sufficient compensation for their vested interest.[1] And indeed the chiefs' first reply, delivered on January 3rd, was mild enough. They asked that the hut-tax should be two rupees instead of three, and that their own share of it should be a third instead of a tenth, for otherwise they would be poor and despised; but they did not challenge the Commissioner's proposal that the unoccupied land in the country should be vested in the Crown.

Johnston had by this time withdrawn from Kampala to his administrative headquarters at Entebbe twenty miles away on the shores of the Lake, leaving the day-to-day conduct of negotiations to Frederick Jackson, the civil officer in charge of the Buganda province.[2] Jackson had great tact, and his experience of the country went back to 1890; none the less he failed on this occasion to hold the confidence of the self-assured Baganda leaders. What he said to them in reply to their note we do not know, but within a very few days of its delivery the atmosphere of calm bargaining had been succeeded by one of panic. Alfred Tucker, the Anglican Bishop of Eastern Equatorial Africa, returned to Kampala from a tour in Ankole on January 8th and found the capital in a state of high excitement. 'The chiefs', he wrote, 'are coming to see me every day and almost every hour of the day.' And their talk was no longer of the hut-tax, but of the proposed land settlement, to which they now declared themselves unalterably opposed. They were ruined, they told Tucker. Their country was being taken from them and their glory had departed.[3]

Already on January 5th Johnston had authorized his deputy to make some minor concessions. To the Regents and the great chiefs he had offered fixed salaries instead of the suggested commission on the hut-tax. He had offered them also personal estates corresponding to the importance of their offices. The remainder of the cultivated land, which was to be confirmed to African possession, he had offered to place under the administration of a Board of Trustees, half the members of which should be Baganda. He had made it plain that even the proposed Crown lands should be available to African purchasers on

[1] Johnston to Salisbury from Kampala 24.xii.99, *F.O.2.204.*
[2] F. J. Jackson: *Early Days in East Africa*, 1930, pp. 387-8.
[3] A. R. Tucker: *Eighteen Years in Uganda and East Africa*, 1908, Vol. II, pp. 254-257; Tucker to C.M.S. 18.i.00, C.M.S. Archives, Uganda Mission 1900, No. 56.

terms at least as favourable as those for immigrants. But it required a far more radical revision of the proposals than this to mollify the Baganda leaders, whose suspicions were now thoroughly awakened. A big meeting of chiefs and senior missionaries convened by Jackson on January 13th broke up without resolving the deadlock. 'It is the land question', Jackson reported, 'that seems to be their bitterest pill, not so much on account of the land itself and its passing out of their hands . . . as the effect it will have on their pride as a governing body.' Power over land was in fact the supreme attribute of chieftainship in Baganda eyes. It was the Kabaka's power over land, delegated by him to the different orders of chiefs, which created the patron and client relationship existing between chief and peasant. Any proposal to interfere with this power, therefore, brought into question the whole system of internal self-government which the Baganda thought they had retained in their previous treaties with the British. Wherein had they offended, the chiefs asked, in a memorandum following the conference of January 13th, that the Kabakaship should be thus abolished and the Council of Chiefs set aside? 'Peevish nonsense,' answered Johnston. When had he ever said that the Kabaka was deposed or the Council abolished?

And yet for all his impatience and lack of understanding, and for all the rough asides in his private correspondence with Jackson about 'the thick skulls of the Baganda nobility', Johnston was not above taking the good advice of the missionaries of both denominations, who cheerfully walked the long, hot miles to Entebbe in order to mediate between the British Administration and their favourite African converts. Bishop Hanlon of the Mill Hill mission was the first to go, and probably it was he who explained to Johnston the importance of conciliating with grants of private land, not merely the dozen or so highest-ranking chiefs, but the subordinate ranks of the feudal hierarchy as well. On January 24th the Commissioner announced that he was prepared to grant estates of fair size to the King, chiefs and petty chiefs to the number of 784. He was prepared, therefore, not merely to buy the support of a few signatories to his treaty, but to consolidate the position of a governing class. For the Baganda negotiators this was a great step forward.

At the end of January Hanlon was succeeded at Entebbe by Tucker. Though by no means an unqualified personal admirer of the Special Commissioner, the Anglican Bishop was fully seized of the immense significance of the opportunity afforded by the new proposals to individualize land tenure. He reminded the chiefs that according to existing customary law all the land in the country, excepting only the *Butaka* land, the burying-places of the several clans, belonged to the Kabaka, who had power to turn any chief out of his office and out of the land that went with the office at a moment's notice. No land, he pointed out, could be properly developed under such a tenure. But he also declared himself openly in support of the chiefs in their shrewd contention that cultivated land alone was of no use to them without a corresponding allowance of uncultivated fallow or *nsiko*, which was indispensable to their system of shifting cultivation. It was this problem of *nsiko* land that Tucker took to Johnston, and out of Johnston's sympathetic study of which there emerged the partition of the land in Buganda between the Crown and the chiefs which was ultimately incorporated in the Agreement. The earlier distinction between cultivated and uncultivated land was now dropped. Assuming, said Johnston, that the total land area of Buganda was 19,600 square miles, he proposed that the Crown should take 9,000 square miles in trust for the people of Uganda as a whole, and a further 1,500 square miles of forested land, which it could exploit at its own discretion. Of the remaining 9,100 square miles, 50 would be set aside for government stations, 92 for the Christian missions, 958 as large estates for the royal family, ministers and senior chiefs, and 8,000 as smaller estates for the minor chiefs and traditional landholders who could establish their claims before the native council or *Lukiko*. In marking out these individual holdings the *Lukiko* might select cultivated or uncultivated land, or a proportion of each: the only condition was that the total area of 8,958 square miles was not to be exceeded.

It had been no part of Johnston's original purpose to create in Buganda a small, privileged aristocracy of African land-owners who, whether or not their legal title amounted to full freehold tenure, had nevertheless the two essential rights, to transfer land by sale, and to charge rent for its use from the peasant occupiers. It would seem, on the contrary, that his first plan had been to confirm the peasants in their occupational rights, and to use the Crown lands as a source from which a more individual form of tenure could be conferred upon progressive African farmers as also upon immigrant settlers from India and Europe. His inclusion of the minor chiefs and his solution of the *nsiko* problem had therefore between them involved a complete change of front. It was the price he chose to pay for the co-operation of the political leaders of the country, in bringing Buganda within the administrative system of the Protectorate as a whole, and in making it the starting-point for taxation and the more detailed control of native affairs which taxation implied. But it did not amount, as some have since supposed, to a betrayal of the poor peasantry of Buganda into the hands of aristocratic oppressors. For at the same time as he changed his policy in relation to the land to be confirmed to the possession of the Baganda, he changed also his policy in relation to the land to be ceded to the Crown. Would-be immigrant settlers could now, if they were willing to pay the price, buy land from the aristocratic estate owners. So also could the more well-to-do peasants not included in the *Lukiko's* distribution. The Crown lands, therefore, need no longer be regarded as the source of land for alienation and sale. They could become instead the safeguard of the poor from the possible oppressions of the rich; their existence as a refuge would ensure that the new Baganda landlords would be unable to charge excessive rents to their tenants. 'I want', he explained to Jackson, 'to secure the greater part of the land to the people of Uganda, and to make it impossible for any greedy King or chief or collection of chiefs to sell large quantities of land to European speculators. I want to be perfectly fair in the matter, so I propose in this arrangment to give the King, Chiefs and petty Chiefs estates of fair size which they can do with as they like—if they choose to be silly and sell them, they can sell them and eat and drink the money they get for them; but the rest of the uncultivated land I wish to secure for the people of Uganda as a whole, by placing it under the control of a Board of Trustees, half native and half European. As to the land uncultivated or forested I wish to place that under the control of the Queen, to be disposed of to the best advantage of the country, the revenue from it to be used in the development of the country and not to be sent to England. . . .'[1]

Without doubt it was Johnston's drastic revision of his proposals for a land settlement, with its strong appeal to the self-interest of the ruling class, which was the decisive move for the success of the negotiations. Thereafter, events moved fast. On February 7th and 8th Johnston spent two long days in personal negotiation with the Regents and principal chiefs at Entebbe. On the 10th a first draft in English of the whole treaty was sent to the Anglican Mission for translation into Luganda. On the 13th a full conference of chiefs, supported by their missionary

---

[1] Johnston to Jackson 24.i.00, cited J. V. Wild: *The Story of the Uganda Agreement*, Nairobi, East African Literature Bureau 1950, p. 78.

advisers, met in Johnston's house at Entebbe to discuss final amendments.[1] The remaining three and a half weeks before the formal signature on March 10th was occupied mainly in translation and printing. And yet, for all the speed of the negotiations, the Baganda leaders were not, as the final document reveals, so concentrated on their own interests that they failed to secure a constitutional and territorial settlement of the greatest significance for their country as a whole. In the first clauses of the Agreement, which regulated the status of the Kingdom within the Protectorate, the Baganda made four substantial concessions. They renounced their claims to tribute from the adjoining tribes; they agreed that Buganda should rank as a province of equal status to any other provinces into which the rest of the Protectorate might be divided; they agreed that revenue collected in Buganda should be merged in the general revenue of the Protectorate; and they agreed that the laws made by Her Majesty's Government for the Protectorate should be equally applicable in Buganda, except in so far as they might conflict with the terms of the Agreement. But in exchange for these concessions they obtained a formal definition of their boundaries which recognized their jurisdiction over the very considerable areas of southern and eastern Bunyoro occupied by their armies since the campaigns of 1894 and which transferred to them in addition the county of Kabula taken from Ankole and the island of Buvuma from Busoga. Buganda, in fact, became part and parcel of the Protectorate, but in doing so doubled the size of its own territories.[2]

The remaining seventeen clauses of the Agreement dealt with the internal administration of Buganda, and here also the negotiating chiefs gained at least as much as they conceded. The land settlement followed very closely Johnston's revised proposals. The Baganda ceded 10,550 square miles to the Crown to be controlled by the Protectorate Administration; the remainder was parcelled out into freely transferable estates to be allocated in the first instance to the royal family and the fortunate few of the chiefs and notables. Minerals became the property of the owners of the land, subject to the payment of a

---

[1] In the foregoing account of the negotiations leading up to the treaty I am deeply indebted to Mr Anthony Low of Makerere College for placing at my disposal an important paper entitled 'The Making of the Uganda Agreement', which is based upon a full study of the relevant documents in the Secretariat Archives at Entebbe.

[2] The text of the Agreement is enclosed in Johnston to Salisbury 12.iii.00, *F.O.2.297.*

ten per cent royalty on their exploitation. The people at large retained their customary rights to hunt and collect timber in the forests ceded to the Crown; they could also, if they wished, settle as tenant occupiers on the unforested Crown land. In the administration of justice the Baganda formally surrendered to the Protectorate Government the right to try all cases involving non-natives of the Kingdom; they allowed a right of appeal from their own courts to the Protectorate courts in respect of all sentences involving more than £100 fine or five years' imprisonment; and they agreed to submit all death sentences for confirmation to the Queen's representative. But, these three exceptions apart, the Baganda remained justiciable only in their own courts. Most important of all, the Baganda secured by this Agreement the constitutional right to be governed directly by their own Kabaka and by their traditional hierarchy of chiefs, acting with the advice of the traditional council of state or *Lukiko*.

Some limitations were indeed imposed upon each of these institutions. The *Lukiko* was curtailed in membership to the three ministers, the 20 *saza* or county chiefs and 66 other notables, all nominated by the Kabaka, who was amenable in the last resort to the advice of the Protectorate Administration. But the *Lukiko*, so constituted, gained the right to debate 'all matters concerning the native administration of Buganda', and to forward to the Kabaka, for reference to the Protectorate Administration, all resolutions adopted by a majority vote. It retained also its traditional right, upon a vacancy in the Kabakaship, to choose a successor from among the eligible princes of the royal house, subject only to the approval of its nominees by the Protectorate Government. Direct taxation, fixed in the first instance at three rupees or four shillings a hut, could only be increased with the *Lukiko's* consent. The three Regents or ministers, and the 20 *saza* chiefs, retained under the Agreement their primary status as servants of the Kabaka's Government, and their traditional functions as magistrates, police chiefs and directors of public works. Their appointments, however, became subject to the approval of the Queen's representative, and they were charged with one new function, in respect of which they were the salaried agents of the Protectorate, not the Buganda Government. For it was upon the *saza* chiefs that there rested the responsibility for collecting the Protectorate hut-tax, and it was upon their efficiency in doing so that, not only their own emoluments but also those of the Kabaka and ministers, depended. 'Should the Kingdom of

Buganda', reads the clause which is the most revealing of the atmosphere in which the Agreement was negotiated, 'fail to pay to the Uganda Administration, during the first two years after the signing of this agreement, an amount of native taxation equal to half that which is due in proportion to the number of the inhabitants; or should it at any time fail to pay the aforesaid minimum ... or should the Kabaka, Chiefs or people pursue at any time a policy which is distinctly disloyal to the British Protectorate, Her Majesty's Government will no longer consider themselves bound by the terms of this Agreement. On the other hand should the revenue exceed two years running a total value of £45,000 a year, the Kabaka and County Chiefs should be entitled to appeal to Her Majesty's Government for an increase in their subsidies.'

It was perhaps fortunate for the success of the negotiations that the reigning Kabaka was an infant, for there is no doubt that it was the Kabaka who in terms of real power lost most by the Agreement. Ultimate sovereignty, of course, he had already lost by the earlier treaties concluded by Lugard and Portal with the ex-Kabaka Mwanga. Under Johnston's treaty, however, the Kabakaship became the constitutional pivot upon which practically the whole control of the Protectorate Government over the Buganda Government was based. It provided that the Queen's representative should have direct access to the Kabaka at all times, and failure to co-operate fully in any detail of policy could be construed as disloyalty, which would render him liable to loss of recognition. Upon a Protectorate Government bent upon active interference in the affairs of Buganda, and prepared to use its influence over the Kabaka to the full, the Agreement imposed practically no check. The Protectorate Government could advise the Kabaka on the choice of his ministers, chiefs and *Lukiko* members: it could thus in the last resort force what measures it pleased upon the acceptance of the *Lukiko*. This aspect of the question did not, however, attract attention for many years. Far more apparent, immediately, was the Kabaka's loss of power in relation to his own people. The Agreement deprived him specifically of the power of life and death, and of the right to mobilize an army—save under the explicit advice of the Queen's representative. It left him potentially a rich man, the master of private estates totalling 350 square miles; but by removing the rest of the land from his control, it reduced very considerably indeed his power over the most powerful of his subjects. It closed the age of absolute monarchy and established the ascendancy of the barons. To a

large extent the real revolution it effected was probably
unnoticed by the Baganda negotiators, who, representing the
baronial interest, doubtless thought that they had added
immensely to the royal dignity by securing for the Kabaka the
style of Highness and the right to a salute of nine guns. Significantly, it was upon this point of protocol that Johnston anticipated the strongest opposition from the Foreign Office. He
begged Lord Salisbury to weigh the importance of an appeal
to native vanity. 'The idea of their Ruler—the grandson of
Mutesa, the descendant of a line of African Kings exceptional
for its continuity, its apparent historical actuality and the area
of country subject to its rule—being placed on the same level of
importance as the Sultan of Zanzibar, has done more than
anything else to reconcile the Regents and Chiefs of this country
to surrender into the hands of the British Government the right
of taxation, the control over the land, and the power of life and
death over the people.'[1]

Curious improvisation that it was, the Buganda Agreement
of 1900 was probably, after the construction of the Mombasa-
Kisumu railway, the most important single event in the history
of Uganda since the founding of the British Protectorate. Its
innovations in land tenure provided a supreme incentive to
the introduction of an exchange economy, and anticipated by
fifty-five years some of the principal recommendations of the
East Africa Royal Commission of 1953-5. On the constitutional
side it established the system of internal administration in
Buganda and the pattern of relations between the Buganda and
Protectorate Governments which endured in all essentials for
half a century. When the Protectorate Government in November 1953 withdrew its recognition from the son and successor of
Kabaka Daudi Chwa and deported him from the country, it
was upon the Agreement of 1900 that it took its stand. It was the
long-overdue revision of the Agreement in 1954-5 which paved
the way for Kabaka Mutesa's return. More immediately, however, the conclusion of the Agreement provided Johnston with
the corner-stone for his radical reconstruction of the Protectorate administration. It was not at all that he wished to reproduce
its provisions in a whole series of similar agreements with other
tribes. On the contrary, he envisaged it as a special alliance
with the Baganda alone, entered into not only because they
were the most progressive people of the Protectorate but also

---

[1] *Op. cit.*, Johnston to Salisbury 12.iii.00.

because they were the only group capable of offering a serious threat to the security of the Protectorate Government. The first and basic purpose of the Agreement was to identify the interests of the Baganda with the support of the British Administration. It was of the essence of such an idea that the Baganda should enjoy a unique and highly privileged position among the other peoples of the territory.

Characteristically, Johnston did not wait to secure the approval of the Foreign Office before proceeding to the formal signature of the Agreement. At the end of December 1899 he had asked permission to introduce a hut-tax in Buganda; but he had made no reference at all to the elaborate negotiations he was conducting with the Baganda leaders in any of the multitudinous despatches written during the two and a half months which followed. All things considered, the official reaction, when faced at the end of April with the *fait accompli*, was at first surprisingly mild. 'This despatch', wrote Hill 'encloses and explains an Agreement which is very ably conceived and of which the first reading impresses me favourably.' On June 6th, however, Hill and Brodrick sat down with Davidson of the Legal Department and Ternan, the former military Commandant and Acting Commissioner who was then on leave in England, to examine the treaty in detail. About the two matters of most immediate practical importance they were profoundly sceptical, Ternan venturing the prophecy that the proceeds of taxation would not even realize the amount of the subsidies guaranteed to the Kabaka and Chiefs, and Davidson questioning strongly the practicability of implementing Johnston's land settlement. The Committee concluded that the Agreement had been 'ably and carefully drawn', but 'they were met by the fact that it had been signed on behalf of H.M.G. . . . and was not therefore susceptible of verbal amendment. This being so, it must either be accepted or disallowed. They were not prepared to recommend the latter step, seeing that those on the spot have better means of judging and are all agreed: consequently they suggest its acceptance.'[1] Johnston, however, received no word of official commendation for his work. Instead, a distinctly chilly draft was prepared by Hill in Lord Salisbury's name, stating in studiously negative terms the Government's unwillingness to invalidate what he had done.[2] It reached him in his camp at Fort Portal in the middle of August, five full months after the Agreement had been signed.

[1] Minutes and Memoranda attached to Johnston to Salisbury 12.iii.00, *F.O.2.297.*
[2] Salisbury to Johnston 15.vi.00, *F.O.2.296.*

Johnston, needless to say, had long before this set in motion all the essential points of his wider administrative reorganization, of which the Buganda treaty was merely the indispensable preliminary. First and foremost, the assurance of the whole-hearted co-operation of Buganda with the Protectorate had cleared the way for a long-overdue redistribution of responsibility between the civil and military arms of the British Administration. The first large task to which he had addressed himself on his arrival in Entebbe in January 1900 had been a searching inquiry into the state of the Protectorate accounts, which proved to be nearly two years in arrears, and which showed an outstanding deficit of something like £100,000. In part he found this to be due to uncontrolled expenditure on the Uganda account by the authorities of the East African Protectorate, who were responsible for all transport arrangements between Mombasa and the Lake. In part also it was due to the fact that customs for both Protectorates were collected at Mombasa, and that only a fraction of its proper share in these revenues was in practice remitted to Uganda. Mainly, however, Johnston attributed the chaotic state of the finances to the inefficiency of military accountancy.[1] 'The fact is', he explained to Lord Salisbury, 'that, except in regard to the Indian Contingent, the British officers employed in the Uganda Rifles have not in all cases given satisfaction to the Administration of this Protectorate. Their military qualities have seldom if ever left anything to be desired, but they are restless, and inclined to be discontented and fretful, unless either allowed to do a great deal of big game shooting or to take part in some native war.'[2] It was above all on the financial side of administration that the sporting inclinations of the military officials had led to the greatest negligence. Accounts had been handed over to half-trained Indian clerks and storekeepers working with little or no supervision. Returns and indents had been forwarded to headquarters late or incomplete. There had been a general assumption that detailed paper work was no part of the duties of an officer and a gentleman. It was clear that before the collection of revenue could be added to the cares of a district administrator it would be necessary to substitute civilian officials for the military. 'I desire', Johnston had written as early as February 1900, 'as soon as possible to take the civil administration of Bunyoro and the Nile districts out of military hands, as the military officers make a nearly hopeless muddle of

---

[1] Johnston to Salisbury from Port Alice 3.iii.00, *F.O.2.297*.
[2] Johnston to Salisbury from Entebbe 17.iii.00, *ibid.*

their accounts, and with the institution of native taxation a more business-like system is necessary.'[1]

The practical problems of converting a mainly military into a mainly civil administration were, however, considerable. Johnston had to keep strictly within his estimates. Any expansion in his civilian establishment had to be balanced by a corresponding reduction on the military side. Possible gains in administrative efficiency had to be weighed against possible losses in military security. The change posed also very delicate problems of human relations. It was the almost universal experience during the early years of administration in Africa that when a military officer and a civilian official were posted alongside in the same district, they quarrelled over the spheres of their respective responsibilities. In Uganda this always explosive relationship was doubly charged in that only a handful of the civilian officials belonged to anything like the same social *milieu* as the military officers. There was, for example, the case of James Martin, an illiterate Maltese of immense force of character, who had graduated from caravan-leading to the charge of a district in the Eastern Province; and there was the extreme case of Francis Spire, who had come to Uganda in 1894 as Colonel Colvile's batman, who had been promoted by Berkeley to the position of Chief Cashier, and who was at last posted by Johnston as Collector in Bunyoro. When the appointment was disallowed by Hill on the grounds that Spire might find himself obliged to issue orders to military officers who were his social superiors, Johnston responded with an angry protest. 'Richard Lander,' he wrote, 'who first definitely traced the outlet of the River Niger, went to that river as valet to Captain Clapperton, and after his master's death performed the services to African exploration which gained him the Gold Medal of the Royal Geographical Society. He was sent back to the Niger by the Government of that day as one of the principal officials in charge of the Niger Expedition. Dr Livingstone was the son of a poor weaver, and worked for years as a factory boy, and yet for many years he was judged worthy to hold Her Majesty's Commission as Consul in Central Africa. Why therefore in Mr Spire's case an objection should be raised to his advancement in the service of the Uganda Protectorate, after six years work in the country, the climate of which he is able to support, and the languages of which he has done more to acquire than most Europeans, I am at a loss to understand.'[2]

[1] Johnston to Salisbury from Entebbe 18.ii.00, *F.O.2.297.*
[2] Johnston to Salisbury from Katwe 26.vii.00, *F.O.2.299.*

All the same, the problem was one which, in his overall plan, he had gone out of his way to face and to solve. The conclusion of the Buganda Agreement made it possible, so Johnston believed, to make a reduction of about 700 men in the fully trained, highly paid, expensively equipped and lavishly officered native force built up by Colonels Ternan and Coles since the outbreak of the Sudanese Mutiny. He was in any case sceptical of the value for colonial campaigning of the spit-and-polish, parade-ground methods practised by the British officers. 'These soldiers', he wrote in a memorable passage, intended no doubt for Lord Salisbury's delectation, but in fact passed by Hill straight to the officer he was criticizing, 'are wonderfully efficient in anything approaching the conditions of civilized warfare, and they do credit to the work done by Colonel Ternan and his officers in organizing them in past times; but the very degree to which Colonel Ternan has succeeded in causing them to resemble civilized troops renders them less efficient in bush warfare. They are beginning to require now military roads on which to tramp, tramp, tramp in their military boots, and, to display their military qualities to the best advantage, they must be met by an enemy on much the same plane as themselves. In our recent expeditions undertaken against the robber tribes of the eastern parts of the Protectorate, the regular soldiers have been of comparatively little use—the real work has been done by the native allies, who were probably quite naked except for a bandolier or a cartridge pouch, but who managed, with the aid of Snider rifles and their own native spears, to encounter and defeat an enemy whom the regular soldiers seldom saw.'

Johnston proposed to keep only 1,100 instead of 1,800 of these regular troops of the Uganda Rifles, and to concentrate the greater part of them, as also of the 400 members of the Indian Contingent, at headquarters as a central, striking force which would be ready to deal with an emergency in any part of the Protectorate. Small garrisons of regular troops under commissioned British officers would remain in Bunyoro and the Nile districts, and also in the Nandi country east of Lake Victoria; but for the rest, the protection required by district officials for the maintenance of ordinary law and order, and the safe conduct of mail and supplies, would be provided by a new force of armed constabulary 1,400 strong, paid at half the rate of the regular soldiers, lightly equipped, and officered by British N.C.O.s, who would be responsible directly to the civilian officers in charge of the districts in which they were

stationed. About a third of the new force Johnston expected to
recruit from among the more elderly and less physically fit of
the Sudanese regulars, who would be retired and then offered
the chance of re-enlistment in the constabulary at the lower
rate of pay. For the rest he proposed what was to most of the
military officers the revolutionary step of employing Baganda.
'I am drafting into this police force', he explained to Lord
Salisbury, 'what may be styled the Regular Militia, which has
hitherto been employed and armed by the King and chiefs of
Buganda, and which has taken a gallant part in our wars
against Bunyoro and the mutinous Sudanese. These men
dislike to settle down to the life of a peasant, yet, at the same
time, it is preferable to give them legitimate occupation under
arms instead of allowing them to remain an unemployed and
turbulent element in the country.'[1]

As with the Agreement, so now with his military reorganization, Johnston acted first and reported later. The opportunity
seemed indeed too good to be missed in that the two senior
British Army officers, Colonel Ternan and his friend Colonel
Coles, were both in England on leave. In Colonel Evatt of the
Indian Contingent he had temporarily a Commandant as
fully sympathetic as Maguire and Edwards had been in Nyasaland. Confidentially, and with absolute propriety, he requested
that neither Ternan nor Coles should be encouraged to return
to Uganda. Repeatedly he urged that the complement of
British officers should be kept down to twenty-nine. 'I am
obliged to say with some frankness,' he remarked on one
occasion, 'that as a rule in Tropical Africa one Indian Staff
Corps officer is worth two British.'[2]

Grimly Hill at the Foreign Office turned over the despatches
to Ternan, whose comments make critical but not very convincing reading. For, even from a strictly military point of
view, Johnston's arguments were difficult to contest. It was
consistent with all sound military theory that a colonial
garrison, if standards of discipline and training were to be
maintained, should as far as possible be concentrated and not
dispersed in small units. It was also a basic military tenet that
troops should only in exceptional circumstances, and then only
very temporarily, be employed as police. Ternan, therefore
could only argue that his own dispositions were being upset, and
that the new police, being under civilian control, would prove

---

[1] Johnston to Salisbury 17.iv.00, 5.v.00 and 29.v.00, *F.O.2.297* and *299*.
[2] Johnston to Salisbury 26.v.00, *F.O.2.299*.

ineffective as a para-military force. He was in fact, though perhaps sub-consciously, pleading for the continuance of military government. To Hill the fact that Johnston was reversing Ternan's arrangements appeared sufficient grounds for obstruction; but Salisbury, in a memorandum which has disappeared from the files, evidently decided to support the man on the spot. With an ill grace Hill drafted one of his most meanly permissive communications. 'Considerable doubt has been expressed by the military authorities, but Lord Salisbury must rely on your assurance that the state of the Protectorate is now such as to justify a reduction of the military establishment.'[1] At the same time he managed to secure the appointment of Ternan as Deputy Commissioner and Commandant in the East Africa Protectorate and of Coles as his successor in Uganda. For himself Hill asked and obtained permission to carry out a tour of inspection of the two Protectorates during the months of October and November 1900.

Long before Hill made his unwelcome appearance, Johnston had begun to be aware of the dangerous influences that were opposing him in Whitehall. The first warning had come from his old friend Sir Villiers Lister, now in retirement, who referred to 'a reign of fuss and worry' in which the personal relations between the men at the office and those serving abroad had lost their old friendliness and intimacy. Shortly after the signing of the Agreement Johnston, writing to his wife, had remarked on a kind and encouraging letter received from Brodrick, the Parliamentary Under-Secretary.

The Ministry evidently attaches the greatest importance to my work out here, and, as Mr Brodrick says, my appointment helps the Government to stave off Opposition attacks on their Uganda policy, because I seem to inspire confidence among Liberal politicians. Of course this sentiment does not affect the present attitude of Hill, —— and —— who still continue trying to put spokes in my wheels. But there are signs that Brodrick and Lord Salisbury are not going to allow fractious opposition to continue. The matter, however, is soon coming to an issue over questions of the Estimates and my scheme of military reorganization. Either Lord Salisbury must allow my views to prevail, or I shall be obliged to resign. But I am grateful for Mr Brodrick's letter. It came at a moment when I needed encouragement. Do not imagine I have broken openly with any of the men to whom I allude. Of course I remain, officially, studiously civil. The war is a covert one. If I prevail, I shall say as little about it as possible.[2]

[1] F.O. to Johnston 10.viii.00, *F.O.2.296.*
[2] Cited by Alex Johnston, *op. cit.*, p. 210. Mr Johnston quotes only two letters from Sir Harry to Lady Johnston; none at all has survived among the private papers.

Not even his worst enemy could have denied that Johnston had enormous pluck. Only a week or two before this letter was written he had been once again in mortal danger with black-water fever. The attack, his fourth, had come within six months of landing in tropical Africa, within three of settling by the mosquito-infested shores of Lake Victoria. It was characteristic of the disease for attacks to recur with increasing frequency. Almost any other man would have packed his bags and left at once for the coast. But Johnston stayed. The matter was never referred to in any despatch, and the daily round of work went on almost without interruption. Accounts, estimates, frontier questions, punitive expeditions, preservation of game, prevention of smuggling, the railway and the Lake steamers, administrative postings, military promotions, supplies, housing, immigration—all these things and many more had to be handled with the assistance of a secretariat of four men, two of whom were likely to be sick at any given moment. But they were handled, as always, at tremendous speed and with a verve which seldom missed the opportunity for a telling phrase or a sally of pungent wit. And there was still time to spare for painting and gardening, for languages and pets. Botanical and ornithological drawings Johnston frequently accomplished while he was dictating despatches to his brother. Curious traces of his other interests survive in the Secretariat archives at Entebbe. 'The Special Commissioner,' reads one communication from Frederick Jackson to the Superintendent of Public Works, 'has sent a note to say that he requires one each of the following tribes . . . in order that their languages may be written down: 1 Lur, 1 Alulu, 1 Lendu. Men who can talk Swahili preferred.' 'Over and above such taxes as you can collect in rupees', reads another from Cunningham, the official Private Secretary, to Stanley Tomkins at Kampala, 'you may collect others in Cauri-shells . . . or ivory, or india-rubber, or in the wild animals mentioned in the Memorandum. Would it not be an awful thing if the Collector and his staff at Kampala were found to be devoured by wild animals collected as taxes? To avoid any such eventuality, if you really do receive animals . . . you had better transmit them with care to Entebbe.' An accompanying schedule authorizes tax remissions of 3 rupees for wild pig in good condition, of 90 rupees for young zebra, partially trained and easy to deal with, of 300 rupees for hippopotamus calves and of 3,000 rupees for young elephants.[1]

[1] Jackson to Pordage 25.iii.01, Cunningham to Tomkins 20.x.00, Secretariat Archives, Entebbe.

Certainly, Entebbe during Johnston's reign had a wild exotic flavour, more akin in some respects to a travelling camp of the Emperor Frederick II than to a centre of British colonial administration. Government House was a low, thatched bungalow with walls of clay and floors of beaten cow-dung. The windows, commanding magnificent views across the sparkling waters of Lake Victoria towards Kome Island and the Sese archipelago, were merely holes in the wall, unglazed and unshuttered. Furniture, other than camp furniture, was the rough and ready work of recently settled Indian and Swahili carpenters. On the rudely white-washed walls Johnston's own water-colours hung surrounded by African shields and spears, quivers, pipes and fetishes. A chimpanzee and a pair of tame baboons made free use of the public rooms, as did a lordly black eagle which on one occasion 'slew with one swift stroke a privileged parrot for mocking him, and then disdained even to look at the carrion'. A baby elephant was allowed into the house for tea, helping itself to jam sandwiches from the common plate but drinking from its private milk-bottle. At the front door there was a large snake-pit, designed, so Johnston said, to deter the more boring class of visitors. On the gentle slopes behind the house the aged but still energetic Alexander Whyte had begun to lay out the botanical garden for which Entebbe is justly famed. A glade of tall forest, cleared only of its under-growth, was left to attest the primeval splendour of the site, and here in Johnston's time lived other members of his private zoo—antelopes and zebra, leopards and serval cats, the last two categories chained but still boisterous. The special pets of the establishment, however, were a group of Congo pygmies, rescued by the Administration from a German kidnapper, who were awaiting repatriation to their native forests. 'Why, I always thought they were *small* men,' the Special Commissioner had remarked to the embarrassed junior official who brought them to Entebbe, 'but I see that they are nearly as tall as I am.'[1]

Johnston in these surroundings could appear to many of his fellow Europeans a remote and forbidding personality, quite wrapped up in his own eccentricities. Certainly he had no time for small-talk, and he made little attempt to exercise the open-handed hospitality expected, not only by residents but also by every passing traveller and sportsman, of the Queen's representative. With a chosen few—Evatt and Jackson among the senior men, and one or two others like Delmé Radcliffe and Hobley, who shared his scientific and anthropological interests

[1] Communicated by Mr F. W. Isaac.

—he was on terms of intimacy. With the rest he was fair, but inclined to be cold and a little intimidating also. He had always disliked alcohol himself and he strongly disapproved of its consumption by others in tropical climates. He was also repulsed by the sexual irregularities openly practised in the absence of white women by many of the best and most hard-working officials. The soldiers had some reason to dislike and distrust him. He was critical of their traditional way of life in Uganda, and entirely unsympathetic towards the desire of many of them to get away and take part in the South African war. The missionaries for their part were slow to overcome their suspicions of the ostentatious unbeliever. 'Sir Harry Johnston is a man who thinks he knows everything,' Bishop Tucker once wrote in a state of some irritation. 'He is so wise in his own eyes', wrote another C.M.S. missionary, John Roscoe, 'that he will not take any advice readily'.[1] Nevertheless it was the missionary element in the European community which commanded from the first Johnston's whole-hearted approval, and it was from them in the end that he won the most open recognition of his services. His first report on the general condition of the Protectorate, which he composed at the end of 1900, was practically a paean in praise of the missions. Remarking that there was only one official, and he in a subordinate position, who had bothered to acquire the Luganda language, which was 'the key to the minds of two-thirds of the population', he proceeded to describe the rapid spread of Christianity over the Kingdom of Buganda and the district of Toro as one of the greatest triumphs to which the advocates of Christian propaganda could point.

It must not be imagined, of course, that the Baganda or Batoro have none of the Old Adam in their composition since they accepted Christianity; they steal, lie and commit adultery much like the Christian peoples of long standing; but, undoubtedly their intelligence is quickened, their ideas are enlarged —to a very notable extent—and their harmful old superstitions are swept away by their acceptance of the new faith. The difference between the Uganda of 1900 and the blood-stained, harassed, barbarous days of Mutesa and his abominable son Mwanga, is really extraordinary; and the larger share in this improvement is undoubtedly due to the teaching of Anglican and Roman Catholic missionaries.

It was a remarkable tribute. True he modified it somewhat in respect of the missionaries' social teaching, but even then only

[1] Tucker to C.M.S. 15.ix.00, Roscoe to C.M.S. 9.vi.00, C.M.S. Archives, Uganda Mission 1900, Nos. 172 and 130.

as a basis from which to illustrate his own ideas on social and economic policy. For he could never forget that his main task in Uganda was to inaugurate an economic revolution which would make the new Protectorate financially self-supporting. He could only succeed if the people of the country could be persuaded to produce for the world market, and so to earn the money incomes from which in turn a local revenue could be derived. He was sure in any case that it was the mission of civilization to inject a certain element of discontent into the complacency of negro societies about the material things of life. The most corrupting asset of the whole Lake Victoria Basin was in his view the banana plantain, which supplied, almost without the necessity of labour, man's food and drink and an important part of his building materials. Where life at a simple level was so easy, there was little incentive to improve it by toil. Yet Johnston was certain above all things that it stood in need of improvement. And he was disturbed to find that the emissaries of Christianity, which he regarded in all sincerity as the handmaid of Evolution, were apparently content to adapt the high superstructure of their ethical doctrines to so mean a foundation in the material circumstances of existence.

I am afraid there is rather a tendency on the part of missionaries, who are devoted to their converts and delighted at the success of their propaganda, to imply in teaching that the Baganda are perfect as they are, and had better remain in the same state of life as that in which they at present find themselves—viz., clothed in comely, fawn-coloured bark-cloth or in snowy white cotton, eating little but bananas, and living in houses made of grass and reeds. The missionaries are quite right about the clothing—right, I mean, to discourage hideous caricatures of European coats, trousers and hats; but in other respects I think they should not teach contentment to their converts. An honest friend of the Baganda would do this for them: he would try to make them adopt the plough (as we are trying to make them do); to harness oxen or donkeys to the plough, instead of sending their women out to hoe the ground; to plant grain crops of every description, instead of confining their dietary mainly to the stodgy banana; and to build far better houses, and to live in far more cleanly fashion than they do at present.

The main interest of the passage lies in the trend of Johnston's own thought. Now that the political stability of the Protectorate was assured through the agreement with Buganda, now that administration, through the adaptation of military and police policy, had been given a new flexibility, Johnston was pre-occupied above all with the problems of economic development which would become capable of solution when the railway was completed. Right through his five months' stay at Entebbe from January until May 1900 he had been engaged with Whyte and Doggett on a study of the natural resources of the country. His preliminary conclusions on the subject were embodied in the April report. He thought that there was a great future in the natural rubber of the forests. He observed that coffee grew wild in many parts of the Protectorate and ventured the pre-diction that Buganda and Busoga, Toro and Bunyoro were destined to become great producers of this crop. He remarked on the existence of cotton of good quality and long staple, but dismissed it from serious consideration, because it would probably never pay to export it by the railway to the coast. He stressed the importance of sugar and grain crops as food for local consumption, and of timber for the improvement of building. But the greatest problem of all would be the enlist-ment of human effort. Taxation would be a spur, but not in itself a sufficient one. The real solution, provided the people were not spoiled by missionary flattery or by the attitude of officials who frequently became 'more Muganda than the Baganda', would lie in the stimulation of new desires. 'When the railway reaches the Victoria Nyanza, when that lake is worked by steamers gathering up all the products from its thousands of miles of coast, when twenty traders (encouraged by these transport facilities) establish themselves where one trader now exists, and when these traders are ready with "cash down" to pay for goods, there is little doubt in my mind that the natives will be roused from their present lethargy and will seek far and wide for such products of their country as may be of marketable value.'[1]

Meanwhile the most urgent task of his Special Commission was to press on with the quest for natural resources by a personal inspection of as much of the territory as he could manage to traverse on foot. Eight months of the twelve that remained to him he spent almost continually on the march. They are dis-appointing months for the biographer in that during them the only despatches he sent to the Foreign Office dealt with specific matters of administrative business that he performed on the way. The main purpose of the journeys was scientific and not

[1] Preliminary Report on the Protectorate of Uganda, in Johnston to Salisbury 27.iv.00, *F.O.2.298.*

administrative. Their results appeared in the magnificent report which he presented at the close of his mission and in the two massive volumes of the *Uganda Protectorate*. But both these documents are secondary and completely depersonalized. Apart from a few acknowledgments, they make no distinction between the information which he acquired himself and the important contributions supplied, for example, by George Wilson in Bunyoro, by Delmé Radcliffe on the Nile, by Hobley in Kavirondo. They offer few clues indeed about the detailed movements and the daily life of unusual interest and activity which made their composition possible. There are some indications that the diary and the notebooks which Johnston had beside him when he wrote the *Uganda Protectorate* may have disappeared by the time he wrote *The Story of My Life*. If not, they must have shared at his death the fate of most of his private correspondence at the hands of a wife who had little appreciation of her husband's place in history, and who felt that the claims of discretion were absolute and extended beyond the grave.

A long-projected visit to Bunyoro and the Nile Province was rightly forbidden by the doctors after Johnston's serious illness: this was to remain the only large tract of country in his vast dominion which he never saw. On May 30th, 1900, however, he set out on a four-months' tramp through the far west. The first stage of about two hundred miles from Kampala to Fort Portal is accomplished by the modern motorist between breakfast and tea: it must have taken the Special Commissioner's expedition between a fortnight and three weeks. 'We looked', wrote Alex Johnston, 'rather like a travelling circus. Harry could not bear to be parted from all his animals when on *safari;* so favoured monkeys, perched on the woolly heads of porters, peered above the waving elephant grass, sunflowers and blazing scarlet *Ekirikiti* trees covering successive hill-furrows which our caravan climbed in single file, to find another and yet another hill beyond.' The travelling commissariat included cows and goats on the hoof, which caused tedious confusion and delay at every unbridged, swampy river. The porters and camp servants were chosen from every people and kindred and tongue, so as to provide material for linguistic study on the march. Six pygmies homeward bound after their kindly detention at Entebbe ranged, with their characteristic independence of human toil and care, up and down the moving file of men. It was a rule of the expedition that the European members took breakfast and tea alone in their tents. In the evening, however, a small dinner-jacketed group gathered round a well-laid table, and the Goanese cook was expected to give of his best. 'Conversation and cards were then encouraged by the camp-fire, the smoke of which somewhat mitigated the swarm of night-flying insects whose object in life seemed to be to commit suicide in the soup. Hyenas might be laughing like maniacs in the outer darkness, the tree-hyraxes be emitting their unearthly screams above the incessant chorus of frogs and crickets. The hideous flying-foxes or fruit-bats might pass like evil spirits above our narrow circle of light. Our porters might sing barbarically of love and of pumpkins; but this was our hour of home-talk of Europe, of mind rather than matter.'[1]

At length the column, having completed the last cycle of swamp and forest and flat-topped hill that makes up the landscape of Buganda, emerged one day in mid-June upon the superb, soft downland of Mwenge, the choicest pasturage of all East Africa, the traditional meeting-place of aristocratic Bahima herdsmen from Bunyoro in the north and Ankole in the south.[2] Ahead, to the west, rose the threatening pile of grey-black cloud that conceals almost perennially the main mass of the Ruwenzori range. They were entering the district of Toro, historically a collection of small hereditary chieftaincies, reorganized by Lugard under the paramountcy of the Mukama Daudi Kasagama, whose dynasty, an offshoot of the royal house of Bunyoro, had ruled in semi-independence for perhaps a century among the western foothills of the great mountain. Two or three more days brought Johnston to Kasagama's capital, perched dramatically as a Rhineland castle upon the steep summit of Kabarole hill. A mile away stood the first rough buildings of Fort Portal crowning the gentle ridge where, to-day, a broad avenue of jacarandas drop their blue flowers upon an emerald lawn. There followed perhaps ten days of meetings with Kasagama and his chiefs, culminating on June 26th in the signature of an agreement as simple as the Buganda Agreement had been complex. The boundaries of the kingdom were defined, as also those of the component principalities. The rulers of these principalities accepted more or less the status of county chiefs under the Mukama, retaining, however, the right to nominate their own successors. The imposition of a hut-tax was provided for; it was to be collected by the county chiefs, who were to retain one-tenth of the proceeds. Justice was to be administered to natives by the county chiefs in their own courts, with a right of appeal to the court of the Mukama, and, in

[1] Alex Johnston: *op. cit.*, pp. 196-8. [2] See Plate 16, facing p. 320.

A MUHIMA FROM ANKOLE, UGANDA

GALLIREX JOHNSTONI

cases involving more than £100, to the European officer in charge of the district; cases involving non-natives were transferred to the jurisdiction of the European magistrate. The agreement provided for the creation of freehold estates on the Buganda pattern, but these were conferred only upon the Mukama and his family and upon the ruling chiefs immediately subordinate to him; for the rest, the inhabitants of the country retained by implication their existing rights over the land in occupation, while vacant and forested lands were transferred to the Crown. The Toro Agreement was thus in the main a reversion to Johnston's treaty practice of Nyasaland days. He had always believed that the assumption of control over land and of the right to levy taxation were matters of such importance that they should, like the original transfer of sovereignty, be written into formal agreements with each of the native peoples in turn. To this list he had now added a formal recognition, and limitation, of the rights of native courts. He had also followed the Buganda precedent to the extent of offering freehold estates to the signing chiefs. But in Toro, as later in Ankole, neither the social and economic development of the country nor the status and bargaining powers of the lesser chiefs seemed to him to justify any further extension of individual tenure. Vacant lands formed a sufficient proportion of the whole for their possession to give the Crown an adequate control over land use, and there was consequently no reason why existing customary holders should be disturbed in their occupational rights.[1]

His business in Fort Portal concluded, Johnston started immediately on another long march which was to take him first a hundred miles southwards along the eastern base of the Ruwenzori range to Katwe on Lake Edward, and thence west and north, as far again, across the Semliki river to the administrative station of the Congo Free State at Fort Beni. He had many reasons for this journey. A long series of disagreeable boundary incidents had suggested the necessity for establishing friendly personal relations with the Congo officials as the preliminary step towards a more exact and more rational definition of the frontier. The perfect opportunity for an informal *rapprochement* had presented itself in the repatriation of the kidnapped pygmies, whose home village was in the forest west of Beni, Johnston hoped to form some first-hand impression of the administrative methods of the state officials, which were

---

[1] The text of the Toro Agreement is in *F.O.2.559*, and Johnston's very brief comments on it in Johnston to Salisbury from Fort Portal 25.viii.00, *F.O.2.299*.

L

already under heavy attack in Europe, and with this end in view he took with him Stephen Bagge, the District Collector at Fort Portal, whom he proposed to send on leave to England by the Congo route. Needless to say, however, Johnston had other motives of a more personal and scientific kind. He wished to add to his linguistic collections examples of the Bantu languages spoken in the eastern Congo. At Beni he would find, in the prison if nowhere else, a representative group of informants. Above all, perhaps, he wished to investigate the rumours, first recorded by Stanley in his account of the Emin Pasha expedition, of a mysterious mammal of horse-like appearance, which was said to dwell in the depths of the eastern reaches of the great Congo Forest. On his march to the west, he had questioned closely his pygmy companions, who had described to him a creature striped like a zebra but with a brown back, which they called *okapi*. On reaching Beni he encountered in Captain Eriksson of the Congo State service, a co-operative and friendly host, who confirmed at once the reality of the *okapi's* existence. When the frontier questions had been discussed and when Bagge had departed westwards bearing a personal letter from Johnston to the Governor-General at Leopoldville, an expedition was organized into the forest to visit the pygmy settlements. Johnston had the satisfaction of personally delivering his charges into the joyful circle of their relatives, but of a live *okapi* no trace was to be found.

> In the impressive and oppressive gloom the soldiers, to keep their courage up, continually sounded their bugles, and in consequence scared away every living creature except gorgeous butterflies and bird-eating spiders with golden webs. The many layers of dense foliage overhead, completely hiding the sky, were bombarded by perpetual and torrential thunderstorms with a sound like musketry punctuated by terrific crashes of heavy guns. Even when this inferno ceased, the atmosphere like the ground was as full of water as a sponge, this being one of the wettest spots on the globe not actually submerged by ocean. At times indeed the illusion was strong in this ghastly gloom, as we staggered half-blinded and choked through the reek of it, that we were being drowned in a thicket of sea-weed in the stagnant zone beneath a storm-tossed sea.[1]

Stricken by fever, the party was forced to retreat with its mission uncompleted. Some months after Johnston's departure, however, Eriksson forwarded to Entebbe the complete skin and skull of an *okapi* killed by one of his soldiers. It proved upon

[1] Alex Johnston: *op. cit.* pp. 201-2.

examination to be neither horse nor zebra, but nearer to the giraffe than to any other mammal. It was classified by Lankester of the British Museum as a new genus, *Okapia—Okapia John-stoni*.[1]

On July 27th the expedition was once more at Katwe: the journey from Fort Portal to Beni and back to Lake Edward had consumed a month. The next lap, from Katwe to Mbarara, the capital of Ankole, and back again to Fort Portal, was to occupy another. It is a month about which less is known than any other in Johnston's African life. A water-colour of one of the striking crater-lakes of Bunyaruguru and a photograph of the Mugabe and his court at Mbarara, both reproduced in the *Uganda Protectorate*, are the only certain indications in any of his published works that the journey was made at all. Among the Foreign Office papers, the postscript of a private letter to Hill announces his impending departure for Ankole, and a despatch from Jackson eighteen months later remarks that Johnston, during his visit to Mbarara, had decided that the country was not yet sufficiently settled to justify the conclusion of a treaty.[2] The fact of the matter was that Ankole proper, like Toro proper, was only the most important of a group of independent principalities, and that in the case of Ankole, unlike that of Toro, the rulers of the peripheral states were not prepared to assume without a struggle the rôle of county chiefs under the paramountcy of their overweening neighbour. There is little doubt that Johnston, in the interests of efficient administration, would have favoured the policy of centralization that was eventually carried out. But in August 1900 he had neither time to negotiate nor force to impose his will, and he could only leave the situation as he found it.

From Mbarara Johnston returned to Fort Portal. An unusually sympathetic observer, the C.M.S. missionary A. B. Fisher, who encountered him there almost daily during the week from August 20th to 26th, has left in his unpublished reminiscences a precious and convincing if not an outstandingly literary portrait. 'H. H. J. much appreciated our welcome and was most friendly. He was a little man with a big head and shock of thick hair, a very high complexion, good-looking. His voice was weak, he never stopped using it . . . he was the cleverest official to visit Uganda. He gave me the impression that there was no branch of human knowledge that he did not

---

[1] *Uganda Protectorate*, pp. 378-83, and Frontispiece.
[2] Johnston to Hill from Mbeni 20.vii.00, *F.O.2.299*; Jackson to Lansdowne 31.x.01, enclosing Ankole Agreement of 25.x.01, *F.O.2.559*.

know. . . . He was so pleasant and agreeable and hospitable and demanding that he kept us all hunting and supplying the information he was collecting. . . . The little Commissioner charmed his large native tea-parties by his numerous inquiries about birds, beasts and flowers. . . . One would like to have seen him outside his tent, surrounded by tables and his collecting plant and assistants, who received from a line of men and women all manner of specimens for his acceptance and reward . . . and his warm gratitude which he put over to them in good Swahili and halting Lunyoro.' . . . 'The commissioner called to have tea', wrote Fisher in another place, 'and told me of his terrible experiences during his visit to Katwe and the Semliki. Sitting in his tent after the day's march, a sudden storm came from the mountain. The tent shook. He called all his servants for help. The storm burst. The camp was flooded. "I clung to the ridge-pole and prayed to Almighty God that if he saved me, I would never return there again." The little man was very distressed at the memory of his terrible suffering and above all the damage to his precious collection.'[1]

At Fort Portal an unpleasant consignment of mail awaited the Commissioner's attention. From Jackson at Entebbe came news of persistent attacks by the Nandi on the engineers engaged on the construction of the railway and telegraph between the Mau summit and Mumia's. In June, twenty-five lives had been lost in small ambushes on supply caravans and bridging parties. In July the losses had risen to fifty, of which at least half had been suffered by fully armed escort patrols of the Uganda Rifles. Evatt had already gone east with reinforcements from Kampala, and to these Johnston now decided to add half of the Toro garrison. 'The native rulers', he commented to Jackson, 'may be vicious in regard to their desire to redeem little girls and give them a Christian home, but they are perhaps more loyal to the British Government than any potentates out here. In case of any disturbance, however, there are troops in Ankole, at Katwe and in Bunyoro.'[2] More serious in a sense than the activities of the Nandi were those of Clement Hill. The post from England had brought Hill's grudging acquiescence in the Buganda Agreement, probably also his first acid comments on the military reorganization. Worse, Johnston suspected that news of his strained relations with his chief had penetrated through Ternan to the junior military officers in Uganda.

[1] I am indebted to Mr H. B. Thomas, O.B.E., for numerous extracts from the Rev. A. B. Fisher's papers.

[2] Johnston to Jackson from Fort Portal 26.viii.00, Secretariat Archives, Entebbe.

The Foreign Office [he confided in his wife] continues not only to oppose most of my reforms, but seems to let its feeling of opposition to them leak out, so that some of my subordinates here hesitate to carry out my instructions. The sort of hint thrown out seems to be 'All right, let him have his way, seemingly. Keep quiet, wait till he has left Uganda for ever, and we can put the old people back'. Brodrick sends me out flattering messages from Lord Salisbury and from Sir Michael Hicks-Beach (who is pleased at my financial work), but I can see that he and Lord Salisbury are leaving everything to Hill, who of course longs for me to leave Uganda.[1]

Neither Hill nor the Nandi, however, could deter Johnston from one more expedition which he had been planning since his arrival in the country. He had always known that the richest stores of botanical treasure in tropical Africa were concentrated upon the slopes of its few high mountains. It was there too, where alpine flora grew isolated by hundreds if not thousands of miles of torrid lowlands from comparable genera and species, that evidence concerning the greatest problems of diffusion and evolution could be found. Johnston had served his botanical apprenticeship on Kilimanjaro; he had broadened his experience on the Cameroons mountain and Mount Mlanje. He was not going to pass Ruwenzori by without a visit. The doctors had in any case ordered it, but scientific curiosity was perhaps the more compelling motive. And so at the end of August the nucleus of the party, strengthened by some sturdy Bakonjo inhabitants of the mountainside, trekked up the Mubuku valley and disappeared into the cloud-belt. For a fortnight they ranged in hail and driving rain at altitudes of between 7,000 and 15,000 feet, floundering in moss and lichen eighteen inches deep and gazing incredulously at arboreal heaths, at giant groundsels, and at twenty-foot lobelias massed like monuments in a cemetery. They returned with examples of 92 botanical species, of which five were new to science. Johnston's highest climb had been to 14,800 feet. So fleeting had been his glimpses of the summit peaks that he overestimated their height by some 3,000 feet at not far short of 20,000.[2]

Refreshed as much as by a spell in Europe, Johnston marched straight for Entebbe, which he reached early in October. The outstanding problem with which he had now to deal was the hostility of the Nandi tribe. Until they were brought to reason

[1] Cited in Alex Johnston: *op. cit.*, pp. 209-10.
[2] *Uganda Protectorate*, pp. 152-89, 323-6.

there could be no peace in the Eastern Province of the Protectorate, and the further progress of the Uganda Railway would
be seriously delayed, if not brought to a standstill. And yet the
Nandi were a peculiarly difficult people either to fight or to
treat with. Like their eastern neighbours the Masai, they had
no chiefs other than the priests, or *laibons*, whose political
influence, though undoubtedly great, was entirely undefined.
Being a semi-nomadic people of pastoralists and warriors, they
were as far as possible from comprehending any advantage in a
settled administration, which would inevitably involve almost
intolerable changes in their traditional way of life. As enemies,
though still primitively armed, they were dangerous, highly
mobile and extremely hard to punish. If their huts were burnt,
they could rebuild them. If their crops were destroyed, they
could trade cattle for grain with their settled Kavirondo neighbours. They were vulnerable only in their cattle, which were as
mobile as they were themselves. For all these reasons past policy
towards the Nandi had been to leave them as far as possible
alone. Supply caravans had been routed by a long détour to
the north of their main strongholds, and isolated depredations
had been punished by cattle-raids undertaken against the
guilty clans, which had not hitherto acted collectively either in
attack or defence. But now that the railway track was being
driven straight through the favourite pastures of the tribe,
there were beginning to be ominous signs of collusion between
the clans, and Johnston was at one with all his advisers that the
only answer to the serious events of June and July was a definite
and final programme of subjugation.

During the months of August and September Evatt, with
some 400 Indian troops and a small force of Masai levies, had
carried out two broad sweeps through the Nandi country, from
Kisumu to the Ravine station and back again. He had carried
off much livestock, but mostly sheep and goats, which were less
mobile and less highly valued than the cattle. To bring the
warriors to an engagement, or to induce them to sue for peace,
something more drastic was necessary. They must lose a sensible
proportion of their cattle. Then and only then would they face
the fact that the conditions of life had changed, and that it was
to their interest to come to terms with the stranger in their
midst, instead of harrying his camps by night and retreating to
the high forests by day. Two days after his return to Entebbe
Johnston sent Jackson to take charge of affairs in the Eastern
Province, with full authority to act in his name, and to correspond if need be, directly with the Secretary of State. 'Every

other consideration', he wrote, 'must give way to that of safe transport and safety for the railway engineers.' For the rest, he left his deputy the full range of choice, 'either to so smash up the Nandi nation that it will be unable to send out parties of raiders anywhere near the Nyando valley, or else to take advantage of a genuine desire on their part for peace'.[1] Meanwhile, in Buganda, he arranged with the Katikiro, Apolo Kagwa, for the recruitment of 2,000 paid porters to speed the assembly of materials for the Nyando valley section of the line, and of 1,000 unpaid military levies who were to be rewarded for their services with Nandi cattle. That he had not overestimated the crisis was proved on October 13th, when Evatt's main encampment, containing most of the captured livestock, was raided at night with the loss of 10 native ranks and of Dr Sherlock, the medical officer of the expeditionary force.[2]

Such was the situation in Nandi when Sir Clement Hill, having consulted with his friend Colonel Ternan in the East Africa Protectorate on his way up country, arrived at Kisumu on October 26th. Jackson, who met him there, was certainly one of the kindliest and most tolerant of English gentlemen, but not even after the lapse of thirty years could he write without asperity of the interview that followed.

He arrived in a very bad temper, told me that the railway was practically at a standstill, which was scarcely correct, as there was a full company of Uganda Rifles as a guard at Londiani; that the soldiers at Fort Ternan, the headquarters of the expeditionary force, were divided among themselves and were quarrelling; and then to my dismay he told me he had ordered Evatt to discontinue operations, and I was myself to go to Nandi and make peace. Nothing could have been worse, and the position was rendered the more difficult and unpleasant, as it was clear as daylight that Sir Clement was violently prejudiced against Evatt and that he had been 'got at' by a man, whose name I forget, who happened to be senior in the army to Evatt and was jealous of him, and was more out to try and down him and do him a bad turn, than do his own job. Sir Clement himself told me that this same man had had the impertinence and bad taste to say 'he considered it *infra dig* for an officer in the British Army to serve under an officer in the Indian Army'. Later on, when Sir Clement had calmed down, I pointed out that to close down operations at such a juncture, and immediately following a bad setback, would only mean further and perhaps worse trouble in the near future, but he was obdurate.[3]

[1] Johnston to Jackson 7.x.00, Secretariat Archives, Entebbe.
[2] Johnston to Salisbury 10.x.00, 21.x.00, 25.x.00, *F.O.2.300.*
[3] F. J. Jackson: *Early Days in East Africa*, pp. 332-3.

Hill's thesis, as he developed it in a despatch sent to the Foreign Office next day, was more discreet and also more cynical. The troops at Evatt's disposal were, he argued, too few both to protect the railway staff and to punish the Nandi. The completion of the railway was the first priority: therefore peace, even a temporary peace, with the Nandi was essential. Had this been the truth, his reversal on purely technical grounds of Johnston's policy, before he had even seen and consulted with Johnston, would have been a strange enough lapse from the ordinary standards of official behaviour. But in point of fact, as Jackson's account shows clearly, Hill's action was not in reality based upon these technical grounds at all, but rather upon a preconceived desire to discredit Johnston's whole military policy in so far as it differed from that of Ternan. 'He arrived here so upset,' wrote Jackson to Johnston, 'and was so anxious to get on to see you, that he was scarcely open to reason or argument. I am still of opinion that his criticisms were not fair to us and were prompted more by Ternan and the E.A.P. people than from personal observation. . . . It would appear that the damage was done before his arrival at railhead, at least that is what I gathered from those who came up with him.'[1] The cost of Hill's premature peacemaking was the major military undertaking of 1905-6, which was serious enough to necessitate the collaboration of troops from both Protectorates. It is ironical that the new Parliamentary Under-Secretary at the Foreign Office used Hill's despatch to defend Johnston from one past misrepresentation. 'It seems clear that the fears at one time expressed of the [Nandi] disturbance having been caused by acts of rash and premature interference by the Administration (imposition of hut-tax, withdrawal or changed disposition of troops) were *not* well-founded.'[2]

Having made his contribution to the Nandi problem, Hill sailed across the Lake to Entebbe, where, in Johnston's small bungalow with the snake-pit at the door and the baboons and other pets entering and leaving by the unshuttered windows, the relations between host and guest must have been as highly charged as any in the history of hospitality. But for one fact there might have been an explosion. Hill had heard on his way up that Lord Salisbury, through retaining the premiership, was at last relinquishing the Foreign Office to Lord Lansdowne. To Johnston it was a bitter blow and probably it prevented him

---

[1] Jackson to Johnston from Kisumu 2.xi.00, Secretariat Archives, Entebbe.
[2] Hill to Salisbury from Port Florence 27.x.00, with minute by Cranborne, *F.O.2.556.*

from pushing his protest against Hill's conduct in the Eastern
Province to the point of telegraphing his resignation. But there
was worse to come. On the third day of his visit Hill moved to
Kampala and there convened a meeting of military officers and
civilian officials, together with the principal missionaries and
the three native ministers of the Buganda Kingdom. To this
strange assembly he 'put the question baldly: "Do you consider
Johnston's work as being successful, his changes of policy
well-founded?" ' This announcement of the agenda took all who
were present, as well it might, completely by surprise. To
Johnston himself it was a moment of agonizing humiliation and
dismay.

> The French Bishop said nothing, only simpered. I do not
> think he understood much English. One of the military officers
> remained silent, and the three Baganda chiefs probably thought
> that they were not expected to speak before the Europeans had
> said their say, if indeed they understood anything about it. But,
> after a minute's pause the English Bishop rose, gave a summary
> of what I had done between Naivasha and the Congo State, of
> the difficulties I had had to meet with, and of the unexpected
> successes which had attended my intervention. I felt intensely
> grateful to him, not so much on my own account, for I had
> realized that my health was failing and I longed to be back in
> England out of reach of malarial fever; but because there were
> so many others associated with me in this work of reform, whose
> futures probably much depended on Foreign Office goodwill.
> Bishop Tucker's speech turned the tide, and for the rest of his
> visit Hill was amiability embodied.[1]

It is unfortunate that the only direct account of this striking
episode is Johnston's own, yet there is no reason to doubt its
essential veracity. Except for the Nandi despatch, Hill put
nothing in writing about his visit to Uganda, and Bishop
Tucker knew the evangelical temper of the Church Missionary
Society too well to burden its committees with details of so
mundane an event. But in the wise and measured phrases of the
Bishop's autobiography it is possible to discern at least the out-
line of the argument he deployed that day. Johnston's land
settlement in Buganda had caused initially a period of great
confusion, while claimants were scrambling for their shares and
while peasant cultivators moved about in despair seeking a
place in which to settle. For the missions it had been a period
of special difficulty, during which congregations were constantly
breaking up and reforming, and during which the enrolment of

[1] Johnston: *Story*, pp. 376-7.

L*

new members temporarily ceased. Yet Tucker, unlike most of his colleagues, had the vision to see beyond 'the game of general post' to the 'peaceful revolution' which he believed would bring serfdom to an end. 'Labour could only be exacted when the penalty of disobedience was eviction from a tenancy at will. A landed proprietorship having been established, such a penalty was no longer possible, Wages and rent, it was clear, must henceforth find a place in the economic system of Uganda.' Again, with the hut-tax there had come at first results by no means pleasing to the Church authorities. To evade it, poor families crowded together in a single hut; insanitary conditions bred epidemics and immorality; young men hesitated to marry when taxation was the consequence of building a home. 'But', said Tucker, 'although having much of evil in it, it had this great merit—it stirred to action and electrified into life the whole nation. Men knew that by a certain date the requisite rupees must be forthcoming. . . . They set to work immediately to raise the needed amounts.' The third phase in the revolution would come, Tucker realized, with the completion of the railway. When produce became marketable, taxation would no longer be a burden to be evaded at the expense of health and decency. Though not himself concerned directly with the growth of the Protectorate revenues, he described Johnston's Special Commissionership as 'the dawn of a new era' destined to bring about 'the relief of suffering, the amelioration of the hard lot of multitudes of souls, and their enlistment in the great army of workers whose faculties, physical and mental, are being employed in the God-given task of subduing the earth'—a task which, he observed, was 'bound up with the eternal purpose of God concerning that complete redemption of the human race, when all that is wrong shall be set right, when there shall be no more death neither sorrow nor crying, and when He will wipe away all tears from all eyes'.[1]

The God-given task of subduing the earth. Truly the difference in outlook between the Christian missionary and the Evolutionist administrator was not so great. The Johnston of twenty-two, in revolt against the hypocritical other-worldliness of the Christianity in which he had grown up, and using the parable of the mustard-seed to illustrate the destiny of man, had already had something of this vision. The Johnston of thirty-two, a diplomat immersed in the politics of the partition of Africa by Europe, who had boasted to Rhodes that his only religion was the extension of the British Empire, had sunk,

[1] A. R. Tucker: *op. cit.*, II, pp. 259-61, 295-6.

momentarily at least, into a despicable perversion of his most
deeply held article of faith. The Johnston of forty-two, with
seven years' experience as head of the Queen's administration
in two of the newly acquired territories, had reverted to a purer
doctrine. He represented no longer primarily the conquering
arm of England, but rather the awakening aspirations of the
Queen's African subjects to subdue their portion of the earth.
During his last three months at Entebbe Johnston lived close to
the Baganda, whom he described in his final report as 'the
Japanese of the Dark Continent, the most naturally civilized,
charming, kindly, tactful and courteous of black peoples'. He
made trips to the Sese Islands and Buvuma in company with
Apolo Kagwa, the *Katikiro*, and established a friendship which
was to be preserved through correspondence for twenty-seven
years. Contacts as close as this had important consequences for
the practical conduct of affairs.

> Prior to our recent investigations [he wrote to Lord Lansdowne],
> the natives knew nothing of the methods of collecting rubber,
> or of its economic value. It occurred to me . . . that it would be
> well to prepare for the advent of the railway, and the consequent
> enlargement of commerce, by having the natives taught on a
> large scale the proper way to collect this rubber, so as not to
> injure the trees or vines that produce it. The Katikiro and the
> other native Ministers and Chiefs of the Kingdom of Buganda
> entered heartily into my views, and sent a number of intelligent
> young natives to be trained by Mr Whyte. . . . These young men
> have now returned to their villages to teach many others on their
> own account. . . . I am entirely opposed to anything like
> monopolies being given to European firms for the collection of
> this rubber, or being retained by the State after the manner
> which prevails on the Congo. It is true that all the forests in the
> Protectorate have now been transferred to the Crown and that,
> technically speaking, the rubber found in them is the property
> of the British Government. . . . I would now propose that
> permission be given to the natives to collect rubber in the Uganda
> forests . . . that they be allowed to sell this rubber to traders at a
> shilling a pound, or whatever amount is a third of the selling-
> value in Europe. If this is done, the trader will be able with
> another third of its value to pay the export duties and the cost
> of its freight to Europe, and the remaining third of its value will
> be a substantial profit, enough to induce him to maintain trading
> stations in Uganda. . . .[1]

The Director of the Royal Gardens at Kew reported en-
couragingly on the samples of rubber he had sent home, so

---

[1] Johnston to Lansdowne from Entebbe 23.xii.oo, *F.O.2.300*.

Johnston was right in his botany. He was not to know that the natural forest rubber of Africa was soon to be outstripped in the world market by the plantation-grown product of south-east Asia, and that it was rather in peasant-grown cotton that Uganda was to find financial solvency and the economic basis for social progress. It was the attitude rather than the particular recommendation that was important; and in Hill's absence it won him a glowing tribute from Lord Cranborne. 'It is in questions of this kind that Sir H. J. has always shown his administrative ability. He can be trusted to devise the measures which will be most likely to open up the resources of the country without leading to the exploitation of the natives.' An examination of his last despatches, including especially his masterpiece, the *General Report on the Uganda Protectorate*, fully bears out this judgment, in the political sphere as well as the economic. Despite his enthusiasm for anthropology and his unique ability—the product of twenty years of linguistic inquiry—to make intelligent contact with the most primitive specimens of humanity, Johnston was never guilty of a sentimental paternalism which desired to leave Africans as they were. He had no doubts at all of the benefits already conferred upon Buganda by British rule.

As regards the condition of the Baganda people before British interference put an end to the cruelties of King Mwanga, those who will consult the works of Speke and Grant, of Stanley, Lugard, various missionary writers Catholic and Protestant, and the letters and records which the Baganda Chiefs themselves have compiled and published, will see the state of things which existed at that time. The vicinity of the King's palace at Mengo was blood-stained almost as the cities of Benin and Dahome, with the constant slaughter and maiming of wives, councillors, pages and slaves. King Mutesa beheaded his wives for forgetting to shut the door. Pages were horribly mutilated for treading on the tail of a pet dog. In Busoga, until the establishment of something like British rule about two years ago, no girl of pleasing appearance was allowed to remain in her own home, or with a husband of the peasant class. She was immediately haled off to swell the harem of a local Chief, or even sent to some magnate in Buganda or Bukedi. Much the same practice prevailed in Bunyoro and Toro. Wars would take place resulting in the complete depopulation of a country, of the domestic animals, and of the cultivation. Take, for example, the Gwas 'Ngishu plateau in the Elgon district. This was at one time inhabited by a powerful clan of Masai, who like their modern descendants the Kwavi, were good cultivators. They established many flourishing villages, and possessed large herds of cattle. Attacked by the Nandi, the Elgeyo, and by another branch of the Masai, they were nearly completely extirpated, and such as escaped the spear of the victorious enemy took refuge in far countries. The result was the complete depopulation of a large and fertile district, which has remained depopulated to this day, all natives being afraid to settle there for fear of the predatory habits of the Nandi and the adjoining tribes. Many parts of the Mau plateau show traces of once numerous villages, which are now without a single human inhabitant.

Yet Johnston did not, like so many apologists of empire, attempt to twist these undoubted facts into an argument, either for a system of direct rule in which the European administrator would squeeze out the indigenous political authorities, or for an economic policy based on white settlement in which Africans could participate only as wage labourers. Instead he laid them alongside the equally undoubted facts of African response to missions and to government, and used them as an index of the African's capacity for progress. 'The natives,' he said, 'especially those speaking Bantu languages—because these Bantu peoples consist of settled agriculturalists—should be assisted and encouraged to govern themselves as far as possible, without too much interference on the part of European officials. The presence of this European element . . . should be restricted . . . to the administration of justice to foreigners, the collection of revenue, the regulation of finance, the management of railways and steamers, and the direction of scientific enterprise in connection with the resources—animal, vegetable and mineral—of the Protectorate.' In the economic field, as in the political, it is clear that Johnston expected the African population, with assistance and encouragement, to work out its own salvation and that of the Protectorate government. He drew attention to the fact that in the Eastern Province there existed a massive highland region where 12,000 square miles of fertile land, situated at between 6,000 and 10,000 feet above the sea, lay almost devoid of population. He went so far as to call it a 'white man's country', where settlement could be encouraged without any fear of infringing native rights. Yet, so far from building his theory of economic development around this region, he treated it as quite peripheral. The main source of national wealth, as also of government revenue, would come from the produce of the peasant from his own lands. 'I think I may say that nothing has tended to bring about friendlier relations between the European administration and the native population than the adjustment of the land question. What the natives dreaded in the advent of European control was that they would lose their lands and become the tenants of European landlords. . . . So long as the natives live loyally under our protection and pay the taxes they have agreed to pay, great tenderness should be shown towards their feelings in regard to the land, for it is they who will, or should in the main, support the charges of administration.'[1]

Johnston's judgment is the more striking in that it was made after three months spent in the 'white man's country', three months very largely preoccupied with problems of transport and economics, the study of which had confirmed him in his conviction that the two East African Protectorates should be amalgamated and ruled from a capital in the Mau highlands. He had left Entebbe for good on January 9th, 1901, and from then on his headquarters was at the Eldama Ravine station. It was there, at the end of the month, that he received the news of Queen Victoria's death. It was in connexion with his arrival there that Jackson, in his reminiscences, tells a story which, though trivial in itself, reveals an aspect of the Special Commissioner about which we have all too little evidence. The Ravine station had been for more than a year past in the charge of James Martin, the illiterate Maltese, who, although in many ways an admirable and useful member of the Administration, was not above combining his official position with a considerable private practice in the ivory trade. To Jackson, who had known and liked Martin for ten years past, had fallen the uncongenial task of investigating the extent of his friend's misdeeds. He had been appalled to discover that not only were all the charges amply substantiated, but that Martin had been in the habit of sending out his private trading agents in his, Jackson's, name. His interview with Martin was, he said, 'a very distressing one for both of us', and after it he had sent a confidential message to Johnston recommending a transfer to a post with fewer temptations. He had little hope, however, that his chief would share the leniency of his views. 'On Sir Harry's arrival, Martin, two others and I went down the hill to meet him, and after greetings and a short *résumé* of his journey, as we began to ascend the hill, he turned to Martin with a beaming face, and said, "And now, Martin, I want to tell you that I have decided to occupy the Sesse Islands and build a station on

[1] *General Report on the Uganda Protectorate*, in Johnston to Lansdowne 10.vii.01, F.O.2.462.

Sagalla, to be named after Stanley, and I want you to build it for me." Nothing could have been neater, and in spite of the stiff climb to the station, we three who were in the know breathed more freely.'[1] Johnston appears from his own writings and from those of his brother as an unfathomable compound of genius and of childish eccentricity. We know that to some of the missionaries he appeared a disagreeable, conceited man, and to some of the soldiers a figure of fun. It is a relief to know that to his nearest collaborator he could appear in a light so human and so adult.

Johnston stayed a fortnight at the Ravine, trying in concert with Jackson to make the best of Hill's Nandi peace. February found him in the Rift valley, at Naivasha and even as far east as Nairobi, engaged mainly in railway business. In March he was back at the Ravine, his eye on the problem of administering the wild Suk and Turkana peoples in the north of the Eastern Province. Throughout all this time, however, his dreams were centred upon his plan for a capital, to be called King Edward's Town, which would be 'the Simla of East Africa', with its Calcutta at Mombasa and its Bombay at Entebbe. It was by no means the far-fetched idea of an imperialist paranoiac. Had it come to fruition, the history of East Africa would have flowed in another and probably a better channel. For a Governor-General residing at King Edward's Town would have seen the problems of East Africa in a proportion that was never possible for a territorial Governor at Nairobi or Entebbe. He would have had within his view not merely the actual length of the Uganda Railway but the whole area which it served. He would have seen Kisumu from the first, not as a terminal, but as the great collecting point for the produce of the Lake Victoria Basin. He would have been in touch with the African peoples most capable of quick progress as well as with those who, by reason of their pastoral culture or their lack of a centralized social organization, were certain to be slower in adapting themselves to the new situation. A man in this position might still have decided, like Sir Charles Eliot in Nairobi, to encourage white settlement in the sparsely inhabited highlands; but he would have seen white settlement for what it was, and for what in East Africa it must always be, a frail incursion, confined to small temperate islands rising from a tropical sea, and dependent for manual and semi-skilled labour upon what must always remain an overwhelming majority of Bantu, Hamitic and Nilotic peoples.

[1] F. J. Jackson: *Early Days in East Africa*, pp. 70-2.

Johnston's official instructions had directed him to bear in mind that the two Protectorates might be merged. Already in 1899, therefore, the policy of the Foreign Office had been tending that way. It seems almost incredible that Hill, in the course of a two months' visit, should have failed to understand the obvious economic unity of the region, that he should in fact have reacted strongly in the opposite direction. In 1899 Colonel Macdonald had submitted recommendations for a new frontier between Uganda and the recently reconquered Sudan. His criterion had been the commercial watershed between the Nile route and the Uganda Railway. The districts from which freightage to a seaport would be cheapest by the Nile route should be in the Sudan; the districts which would import and export via Mombasa should be in Uganda.[1] Yet in March 1901 we find Hill, in a memorandum on transport, exhibiting the most astounding ignorance of commercial geography. 'My own impression at present is that we shall have to put East Africa, up to the eastern shores of Lake Victoria, under one Chief, separating it from the Zanzibar post, and leave all west of that to another Chief whose relations will in future lie largely with the Nile route and all the problems which that indicates: Belgium, Congo, Sudan.'[2] It was on the basis of this grave misapprehension of the facts, inexcusable in the head of the Foreign Office African Department, that East Africa was in 1902 to be re-partitioned, the two Protectorates remaining, but with the Eastern Province of Johnston's Uganda transferred to the East Africa Protectorate. 'On further consideration,' wrote Hill, 'I am inclined to think it is premature to take the King's pleasure in regard to the name of the new township which Sir H. Johnston proposes to lay out. It may turn out that it is for some reason or other . . . not a suitable site, and it would be unfortunate to associate H.M.'s name with an abortive scheme. Shall we delay for the present?' Lord Lansdowne, who had been but five months in office, can be forgiven for replying 'Very well.'[3]

It is fitting that Johnston's last six weeks in Uganda should have been spent once more upon the march, as much in the cause of science as of administration. On April 1st he left the Ravine station in company with C. W. Hobley, the most congenial to him of the younger officials and as enthusiastic an anthropologist and linguist as himself, and travelled in a slow

[1] Intelligence Division to F.O. 2.xii.99, *F.O.2.241*.
[2] Memorandum by Hill 28.iii.01, *F.O.2.465*.
[3] Minute by Hill, dated 12.iv.01, on Johnston to Salisbury 18.ii.00, *F.O.2.297*.

circle round the base of Mount Elgon. He found, to his great
delight, examples of Bantu speech still employing the archaic,
reduplicated prefixes, the existence of which had been postu-
lated by the egregious Dr Bleek from his library in Cape Town
half a century before. He collected 111 different species of the
flora of the mountain. He shot the first identified specimen of
the five-horned giraffe. He painted assiduously. He photo-
graphed.[1] And all the time, no doubt, the content of his
General Report on the Uganda Protectorate was taking shape in his
mind. At the Ravine, on his way through to the coast, he
received from Jackson in Buganda the news that receipts from
the first year's hut-tax had totalled £34,000 in cash and goods
besides a very considerable amount of labour given in commutation of tax, which had been employed on the building of
roads, rest-houses and other public works. With this augmenta-
tion of the revenue on one hand, and with a saving of £18,000
a year in military expenditure on the other, Johnston could
rightly feel that he had fulfilled the principal objectives of his
appointment.[2] On May 27th he boarded the French steamer at
Zanzibar, leaving it again at Suez in order to stay with Lord
Cromer in Cairo. His long-suffering brother had to look after
the travelling menagerie alone. A leopard broke loose during
the voyage through the Mediterranean. 'At Marseilles the
Customs authorities refused to admit the existence of aye-ayes,
kinkajous and hyraxes, and a special room had to be engaged
and paid for at a Paris hotel under the heading *Appartement de
Singe*.'[3]

[1] Johnston: *Uganda Protectorate*, pp. 326-9, 375, 892-3.
[2] Johnston to Lansdowne from Ravine 18.v.01, *F.O.2.462*.
[3] Alex Johnston: *op. cit.*, p. 190.

Chapter 11

TWENTY-SIX YEARS

IT took Johnston some time to realize that he was being squeezed out. His initial welcome indeed surpassed all expectations. Sir Clement Hill gave an official dinner. Lord Salisbury asked him to Hatfield. The King's interest in his mission seemed more than perfunctory. An outstandingly appreciative letter from Lord Lansdowne followed him to Guernsey, whither he had retreated for the summer months to rest and to write. The high honour of the G.C.M.G. came in due course. Yet already by the autumn of 1901 the future was beginning to look a little ominous. He had returned from Guernsey in October and was living in a borrowed house near Shere in Surrey, writing *The Uganda Protectorate* and waiting for his next appointment. He had made it clear that he could not serve again in any part of the tropics where he might be liable to a recurrence of blackwater fever. This made him, he realized, more difficult to promote. Even if East Africa had been unified according to his recommendations, he could not have consented to be the first Governor-General. Still, he thought he could reasonably hope for one of the minor Colonial office governorships—Cyprus, perhaps, or Malta—or, that failing, at least for one of the lesser Legations, perhaps not even necessarily as far afield as Bangkok or Bagota.

But he was wrong. Chamberlain was still at the Colonial Office and determined to exercise his patronage without assistance from an ageing Prime Minister or a new Foreign Secretary. And at the Foreign Office things had changed distinctly for the worse. It was not only Hill in place of Anderson and Lansdowne in place of Salisbury. Barrington still ruled the Private Office, but it was a Barrington who was noticeably less cordial than he who had served Lord Salisbury. It was not that Lansdowne himself was unfriendly, but that the permanent officials were once more firmly in control of appointments. In December Lady Johnston's uncle, Lord de Saumarez, warned him not to expect too much. 'The Office as a body hates the introduction of new blood into the service, and I am not surprised that you find the officials hostile. I saw Edward Malet last week in Paris, and in talking over sundry changes in the heads of missions, I asked him what he thought you would be likely to get. "Oh," he said, "Johnston does not belong to the Service. I don't think he is likely to get anything."' No Legations, therefore, for a man who had been ruling provinces in Africa instead of being a Second Secretary in Bucharest or Montevideo.

Two Consulates-General were in fact all that were offered: Somaliland, which Johnston refused, and Beirut, which he accepted, but from which the previous incumbent subsequently withdrew his resignation. Meanwhile the autumn of 1901 had become the spring of 1902, and he had been six months without pay. Not altogether reluctantly he decided to negotiate for a pension. He should get, he calculated, about £670 a year: with some additional earnings from books and pictures, he should be able to live modestly in England, and perhaps even, as some of his friends were already suggesting, to consider standing for Parliament. Still, retirement at forty-three left a wound, and the Treasury in its lordly way rubbed salt in it, by arguing that Special Commissions were too *special* to affect pensions, and by thus reducing the figure to £500 a year. For an administrative career twice blighted by blackwater, for a diplomatic substitute blocked by the vested interests of the regular profession, it was scarcely a generous compensation. Certainly Johnston had not the moral qualities necessary to overcome such an opportunity for lasting grievance. Till he took to writing novels in his late fifties, he retained a strong streak of bitterness against the Government, which no doubt closed many possible avenues to influence and useful activity.

On his retirement, the Johnstons moved at last from their cramped London *pied à terre* at Queen Anne's Mansions to a comfortable family house in Chester Terrace, Regent's Park. It was a good choice, and it could easily have been the start of a new and happier chapter in their lives. It was a convenient base both for free-lance literary work and for semi-political entertaining. It was close to the Zoo, the scene of Johnston's oldest and most serious scientific interests, and of which he had now appropriately joined the Council. There was room at Chester Terrace for Alex Johnston, who still worked for his brother as secretary and factotum. Above all, there was room for children, now at last expected: nothing would have done more to reconcile the Johnstons to retirement; nothing would more likely have given them the patience to build afresh. He was indeed already making an excellent recovery. He had been much delighted by the award of an honorary Doctorate of Science at Cambridge for his services to ornithology, and he was working with unprecedented speed and gusto. *The Uganda Protectorate* appeared in June and brought a pleasing flood of tribute and congratulation. Two more volumes were on the stocks—an illustrated work on *British Mammals* for a series edited by the Duke of Bedford, and *The Nile Quest*, a history of exploration in Abyssinia, the Sudan and Uganda, which was to be the best and the most artistically finished of all the books he wrote.

The text of *British Mammals* shows a peppery character, as strongly given to controversy as ever, the wit mordant through adversity, but still very much alive. 'It should be pointed out that whereas the wolf lends a certain picturesqueness to the forests of France and Germany, it seldom interferes with man except during the height of the winter. Its presence in Epping Forest, in the New Forest, and in other domains increasingly affected by pleasure-parties, would add greatly to their romantic interest, and at the same time might wholesomely check the gambols of the bean-feaster and his mate without subjecting them to any worse punishment than a scare.' *Homo sapiens caucasiana* was, he drily observed, 'the commonest mammal in the British islands to-day, with the doubtful exception of the long-tailed field mouse'; and his strictures upon the depredations committed by this mammal upon its fellows in the class must have occasioned, one feels, some twitching of moustaches and readjustment of monocles among many of the purchasers of the Woburn Library. 'The otter is being rapidly extinguished in Wales, Devonshire and Sussex by unreflecting, red-faced, well-meaning, church-going, rate-paying persons, on the plea that it eats salmon or trout. . . . It would be a shame if this remarkable aquatic weasel . . . were extirpated . . . to gratify the angler's craze—a craze nearly as modern as golf or cricket, but not so picturesque or beneficial to athletic development.'

Unfortunately the bright new associations of Chester Terrace were soon clouded by a domestic tragedy more searing than the public failure. In July 1902 Winifred Johnston had a fall and was delivered prematurely of twin boys. Both died within a few hours. There were not to be any more children. Unnerved, the parents fled away to a house by the river near Chertsey, lent by Harry's old friend Carmichael Thomas of *The Graphic*. There they boated much, they went driving often, and he worked furiously at *The Nile Quest*. It was his fourth large volume within a year, and his eyes began to feel the strain. Once again Thomas came to the rescue, and after attending the postponed coronation of King Edward in August, the Johnstons removed

AN AFRICAN RIVER IN THE GOOD OLD DAYS

JOHNSTON IN LATER YEARS

for four months to Ireland, he as the Special Correspondent of *The Daily Graphic*.

At last, at the beginning of 1903, they felt able to return. They had been hoping against hope for some new offer of active service from the Foreign Office, but none had come. The question of Parliament could therefore no longer be deferred. The trouble was that English politics placed Johnston in a sad dilemma. His oldest political friends were Conservative: Salisbury, Hicks-Beach, Brodrick, Cranborne. His expansionist creed, too, was Conservative. It had been the victory of Gladstone over Disraeli in 1880 which had prompted his African career. Yet temperamentally he was not merely a Liberal but a Radical. He belonged by nature to the outspoken and rebellious group in any company. The men really congenial to him in the House of Commons were Harcourt, Dilke and Labouchere, the men who had consistently opposed expansion, so long as opposition had been a practical policy. There was this amount of logic in the paradox, that it was the men who had opposed expansion while it was taking place who, when it was irreversible, often became the most enlightened and most forward-looking of colonial statesmen, because, if they were interested at all, it was not in national prestige, nor yet in dividends, but in the progress of colonial peoples. Among Johnston's closest friends during that spring of 1903 the Thomases were urging him to the right, while W. T. Stead of the *Review of Reviews* was pushing him hard to the left, flattering him with the suggestion that he was a potential Liberal Viceroy of India. In the choice the personality of Joseph Chamberlain must have been a strong repellant from the claims of the right: to be anti-Chamberlain was perhaps the first article of Johnston's political creed. The moment of decision came, ironically enough, with Salisbury's death in August 1903, which left a vacancy in Lord Cranborne's seat at Rochester. The Rochester Liberals asked Johnston to be their candidate; Sir Alfred Harmsworth, favouring the growth of imperialism in all parties, promised him the full support of the *Daily Mail*; in the opinion of many who wished him well he made, in accepting, the greatest mistake of his life.

Johnston lost the Rochester by-election. There had been a Conservative majority of 500, and he failed even to reduce it. As he himself was well aware, he was a bad parliamentary candidate, unimpressive in addressing large audiences, inexperienced and incautious in dealing with the fanatic fringe of teetotallers and sabbatarians, who made such a large proportion of the Liberal noises at election-time, and whose unrestrained pronouncements frightened away the centre voters on whom a Liberal victory in a marginal constituency must turn. His imperialist yet free-trade platform, however, was widely reported, and won him several invitations to contest constituencies at the next General Election. Had he chosen warily and nursed well, he could hardly have failed in the Liberal landslide of January 1906. But Rochester had cost him more money than he could afford, and he decided that another fight was only possible if it could take place within walking distance of his home. In January 1904 he settled with the West Marylebone Liberal and Radical Association in a constituency which had a large Conservative majority. Nevertheless in Marylebone he did much better than at Rochester. As luck would have it he was out of the country when the General Election took place and for three months beforehand, and his wife and friends, working in his absence, reduced the Conservative majority by four-fifths. Nevertheless, with such an opportunity missed, and with 377 successful Liberal candidates to scramble for places at the next Election, it was not to be thought of that he should continue in the attempt. Parliament, the classic remedy for an able man who had met with a reverse in the public service, had failed.

Only one further disaster was needed to extinguish finally Johnston's taste for practical affairs and to drive him into full retreat as a scholar and a man of letters, and this was supplied by his association from 1904 till 1909 with two companies formed for the economic development of Liberia. The Liberian Rubber Corporation and the Liberian Development Company, Chartered and Limited, were both the children of an English syndicate under the chairmanship of a Colonel Cecil Powney, who had been investigating commercial possibilities in Liberia since 1901. The object of the rubber company was on the one hand to establish its own plantation of Para rubber at Mount Barclay, ten miles inland from Monrovia; and on the other hand to organize the collection of the natural forest product by setting up forestry stations, where the natives could be taught to recognize and tap the various species of rubber-bearing lianas, and whither they could bring for sale the produce collected.[1] An arrangement negotiated by Johnston during a visit to Liberia in July and August 1904 provided that a royalty of eightpence a pound on natural rubber should be equally divided between the Company and the Liberian government.[2] It was an experiment in which he had been deeply interested since his Uganda

[1] H. H. Johnston: *Liberia*, 1906, pp. 424-5.
[2] *Ibid.*

days; but it could hardly have been launched at a more unfortunate moment. Operations began just when the value of
African *Landolphia* rubbers were falling sharply below those of
Para *Hevea*. By the time the *Hevea* plantations at Mount Barclay
were coming into bearing, the competition from Malaya was
severe and *Hevea* prices were falling fast.[1] The Company,
therefore, maintained an increasingly precarious existence until
its absorption by the American Firestone Company in 1923.

The story of the rubber company and the reasons for its
failure are clear enough. The same cannot be said of the
Liberian Development Company, about which even the most
elementary facts are extremely obscure. No word on the
subject survives in Johnston's private papers, and the Foreign
Office records of these years, which must contain most of the
necessary information, are not yet open to inspection. Roughly,
however, it may be said that since the turn of the century the
Liberian government had been under increasing pressure to
extend the range of its administration from the narrow, coastal
belt occupied by the American negro immigrants, to the vast,
forested hinterland populated by indigenous tribes which it
had hitherto left severely alone. Since the expansion of the
surrounding British and French protectorates in Sierra Leone
and the Ivory Coast these tribes had become ever more
frequently involved in frontier incidents, as a result of which
Monrovia had found itself faced with heavy demands for
compensation, coupled sometimes with brazen proposals for the
cession of territory. And yet Monrovia had not the financial
resources to open up the interior, to make roads through the
forest, to establish an administrative organization and to
maintain a frontier force. It would appear that it was the
object of the Liberian Development Company to obtain very
extensive concessions for mineral development, railway and
telegraph construction and banking, in exchange for practical
assistance to the Liberian government in extending its jurisdiction to the interior districts. In respect of the native-occupied
hinterland it was intended to acquire something like the powers
and responsibilities of a Chartered Company.

What were the full propositions discussed with President
Barclay and his Cabinet, the evidence at present available does
not show. All we know is that during a second visit to Liberia in
December 1905 and January 1906 Johnston negotiated the
terms of a loan to the Liberian government of £100,000,
which was to be secured on the customs revenues by vesting the

[1] R. C. F. Maugham: *Liberia*, pp. 114-15.

appointment to the controllership of the Liberian customs in the British Foreign Secretary. The loan, which was to be advanced by the London banking house of Erlanger's, was to be made available to the Liberian government only through Johnston's company, and was to be employed, after redeeming the internal floating debt, only upon certain development projects in which the Company was also concerned. We know also that in the course of 1906 and 1907 there were quarrels and recriminations between the Liberian government and the Development Company, as a result of which, in 1908, the Company withdrew from its position as middlemen in the transaction, leaving the Liberian government in full control of the unexpended balance of the loan and responsible directly to the Erlanger group for its servicing and repayment.[1]

It has been suggested by a series of American writers, basing their statements ultimately upon the Liberian versions assimilated by members of the American Commission of 1910, that the quarrel was due to misappropriation of the loan funds by the Company.[2] Johnston in his autobiography gives the outlines of a more complex and also a more convincing explanation, which suggests that the loan was merely part of a much wider arrangement between the Company and the Liberian government, and that the causes of the breakdown in relations were political rather than economic. Johnston says that in 1905 he went to Paris for discussions with Colonel Binger at the Quai d'Orsay on a Franco-Liberian frontier settlement. He says that, after the change of government in England in January 1906, the French stiffened their terms. He says, finally, that high-handed action by the British Governor of Sierra Leone engendered hostility at Monrovia at a critical stage in the negotiations.[3] All this suggests a Company angling for a Charter and a sphere of operations in the Liberian interior, a transaction in which the loan was only a preliminary manœuvre. It suggests a Liberian government, traditionally xenophobic, taking fright at the last moment on the broadest political issues, and then, since it was going no further with the Company in other ways, fighting to get the loan into its own hands.

Whatever the exact nature of this project—and there will certainly be more to learn about it when the Foreign Office records become available—there is no doubt that its failure was

[1] R. C. F. Maugham: *Liberia*, 1920, pp. 93-4, etc.

[2] R. L. Buell: *The Native Problem in Africa*, New York 1928, p. 799; G. W. Brown: *The Economic History of Liberia*, Washington 1941, pp. 164-7, etc.

[3] Johnston: *Story*, pp. 407-8; cf. L. Jore: *La Republique de Libéria*, Paris 1911, p. 99 *sqq.*

to Johnston a disappointment much wider than any financial loss he may have incurred. He had no capital to speak of; his own investment in the two companies must have been almost nominal; we learn from his brother that, except at the very beginning, he had refused to accept any remuneration for his work as a Director.[1] His interest was not, therefore, mainly financial. It was rather a matter of having once more a province to govern. He had been pushed out of his profession at the height of his powers: in Liberia he had hoped to re-enter African administration by a side door. Kirk, too, had been retired before his time and had found more than financial compensation on the boards of the East and South African Chartered Companies: it was natural that Johnston should seek a similar solution. The real clue to his motives is perhaps to be found in the incautiously grandiloquent summary which slipped undetected into the autobiography. 'I considered I had settled the case of Liberia on very favourable lines, and that I should have a task of great interest in developing her resources and steering her to affluence and good government.'[2] By the end of 1906 the castle in the air had been demolished, and only the débris remained. Already, after the failure in West Marylebone, Johnston had decided to live in the country. But he had imagined himself as a regular mid-week visitor to the metropolis, a busy and respected figure, well known to the drivers of hansom cabs and the doorkeepers of clubs and government offices. Now there would be little to bring him up: the Academy, his publishers, an occasional lecture to a learned society. And he was still only forty-eight.

It was, unexpectedly enough, the retreat itself which provided the healing and the satisfaction. The hamlet of Poling lies about two miles to the east of Arundel and about four miles inland from the sea, just where the South Downs drop finally through an encircling belt of woodland into the rich farming country of the coastal plain. St John's Priory stands a little to the north, on the last shelf of raised ground, overlooking the village and the plain. Originally a small stone-built house and chapel, inhabited for nearly four centuries by knights of the order of St John of Jerusalem, it had passed in Elizabethan times to yeoman farmers, who had surrounded it gradually with a pleasing medley of brick walls and thatched outbuildings. It was already a mellow spot, timbered and very sheltered. The Johnstons, though they held it only on a life tenancy from the

[1] Alex Johnston: *op. cit.*, p. 256.   [2] Johnston: *Story*, p. 407.

Duke of Norfolk, must have spent lavishly in converting it into a small country-house of eight or nine bedrooms, standing in two or three acres of meticulously kept gardens and orchard. Here Winifred Johnston was from the first in her element. She had always run a good house. Now she added steady, dutiful work for the parish church, and long, active service in local government. She knew everybody, went about constantly, lived with unusual intensity the conventional life of a woman of her class. It was a life which was, in a perfectly friendly way, utterly detached from his.

But Johnston, too, found real contentment at Poling. He loved the house and the surrounding country. He became a benevolent despot in the garden. He also worked very hard indeed, and with increasing satisfaction, at his books and pictures. A hundred yards from the Priory, on the other side of the lane leading down to Poling village, there was a pretty little two-roomed thatched cottage, older even than the house, standing in its own orchard with a hedge of roses and a tinkling stream. Here Johnston had his library and studio, and here he spent long working days, returning to the big house only for meals. In the intervals of composition he liked to work at the cottage garden with his own hands, and an old family servant still living in the village remembers him constantly pushing a wheel-barrow while engaged in small tasks, levelling his lawn or bridging his stream. Within the household he was sometimes exacting in his demands for absolute tidiness and perfect punctuality, but usually he was gay and amusing and gave the impression that he was enjoying his life to the full.

> *He's witty and he's wise,*
> *And a terror for his size.*

was a couplet which, if not actually composed in the servants' hall, was much appreciated and long remembered by its inmates. More and more, however, he excused himself from the social round in which his wife was engaged. He grumbled even at his rare visits to London. He liked to lead his life of intense activity in private and with the least possible interruption.

His brother Alex moved down with the family to Poling and continued to work for him until 1909: after that a secretary came out daily from Brighton. At Priory Cottage, no less than at Entebbe or Zomba, Johnston was a hard taskmaster, maintaining his power of very rapid dictation until the last year or two of his life. He was thus able to accept most of the literary work that he was offered, and in addition to his annual output of two or three books, he contributed a steady flow of articles to the daily press, the monthly reviews, and also to such publications as the *Encyclopaedia Britannica* and the *Harmsworth Natural History*. The first large task to be finished at Poling was his two volume work on *Liberia*. It has been seriously suggested by at least one of the American authorities on Liberia that Johnston wrote this book as a prospectus for his companies.[1] But prospectuses do not usually run to 1,200 pages, nor perhaps would they exercise the desired influence on investors if they did. And the born prospectus-writer, one feels, would hardly have bothered to recount the history of the West African coast from the times of Hanno the Carthaginian, to have printed careful facsimiles of the Vai system of handwriting, to have mercilessly badgered the authorities at the Natural History Museum into identifying his collection of Liberian scorpions and spiders.[2]

> My dear Johnston [wrote the recently retired Director of the Royal Botanical Gardens], I take it as extremely kind of you to send me a copy of your fine book on Liberia: it is a splendid addition to your monumental series of books on tropical Africa. I confess I look on them with pride, as I had the good fortune while I was at Kew to see the gradual evolution of your whole official career, and perhaps to be a little helpful in it. I think posterity will confirm my opinion that it is unique. Administrator, diplomatist, artist, man of science, linguist, literateur, you have focussed on your kind every possible impulse of enthusiasm. Looking back as I do to the little handful of plants, the first samples procured by Kew of the vegetation of Kilimanjaro, the progress of our knowledge is really stupendous, and how large a part is due to yourself and your never-flagging interest. . . . I have just brought out another part of *The Flora of Tropical Africa* that completes eight volumes. There are still three more required and even then the whole thing is only a beginning.[3]

It was hardly surprising that during the years from 1904 to 1908 Johnston should have been involved in the great agitation raging in England over the malpractices of King Leopold's administration in the Congo. It is significant that he tried to avoid committal for as long as possible, and that even when he could no longer conscientiously stand aside, he remained a moderating influence among the ranks of the reformers. In particular he played a notable part in converting the leaders of

[1] R. L. Buell: *op. cit.*, p. 799.
[2] H. H. Johnston: *Liberia*, 2 vols, 1906: Johnston to Chubb (Natural History Museum) 20.iii.06.
[3] W. T. Thistleton-Dyer to Johnston 8.vii.06, *Johnston Papers*.

the Congo Reform Association to support of the annexation of the Congo by Belgium. Obvious and inevitable as this solution may nowadays appear to have been, it was by no means easily accepted by men like Morel, Fox Bourne and Dilke, who felt that substantial Belgian interests had been implicated in the King's régime, and who were advocating a form of international control to be established by the signatories of the Berlin Act of 1885. Johnston did not believe in an international solution, because there was, he said, no such thing as an international conscience. Half the trouble with King Leopold's administration was that it was internationally recruited and therefore lacked the *esprit de corps* and the sense of public accountability which would have existed in a national service. And many of the faults of the Congo system had been anticipated under the similarly internationally recruited service employed by the Khedive Ismail to govern the Sudan.

These were the arguments which Johnston pressed upon Morel and his friends when he took the chair at one of the largest public meetings promoted by the Congo Reform Association in June 1905,[1] and it was to this theme that he returned in the important preface which he wrote for Morel's *Red Rubber* in the autumn of 1907. 'I wish', he wrote, 'to testify to the good work which has been done by Belgians in the Congo Free State, and to dissociate the country of Belgium from the odium with which her Monarch is now regarded by educated people in Europe, Africa and America. . . . If there have been bad Belgians on the Congo, there have been bad Englishmen, ruthless Frenchmen, pitiless Swedes, cruel Danes, unscrupulous Italians. Belgium has only to bear the brunt of the movement which is now threatening the existence of the Congo Free State in its present form, because the Sovereign of that misgoverned state is also King of the Belgians. Many of us have felt, and still feel, that when the King's autocratic rule as Sovereign over this African dominion had been proved to be such an appalling blot on the history of European intervention in Africa as to be no longer tolerated, that the individual sacrifices made by Belgium and by the Belgian people should be recognized by the handing over of the Congo Free State to Belgium as a Belgian Protectorate.'[2]

In 1907 Johnston's Congo interests were heavily reinforced through his being entrusted by the Baptist Missionary Society

[1] Dilke to Johnston 18.ii.08, *Johnston Papers*, refers to 'our having accepted Belgian annexation at your suggestion. . . .'
[2] E. D. Morel: *Red Rubber*, p. x.

with the immense collection of papers left by the great Congo pioneer, George Grenfell. It was difficult material, but handled with the scholarship and the artistry of which he was at times capable, Johnston could have written a biography which would have made a deep impression on the England of his day. For there was no doubting Grenfell's complete dedication to the Congo and its peoples, and yet he had been for nearly twenty years the Free State's most loyal citizen and supporter.

It has been given to me [Grenfell had written in June 1904] to enter upon the thirtieth year of my African life. For the first ten years I lived under native rule, and the bitter experiences of that time have burnt themselves indelibly into my mind and memory. I saw the havoc made by the liquor traffic over wide stretches of the country, where bottles of gin and rum were the staple currency, and where it was useless to go to market to buy food without them. It has fallen within my experience to see slaves brought down to the white man's store and sold for gin and rum and barter goods paid over the counter; and I have been in the midst of an Arab raid in the centre of the continent, and within 24 hours counted 27 burning or smoking villages, and had myself to face the levelled guns of the raiders. I have seen the cruel bondage in which whole communities have been held by their superstitious fears—fears that compelled them, lest a witch might be suffered to live, to condemn their own flesh and blood and to inflict the most horrible cruelties upon them. And I have, all unavailingly, stood by open graves and tried to prevent the living being buried with the dead, and altogether have seen more of the dark side of human nature than I care to think about. I claim to know better than a great many what is meant by native rule. After ten years of it, I knew enough to make me grateful beyond measure when I learned that King Leopold of Belgium was taking upon his shoulders the burdens involved by the administration of the Congo territory. A marvellous change, during the second decade of my African life, came over the distracted country I had previously known under the chaotic sway of hundreds of independent chiefs. . . .

The revelations concerning cruelties inflicted upon the people that were made known by Consul Casement, by the Revd. J. H. Weeks and others of my colleagues at the close of 1903 compelled me to believe in the existence of a condition of affairs that I had come to regard as belonging entirely to the old régime and impossible under the new one. It was with nothing less than the most profound consternation that I was compelled to accept the evidence and to believe what looked like the incredible. . . . Defenders of the Government say these terrible things are the acts of madmen, for which the Government is not to be condemned. . . . Seeing the number of lonely outposts occupied by

single white men with a mere handful of native soldiers in the
midst of half-subjugated and altogether cruel and superstitious
people, it would not be surprising if more madness came to light.
It is the *system* that is to be condemned rather than the poor
individual, who, overcome by his fever-heightened fears, loses
control of himself and resorts to awe-inspiring acts of vengeance
to uphold his authority.[1]

Clearly there was here a life of the deepest interest and
historical significance. But it was not one that could be
adequately portrayed by a Johnston who was concerned to
prove that all good missionaries were, like himself, primarily
emissaries of science, and whose curious biographical method
was to depersonalize all Grenfell's observations and to sort
them under a series of geographical and ethnographic headings
into a book that might properly have been called 'All that
Grenfell knew about the Congo and some more besides'. It was
not at all the mere failure of an agnostic to understand the
outlook of a believer. It was that Johnston was still the prisoner
of the encyclopaedic literary form which he had evolved in
British Central Africa and which he had employed again in *The
Uganda Protectorate* and *Liberia*. For *George Grenfell and the Congo* it
was singularly inappropriate. In the Grenfell papers he had a
great literary opportunity, and he killed it dead.

The winter of 1908-9 Johnston spent touring in the southern
states of America, and in the West Indies, collecting material
for his next large work, *The Negro in the New World*. The
initiative for his journey had come from President Theodore
Roosevelt, who shared a surprising number of his many
interests, who knew and admired his writings, and who wanted
his assistance in planning the East African holiday which he
was to take on laying down the presidency in 1909. With such a
sponsor, invitations to lecture arrived in shoals, and a judicious
selection easily covered all the expenses of the trip. The midnight talks in the President's private studio, which followed the
formal White House dinners, were a huge success, and gave
rise to three or four years of boisterous correspondence. 'I am
confident', wrote Roosevelt in an unusually serious sentence,
'that in Africa I shall come to substantially your judgment on
the race problems; but oh what slow work it is to get a working
hypothesis for race out of such conflicting passions as violent
and brutal race prejudices, maudlin sentimentality and utter
indifference.'[2] As for Johnston, the intensive travelling through

---

[1] H. H. Johnston: *George Grenfell and the Congo*, Vol. I, pp. 375-8.
[2] Roosevelt to Johnston 9.iv.09, *Johnston Papers*.

Virginia and the Carolinas, Georgia, Alabama, Louisiana, Mississippi and Florida, and then on through Cuba, Haiti, San Domingo and Jamaica, marked an important stage in his thought about Europe and the colonial territories.

As regards the Negro or any other backward race [he had written in 1907], I am not a sentimentalist. I have no pity in retrospect for the sufferings of the Celtic and Iberian inhabitants of Great Britain during their conquest by the Romans. I do not regret the Norman remodelling of England. These movements have done much to make the United Kingdom one of the foremost among the civilized free nations. The greater part of Africa has got to submit to a similar discipline. There are many tribes of Negroes of the present day who are leading lives not much superior in intellectual advancement to those of brutes; *but there is not an existing race of man in Africa that is not emphatically human and capable of improvement.*[1]

America in 1908 gave Johnston the vision of how much more rapidly than he had ever imagined this improvement might be achieved. In Alabama, two generations from the abolition of slavery in the southern states, he met negroes who were by any standards of judgment distinguished men—Booker Washington, the celebrated Principal of Tuskagee, and G. W. Carver, his Professor of Botany, than whom, Johnston wrote, 'no one I ever met in the New World taught me so much about the plant distribution in North and South America'. Undoubtedly the experience revolutionized his outlook. So also did the spectacle of ordinary negro men and women who were beginning to take full and free part in the life of a civilized society. In New York, in New Orleans and a host of smaller towns where Johnston seems to have pressed his sociological inquiries to the point of house-to-house visiting, he found that he could see no difference 'in surroundings, in culture, in decorum, between the lives of these absolute negroes, or of the many different degrees of negroids, and the lives led by Anglo-Saxon white people earning the same wages . . . while there was indeed a balance in favour of the negro if you compared his life with the lowest class of recently arrived Irish or Italian immigrants.'[2]

After his visit to America Johnston's anti-racialist propaganda began to assume a new note of urgency and of prophetic warning. In two articles first published in the *Nineteenth Century* he strongly attacked 'the arrogant, imperfectly educated, unobservant, White Man of England, the United States, Belgium

---

[1] E. D. Morel: *Red Rubber*, pp. xii-xiv. Johnston's italics.
[2] H. H. Johnston: *The Negro in the New World*, p. 475.

or South Africa, who would continue to assert that the coloured races have made no progress towards the white standard'. They were living, he said, in a fool's paradise, and so also were those who rested their hopes of a permanent superiority upon a theory of the survival of the Whitest race. It was a theory which had come into the world too late to have any practical influence upon the conduct of men. Christianity had been defying it with impunity for nearly two thousand years; and already in Asia and Africa Christianity had sown the dragon's teeth of education among the backward peoples.

In the 'eighties of the last century, when the Imperial spirit in the United Kingdom received another renaissance, the prospect seemed a most attractive one. The black and yellow world was to be governed with a genial despotism that smacked the naked negro on the back in half contemptuous admiration of his big muscles and satisfaction that they were going to be employed in the White Man's work. . . . The idea that there would ever be any serious demand on the part of the coloured peoples for a voice in their own taxation and government scarcely disturbed the forecast of any average imperialist. . . . But unfortunately for the ideals of the imperialist Britain of twenty years ago, education was permeating the British Empire in all directions. . . . Missionary societies were everywhere founding schools, colleges and universities, attempting to make black, brown and yellow peoples think and act like white Christians . . . impressing on them over and over again that once they were Christian and civilized, or even civilized without actually being Christian, they were the equal of any man, no matter of what colour or race.[1]

As the years passed, Johnston's views on the policy to be pursued towards the indigenous population of the African colonies and protectorates became steadily more advanced. In 1917 he wrote a substantial pamphlet setting out the black man's contribution to the war, and emphasizing the obligation of the Imperial Government, as soon as the war was over, 'to recognize and affirm his rights as a citizen of the Empire'. The Zambezi, he argued, should be accepted as a great political boundary, north of which the white immigrant's claim to dominate was baseless. British Africa north of the Zambezi should be administered in four 'vice-royalties'—Central Africa, East Africa, the Sudan and West Africa—in which the principles must be recognized that occupied land was secure from

---

[1] H. H. Johnston: *Views and Reviews*, 1912, pp. 232-4, 258-9; cf. 'South African Union and the Colour Question', *The Nineteenth Century*, Vol. LXVI, p. 245, and 'The Negro and Religion', *ibid.*, LXVII, p. 995.

expropriation, that economic resources must be developed solely for the benefit of the territory concerned, and that there must be from the first native representation in the governing councils. 'Not only must education be pushed resolutely, but the results of education must be faced and accepted. . . . We must remove the disgrace of not having anywhere on the African continent a University to which Black and Yellow students may repair for their higher education.'[1]

The Coloured man [he wrote in a passage which belongs in sentiment nearer to 1950 than to 1920] must remember that his lands cannot properly be developed without . . . the White man's capital; and the White man in Europe and North America is not going to risk his money and effort where there is no security and where he runs the danger of losing his capital and the investment of his energy. Without the tapping of wealth in rock and soil and desert sand, the Coloured man will always remain poor and futile. But the White people must try to realize that the still Backward races, the once decrepit nations, have travelled far in intellectuality since the middle of the nineteenth century, and that the continuance of an insulting policy towards them will join them some day in a vast league against Europe and America, which will set back the millennium and perhaps even ruin humanity in general. Nature will have conquered by setting one half of mankind against the other.[2]

During the three years which followed his journey to America Johnston experienced much anxiety about his health. For a year or more he was suspected of having Bright's disease. Then the symptoms disappeared, but gave place to *migraines* of alarming violence. His time was much interrupted by travelling in search of mineral springs and winter sunshine. He managed nonetheless to write, besides *The Negro in the New World*, a large illustrated *History and Description of the British Empire in Africa* and a smaller volume called *The Opening-up of Africa*; he managed to revise and greatly enlarge his *History of the Colonization of Africa by Alien Races*, and to compose the series of articles and lectures which was later published under the title *Common Sense in Foreign Policy*. The last was indeed much more than a literary engagement. At the White House in 1908 Johnston had found a sympathetic listener in the German ambassador in Washington, Baron von Speck von Sternberg. At the dinner-table or after, they had developed in conversation with the President and Senator Root the outlines of a scheme whereby Germany

[1] H. H. Johnston: *The Black Man's Part in the War*, 1917, pp. 103-120.
[2] H. H. Johnston: *The Backward People and our Relations with them*, 1920, p. 61.

M

in exchange for the retrocession of Alsace-Lorraine, should be given a free hand to extend her influence in the Near East: Austria was to be compensated in the Balkans, Russia in Mesopotamia. The Baron was interested enough to communicate with the German Embassy in London, where the Councillor, von Kuhlmann, greeted the scheme with applause and kept on close terms with Johnston almost until the outbreak of war in 1914. The years from 1909 till 1911 were, however, the period of greatest activity. Johnston spoke at Anglo-German meetings and dinners in London. In the autumn of 1910 he went at the invitation of the King of Württemberg to lecture at Stuttgart. In the following year he made plans to canvass his views more widely, in Cologne and Munich, Berlin and Hamburg. But the Agadir incident had created an atmosphere most unfavourable to his message, and at Cologne he was actually paid for his lectures and asked not to deliver them.[1]

Those tours in Germany had, however, one very important consequence for Johnston's life. At Hamburg he visited on each occasion the great Bantu scholar Carl Meinhof, whose publications he had long admired, and whose reputation as the leading authority on the subject he had hitherto regarded with some awe. He could never forget that he himself was only an amateur, that his only University degree was an Honorary Doctorate of Science. He had had it in mind to wonder whether the great work for which he had been preparing all through his adult life should not be abandoned to the trained hand. Contact with the great man, however, speedily put an end to his inhibitions. He saw at once that Meinhof's knowledge was fragmentary beside his own. He found that Meinhof's plans for future work were vague, and that at least they were prompted by no overmastering ambition to produce a comparative grammar that should be the successor to those of Koelle and Bleek. And so, in 1912, feeling his health suddenly very much improved, Johnston rearranged the furniture at Priory Cottage to accommodate the great task which was to occupy the main part of his time for ten years to come. He had still, of course, to earn a part of his living with his pen, and even during 1912 and 1913, the years of his most intensive linguistic work, he produced six volumes of popular empire history, as well as articles and smaller pieces.[2] War conditions slightly checked the flow:

---

[1] Johnston: *Story*, pp. 445-56; *Common Sense in Foreign Policy*, p. 50 *sq.*
[2] *Pioneers in West Africa, Pioneers in Canada, Pioneers in India, Pioneers in Australasia. Pioneers in Tropical America, Pioneers in South Africa*, London, Blackie, 1912-14.

between 1914 and 1918 he published only five comparatively small volumes.[1] After the war he turned to fiction and wrote, besides his autobiography, a novel a year from 1919 until 1924.[2]

In all his scientific work Johnston was first and foremost the indefatigable collector, and the *Comparative Study of the Bantu and Semi-Bantu Languages* is perhaps above all else a unique and important collection of words. Of its 1,350 quarto pages, 750 are filled with illustrative vocabularies, setting out the equivalents of about 250 common words in 300 languages and dialects. The remaining 600 pages are divided between classificatory analysis and grammatical studies of the various parts of speech. A glance at the bibliography shows that the vocabularies represent no ordinary work of compilation. Rare indeed is the reference to an adequate dictionary or grammar. A brief vocabulary printed by a missionary society, some additional phrases noted by a passing traveller, a fleeting reference in some philological journal, these were normally the only published sources at his disposal. Often these were supplemented by manuscript notes supplied by correspondents. In an astonishing number of cases, perhaps more than half, the main source of information was in Johnston's own notes or in the vocabularies which he had printed in every one of his descriptive works from *The River Congo* to *The Uganda Protectorate*. In 1915 he took advantage of an invitation by the French Government to make further collections of West African, Semi-Bantu vocabularies from African soldiers serving in southern France.

In spite of all efforts at accuracy it was inevitable that in a work of this size some serious errors should remain. Often there was no means of assessing the quality of the informants on whom he had to rely: not even the best of them had any real knowledge of phonetics. If Johnston's own standard of lexical accuracy were high, his ear was most imperfect. The vowels in *Kongo*, for example are identical and short, yet Johnston invariably wrote *Kongω*. Inevitably such failures in phonetics led to mistakes in analysis and classification. Johnston subdivided his 300 illustrative vocabularies into 40 main groups. In doing so he was frequently forced to adjudicate between the claims of conflicting sets of criteria; and on the whole his classification was not, perhaps, much more rough and ready than any other that has since appeared. But when, for example,

[1] *East Africa*, 1914; *A Gallaxy of Heroes and Heroines*, 1915; *The Truth about the War*, 1916; *Science and Religion*, 1916; *The Black Man's Part in the War*, 1917.
[2] *The Gay-Dombeys*, 1919; *Mrs Warren's Daughter*, 1920; *The Man who Did the Right Thing*, 1921; *The Veneerings*, 1922; *Little Life Stories*, 1923; *Relations*, 1926.

he placed the Luganda and Kinyaruanda languages in the same group, failing to realize that one had five vowel-sounds and the other seven, he made what is in modern eyes a serious blunder. And likewise, in basing his classification to some extent on lexical affinities which phoneticians have proved to be untrustworthy, Johnston offended frequently against modern linguistic theory. Nevertheless, when all has been said, Johnston's linguistic critics are probably to-day his staunchest admirers. The circle is small indeed of those who have attacked the Bantu problem as comprehensively as he did, and its members pause to recognize how much they owe to his pioneering efforts. He is the undoubted father of the Bantu studies now flourishing in several English universities. Had he followed the advice of Flinders Petrie, and applied in 1916 for the Directorship of the newly founded School of Oriental Studies, the circle of his intellectual progeny might be wider and more widely known.[1]

When the second volume of the *Comparative Study* emerged finally from the Clarendon Press in the summer of 1922, Johnston was sixty-four years old and already frail. His health, which had been excellent from 1912 until 1917, had begun to fail after an attack of mustard gas, which he suffered while lecturing to troops under the auspices of the Y.M.C.A. In 1918 and 1919 he had had to undergo two fairly serious operations for a liver complaint. For a year he was restored, but by the end of 1920 he was becoming easily fatigued and had to modify drastically his habits of work and of physical exercise. Evening engagements, long resented, were now put definitely aside. Apart from a very few close and congenial neighbours like Israel Zangwill and Lady Maud Parry, the widow of the composer, the only visitors he welcomed at Poling were his numerous brothers and sisters, to all of whom he remained very deeply attached. In his sixty-sixth year he completed his autobiography. In his sixty-seventh he began his fortieth volume, a novel called *Relations*. He was writing at it one morning in 1925 when suddenly his hand refused to obey him. His wife being away on a visit to her family, he stumbled through to the kitchen complaining that his pen was out of order. It was in fact a slight stroke which, recurring a few months later, paralysed the right side of his body and affected his mental powers. 'When for any length he dictated to me,' wrote his brother Alex, who returned to Poling to help Winifred Johnston with the nursing, 'it was

[1] Flinders Petrie to Johnston 18.viii.16, *Johnston Papers*.

piteous to see his once quick and brilliant brain fumbling and groping for expression where once it had taxed the capacity of the quickest stenographers.'[1]

A precarious régime of bed and bath-chair, with motor drives on fine afternoons, was maintained for nearly two years: then Johnston kicked over the traces. He was determined to visit his favourite sister, a Mrs Henderson, who lived in the country in Nottinghamshire. In a weak moment the doctor gave permission. The journey was organized with the greatest care, but it was too much for him. Soon after his arrival he had another stroke, and there at Woodsetts House, near Worksop, on July 31st, 1927, he died. His body is buried in the church-yard at Poling. Winifred Johnston, who died six years later, lies beside him. The tombstone is inscribed with a tribute from the Kabaka and people of Buganda. *Amazimage ku Buganda galaga nti Bungereza eyagala bona bekuma babere ne dembe*—'His faithfulness to Buganda shows that England wishes all whom she protects to be free.' In the church a tablet of pleasing simplicity reads:

IN MEMORY OF

SIR HARRY JOHNSTON

G.C.M.G., K.C.B., D.SC.

ADMINISTRATOR SOLDIER

EXPLORER NATURALIST

AUTHOR AND PAINTER

1858–1927

VIR FORTIS AUDAX MITIS INGENIO MAGNO

[1] Alex Johnston: *op. cit.*, p. 336.

LOCATION OF MANUSCRIPT SOURCES

British South Africa Company, Cape Town (Kimberley) Office Papers, Central African Archives, Salisbury, Southern Rhodesia. Some microfilms in Library of the Royal Empire Society, London.

Cawston Papers, Rhodes House, Oxford.

Church Missionary Society's Archives, 6 Salisbury Square, London, E.C. 4.

Foreign Office Archives, Public Record Office London. Series : *F.O. 2* (Africa), *F.O. 27* (France), *F.O. 63* (Portugal), *F.O. 64* (Prussia), *F.O. 83* (Miscellaneous), *F.O. 84* (Slave Trade).

Johnston Papers, Central African Archives, Salisbury, Southern Rhodesia. Microfilm copies in Library of the Royal Empire Society, London.

Mackinnon Papers, School of Oriental and African Studies, University of London.

Rhodes Papers, Rhodes House, Oxford.

Royal Geographical Society's Archives, Kensington Gore, London, S.W. 7.

Salisbury Papers, Christ Church, Oxford.

Uganda Secretariat Archives, Entebbe, Uganda.

INDEX

Abercorn, Duke of, 165, 174, 178, 179, 187, 188n
Abercorn, N. Rhodesia, 175
Aberdare, Lord, 46-7, 85, 99
Accra, 94, 117, 118, 122
Aden, 47, 53-4, 94, 142, 156
African Association, of Liverpool, 109-10, 130
African International Association, see International
African Lakes Co., 140, 143, 149, 157, 169, 178, 203, 205, 207; relations with Nyasa Arabs, 145, 161-5, 215, 261; proposal for Charter, 151; proposed amalgamation with B.S.A. Co., 155, 173-4, 182-8, 198-200; land claims of, 222, 224
Akassa, 25
Alexandra, Queen, 284-5
Algeria, 9, 11, 14, 141-2, 282-4
Ambriz, 31
Ambrizette, 25, 31-2
Anderson, Sir Percy, 17n, 53, 54, 76, 89, 91, 96-9, 101, 103-104, 105n, 110n, 114, 118, 124, 135, 146, 155-6, 171-2, 177, 194, 224, 225n, 231, 232, 234, 255-6, 264, 272; interest in the Congo, 47-9; delimits spheres in E. Africa, 83-7; first discussions with Rhodes, 152-3; negotiates subsidy for Nyasaland, 184-90; separates Nyasaland and N. Rhodesia, 245-50
Angola, 21, 24, 27-31, 40, 70, 101, 139, 148, 281
Angra Pequena, 70
Ankole, 300, 320-1, 324
Arabs, in East Africa, 52; in Kilimanjaro area, 59-60, 125; L. Nyasa area, 140, 145, 161-164, 224, 263-8

Arnold, Sir Edwin, 77, 99
Arnot, F. S., 162
Austin Lee, Henry, 47

Bagge, Stephen, 322
Balfour of Burleigh, Lord, 151
Banana, 25, 32, 45
Bangweolo, Lake, 161
Bantu languages, see Johnston
Baptist Missionary Society, 25, 32-5, 94-6
Baring, Sir Evelyn, see Cromer
Baringo, Lake, 295
Barotse, the, 154, 174-5, 237
Barrington, Sir Eric, 185, 186n, 276-7, 328
Barros Gomez, Senhor, 146, 148
Basel Missionary Society, 94-6
Bates, H. W., 54, 58, 61-3
Beaconsfield, Lord, 10, 15, 17, 341
Bechuanaland, 139, 144, 154-5, 173-4, 226, 233
Beecroft, John, 89
Beira, 180, 243
Beit, Sir Alfred, 179
Bemba, the, 261
Beni, 321-3
Benin River, 93
Benue River, 93, 97, 105, 131
Berkeley, E. J. L., 286, 290, 310
Berlin Act, 71, 91, 94, 130, 132, 190, 217
Bismarck, Prince, 71, 86-8
Black Man's Part in the War, The, 352-3
Blantyre, 150, 159, 168-9, 202, 210-13, 231, 253, 262, 266, 270
Bleek, W., 22, 286, 337
Bolobo, 37, 39
Bombay, 231, 257
Bonny, 25, 90, 100, 114, 119, 120, 121
Boyce, Sorabji, 207, 214, 274